The Modern Spanish Economy

Transformation and Integration into Europe

Keith Salmon

PINTER
London and New York
Distributed Exclusively in the United States by St. Martin's Press

PINTER
An imprint of Cassell Publishers Limited, Wellington House, 125 Strand, London WC2R 0BB, England.

First published in 1995

Distributed exclusively in the USA and Canada by St. Martin's Press, Inc., Room 400,175 Fifth Avenue, New York, NY10010, USA

Keith Salmon is hereby identified as the author of this work as provided under Section 77 of the Copyright, Designs and Patents Act 1988.

British Library Cataloguing in Publication Data
A CIP catalogue record for this book is available from The British Library

ISBN 1 85567 153 0 (hbk)
ISBN 1 85567 154 9 (pbk)

Library of Congress Cataloging-in-Publication Data
Salmon, Keith G. , 1947-
The modern Spanish economy: transformation and integration into Europe/ Keith Salmon.
p. cm.
Includes bibliographical references and index.
ISBN 1-85567-153-0. -- ISBN 1-85567-154-9 pbk.
1. Spain -- Economic conditions -- 1975. 2. Spain -- Economic policy. 3. European Economic Community -- Spain. I. Title.
HC385. S25 1995
338. 946 -- dc20 95 - 3878
CIP

Typeset by Patrick Armstrong, Book Production Services
Printed and bound in Great Britain by Biddles Ltd, Guildford and King's Lynn

The Modern Spanish Economy

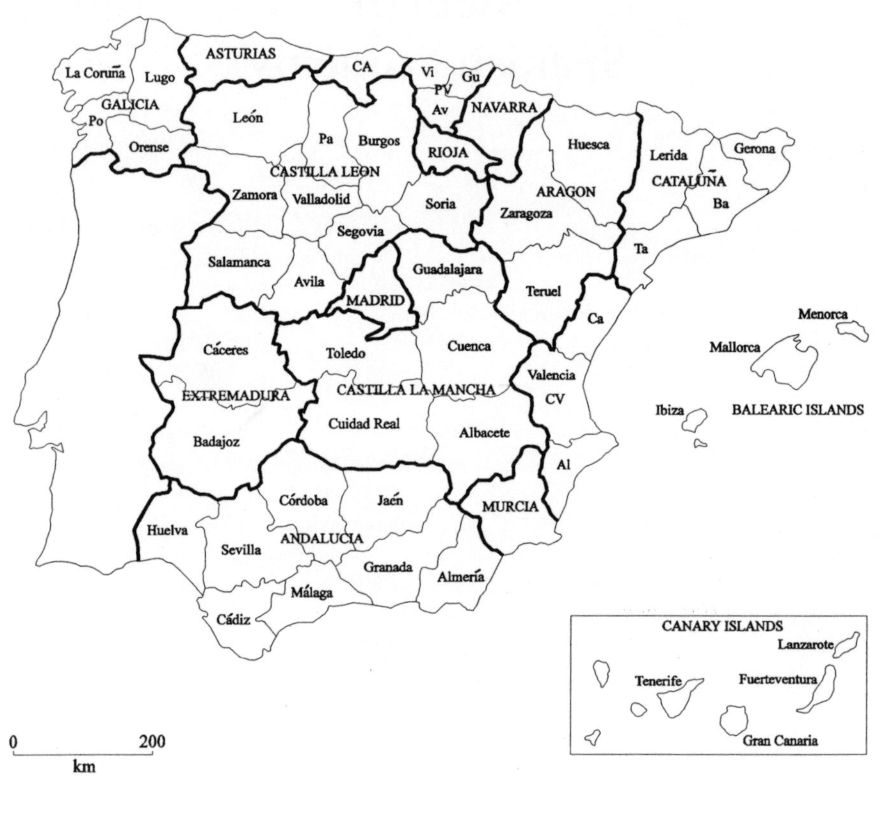

PROVINCES		REGIONS	
Al	Alicante	CA	CANTABRIA
Av	Alava	CV	COMUNIDAD VALENCIANA
Ba	Barcelona	PV	PAIS VASCO
Ca	Castellón		
Gu	Guipúzcoa		
Pa	Palencia		
Po	Pontevedra		
Ta	Tarragona		
Vi	Vizcaya		

Frontispiece Regions and Provinces of Spain

Cuando pasas por mi lado
sin echarme una mirada
¿ no te acuerdas de mi nada,
o te acuerdas demasiado?

Ramón de Campoamor

Where three roads joined it was green and fair,
And over a gate was the sun-glazed sea,
And life laughed sweet when I halted there;
Yet there I never again would be.

Thomas Hardy

To all those who have sacrificed their time and provided invaluable encouragement and assistance in the production of this book; especially Jenny, Alfonso Pajuelo, Rogelio Velasco, Francisco Mochón, Francisco Zambrana, Vicente Granados, Damian López Cano, Ray Skipp for drawing the maps, as well as my parents and many friends.

Keith Salmon

September 1994

Contents

List of figures

List of tables

Notes

Throughout the book the following conventions are used:
One billion refers to one thousand million
'pta' is used as the abbreviation for peseta
The European Union refers to the twelve member states as in mid 1994

Chapter 1

Evolution and structure of the Spanish economy

1.1 Evolution of the Spanish economy

The contemporary structure of the Spanish economy reflects its own peculiar evolution perhaps more than that of other western economies, in part a result of previous isolation from the global economy and from modern western currents of social change. The roots of this individualism can be traced to the Reconquest and the formation of the Spanish state in the Middle Ages. Wealth and power were polarised as a land-tenure system emerged that left central and southern Spain dominated by large estates. This power base was then protected through successive centuries by the Church, the large landowners, the army and the central government (composed essentially of the same élite group of people). Between them these groups suffocated innovation and social mobility, preventing the emergence of a significant group of urban industrial capitalists who might have challenged the system, and maintaining the elements of a traditional society into the mid twentieth century: 'If the process of economic modernization is characterized by a systematic effort to implement more efficient ways of production and distribution, then Spain did not start modernizing until the early 1960s' (Lieberman 1982, pp. 7–8). There was no Spanish Renaissance in the sixteenth century, no social revolution as in France in the eighteenth century or social evolution as in England, neither was there any agricultural or industrial revolution.

While a sense of history is important in understanding contemporary economic development, it is equally important that images of the past do not obscure current reality. This is especially true where economic change has been rapid and past images have been very strong, as in Spain. Thus, an analysis of the contemporary economy must incorporate history in so far as it explains current processes, but it must simultaneously extricate itself from out-dated perceptions.

1.2 The Francoist economy: autarchy 1939–59

In the decade or so after the Nationalist victory in the Civil War, the system of intervention and protection that had been built up in the early twentieth century was reinforced around the political dictatorship of General Franco. The semi-fascist Falange provided the dominant ideology, the Movimiento (Falangists and Carlists) providing most of the ministers and high functionaries of the major government economic departments. Clearly rejecting *laissez-faire* principles, in retreat since 1891, the huge interventionist apparatus was aimed at establishing complete control over the economy. Controls covered wages, prices, agricultural output, trade (through quantitative restrictions on imports, foreign exchange and investment controls) and direct state participation in the economy. The latter was most clearly demonstrated in the formation of a series of state companies (for example in energy, Endesa, and in transport equipment, E.N. Bazán, Enasa and Seat), mostly under the umbrella of the state holding company, the National Industry Institute (Instituto Nacional de Industria, INI). Alongside this restrictive economic regime was a repressive political system that denied civil liberties and quashed initiative. Free trade unions were banned, replaced by 'sindicatos' that represented both employers and employees in a given field of economic activity and operated, in effect, as organs of the government, principally serving the interests of the state. The highest development priority was given to the quest for self-sufficiency, promoted through such legislation as the Law of Protection and Development of National Industry (1939): 'during the period 1939–59, Spain presents the historian with an almost unique study in autarchic development.' (Lieberman 1982).

Autarchic development was centred around a policy of rapid industrialisation based on import substitution and guided by the desire for self-sufficiency. Public enterprises were set up to achieve this objective. The policy also meant a decoupling of Spain from the international economy. Thus in 1950 trade represented only 5 per cent of the gross national product. However, this extreme level of isolation was not only the outcome of internal policy but resulted too from decisions taken by the international community, as illustrated by the United Nations decision to institute an economic boycott of Spain (taken in 1946 and not rescinded until 1953) and by the exclusion of Spain from the European Recovery Programme (Marshall Aid in 1948).

Reconstruction of the Spanish economy after the Civil War was long drawn out both because of the damage wrought by the Civil War itself and because of the international environment faced by the country in the 1940s and early 1950s. The Civil War brought immense human loss in terms of the dead and injured (perhaps one million dead during and immediately after the Civil War), losses through emigration and a bitter human legacy. There was also widespread damage to buildings and infrastructure. Following the Civil War there was a severe shortage of materials occasioned first by the Second World War and then by the international isolation of Spain. Not until 1950 did the index of industrial production rise above its level in 1929, and in agriculture regeneration was even more tardy, remaining below its late 1920s level of production until 1958 (Carreras 1989a).

During the 1940s and 1950s the Spanish economy struggled to survive, isolated from the mainstream of development building in the western economies. In 1950 manufacturing industry still represented only a small part of the economy (about 18 per cent of the economically active population), while almost 50 per cent of the economically active population remained in agriculture. The population was essentially poor, with real incomes per capita only about one third of those in 1980 (Carreras 1989b). This small domestic market (28 million people in 1950), energy and raw material shortages, as well as poor communications, combined to frustrate autarchic development. Costly industrialisation and agricultural policies created consumer goods shortages and inflation (rising to 15.5 per cent in 1957). The balance of trade recorded a series of deficits (Tena 1989), running down foreign-exchange reserves and reflecting an overvalued currency. By the late 1950s these problems had reached crisis proportions. There was a high level of inflation. The value of the peseta was in decline outside of Spain. Balance of payments deficits, coupled with the lack of foreign-exchange reserves, threatened to bankrupt the country.

1.3 The Francoist economy: economic miracle 1959–73

The keys to the 'economic miracle', which propelled Spain from the ranks of the less developed countries to an industrialised country, were changes in the political outlook of those controlling the economy and the desire by Spaniards for modernisation (Fuentes Quintana 1988), together with a break in the extreme isolation and autarchy of the early 1950s. An initial break in isolation came in 1953 with a defence agreement enabling United States military bases to be established in Spain. In return Spain received substantial economic aid (estimated at $625 million between 1951 and 1957). Cabinet changes in 1957 brought to prominence a new group of technocrats (associated with the Opus Dei) less wedded to autarchic policies than their predecessors. In 1958 Spain became a member of the World Bank and in 1959 a member of the International Monetary Fund (IMF), and subsequently part of the Organisation for European Economic Co-operation (OEEC).

The prelude to economic growth in the 1960s and early 1970s was thus set in changing internal economic perspectives and increased international recognition of the Spanish regime: changes that were marked by the adoption of the Stabilisation Plan of 1959 (Plan Nacional de Estabilización Económica), which heralded a significant change in Spanish economic policy and the end of autarchy. The Plan emerged following visits and recommendations from the OEEC and the International Bank for Reconstruction and Development. The Plan (underwritten by foreign aid) was characterised by deflationary and tight monetary policies embracing: i) a reduction in public expenditure and lending to the public sector; ii) restrictions on lending to the private sector; iii) increased prices for public services; iv) higher interest rates; v) devaluation of the peseta exchange rate within Spain and an end to multiple exchange rates; and vi) measures to liberalise foreign investment and trade. The immediate impact of the Plan was an improvement in the balance of payments coupled with a severe recession (increased unemployment and reduced demand).

The fact that measures taken under the Stabilisation Plan did not trigger a long drawn out recession but were followed by an 'economic miracle' was due to favourable external factors. The international economy (especially that of north-west Europe) was growing, providing a market for Spanish goods and direct employment for substantial numbers of Spanish migrants (remitting equally substantial sums of money back to Spain). Tourism was emerging as a leading sector, generating considerable direct employment and income together with important multiplier effects in related industries such as transport and construction. In addition, foreign investment had returned. Thus a Plan that was designed to promote stability in the economy actually contributed to a period of rapid growth (Fuentes Quintana 1988)!

Despite the pronouncements made in the Stabilisation Plan to liberalise the economy and some moves in this direction, in practice protectionism remained alongside new forms of intervention. For example, 'acción concertada' involved joint action between the private sector and the government, which gave discretionary assistance. Government assistance was also given, especially to the traditional sectors of shipbuilding and steel. The involvement of INI in the economy expanded, for example in the Asturian steel complex Uninsa and the coal mining group Hunosa. Nationalisation of the Bank of Spain in 1962 provided increased government control over the banking system. In trade the tariff structure was carefully graded to give most protection to consumer goods with lower tariffs for intermediate goods and the lowest tariffs for capital goods. There were also incentives to export, including tax rebates, official credit and insurance. This continuing excessive protectionism distorted the market and stored up problems for the future.

Indicative national planning (through a series of National Development Plans (Planes de Desarrollo Nacional) and regional planning were embraced by the government in the 1960s. Planning was not very successful, partly due to a weak technical base and the existence of a large, inefficient public sector. Indeed, it may have been detrimental in that it directed attention away from fundamental institutional reform and a more efficient allocation of resources. An enormous apparatus of complex discretionary grants and loans was set up favouring those within the privileged circle (*cir-*

cuitos privilegiados de crédito). Public investment in the 1960s was directed particularly at those sectors suffering problems of adaptation to the changing economic climate or at basic industry: for example, chemicals, steel, shipbuilding and transport equipment, which were often not very technologically advanced but were experiencing rapid economic growth. Thus while development was stimulated by the Stabilisation Plan, it was hindered by the National Development Plans (Fuentes Quintana 1988)!

The Spanish 'economic miracle' of the 1960s is clearly documented by both the growth and changing composition of the gross domestic product (GDP). Between 1959 and 1971 the average annual growth of GDP was about 7 per cent (Figure 1.1), surpassed at the time only by Japan. GDP doubled in real terms during the 1960s, narrowing the development gap with other countries; thus in 1953 GDP was 14 per cent that of France and 22 per cent that of Italy, in 1965 it was 22 per cent that of France and 39 per cent that of Italy, and in 1974 it was 23 per cent that of France and 40 per cent that of Italy. The growth of gross domestic industrial product (value added by the industrial sector) was even more rapid, growing in real terms at an annual average rate of 9.4 per cent between 1960 and 1973.

Growth was matched by structural and spatial change in the economy. The proportion of the labour force employed in agriculture declined

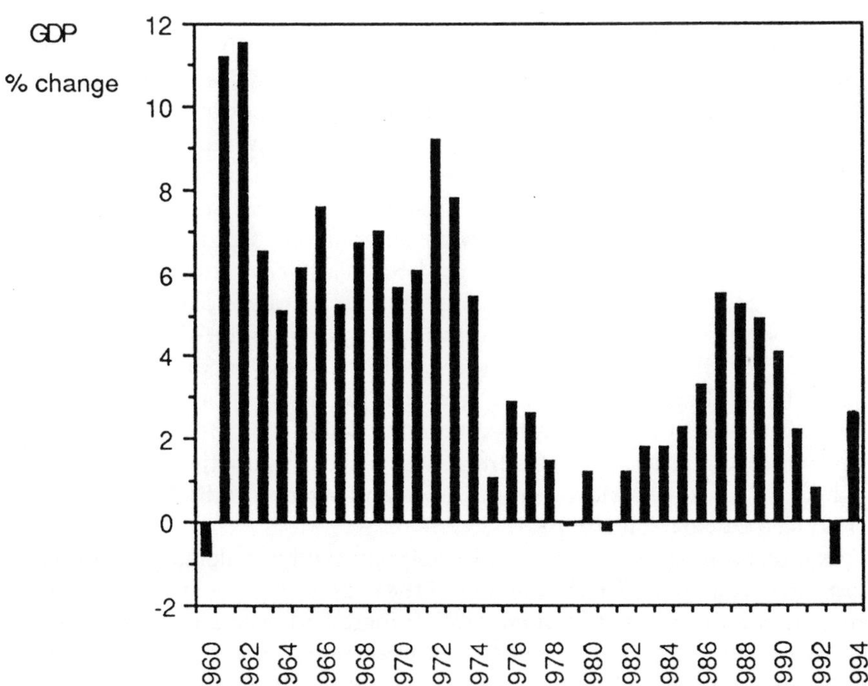

Figure 1.1 Evolution of the economy, 1960–94
Source: Banco de Bilbao 1980; Banco Bilbao Vizcaya 1993a

sharply, while that in services grew. Energy consumption switched decisively from coal to oil and increasing use was made of capital in place of labour. In industry, synthetic materials replaced many traditional products and the composition of production changed towards the greater importance of capital goods industries: metallurgy, construction materials, chemicals and transport equipment. Spatially, a new prosperity began to emerge around the coast, led by tourism but also including new agricultural and industrial developments. These patterns of economic change were accompanied by rural out-migration and depopulation of the interior, urbanisation and the growth of coastal populations.

However, broad expanses of industry (including steel and textiles) remained technologically backward, small in size and protected by high tariffs. There was excessive geographical concentration of growth, which was at the root of wide spatial variations in per-capita incomes. Unemployment was contained only by mass emigration (a process sponsored by an active government emigration policy).

Increased foreign trade and foreign investment were important features of economic growth: 'The rapid growth of foreign trade and of foreign investment constituted the most salient features of the evolution of the Spanish economy in the 1960s.' (Lieberman 1982). Imports rose from 7 per cent of GNP in 1960 to 17 per cent in 1970, and exports from 10 to 15 per cent of GNP. The growth of imports was associated with rapid industrialisation and rising incomes: thus industrial raw materials, semi-finished and finished goods increased in importance to represent 75 per cent of total imports in 1970. Exports of manufactured goods increased, with industrial equipment and consumer goods becoming more important relative to raw materials and agricultural products. The massive growth of imports and deficits on the balance of trade were largely financed by tourism earnings, migrant remittances and foreign investment, which ensured that the balance of payments current account was generally in surplus.

Foreign investment (especially by US, West German and Swiss firms) was directed towards high-technology industry and services, and was spatially concentrated in Madrid and Cataluña. Investment was attracted by labour force considerations (abundant labour and low labour costs) and the protected and expanding market (for example, in the motor-vehicle industry, authorisation for foreign investment was given only on condition that the domestic market would be protected). Other multinationals were established in sectors with low import duties and where products could not be produced by Spanish companies.

Rapid economic growth in the 1960s masked problems embedded in both the organisation and structure of the economy. The Stabilisation Plan had not led to a market economy; rather there had been a further evolution of corporate capitalism permeated by state intervention. Factor markets, especially the labour market, were inflexible. The taxation system was poorly developed (resulting in a noticeable lack of public goods, contributing to private affluence amidst public squalor) and many institutions (for example accountancy and insurance) were antiquated. Problems in the industrial structure were fundamentally those of small scale and the prevalence of traditional industries using traditional technologies. Hence the character of Spanish industry was midway between that of a newly industrialising country and an advanced industrial one, with competitive advantage often based on relatively low labour costs in traditional industries.

Public policy measures, developed within the context of the rapid economic growth of the 1960s, further emphasised the concentration on traditional industries through investment in increasing their capacity, while giving little attention to stimulating innovation and technological development. An example of the lack of attention given to promoting a climate of technological change was that associated with the law governing patents. Until 1985 patents were covered by the Industrial Property Law 1929 (Estatuto de la Propriedad Industrial), which provided inadequate protection for the inventors of new products.

1.4 Economic crisis, political transition and preparation for membership of the European Community, 1974–85

Following the death of General Franco in 1975 it was inevitable that in the late 1970s economic problems were subordinated to political considerations as the political system moved cautiously towards democracy. Policy measures were also increasingly overlain by preparations for entry into the European Community and the adoption of a liberal and more open economy. The decade was characterised by fundamental shifts in the nature of the political economy: from dictatorship to democracy, from centralism to regionalism, in the introduction of a welfare state and in the competitive position of Spanish industry in the world economy.

In the early 1970s the economic miracle ground to a halt. Growth of the industrial product, which had been running at an annual average rate of 9.4 per cent between 1960 and 1973, fell to an average annual rate of 0.8 per cent between 1975 and 1983 (Pérez Simarro 1986). Recession was broken by signs of recovery in 1978 (helped by a 20 per cent devaluation), renewed growth in tourism and increased foreign investment. But this recovery was quashed by further steep oil price rises at the turn of the decade that threw the economy into a severe crisis.

Economic problems in Spain were linked to those in the international economy, which were triggered by oil price rises commencing in 1973. Between January 1973 and January 1974 the Organisation of Petroleum Exporting Countries (OPEC) succeeded in raising the price of crude oil by almost 500 per cent. At that time crude oil constituted 55 per cent of Organisation for Economic Co-operation and Development (OECD) energy sources, of which about 75 per cent was imported. The shock to the international economic system of these sharp price increases was to reverberate through the following decade, spawning a reappraisal of production processes which led to de-industrialisation in traditional manufacturing areas, shifts in the international division of labour and a reorganisation of energy use; in OECD countries unemployment increased and the phenomenon of stagflation (stagnation in growth accompanied by inflation) appeared.

Lack of domestic energy resources and consequent dependence on imported energy left the Spanish economy particularly vulnerable to increased oil prices. Industrial expansion in the 1960s and early 1970s had relied heavily on cheap oil; oil accounting for 68.3 per cent of Spain's energy requirements in 1973. Yet, while in other OECD countries the consumption of primary energy per unit of GDP decreased from 1973, in Spain it continued to increase until the end of the 1970s. By 1978, 72.6 per cent of all energy requirements were based on oil; almost all of which was imported (Harrison 1985). Energy imports as a proportion of the total import bill increased from 13 per cent in 1973 to 26 per cent in 1975 (Table 1.1). In 1978 the cost of Spanish energy imports was equivalent to 41 per cent of the value of merchandise exports (Lieberman 1982). After the second oil shock in 1979 the costs of imported energy rose even higher. By 1981 Spain spent pta 1,259 billion on energy imports, equivalent to 42.4 per cent of the total

Table 1.1 Evolution of energy imports in merchandise trade, 1973–93

Year	Total imports (pta billion)	Energy (pta billion)	Energy/Total (%)
1970	332	44	13.3
1973	562	73	13.0
1975	932	240	25.8
1980	2,451	943	38.5
1981	2,970	1,259	42.4
1982	3,466	1,376	39.7
1985	5,115	1,835	35.9
1987	6,051	978	16.2
1988	6,989	790	11.3
1990	8,898	1,051	11.8
1993	9,999	1,105	11.1

Sources: Alonso 1988; Banco de España 1994

merchandise trade import bill and 67 per cent of the total value of merchandise exports.

Inflation accompanied economic stagnation in the 1970s (Table 1.2), reaching an annualised rate of 37 per cent in the summer of 1977. High inflation resulted from the sustained increase in oil prices, huge public sector deficits, a permissive monetary policy and social peace bought at the cost of large rises in monetary wages in advance of increased productivity. Real wages in industry increased by 130 per cent between 1970 and 1982, more than in any other European country, while productivity increased by only 42 per cent. Simultaneously, negative real rates of interest (with inflation higher than interest rates) contributed to increased borrowing and higher levels of company debt, which would result later in crippling financial burdens.

Unemployment increased sharply to become the most pressing social problem. This sharp increase was partly the result of economic problems. Agriculture and industry each shed over one million jobs between 1974 and 1982 (Harrison 1985). But it was also the outcome of social change, including an expanding population of working age, a continued increase in female labour participation rates and the curtailment of emigration coupled with the return of many former migrants (following growing employment problems in north-west Europe).

Table 1.2 Evolution of the economy, 1973–94

Year	GDP growth %	Inflation %	Current account balance (pta bn)	Year	GDP growth %	Inflation %	Current account balance (pta bn)
1973	7.8	11.8	35	1984	1.8	9.0	355
1974	5.4	15.7	-179	1985	2.3	8.1	397
1975	1.1	17.0	-177	1986	3.3	8.3	523
1976	2.9	17.7	-284	1987	5.5	4.6	32
1977	2.6	26.4	-160	1988	5.2	5.8	-433
1978	1.5	16.6	115	1989	4.9	6.9	-1,454
1979	-0.1	15.5	62	1990	4.1	6.5	-1,596
1980	1.2	15.2	-364	1991	2.2	5.5	-1,832
1981	-0.2	14.4	-458	1992	0.8	5.4	-2,411
1982	1.2	14.0	-487	1993	-1.0	4.9	-649
1983	1.8	12.2	-338	1994	2.0	4.6	-350

Figures for 1994 are forecasts

GDP growth at constant market prices

Inflation figure based on retail price index (Indice de Precios al Consumo), December to December

Sources: *El País* 1994; BBV 1993a; Banco de España 1994; OECD 1994

The economic crisis brought a change in the comparative advantage of Spanish industry, as both energy and labour costs increased (Maravall 1987; Pérez Simarro 1986) and as Newly Industrialised Countries (NICs) emerged. Thus the economic crisis of the late 1970s and early 1980s was centred on those industries in which Spain had specialised in the 1960s, such as steel, shipbuilding, textiles and heavy chemicals.

Economic policy was directly related to the evolving domestic political situation. The extent to which the government intervened directly in the economy and the rigidity of institutions and factor markets impeded automatic market responses and placed particular importance on government policy. In 1974 there was a climate of uncertainty following the assassination of Carrero Blanco and the illness of General Franco. Hence the policy response was to buy time by attempting to isolate the economy from the international recession (*política compensatoria;* abandoned in 1975). There was also a vain hope that recession would be short lived. Measures were implemented to stimulate internal demand and prevent domestic oil prices from rising. The immediate impact was a sharp deterioration in the balance of payments, exacerbated by a continued increase in oil consumption. Following the death of General Franco in November 1975 the political situation became even more delicate, haunted by the spectre of the previous attempt at democracy in a similarly adverse economic climate in the 1930s. Thus a highly permissive economic policy was adopted (*política permisiva,* 1976 to 1977) clearly linked to securing the transition to democracy. Wages were allowed to rise ahead of inflation, monetary policy was lax and the peseta was devalued by 20 per cent in 1977, with no attempt to reduce domestic demand (Fuentes Quintana 1988).

The first democratic elections in 1977 finally brought measures to adjust the economy to the recession and begin the difficult process of economic liberalisation. The policy of adjustment began with the Moncloa Pacts (Los Pactos de la Moncloa), agreed between all political parties, employers and trade unions: agreements that above all represented a commitment to democracy.

The Moncloa Pacts also announced the broad direction of economic policy that was to continue through the years of crisis: a policy that proclaimed an overall commitment to a liberal and open market economy oriented especially towards eventual membership of the European Community, while providing for the continued macro-economic management of a protected economy. Policy was designed primarily to fight inflation and to create an economic environment in which the economy could grow and unemployment could be reduced. Strategy attempted to combine measures to control the money supply (monetary policy), measures to control government expenditure and reduce the public sector borrowing requirement (budgetary policy), and measures to control wages (incomes policy). In addition, steps were taken to improve the competitiveness of Spanish industry, to reform economic institutions and to increase the flexibility of factor markets.

An important shift in the management of the economy was the adoption of modern monetary policy from the early 1970s (Aríztegui 1988), following the public pronouncements of the intellectual leader of monetarism, Milton Friedman, in the United States. Policy was framed within a system of floating exchange rates and became the main instrument of demand management.

> Control over the monetary aggregates ... [was] sought through the regulation of bank reserves. In order to keep bank reserves on a path consistent with desired M3 growth, which ... [was] the main intermediate target from 1973, the Bank of Spain either ... [supplied] funds in the form of loans or else ... [drained] funds from the market by placing short-term certificates of monetary regulation (créditos de regulación monetaria, CRMs) or government paper (short-term Treasury Bills, Pagarés del Tesoro) with private banks and other authorised financial intermediaries. In this process, money market interest rates ... [were] allowed to fluctuate widely. (OECD 1984, p. 20).

By the late 1970s target ranges for money supply (M3, broad money including cash, sight and time deposits) growth were being set, although these were high and often exceeded. Monetary policy was tightened in the early 1980s to contain the high level of inflation and wage settlements and reduce the balance of payments deficit. The target range for the broad monetary aggregate ALP (Activos Líquidos en manos del Público, liquid assets in the hands of the public or M4) was progressively reduced from 14–18 per cent in 1983 to 6.5–9.5 per cent in 1987, and actual monetary growth slowed within these ranges until early 1987.

Continued government intervention was deemed necessary to dismantle the existing system of widespread regulation (required for entry to the European Community), to promote new industry and new labour force skills, to increase the flexibility of institutions and factor markets, to introduce the reforms necessary to harmonise economic practices in Spain with those in other western industrialised countries (especially those in the European Community), but above all to secure an orderly economic restructuring process in the face of the increased competition occasioned by a more open economy. A large slice of the Spanish economy remained uncompetitive and without continued government intervention may have disappeared.

Following the election to government of the Socialist Party (PSOE) in 1982, a new urgency crept into economic policy, prompted by the imminence of entry into the European Community. Industrial reconversion plans were strengthened (while providing safeguards for the social costs involved). Measures to liberalise the economy, increase flexibility (especially in the labour market) and adopt international economic practices were accelerated. The proclaimed objective was to restructure the sectors in crisis and channel resources into new, more profitable, sectors. Liberalisation of the economy was to be achieved through a thorough overhaul of economic institutions. In practice, political necessities ensured that the main emphasis throughout the decade from 1975 remained on cushioning the effects of the restructuring process on traditional industries. Despite this emphasis, unemployment continued to rise from 9 per cent in 1979 to 22 per cent in 1985.

1.5 Economic growth and closer European integration, 1986–92

The period 1986 to 1992 was dominated by the integration of Spain into the European Community, and more widely into the world economy, through the dismantling of barriers to the movement of merchandise and capital and the incorporation of Spanish business into the corporate space of foreign multinational companies (Almarcha Barbado 1993; Salmon 1995; Tovias 1995). Until the turn of the decade it was also characterised by strong economic growth. Politically it was associated with a succession of PSOE governments adopting more market-centred economic policies and seeking to be in the vanguard of European integration, policies which led to a growing split with its traditional trade union support in the General Workers Union (Unión General de Trabajadores, UGT), marked by the first general strike in December 1989.

From 1986 to 1990 (inclusive) the Spanish economy grew faster than most other European Community countries, at an annual average rate of 4.5 per cent (BBV 1993a). Growth was accompanied by imbalances such as a growing current account deficit, spiralling property prices and above all inflation. The containment of inflation became the key policy objective resulting in measures to slow the growth of demand, moderate salary increases and achieve higher productivity.

Growth was driven by an expansion of domestic demand (both private and public) within the context of a growing world economy and further opening of the Spanish economy to trade and foreign investment. Private consumption benefited from real increases in wages (above the level of inflation), an expansion of credit (including money supply targets that were regularly exceeded), increased social security transfers and higher employment. Between 1985 and 1991 two million net jobs were created, the occupied population peaking at 12.7 million in the third quarter of 1991. Buoyant consumer demand was matched by growth in company investment, industrial production and corporate profits and reflected in a rapid rise in car registrations to 1.1 million in 1989. Public consumption (including the consumption of public goods, increased social security payments and increased administration costs) also grew strongly in the late 1980s, propping-up faltering private consumption at the turn of the decade. For example, authorisations for public sector construction projects increased in value from pta 725 billion in 1987 to pta 2,079 billion in 1990 (Banco de España 1993a).

However, the Spanish economy could not defy the gravity of recession in the industrialised economies, commencing in the United States and Britain at the end of the 1980s and spreading throughout western Europe in the early 1990s, nor could it defy the high interest rates (around 14.5 per cent between 1989 and 1992), tight monetary and fiscal policy prevailing at the turn of the decade, topped by public expenditure cuts (including cuts in contracts for construction projects and in defence spending). Growth began to slow from late 1989, the slowdown gathering pace and turning into recession in the second half of 1992. Even as the last bars of 'Barcelona' were fading from the Olympic Games and the last fireworks were lighting the night sky in Seville, the carefully embroidered image of a strong Spanish economy was cracking to reveal serious weaknesses.

1.5.1 European integration

Measures to achieve European integration dominated economic policy. There was widespread popular support in Spain for closer integration, which was seen as being part of the process of modernisation, a way of locking Spain into a prosperous economic region and a release from the isolation and claustrophobia of the old regime.

Following a lengthy period of negotiations (dating back to the late 1970s) the Treaty of Accession to the European Communities (Tratado de Adhesión a las Comunidades) was ratified by Spain in September 1985, coming into force on 1 January 1986. In the same year the Single European Act set the timetable for the creation of the Single European Market from 1 January 1993.

Membership of the European Community brought increased external pressures to bear on the political economy, stimulating measures to liberalise the economy, harmonise the regulatory framework of business with that in other member states and directing the increasing external transactions of the Spanish economy towards the EC. For example, the taxation system shifted towards a more European model with a greater reliance on direct taxes (the ratio of direct to indirect tax revenue rising from 98 per cent in 1985 to 122 per cent in 1992; OECD 1994), and the replacement of the former sales taxes with Value Added Tax (VAT). Further external pressure was applied through the agreement on the first phase of monetary union made in Madrid in June 1989 and the simultaneous entry of Spain into the Exchange Rate Mechanism (ERM) of the European Monetary System. In joining the ERM Spain hoped to gain a monetary discipline inside which inflation could be contained and a place at the heart of Europe.

The wave of European integration culminated in the signing of the Maastricht Treaty in December 1991 (ratified in Autumn 1993), committing Spain to the 'convergence criteria' in the Treaty. These criteria were: i) a public sector deficit of not more than 3 per cent of GDP (in 1991 it was 4.4

per cent and rising); ii) public debt no more than 60 per cent of GDP (in May 1992 it was 45.6 per cent); iii) interest rates no more than 2 per cent above the average of the three lowest rates in the EC (Spain had the highest interest rates in the EC at about 13 per cent in July 1992); iv) inflation no more than 1.5 per cent above the three lowest in the EC (in May 1992 it was 4.1 per cent adrift); and v) remain in the narrow band of the ERM for two years (Spain was in the wide band). Thus, at the time the Treaty was agreed Spain met only one of the objectives.

In joining the ERM and committing itself to the convergence criteria the Spanish government not only lost its previous autonomy over monetary policy (tying future domestic monetary policy to that of other EC countries, especially Germany), but also limited its room for manoeuvre on broader economic policy issues such as economic growth and unemployment. Spain entered the ERM at an EC central rate of pta 133.804: Ecu (pta 65: DM) within a wide band allowing a fluctuation of plus/minus 6 per cent. Prior to joining, the government had deliberately held the peseta to a 6 per cent band of fluctuation, broadly the same discipline as in the ERM. After one year the peseta was trading near the ceiling of its value, at pta 62: DM, a position which it held until midway through 1992. The explanation for this strength lay in the continued demand for pesetas (heightened by further liberalisation of capital movements). This in turn was a reflection of high real interest rates, the difference between high nominal interest rates (thought necessary to restrain inflation) and inflation, and a nominally guaranteed exchange rate.

The strong peseta increased the competitiveness of imports (especially those from non-EC countries) and decreased that of exports (simultaneously contributing to the redirection of exports towards EC countries), swelling the current account deficit. It also placed severe pressure on domestic economic activity, contributing to de-industrialisation, the decline in tourism at the turn of the decade and rising unemployment from mid 1992. On the other hand, the inflow of foreign capital offset the deficit on the current account, inflation was contained and economic growth was above that of most other EC countries.

Constraints on economic policy were tightened even further when Spain signed-up to the Maastricht Treaty (December 1991) and set out on a path to meet the convergence criteria for economic and monetary union in 1997. To achieve these objectives a Convergence Plan (Plan de Convergencia) was agreed in March 1992 under which macro-economic policy (monetary and budgetary) was refocused and structural measures, such as greater flexibility in factor markets and the break-up of monopolies, pursued more vigorously. The limitations placed on monetary policy by the ERM and failure to reach an incomes policy with the unions (failure with the Pacto de Competitividad in 1991) meant that the emphasis had to be placed on budgetary and fiscal policy. Hence tax increases and public expenditure cuts were introduced. In July 1992 it was announced that the standard rate of

VAT would be increased from 13 to 15 per cent from 1 August 1992 (bringing into line with the EC standard rate) and that income tax would be increased except for those on very low incomes. Cuts were also announced in government spending (including freezing employment recruitment and salaries in the civil service).

Whereas interest rate policy in Spain was largely dictated by domestic considerations up to 1991 (helping to combat inflation, finance the general government deficit in a non-inflationary way, and keep the peseta near the top of its ERM band, fostering confidence in the economy), in 1992 it became overshadowed by external considerations and the need to keep the peseta in the ERM and therefore maintain the central plank of Spanish economic policy built around meeting the convergence criteria for economic and monetary union described in the Maastricht Treaty (OECD 1993). Thus monetary policy in 1992 through to the collapse of the ERM in August 1993 (and its reorganisation with exchange rate fluctuation bands of plus/minus 15 per cent) was dominated by exchange rate considerations. During the currency turmoil in September 1992 the peseta fell very quickly from the top of the ERM band to the bottom (as a thinly traded currency once it came under pressure its value moved very quickly). The currency was devalued immediately (on the 16 September) by 5 per cent but remained within the ERM. As a further measure to support the exchange rate, capital controls were reintroduced as an alternative to raising interest rates (above their existing high levels) or further devaluation. Continuing downward pressure on the peseta forced another devaluation in November 1992 (6 per cent devaluation was accompanied by the lifting of capital controls), but pressure continued forcing yet a further devaluation (this time of 8 per cent) in May 1993. External factors were thus dictating economic policy (especially German economic policy of maintaining high interest rates to contain inflation sparked by German reunification). High interest rates and clear indications of a tight budget in 1994 were required by the capital markets as the price of maintaining the exchange rate in the ERM.

The measures outlined in the Convergence Plan (especially cuts in unemployment benefits on top of restrictive monetary policies cutting investment and thus employment) and further employment flexibility proposals were strongly opposed by the unions, by many political factions and a growing body of public opinion. Even in mid 1992 there was serious concern over the social costs for the Spanish economy of meeting the timetable for convergence: 'no se cuestiona la necesidad de converger con los países más estables de Europa ... Lo que se cuestiona son los plazos de entrada en la UEM y sobre todo el someter a la sociedad española a la enorme tensión que supone conseguir la convergencia de Maastricht en cuatro años y medio. Este no es ... el Tour de Francia .... Valga la metáfora deportiva para comprender que no necesitamos machacar al tejido social español para gana la copa de Maastricht.' (Sebastián 1992). Concern was manifested in sporadic strikes and protests (for example by miners, workers in heavy industry, the public sector and farmers) and a general strike on 28 May 1992. With the general election approaching the political pressure was rising.

Hence, economic policy became locked into the measures necessary to maintain the exchange rate and meet the convergence criteria, thereby keeping Spain at the heart of European integration. A stream of economists visiting the country spoke out at the contradiction of maintaining high interest rates while the economy had entered a recession, inflation was falling and unemployment was over 20 per cent and rising.

1.5.2 Opening of the Spanish economy

Opening of the Spanish economy and increased integration into the world economy was documented by the increased real value of current account transactions, but much more significantly by the explosion of international capital movements and the accompanying incorporation of Spanish business into the corporate space of foreign multinationals (Salmon 1995).

On the current account merchandise trade grew strongly, its composition shifting towards a greater concentration on consumer goods (especially consumer durables, notably vehicles). Imports flooded in, while exports grew more slowly, impeded by the high value of the peseta. The result was a growing balance of trade deficit, amounting to 6.5 per cent of GDP in 1989. Trade in motor-vehicles illustrated the trends and highlighted the role of foreign multinational companies in exports. Motor-vehicle products represented almost a quarter of the value of all exports in 1992. However, while exports of cars rose by less than half between 1985 and 1992 imports rose over six-fold, import penetration growing from 16 per cent to 50 per cent.

Trade in services grew faster than merchandise trade and showed a surplus throughout the period, frequently sufficient to cover the annual deficits on merchandise trade. However, the surplus was gradually evaporating with import coverage falling to 117 in 1992 (Banco de España 1993b), leaving a current account deficit amounting to over 3 per cent of GDP in the three years 1989 to 1992. Travel and tourism was the source of the surplus on services (outside of travel and tourism there was a growing deficit), accounting for over half of all exports of services. The corollary of the dependence on tourism was the notable lack of income from financial or producer services (a large slice of the rest of the income from services arising from current account investment flows).

Both merchandise and service transactions were increasingly focused on the European Community. Hence, the proportion of imports arising from within the Community increased from 37 per cent in 1985 to 61 per cent in 1993, while exports to the Community increased from 52 per cent to 68 per cent (Table 1.3).

Capital flows (international transactions in financial assets, notably foreign investment and foreign credit) escalated after 1986. Membership of the

Table 1.3 The direction of trade, 1982–93

Imports	Total	OECD	%	EC	%
1982	3,466	1,884	54	1,100	32
1985	5,115	2,890	57	1,870	37
1987	6,051	4,471	74	3,300	55
1988	6,989	5,418	78	3,969	57
1989	8,396	6,521	78	4,780	57
1990	8,898	6,985	79	5,264	59
1991	9,637	7,602	79	5,780	60
1992	10,205	8,077	79	6,214	61
1993	9,999	7,826	78	5,965	60
Exports					
1982	2,258	1,391	62	1,098	49
1985	4,109	2,872	70	2,139	52
1987	4,212	3,338	79	2,681	64
1988	4,659	3,770	81	3,056	66
1989	5,134	4,188	82	3,433	67
1990	5,631	4,631	82	3,907	69
1991	6,065	5,073	84	4,392	72
1992	6,658	5,472	82	4,725	71
1993	7,576	5,975	79	5,054	67

Figures in pta billion

Sources: Banco de España 1990 and 1994

European Community swept away investment controls (especially on inward foreign investment) and introduced a timetable for the elimination of all controls on capital movements by 1993. The removal of controls contributed to Spain becoming the fourth most attractive country in the world for foreign direct investment in the late 1980s (after the much larger economies of the United States, the UK and France). The attraction of Spain as a destination for long-term capital was based on expectations about the strength of the domestic economy, the profitability of fixed investments (including relatively low labour costs) and the position of Spain within the EC. Short-term flows were attracted more by interest rate differentials and expectations over exchange rate variations with the currency being underpinned by the floor of the ERM.

Inward foreign investment enabled the Spanish economy to sustain growth above that of other OECD countries by offsetting the balance of payments deficit, swelling foreign exchange reserves and supplementing domestic investment. It was also associated with the transfer of business ownership out of Spain, increased reliance on foreign technology and spiralling property prices. From 1987 until 1991 (inclusive) the net inflow of foreign long-term capital was greater than the deficit on the current account (BBV 1993b). Foreign exchange reserves rose from $13.3 billion in 1985 to $66 billion in 1991.

Investment flows are subdivided into foreign investment (purchases and disinvestment) and Spanish investment abroad (purchases and disinvestment), and into public and private sector transactions. They are further categorised into direct, portfolio and property investment.

Total private sector investment flows (foreign purchases and disinvestment plus Spanish purchases and disinvestment abroad) increased from pta 836 billion in 1985 (3 per cent of GDP) to pta 8,963 billion (15 per cent of GDP) in 1992. Net foreign investment in Spain increased from pta 413 billion in 1985 to pta 1,235 billion in 1992 (reaching pta 1,845 billion in 1990; Table 1.4).

The three outstanding features of private sector investment flows were their enormous growth, the imbalance between foreign investment in Spain and Spanish investment abroad and their changing composition. Foreign purchases doubled from 1985 to 1986 and then doubled again from 1986 to 1987. In 1986 the value of foreign purchases was roughly half that of all

Table 1.4 Evolution of net foreign investment in Spain, 1970–93

Year	Direct	Portfolio	Real estate	Other	Total
1970	16	-1	10	—	25
1975	18	-4	16	6	35
1980	66	1	42	-1	108
1982	106	1	73	19	199
1983	117	7	114	6	243
1984	156	37	138	-9	322
1985	164	82	159	8	413
1986	284	235	191	7	717
1987	321	435	221	19	997
1988	521	246	267	29	1,063
1989	667	733	303	27	1,730
1990	1,073	451	244	77	1,845
1991	898	501	160	25	1,584
1992	739	404	104	-12	1,235
1990	1,164	1,024*	247		2,435
1991	1,128	2,276*	166		3,570
1992	1,254	1,256*	113		2,623
1993	931	7,089*	100		8,120

Figures in pta billion and refer to long-term private capital movements; new data series from 1990

*: marketable securities

Foreign direct investment in the bottom half of the table is derived from foreign investment less marketable securities and real estate

Sources: Alonso 1988; *Anuario El País* various dates (data from Banco de España, Registro de Caja); 1990 to 1993 figures from Banco de España 1994

foreign purchases 1970 to 1985 (inclusive). After 1987 foreign purchases continued to grow strongly until in 1991 their value was equal to all the income from services on the current account. Similarly, in terms of net foreign investment (purchases less disinvestment), that accumulated between 1986 and 1992 (inclusive) was four and a half times larger than that accumulated between 1970 and 1985 (inclusive). Spanish investment abroad also grew but remained substantially below that of inward foreign investment.

In terms of the composition of foreign investment, growth in purchases after 1985 were accounted for by an explosion in portfolio investment superimposed on strong growth in direct investment. From 1986 onwards portfolio investment became the largest element of purchases, accounting for almost 70 per cent of the total in 1992. In contrast, property investment remained relatively small and fell away at the end of the 1980s. The evolution of the structure of Spanish purchases was rather different. In the mid 1980s portfolio investment exceeded direct investment but direct investment regained its dominant position in the late 1980s, to be overtaken once more by portfolio investment in 1992. As with foreign investment, Spanish property investment remained very small.

Foreign direct investment was the most visible element of foreign penetration of the Spanish economy. From a value of pta 194 billion in 1985, foreign direct investment (purchases) surged to pta 1,257 billion in 1990. Similarly, net foreign direct investment rose from pta 164 billion in 1985 to pta 1,073 billion in 1990. However, only a proportion of this direct investment was in new production facilities. Frequently, such investment was made to secure markets and distribution channels through the acquisition of Spanish companies.

The destination by sector of foreign direct investment shifted over time from manufacturing industry (prior to the mid 1980s) to services (Ontiveros 1991). Within the service sector financial services attracted particular attention as liberalisation proceeded. Foreign direct investment also originated increasingly from within the EC (in 1992 over 85 per cent arose in the EC; *El País* 1993). Within Spain the bulk of foreign investment flowed into Madrid and Cataluña (about 80 per cent), and to a far lesser extent Andalucía, Aragón and Comunidad Valenciana, underpinning the dynamism of these areas.

Spanish direct investment abroad was on a much smaller scale. Purchases increased from pta 67 billion in 1985, peaking at pta 392 billion in 1991. Net investment grew from pta 54 billion in 1985, peaking at pta 314 billion in 1991. The structure of Spanish direct investment abroad was dominated by investment in financial services, distribution and commerce, only a small proportion going into manufacturing industry (12 per cent in 1992). Most of the investment originated in Madrid and Cataluña (reflecting the distribution of business headquarters in Spain). By destination, investment was increasingly channelled into the European Community.

Foreign portfolio investment (purchases) exploded after 1986 to reach pta 2,716 billion in 1992, having been only pta 120 billion in 1985. Net portfolio investment rose from pta 82 billion in 1985 and thence upwards to pta 733 billion in 1989, after which net investment tended to fall (reaching pta 404 billion in 1992). Spanish portfolio investment abroad was on a much smaller scale, restrained by regulations which were not fully removed until 1992. The growth of foreign portfolio investment left the Spanish economy more sensitive to speculative short-term capital movements.

Foreign property investment in Spain grew consistently in nominal terms from 1986 to 1989 adding further upward pressure on property prices in the late 1980s. It then collapsed by 60 per cent in the three years to 1993. Foreign investment in property was concentrated around the Mediterranean coast (in tourism facilities and residential property) and in Madrid. Most of the money was channelled through foreign tax havens or originated in the EC. Spanish property investment abroad was negligible.

Growth in the external debt of Spain also illustrated the process of integration into the world economy. In dollar terms and at current values, external debt grew from $24 billion in 1986 to $78 billion in 1992 (*El País* 1994). About half the debt in 1992 related to private companies, notable among which were the electricity utilities. Increases in external debt reflected the lack of adequate funds in Spain to meet the demands of private and public sector expenditure (for example, as the state sought to meet its social services obligations and all levels of administration sought to finance investment in the late 1980s and early 1990s). The increases also reflected the improved international risk rating of the Spanish government (Moody's sovereign risk assessment for Spain was Aa2 between 1988 and 1992) and Spanish companies. However, higher external debt meant growing debt servicing costs, costs which were sensitive to foreign exchange movements as well as international interest rates.

Another dimension of integration into the world economy was illustrated by the growth of foreign-owned multinational business in Spain, visible evidence of the influx of foreign direct investment. In 1975 Seat cars, Pegaso commercial vehicles and Cruz Campo beer were emblems of Spanish-owned manufacturing. By 1992 all of these were owned by European multinationals. Foreign companies were particularly prominent in exports. Nine of the leading ten exporters in 1992 were foreign multinationals. In the tourism industry, foreign inbound mass tourism was controlled from its inception in the late 1950s by a small number of foreign tour operators.

Foreign capital spread throughout the economy to dominate key areas, especially those characterised by a high proportion of exports. In the late 1980s the title of Francisco Jurdao's book 'Spain on sale' (Jurdao Arrones 1979) could have been applied to almost the entire economy. A survey undertaken by the Ministry of Economy in June 1989 recorded almost 22,000 companies with foreign capital. In 10,000 companies foreign participation was equal to or greater than 50 per cent (BBV 1991). This represented a significant transfer of control over the economy to foreign-owned (especially European) multinational companies and a reorganisation of trade such that an increasing proportion occurred within multinational company networks.

In contrast to the enormous increase of foreign multinationals in the Spanish economy, there were relatively few examples of Spanish multinationals. Although there was evidence of growth in Spanish direct manufacturing investment abroad in the early 1990s, it remained small. Investment in distribution facilities (especially in Belgium and Holland) was more common than in production plants. Manufacturing investment was concentrated in labour-intensive activities, especially textiles and shoes, and geographically in the low labour cost countries of Portugal and Morocco. The attraction of these countries was in their geographical proximity, lower labour costs and, in the case of Portugal, a similar business culture.

The modest presence of Spanish direct investment outside of Spain was also a characteristic of services (with a few exceptions such as Endesa, Iberia, Repsol, Telefónica and some of the larger hotel groups). For example, despite the high profile of Spanish commercial banks within Spain, their presence outside Spain was relatively modest. Furthermore, despite mergers in the 1980s and early 1990s, no Spanish bank in 1992 was large enough to develop a fully global or even pan-European presence, instead they opted for regional alliances. In general, the major Spanish commercial banks had the largest proportion of their foreign assets in Europe (Portugal having been a particular target), followed by smaller investments in Latin America. Similarly, the savings banks had a negligible presence abroad.

Spain was extremely successful in attracting foreign investment in the 1980s. Although there were understandable concerns related to the transfer of control of business, increased foreign investment was generally accepted as an integral part of the process of modernisation, liberalisation and integration into the world economy. Issues such as the loss of sovereignty and control over national resources, the risks of a branch plant economy, the long-term outflow of capital and the impact of a cessation of inward investment (portfolio investment being particularly volatile) appeared academic alongside the immediate benefits of increased investment and employment, technological transfer, new management practices, access to international distribution networks and general access to the resources of multinational companies. In 1981 Tsoukalis stated that the opening of the Spanish economy to foreign investment had played a crucial role in terms of the balance of payments, its contribution to fixed capital formation and employment as well as the transfer of technology (Tsoukalis 1981). This remained true in 1992.

1.6 The contemporary political economy

In the mid 1990s Spain is a medium-size economy embedded in the European Union, experiencing many similar problems to those of other west European countries. Lower interest rates coupled with a substantial depreciation in the peseta (some 50 per cent against the dollar and 20 per cent against most other EU currencies between 1992 and the end of 1993) helped bring recession to an end in 1993, allowing growth to return from 1994 led by a dramatic improvement on the current account and in trade performance.

Spain is less wealthy than many of its EU partners, with GDP measured at current market prices of pta 64,000 billion in 1994 and GDP per head only 75 to 80 per cent that of the EU average, greater only than that of Ireland, Greece and Portugal. Structurally the economy is increasingly dominated by services, which are primarily oriented towards the domestic market (with the notable exception of tourism). In manufacturing, substantial employment remains in traditional industries, while high-technology industry and exports are dominated by foreign multinationals.

The global reach of Spain is restricted by the size of the economy and the paucity and modest size of its multinational companies. Within Europe the political weight of Spain (and of the Mediterranean region in general) has been diluted by the northern enlargement of the EU to fifteen members. The attention being given to eastern Europe in the mid 1990s poses real concerns in relation to the locational, political and economic position of Spain. Much may depend on its position on the southern flank of Europe, a position likely to become of increasing strategic importance in the light of political and socio-economic changes around the Mediterranean and the enormous development gap with the countries on the southern and eastern shores of the Mediterranean in north Africa and the Middle East. Whether this position proves negative or positive depends on how political events unfold in this region. Beyond Europe the political and economic presence of Spain is concentrated on Latin America, where it continues to enjoy a valuable cultural advantage that is being translated into significant economic ties.

Within the country there are wide spatial variations in levels of development, from the rich and economically diversified regions of Cataluña and Madrid (with per capita incomes above the EU average) to the poorest regions of Andalucía and Extremadura (per capita incomes below 60 per cent of the EU average). At a sub-regional level more wealthy coastal and urban areas contrast with the continued poverty of many inland and rural areas (especially rural mountainous areas). However, as in other western societies, the sharpest contrasts in affluence are in the cities, where acute poverty rubs shoulders with conspicuous affluence and the problems of modern western societies are evident.

The political economy of the mid 1990s is fundamentally different from that a decade earlier. At home the political certainties of the 1980s have evaporated, leaving a Socialist Party (PSOE) weakened by a rift with the trade unions, internal ideological struggles and a stream of corruption allegations. Domestic policy is set within a political system of stronger regional government. On a broader front, government policy must now be formulated within the context of the European Union and international agreements (such as the Uruguay Round of GATT). The nature of the European Union itself is changing with enlargement and the opening of trade to the east. Beyond Europe, the balance of economic power is shifting towards the emerging economies, with China waiting in the wings poised to become an economic superpower of the twenty-first century. Multinational companies continue to force the pace of global economic integration, constantly adjusting the spatial pattern of their operations to gain maximum competitive advantage. Overhanging future world development is world population growth, adding more than twice the population of Spain to the world each year.

Economic policy in the coming years will continue to seek to meet the convergence criteria in the Maastricht Treaty and to achieve real convergence with other EU member states, but on a slower time-scale than envisaged at the beginning of the 1990s. Growing environmental awareness is raising the profile of sustainable development policies, such that they may form the paradigm for economic policy in the next century. Measures to promote employment are likely to gain prominence as the threat of inflation subsides. Other aspects of economic policy will follow the orthodoxy in the European Union, with a continued emphasis on the liberalisation of factor markets and the further privatisation of public sector companies. Four interrelated issues are likely to underlie economic policy through to the end of the century: nationalism versus internationalism, dealing with unemployment, reorganising the welfare state and incorporating sustainable development into economic policy objectives.

1.6.1 Human resources

The human resources of a country represent its most important asset, providing the drive and vitality on which economic change is based. From the population emerge the entrepreneurs to lead development, the administrators and the managers, the engineers and the designers. A successful economy and a healthy society must make adequate provision for developing the potential of its population to fulfil these roles and to contribute fully to society. In this respect a comprehensive and efficient system of education and training is essential, linked to a democratic meritocracy. From the population too springs the demand for goods and services, the magnitude of which is determined by the size of the population and per-capita incomes, while changing patterns of consumer preferences are bound up with cultural change.

Official estimates put the size of the population in Spain at 39.2 million in 1995, which when set against the geographical area of the country (504,750 sq. km) yields one of the lowest population densities in western Europe (77 persons per square kilometre). The market, however, is larger than that for the resident population alone, as to it must be added over 60 million visitors a year, adding several million to the population in the summer months.

The distribution of population is very uneven, concentrated around the coast and in dispersed population clusters in the interior, notably in the capital city of Madrid and other provincial capitals. The provinces of Barcelona and Madrid, covering just 3.1 per cent of the area of Spain, contain one quarter of the national population (INE 1992). Provinces with a coastline account for 56 per cent of the normally resident population (on 31 per cent of the area); the majority of these people are crowded along the coastal littoral. In practice, the actual population around the coast is over 60 per cent, swollen in summer by Spanish and foreign tourists. Two of the three provinces with population densities in excess of 500 persons per square kilometre are found along the coast: Barcelona and Vizcaya. The choice of Madrid as the national capital has served to retain a dynamic focus of population and economic activity at the geographical heart of Spain. Outside of Madrid the interior is characterised by provinces in which population densities are less than half the national average, falling to only 10 per square kilometre in Soria and Teruel. Indeed, outside of the major towns in the interior, the absence of people is aptly described by the term 'population desert'. This pattern of population, together with the topography of the country, has fundamental implications for the provision of infrastructure, for the costs and organisation of national distribution. It has also contributed to the maintenance of strong regional markets.

As elsewhere in Europe national population growth has virtually ceased. Spain is a country of net migration gain, facing increasing pressure from immigrants from Africa; the southern migration frontier in Europe having shifted from the Pyrenees to the Mediterranean. Although not a major problem in the early 1990s, the issue of immigration is likely to grow and require further policy measures by the European Union.

Spatial variations in population change have varied through time. The haemorrhage of people from the interior and the south to the industrial areas both inside and outside Spain in the 1960s (Bradshaw 1972; Campo 1979) subsided in the mid 1970s as economic problems enveloped European economies. This left the main areas of population growth concentrated around the Mediterranean coast, especially in the south, buoyed up by a combination of net migration gain (including return migrants and retirement migrants) and higher rates of natural population growth.

Changes in the population structure constitute a crucial factor underlying changing patterns of demand, labour supply, and even political perspectives. In 1995 the population of Spain was relatively youthful in comparison with other west European countries. An estimated 18.2 per cent were aged less than sixteen and 14.9 per cent aged sixty-five and over (Figure 1.2). There are significant spatial variations around the national structure, reflecting variations both in demographic history and culture. In general, population structures in the south and around the coast are more youthful than those in the north and in the interior. The Canary Islands, Ceuta and Melilla, Andalucía and Murcia have the most youthful populations.

Fertility rates have changed abruptly. High birth rates during the 1960s (crude birth rates averaging over 20 per thousand of the population) ensured an increasing number of people reached working age during the late 1970s and 1980s, exacerbating unemployment problems and placing severe strains on the education system. Then towards the end of the 1970s and into the 1980s fertility rates plummeted, transforming the pattern of fertility from one of the highest in western Europe to one of the lowest(fertility rates falling from 2.2 in 1980 to 1.2 in 1994), such that the estimated number of children in the single year age cohort less than one in 1995 was only two-thirds that of the total number of people aged twenty-one and those aged under five were fewer than those aged sixty to sixty-five. This decline in fertility rates reflects important social changes, including the increase in female participation in the labour force, urbanisation of the population, the break-up of the extended family, the widespread adoption of contraception, and possibly the postponement of childbirth.

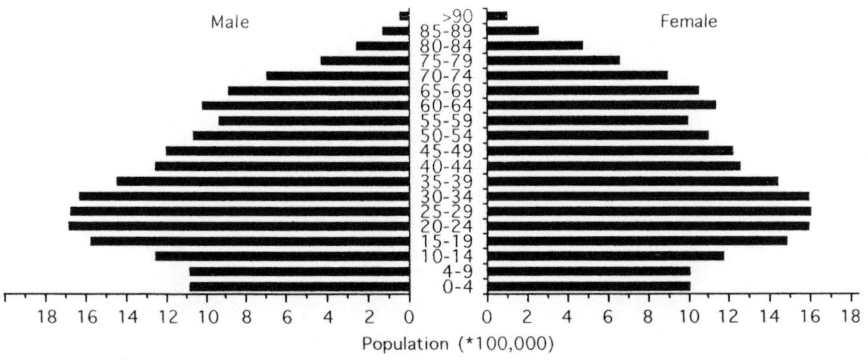

Figure 1.2 Population structure of Spain, 1995
Source: INE (population projections)

Table 1.5 Evolution of the labour force, 1960–94

	Economically active population					
Sector	1960	(%)	1965	(%)	1970	(%)
Agriculture	4,922,700	41.7	4,039,900	33.2	3,706,300	29.1
Industry	2,919,500	24.7	3,359,700	27.6	3,650,100	28.7
Construction	837,100	7.1	964,700	7.9	1,096,300	8.6
Services	3,137,300	26.5	3,812,600	31.3	4,279,500	33.6
Nc	—	—	—	—	—	—
Total	11,816,600	100.0	12,176,900	100.0	12,732,200	100.0
	1975	(%)	1980	(%)	1985	(%)
Agriculture	2,852,600	21.5	2,362,700	17.8	2,242,500	16.5
Industry	3,695,000	27.8	3,429,800	25.9	3,135,300	23.0
Construction	1,387,500	10.4	1,359,000	10.2	1,208,500	8.9
Services	5,208,800	39.2	5,571,600	42.0	5,908,300	43.3
Nc	148,300	1.1	540,700	4.1	1,135,600	8.3
Total	13,292,200	100.0	13,263,800	100.0	13,630,200	100.0
	1990	(%)	1994	(%)		
Agriculture	1,766,400	11.8	1,417,900	9.2		
Industry	3,273,400	21.8	2,990,000	19.4		
Construction	1,398,000	9.3	1,464,700	9.5		
Services	7,409,300	49.4	8,194,300	53.1		
Nc	1,145,200	7.6	1,361,200	8.8		
Total	14,992,400	100.0	15,428,100	100.0		

Occupied population

Sector	1960	(%)	1965	(%)	1970	(%)
Agriculture	4,855,800	41.7	3,968,800	33.1	3,662,300	29.2
Industry	2,874,400	24.7	3,306,100	27.6	3,583,100	28.6
Construction	797,000	6.8	933,900	7.8	1,042,000	8.3
Services	3,113,700	26.7	3,785,100	31.6	4,251,900	33.9
Total	11,640,900	100.0	11,993,900	100.0	12,539,300	100.0
	1975	(%)	1980	(%)	1985	(%)
Agriculture	2,751,100	21.7	2,253,600	19.1	2,023,300	19.0
Industry	3,599,000	28.4	3,188,400	27.1	2,612,500	24.6
Construction	1,238,600	9.8	1,050,700	8.9	744,100	7.0
Services	5,084,300	40.1	5,284,300	44.9	5,257,200	49.4
Total	12,673,000	100.0	11,777,000	100.0	10,637,100	100.0
	1990	(%)	1994	(%)		
Agriculture	1,574,600	12.6	1,209,000	10.4		
Industry	2,981,400	23.9	2,466,600	21.2		
Construction	1,174,200	9.4	1,003,300	8.6		
Services	6,751,800	54.1	6,956,300	59.8		
Total	12,481,900	100.0	11,635,300	100.0		

Figures refer to the first quarter of each year

Nc: non-classified

Source: INE (*Encuesta de la población activa*, various dates)

Lower fertility and mortality rates (as exemplified by infant mortality rates close to seven per thousand) and increasing life expectancy (expectation of life at birth approaching eighty years) have firmly established another demographic characteristic evident for some time elsewhere in Europe, that of demographic ageing. In 1960 only 6.4 per cent of the population were aged sixty-five and over, in 1981 11.3 per cent, in 1991 13.8 per cent (5.4 million people), by the year 2000 15 per cent (6.2 million) and by 2026 perhaps 20 per cent (7.4 million).

Demographic ageing has fundamental implications for social and economic development. The growing elderly population requires a policy not just for the Third Age but also one for the Fourth Age (seventy-five and over): a policy that will centre around retaining the elderly in the community and perhaps in some form of work. Among the economic implications are the shifts in the pattern of demand resulting from a more elderly population and the resources that will have to be made available to support them. For although dependency rates have remained about the same, with increased numbers of elderly people complemented by smaller numbers of children (the dependent population defined as those aged less than sixteen and those aged sixty-five and over, 36.4 per cent of the total population in 1986 and 33.1 per cent in 1995), the problem is that more public expenditure per head is required for the elderly than for children.

A crucial aspect of resource provision for the elderly centres on the social security and welfare system. In the past only a relatively narrow section of the community had the right to draw a state retirement pension and for these people pensions were generally low. Thus for many elderly people their only security lay with their families. But pension rights have now been extended to most workers (such that payments for pensions accounted for 60 per cent of all social security payments in 1993) and the social security system expanded. The increasing drain on government resources that the present system is now creating (public expenditure on social security benefits doubled between 1988 and 1993), the problems of resourcing the system in the future and the disincentive that high employer contributions have on employment creation have led the government, as in other EU countries, to seek reforms.

1.6.2 Employment

The labour force (economically active population) expanded rapidly in the late 1980s (Table 1.5), reaching 15.4 million in the first quarter of 1994, an increase of half a million on the 1990 figure and almost two million on 1985. Growth reflected an increase in both the population of working age and female economic activity rates. Between 1985 and 1994 the number of people aged sixteen to sixty-five grew by over one and a half million and female economic activity rates from 28 to 35 per cent (as measured by the number of economically active females to the total number of females aged sixteen and over) . These factors will sustain further growth of the labour force to the end of the century. However, within the labour force less than twelve million were in employment in 1994 (the occupied population), a measure of the unemployment problem and, despite a three-fold expansion of the economy in real terms and an increase of one quarter in the population, remarkably little changed from the number employed in 1960 (although the real figure for employment is thought to be above that recorded in the Employment Survey, Encuesta de la población activa).

As in other OECD countries the trend has been towards a progressive accumulation of employment in the service sector of the economy (60 per cent of the occupied population in 1994) and a decline of the proportion employed in the primary and industrial sectors (10 and 21 per cent respectively; Figure 1.3). In 1960 only 3.1 million people (27 per cent of the occupied population) were recorded as working in the service sector, by 1994 the figure had more than doubled to over 7 million. Between 1985 and 1994 alone the number of jobs in services increased by one and a half million. In contrast, the number working in agriculture has continued to fall. In 1960 4.9 million people worked in the sector (42 per cent of the occupied population), by 1994 the figure was down to just over one million; half a million jobs being lost between 1985 and 1994. Employment in industry (including mining, gas, electricity and water) peaked in the early 1970s at close to 3.3 million (one quarter of the labour force), thence falling to 2.5 million in 1994. Employment in the sector displayed strong growth in the late 1980s (reaching three million in 1990) before dropping sharply in the early 1990s. Outside of these sectors a notable characteristic of the employment structure is the large proportion classified to construction (8–10 per cent), a group particularly vulnerable to cyclical changes in the economy. These employment trends appear set to continue.

A large sector of the economy remains hidden from official statistics, variously described as the black, submerged or underground economy (*la economía sumergida;* Benito 1987). Although by definition the magnitude and importance of this sector is unknown, it is generally recognised to be considerable (possibly one fifth of the economy employing 2 million people). It is of particular importance in the service industry, in construction and in those manufacturing industries where entry is easy (for example in textiles, toys and food); significant employment in the black economy is therefore likely to exist in tourism, in the shoe and toy industries of Alicante and Valencia, in the textile industry of Cataluña and the food industries of Andalucía. Its existence is deeply embedded in social attitudes to the payment of taxes, in informal working arrangements and in the widespread existence of small family firms. Many people work in the visible economy for long enough to gain entitlement to unemployment benefit, then seek work in the black economy where they are exempt from taxation. Simultaneously, employers avoid both having to make social security payments and the difficulties of complying with employment legislation, allowing them to cut labour when necessary. Thus the black economy has long provided a flexible employment system.

A particular feature of the labour market has been its rigidity, maintaining uneconomic overstaffing, discouraging employment creation and pushing up wages (OECD 1994). There has been a long tradition of job security dating back to legislation passed during the Franco era (Ordenanzas de Trabajo) and revised in the Basic Employment Law (Ley Básica de Empleo) and Workers Statute (Estatuto de los Trabajadores) in the early 1980s. Dismissals necessitated a lengthy redundancy procedure involving agreement from the government and trade unions (*expediente de regulación de empleo*) and large redundancy payments (often much in excess of that stipulated by labour legislation). These factors tended to strengthen workers' bargaining power in collective wage negotiations (*convenios collectivos*). Moreover, the trade unions exercised far greater power than their small

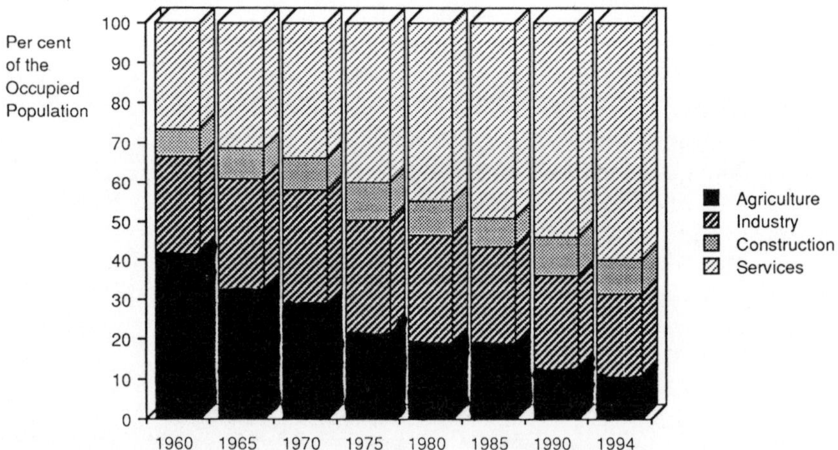

Figure 1.3 Evolution of the employment structure, 1960–94
Source: INE (*Encuesta de la población activa*)

membership (estimated to be around one million) would suggest. This power was exercised through their control over collective wage negotiations, which once agreed within a sector applied throughout that sector. Inadequate training facilities, rent controls and strong regional attachments further hindered labour mobility. Thus, rigidity was supported by the legal framework of employment and by labour market practices.

Successive governments from the late 1970s onwards were unable to introduce fundamental labour market reforms, needing to retain the support of the trade unions. Progress on increasing flexibility in the labour market was limited mainly to introducing new types of employment contracts. Until 1981 the only form of contract was that for indefinite employment (*contrato fijo*). The introduction of a variety of temporary contracts during the 1980s led to these covering about one third of the occupied labour force in 1994. They enabled employers to dismiss workers without the difficulties and costs entailed with indefinite contracts. Simultaneously, they undermined workers' rights and encouraged employers to take on employees on temporary contracts only. Thus the labour market developed a dual character with rigid and flexible segments.

Following fruitless discussions with trade unions in 1993 the government decided to push labour market reforms through parliament in 1994 without the support of the trade unions. Reforms were aimed at employment creation and increasing the flexibility of the labour market. They spanned all aspects of the operation of the labour market, including reform of the basic labour legislation embraced in the Workers Statute and Basic Employment Law (covering such issues as dismissal procedures, collective bargaining and new legislation covering strike action), reforms to the system of employment contracts, measures to stimulate geographical and occupational mobility and legislation to end the state monopoly over job placement (exercised through the National Employment Institute, INEM) allowing in private employment agencies.

1.6.3 Unemployment

The apparent low level of employment (including high unemployment and low economic activity rates) is the most serious socio-economic problem in Spain. Unemployment began to rise in the early 1970s and continued rising almost inexorably through to the mid 1990s (Figure 1.4). Throughout the 1980s unemployment was above 14 per cent, topping 20 per cent in the mid 1980s and reaching a historic high of one quarter of the labour force (3.8 million people) in the first quarter of 1994 (based on statistics from the National Employment Survey). These extraordinarily high levels of unemployment occurred against a background of economic activity rates below the average for the European Union (notably low female rates). The real rates of unemployment, when employment in the black economy was taken into account,

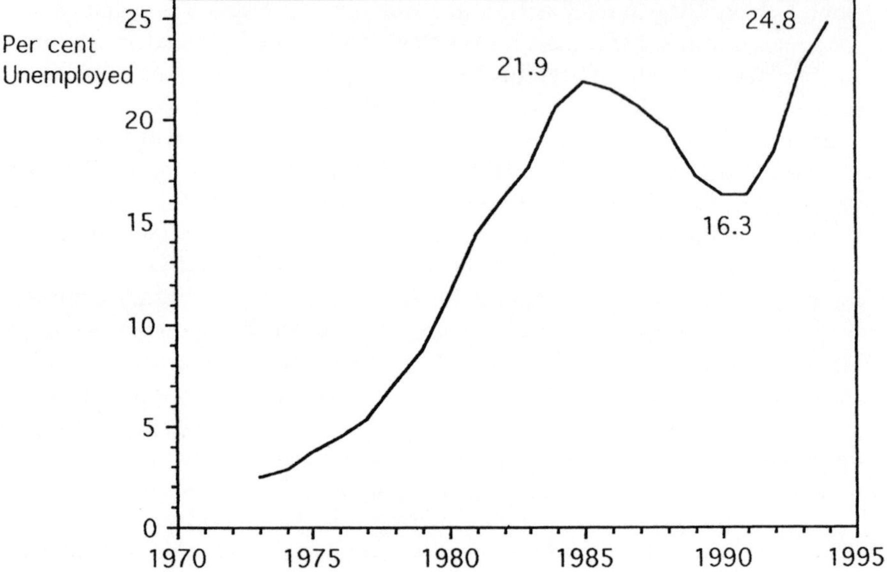

Figure 1.4 Evolution of unemployment 1973–94
Source: INE (*Encuesta de la población activa*)

were somewhat below these figures (perhaps six percentage points below). Nevertheless the scale of unemployment constitutes the most serious socio-economic problem facing Spain (and indeed Europe) in the 1990s.

Pressures underlying the growth of unemployment can be traced to the expansion of the population of working age, the end of large-scale emigration and the appearance of return migration, higher female economic activity rates, the existence of widespread multiple employment (*pluriempleo*) and overtime working, and factors related to structural change in the economy (notably the continued decline of employment in agriculture and in traditional manufacturing and the more recent shake-out in employment in services). But the weakness of the economy to create legitimate jobs had also to be attributed to the rigidity of the labour market (OECD 1994). Prior to labour market reforms in 1994 the economy had to grow by over 2 per cent before there was net job creation.

Particular characteristics of unemployment have been the high rates among young people, women and the less skilled (54 per cent in the age group 15–19 in the first quarter of 1994; 59 per cent among women of this age; INE 1994), plus the high levels of long-term unemployment (over half the unemployed in the ten years before 1994 had been unemployed for longer than one year). Moreover, there are wide spatial variations in unemployment, with rates significantly above the national average in the south

(34 per cent in the first quarter of 1994 in Andalucía), reflecting historical and structural factors, the composition of output, the level of economic development, the mobility of labour, social characteristics and possibly a larger black economy.

1.6.4 Structural reform

Structural reform linked to creating flexibility in the economy became a central tenet of economic development strategy in the 1980s. In Spain traditional institutions and practices have given the country its distinctive image and arguably contributed to a stronger sense of social cohesion than in many northern European countries. But they have also inhibited change and greater efficiency, and been an important factor underlying high inflation and the waste of resources (OECD 1994). Thus in the early 1990s a more determined effort was made to increase flexibility in the land and labour markets and in the institutions regulating the economy. In general, where markets and institutions are covered by international arrangements, liberalisation has made substantial progress. For example, the capital markets have been liberalised and in 1989 a new competition law was passed, strengthening the independence of the Competition Court and increasing the responsibilities of the government Service for the Defence of Competition. But where markets and institutions have been subject mainly to domestic pressures, change has been much slower. Legislation to seriously reform the labour market was only initiated in 1993 as detailed above. Similarly, legislation was only just passing through parliament in 1994 to reform the land market in the guise of the Urban and the Rural Land Rental Laws (Leyes de Arrendamientos Urbanos and Rústicos). The intention is gradually to liberalise the market for old leases (dating from before 1985), bringing regulated rents, which are now sometimes 90 per cent below those of new leases, slowly back to market-related levels over the next ten years. Moreover, the legislation considerably curbs the possibility of transferring leases to descendants and proposes a minimum of four years for new leases. Finally, in the professions anti-competitive practices and rigidities in general have abounded; membership is obligatory in order to practice, there are barriers to entry, competition within a set geographical area (for example a municipality or province) is severely restricted and minimum price fixing is common (OECD 1994).

1.6.5 Continued internationalisation

The process of integration into the international economy will continue through the 1990s with the further incorporation of European Union regulations and the GATT agreements into business practice in Spain and further penetration of the economy by foreign capital through acquisitions and equity holdings in newly privatised companies and those floated on the stock market. In 1993 there was an enormous surge in inward foreign investment, investment rising by 200 per cent on 1992 (Banco de España 1994). The surge resulted from a growth in marketable securities, corresponding largely to the growth in public debt held by non-residents prompted by interest rate reductions. There was also further growth in outward foreign investment, once again dominated by securities. International financial markets are now highly integrated, accommodating large financial flows, the volume and direction of which are likely to be unstable. As was demonstrated during the collapse of the ERM, these financial markets now have the power to overturn government policy.

Net inward direct investment appeared to decline from 1990 to 1993 inclusive (in 1993 a new classification of the capital account items was introduced making historical comparisons difficult). In part this was associated with a number of highly publicised examples of disinvestment. Prominent among these were the withdrawal of support by the Kuwait Investment Office from its Spanish holdings, the decision by Volkswagen to stop assembling cars at its Zona Franca plant, the threatened closures of the Suzuki motor-vehicle plant at Linares and of the Gillette factory in Seville and the closure of the Ebro-Kubota tractor plant in Madrid. Given the stage of the business cycle in industrialised economies, these may be isolated examples which do not constitute a trend. However, the horizons of international capital are now wider than they were in the 1980s, with greater competition for mobile investment from other OECD countries, from eastern Europe and around the Mediterranean basin, and from the 'emerging markets' of South-east Asia and Latin America. In relation to disinvestment, in some cases companies appeared to be shifting production to lower labour cost regions (for example Colgate Palmolive moving to Portugal, moves by Grundig and Philips away from Barcelona and investment by VW in eastern Europe). With the completion of the European Single Market company strategy was also shifting towards the rationalisation of activities to serve the European, as opposed to just the Spanish market (as appeared to be the case with Gillette).

Spanish outward foreign direct investment has also gradually been gaining ground. Although once again it is difficult to separate the short-term response to a depressed domestic market from a longer-term trend, overseas expansion will be essential to offset increased competition at home and to gain access to the economies offered by overseas locations. Initially restricted to a few, often public or mixed public/private companies and to the neighbouring markets of the European Union, north Africa and Latin America, activity outside Spain has been spreading to embrace a larger number of businesses operating in a broader geographical area.

1.7 Restructuring of the Spanish economy

What distinguishes the pattern of economic development in Spain from that of other west European countries in the second half of the twentieth century is the late arrival of industrialisation, the late opening of the economy to international business and the late adaptation of Spanish business culture to operating in a competitive international environment; characteristics which can largely be explained in terms of the profound influence of a history of autarchy, government intervention and protection. To these characteristics may be added the pace of institutional change in the last quarter of the century: from dictatorship to democracy, from centralism to regionalism, from protectionism to liberalism, from nationalism to internationalism and from state corporate capitalism to an open mixed market economy, compounding the changes induced by technological developments and precipitating restructuring throughout the economy. This process of restructuring has involved changes in the institutional and regulatory setting of business, the composition and spatial distribution of economic activity, the size structure and ownership of business and the level of international integration; a process which is documented sector by sector in the following chapters of this book.

Development has been rapid but uneven in time and space, changing the composition of employment while leaving a legacy of business structures shaped by a former business environment, creating urban industrial centres while leaving other areas dependent on a crumbling agricultural or mining base. In 1950 Spain displayed many features akin to those of a less developed country. Half the labour force were in agriculture, forestry and fishing, and the infant mortality rate was over sixty per thousand. Autarchic policies in the first half of the twentieth century had fashioned the economy into one lacking competitiveness and dominated by small businesses, using cheap labour and traditional technologies. Relaxation of these policies at the end of the 1950s contributed to the 'economic miracle', characterised by rapid economic growth and industrialisation based on cheap energy. But inefficient production structures were sustained by protectionism, while innovation was discouraged by extensive government intervention. The long period of suffocating political inertia under the Franco regime was finally broken in the mid 1970s, political metamorphosis coinciding with worldwide economic adjustment to accommodate the escalation in oil prices. The extent and profound nature of these changes were then magnified by the integration of the economy into the European Community and a wider opening to the world economy, reshaping the economy to one dominated by employment in services, especially reliant on tourism and increasingly dominated by foreign capital, altering the way in which people earn their living, the way in which they live and the public and private power relations of the Spanish political economy.

The pace of change provided an eloquent commentary on the new business environment of greater international integration, especially as expressed in the transfer of technology, liberal capital markets and mobile capital, enabled by new information technologies. It illustrated the dramatic impact that the opening of economies to international capital can have at the end of the twentieth century; an example in western Europe of the actual and potential for transformation in the emerging economies.

Integration has been a key feature in recent development, especially integration into the European Union, tying the economy more closely into complex international systems through economic and institutional arrangements. Each round of trade liberalisation has been associated with economic growth: in the 1960s following the Stabilisation Plan, in the early 1970s following the preferential trade agreement with the EEC, and in the late 1980s following membership of the EC. But a more open trading system has also accelerated the process of structural change, outstripping the capacity of the economy to adapt and to create new employment. Furthermore, it has been accompanied by an increasing transfer of power and control over development to supranational and multinational institutions, such that economic development is now strongly influenced by international forces and decisions made outside of Spain in international political forums and the headquarters of foreign multinational companies. These changes, which to a greater or lesser degree affect all states, undermine the traditional notion of the nation state (externally independent and internally omnipotent) and national sovereignty, threatening national identity as many of the distinctive features of Spanish culture are swept away and replaced by a more homogeneous European culture. Concerns over these issues were heightened in the early 1990s by recession, by examples of foreign disinvestment and the spectre of Spanish companies 'exporting' jobs by shifting production overseas. Such concerns pose questions over how far Spain (and other European economies) will be willing to travel along the road of internationalism and open economic systems, what degree of 'management' will be imposed and whether there will be a return to some form of economic nationalism.

Throughout the economy the size structure of business is characterised by a large proportion of small businesses and a paucity of major Spanish multinational companies (in September 1994 there were only three Spanish companies in the Financial Times top one hundred European companies by market capitalisation; Financial Times 1995). While small businesses make a valuable contribution to the economy they are nevertheless frequently unable to compete internationally with larger firms. In most sectors market pressures (sometimes with government encouragement) are now inducing the formation of larger firms and businesses are establishing an international presence, especially in Latin America where Spanish firms have a cultural advantage. However, foreign capital continues to gain ground absorbing an increasing proportion of business in Spain. It is a cause for concern that relatively few major multinational companies are headquartered in Spain, since these are powerful decision-making centres in the world economy and it has been argued that it is at headquarters locations that a complex of high value-added activities develop (Hoggart 1991). The paucity of major multinational companies also restricts the ability of Spain to project itself on the world stage.

An important element of restructuring relates to changes in the spatial organisation of economic activity. Of concern here is that a reworking of spatial patterns of specialisation within the European Union will concentrate decision making, research and development, and many high value-added activities, in the existing core area of north-west Europe, only permitting a scatter of new centres (for example in southern Germany, southern France and Cataluña). Within Spain, self-sustained development appears well established in Cataluña, Madrid, along the Ebro Valley and down the Mediterranean coast at least as far as Valencia. Elsewhere development is much more sticky. Furthermore, a unified Germany and the emergence of market economies in eastern Europe open up an eastward dimension to future European development. In the context of this and previous remarks, the position of Spain looks peripheral, both geographically and in terms of economic power: a magnificent sunny property on the edge of the European Community: 'España es un magnífico solar [soleado] al lado del Mercado Común Europeo.' (Fuentes Quintana 1988, p. 68).

In the rapidly changing world political economy of the last quarter of the twentieth century there was little alternative for Spain other than to open its economy and anchor itself to the neighbouring countries of Europe. In so doing, a respectable level of economic development has been achieved together with a more liberal and dynamic society. The principal problem has been the rise of unemployment, the causes of which, as was argued above, lie partly in the institutions and culture of the country. Adapting these institutions to accommodate the new economic environment was always going to be a painful process and therefore relatively slow within a democracy, especially within a society that has hung on to many of the customs and traditions of the past.

As the end of the twentieth century draws nearer the distinctiveness of the Spanish economy is fading to leave an economy moulded in a pan-European style, embedded in European and wider international business and political systems, and faced with similar problems to those elsewhere in western Europe. International economic forces and European Union policies constitute the context within which the contemporary story of economic development in Spain is unfolding, hence an active policy of external relations is crucial to protect and enhance national interests. But domestic policy continues to have a crucial role to play in seeking to create a business environment that will attract and sustain internationally competitive business while ensuring an attractive social environment for its citizens. Given further investment in amenities, education and infrastructure, a cohesive society, a stable political environment and further liberalisation, Spain should be able to attract its share of new internationally competitive business and new investment, and to achieve a respectable level of development into the next century.

References and bibliography

Almarcha Barbado, A. (ed.) (1993) *Spain and EC membership evaluated.* London: Pinter Publishers

Alonso, J. (1988) 'El sector exterior', in J. García Delgado (ed.), *España: Tomo II, Economía,* pp. 273–365. Madrid: Espasa-Calpe SA

Aríztegui, J. (1988) 'La política monetaria', in J. García Delgado (ed.), *España: Tomo II, Economía,* pp. 903–26. Madrid: Espasa-Calpe SA

Banco de Bilbao (1980) *Informe económico 1979.* Bilbao

Banco Bilbao Vizcaya, BBV (1991) 'Inversión extranjera en España', in *Servex, boletín de comercio exterior,* No. 38, February, pp. 4–6. Bilbao

Banco Bilbao Vizcaya, BBV (1993a) *Informe económico 1992.* Bilbao

Banco Bilbao Vizcaya, BBV (1993b) 'The Spanish economy in 1991 and 1992', *Situacion,* international edition. Bilbao: BBV

Banco de España (1990) *Boletín estadístico,* April. Madrid

Banco de España (1993a) *Boletín estadístico,* May. Madrid

Banco de España (1993b) *La balanza de pagos de España en 1991 y 1992.* Madrid

Banco de España (1994) *Boletín estadístico,* June. Madrid

Benito, S. (1987) 'La economía sumergida en España', *Revista del Instituto de Estudios Económicos,* No.1, pp. 254–88

Bradshaw, R. (1972) 'Internal migration in Spain', *Iberian Studies,* Vol.I, No. 2, pp. 68–75

Campo, S. del (1979) 'Spain', in R. Krane (ed.), *International labour migration in Europe,* pp. 156–63. New York: Praeger Publishers

Carr, R. and J. Fusi (2nd edn, 1981) *Spain: dictatorship to democracy.* London: Unwin Hyman

Carreras, A. (1988) 'La industrialización española en el marco de la historia económica europea', in J. García Delgado (ed.), *España: Tomo II, Economía,* pp. 79–118. Madrid: Espasa-Calpe SA

Carreras, A. (ed.) (1989a) *Estadísticas historicas de España: Siglos XIX–XX.* Madrid: Fundación Banco Exterior

Carreras, A. (1989b) 'La renta y la riqueza', in A. Carreras (ed.), *Estadísticas historicas de España: Siglos XIX–XX,* Chapter 13. Madrid: Fundación Banco Exterior

Chislett, W. (1992) *The internationalisation of the economy.* London: Euromoney publications

Clark, R. and M. Haltzel (eds) (1987) *Spain in the 1980s: the democratic transition and a new international role.* Cambridge, Mass: Ballinger Publishing Company

El País (1993) *Anuario El País,* 1993. Madrid

El País (1994) *Anuario El País,* 1994. Madrid

Financial Times (1995) *FT 500,* special supplement, 20 January. London

Fontana, J. and J. Nadal (1976) 'Spain 1914–1970', in C. Cipolla (ed.), *The Fontana economic history of Europe,* Vol. 6, Pt. ii, pp. 460–529. London: Collins

Fuentes Quintana, E. (1988) 'Tres decenios de la economía española en perspectiva', in J. García Delgado (ed.), *España: Tomo II, Economía,* pp. 1–75. Madrid: Espasa-Calpe SA

García Delgado, J. (ed.) (6th edn, aumentada y actualizada 1993) *España: economía.* Madrid: Editorial Espasa-Calpe

Gilmour, D. (1985) *The transformation of Spain.* London: Quartet Books

Harrison, J. (1985) *The Spanish economy in the twentieth century.* London: Croom Helm

Harrison, J. (1993) *The Spanish economy: from Civil War to the European Community.* London: Macmillan Press

Hoggart, K. (1991) 'The changing world of corporate control centres', *Geography,* April, pp. 109–20

Hooper, J. (1987) *The Spaniards: a portrait of the new Spain.* Harmondsworth: Penguin

Información Comercial Española (1990) '50 años de economía española 1939–1989, 2 vols, Nos 676 and 677, diciembre 1989–enero 1990. Madrid: Ministerio de Economía y Hacienda

Instituto Nacional de Estadística, INE (1992) *Censo de la población 1991.* Madrid

Instituto Nacional de Estadística, INE (1994) *Encuesta de la población activa, primero trimestre* 1994. Madrid

Jurdao Arrones, F. (1979) *España en venta.* Madrid: Editorial Ayuso

Lieberman, S. (1982) *The contemporary Spanish economy.* London: George Allen and Unwin

Maravall, F. (ed.) (1987) *Economía y política industrial en España.* Madrid: Ediciones Pirámide

Mochón, F., G. Ancochea and A. Avila (1988) *Economía española 1964–1987: introducción al análisis económico.* Madrid: McGraw-Hill

Nadal, J. (1973) 'The failure of the industrial revolution in Spain, 1830–1914', in C. Cipolla (ed.), *The Fontana economic history of Europe,* Vol. 4, Pt. ii, pp. 532–626. London: Collins

Nadal, J., A. Carreras and C. Sudria (eds) (1987) *La economía española en el siglo XX: una perspectiva histórica.* Barcelona: Editorial Ariel

OECD (1984) *OECD economic surveys: Spain 1983–1984.* Paris

OECD (1993) *OECD economic surveys: Spain 1992–1993.* Paris

OECD (1994) *OECD economic surveys: Spain 1993–1994.* Paris

Ontiveros, E. (1991) 'Penetración extranjera', *El País* (sección negocios), 30 June, p. 2

Paloma Sánchez, M. (ed.) (1993) *Los grandes retos de la economía española en los noventa.* Madrid: Ediciones Pirámide

Pérez Simarro, R. (1986) 'Situación comparativa de la industria española', *Economía Industrial,* No. 246, pp. 21–31. Madrid

Porter, M. (1990) *The competitive advantage of nations.* London: Macmillan Press

Roman, M. (1971) *The limits of economic growth in Spain.* New York: Praeger Publishers

Salmon, K. (1995) 'Spain in the world economy', in R. Gillespie and J. Story (eds), *Democratic Spain: reshaping external relations in a changing world.* London: Routledge

Sebastián, L. de (1992) 'El barca, Induráin y Maastricht', *El País,* 2 June, p. 54

Tamames, R. (1986) *The Spanish economy.* London: C. Hurst and Company

Tamames, R. (22nd edn, 1993) *Estructura económica de España.* Madrid: Alianza Editorial

Tena, A. (1989) 'Comercio exterior', in A. Carreras (ed.), *Estadísticas historicas de España: Siglos XIX–XX,* Chapter 8. Madrid: Fundación Banco Exterior

Tortella, G. (1994) *El desarrollo de la España contemporánea. Historia económica de los siglos XIX and XX.* Madrid: Alianza Editorial

Tovias, A. (1995) 'Spain in the European Commuity', in R. Gillespie and J. Story (eds), *Democratic Spain: reshaping external relations in a changing world.* London: Routledge

Tsoukalis, L. (1981) *The European Community and its Mediterranean enlargement.*

London: Croom Helm
Velarde, J., J. García Delgado and A. Pedreño (eds) (1991) *Apertura e internacionalización de la economía española.* Madrid: Economístas Libros
Vicens Vives, J. (1969) *An economic history of Spain.* Princeton: Princeton University Press
Vilar, P. (2nd edn, 1977) *Spain: a brief history.* Oxford: Pergamon Press
Wright, A. (1977) *The Spanish economy 1959–1976.* London: Macmillan

Chapter 2
The public sector

2.1 The public sector

In an increasingly integrated world economy, and a closer European Union, it is easy to underestimate the role of national governments in influencing the pattern of economic development within their jurisdiction. Yet, national governments continue to exercise a crucial role in shaping the business environment and in allocating resources within their economies. In terms of resources, total public expenditure in the 1994 budget in Spain was forecast at pta 28,631 billion, some 45 per cent of forecast GDP. Clearly the allocation of this expenditure has fundamental implications for the evolution of the economy. The total public debt in circulation at the end of 1994 was estimated at 60 per cent of gross domestic product (BBV 1994). Simply servicing this debt cost 5 per cent of GDP and 10 per cent of public expenditure, contributing to a large public sector deficit (close to 7 per cent of GDP in 1993 and 1994), diverting investment funds away from productive investment and putting upward pressure on interest rates. Part of public sector revenue and expenditure is related to the direct participation of the public sector in the economy through public enterprises. It is these public enterprises, especially state enterprises, that form the focus of this chapter.

The history of the Spanish economy in the twentieth century is one of extensive state intervention. All aspects of the political economy, including administration and a wide range of prices, wages and trade, were highly centralised and closely regulated from Madrid. Simultaneously, Spain was a country of low public expenditure and low taxation. In 1964 public expenditure and revenue from taxation were each only 19 per cent of GDP (Mochón et al. 1988).

During the late 1970s and 1980s the public finances were transformed as Spain moved towards a welfare state. Public expenditure (embracing responsibilities for administration, the legal system, social security and public enterprises; Figure 2.1) as a percentage of GDP rose from 25 per cent

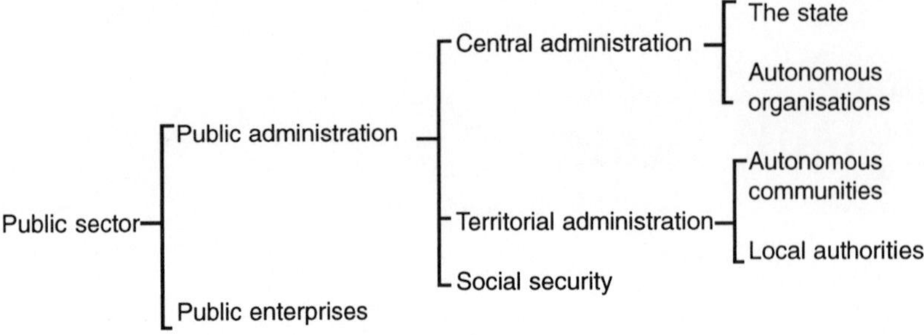

Figure 2.1 Structure of the public sector
Source: Adapted from Mochón et al. 1988

in 1975 to 45 per cent in 1994 (inflated especially by higher social security payments and larger local authority spending bills, but bringing Spain roughly into line with other EU countries). Tax receipts as a proportion of GDP (the tax burden) rose in parallel from 22 per cent in 1975. Indeed, during the 1980s the tax burden in Spain (direct and indirect taxes plus social security contributions) increased more than in any other OECD country, rising from 26.6 per cent of GDP in 1980 to 36.6 per cent in 1992 (OECD 1984 and 1993; Segura 1988).

Public sector activity began to be realigned in the late 1980s and early 1990s, reflecting a tendency throughout western Europe for governments to retrace their role in the economy, withdrawing from many traditional forms of intervention (especially from direct participation through public enterprises; Jonquiéres 1990; Vickers and Wright 1988), while high levels of expenditure on administration and services continue despite efforts to contain them. Thus public expenditure as a percentage of GDP in Spain stabilised at around 42 per cent, numerous public enterprises were privatised and many forms of state regulation dismantled. Simultaneously, new systems of intervention emerged both at the supra-national (European Union) level and at the sub-national (regional) level. For example, the national system of agricultural price support in Spain was replaced by that operating under the Common Agricultural Policy and responsibility for planning development control was devolved to the regions and local authorities. Less direct state participation in economies allowed the advance of capitalism and further integration of the international economic system. A corollary of this change was the retreat of Socialism, not just in western Europe but also in eastern Europe, the former Soviet Union and the Far East.

The broad shift towards market capitalism followed from disillusion in certain circles with earlier economic policies to deal with the economic crisis of the 1970s, coupled with a reassertion of individual freedom over the state. Disenchantment with *dirigisme* and Keynesianism was bound up in ideological and economic arguments, which embraced the perceived bureaucratic inefficiency of the public sector, the appearance of stagflation, the strains of higher public debt, a reaction against the high levels of taxation needed to support weighty public sectors and the political risks associated with managing a large public sector labour force. Nationalised industries were left in a weaker position by more international forms of production, marketing and finance, and by EC competition policy. The private firm operating within a market economy was held to be the means of achieving wealth creation. Thus policies emerged to secure changes in the economic environment: more restrictive budgetary policy, tighter control on public expenditure, attacks on regional policy, tax reforms, labour market policies designed to increase flexibility, and reductions in the size of public administrations and subsidies to 'lame duck' industries.

European Union initiatives, especially competition policy and the creation of the Single European Market, have heightened the pace of withdrawal from direct public sector participation in the economy. These initiatives have required the removal of barriers to trade and competition within the Union, necessitating measures to increase competitiveness within member countries. In some countries, notably Britain under successive Conservative governments, this emphasis on reduced state involvement has been underpinned by a clearly stated ideological position. It is not surprising therefore that Britain has witnessed the most radical revision of the public sector (with all saleable public enterprises, including public utilities and defence industries, being privatised). In other countries, including Spain, the process of change has been more a pragmatic response to circumstances. Once Spain opted to join the European Community and open its economy there was little choice but to adopt the reforms necessary to participate (and survive) within the new economic environment; the march of international capitalism and the desire to be at the heart of Europe were irresistible. An increase in the public sector deficit in the early 1990s provided a further argument for the sale of public assets.

2.2 Public enterprises

Public enterprises are an important component of the public sector and among the most visible elements of it. They are none the less difficult to define precisely. In Spain they have evolved through the acquisition of enterprises for various reasons rather than being the product of a single coherent policy. Thus, public enterprises in Spain have not been concentrated in the field of utilities and strategic industries (sometimes considered as areas of natural state monopoly where the market mechanism is inappropriate). They have emerged across the whole spectrum of economic activity, their composition changing through time as companies have passed to and from the private sector.

The limits of the public sector are drawn according to the extent of public ownership in companies (from 1 to 100 per cent) and the extent of control (from minority participation to full control). A rough guide to the definition of a public enterprise is an organisation whose main purpose is to produce goods and services for the market and in which there is more than 50 per cent ownership by the public administration, or where the public administration has a significant role in the management, as in Telefónica (where the state had only a 32 per cent holding in 1994; Myro 1988). These companies are listed by the government in official statistics (IGA 1988). However, many companies in which the state has some influence are excluded from this list, as are the many enterprises that have been created, transferred to or invested in, by lower tiers of government.

Once enterprises that belong to the public sector have been defined, there is then the problem of their classification. Initially this may be based on the tier of government within which they are located: within the central, regional or local administration. Then, for those enterprises dependent on the central administration, further classification can be made according to: i) whether they fall into one of the major state holding companies: Corporación Bancaria de España (CBE), Grupo Patrimonio (Dirección General del Patrimonio del Estado, DGPE), Instituto Nacional de Hidrocarburos (INH) and Instituto Nacional de Industria (INI) or depend directly on one of the ministries (for example, the railway company Renfe and the postal service Correos on the Ministry of Public Works, Transport and Environment); and ii) the type of activity undertaken.

The Ministry of Economy and Finance makes a broad division of the public sector into: i) the administration of the state (ministerial departments); ii) the administration of social security; iii) constitutional bodies (such as the parliament); iv) the institutional administration of the state; v) organisations with a special legal status; and vi) state enterprises. Public enterprises of various types are concentrated in the latter three classes. In legal terms the organisations in (iv) and (v) are autonomous organisations of the state while those in (vi) are state enterprises.

Autonomous organisations are subdivided into: a) administrative organisations; b) commercial, financial and non-financial organisations; and c) organisations with special legal status (*entidades con estatuto jurídico especial*). In 1992 there were 38 administrative organisations (for example the National Statistics Institute) and 63 commercial, financial and industrial organisations. Commercial services were provided by the postal and telecommunication service (Dirección General de Correos y Telecomunicaciones). An example of a financial organisation was the insurance group Consorcio de Compensación de Seguros. Non-financial organisations included the water authorities (*confederaciones hidrográficas*), seaport authorities (*juntas de puertos*), the Official Bulletin of State (*Boletín Oficial del Estado*), the National State Lottery Organisation (Organismo Nacional de Loterías y Apuestas del Estado) and agricultural organisations such as

Forppa, From, Icona, Senpa, etc. Finally, autonomous organisations with a special legal status included the national radio and television service (Radio y Televisión Español), the Bank of Spain (Banco de España), the Trade Institute (Instituto de Comercio Exterior) and the Spanish airports authority (Aeropuertos Españoles).

State enterprises (trading organisations) can be subdivided into two types: a) organisations with a public legal status (*entidades de derecho público*), within which there are financial and non-financial organisations (an example of the former being the Instituto de Crédito Oficial and examples of the latter being the railway companies Feve and Renfe and the INI); and b) trading companies (*sociedades mercantiles*), which can also be subdivided into financial and non-financial companies (examples of the former being all the state banks in the CBE and the public insurance company Sociedad Mutua de Seguros of the INI; examples of the latter being all the companies with majority participation by the state holding companies Grupo Patrimonio and INI). In 1992 there were 17 organisations with a public legal status and 481 state trading companies (MEH 1992).

2.3 Public enterprises in the Spanish economy

Public enterprises have operated throughout the Spanish economy but they have been particularly prominent in coal mining, mercury, oil and gas, electricity and water, iron and steel, aluminium, tobacco, shipbuilding, transport materials, transport and communications. In 1986 there were 180 companies in which the state had a direct majority holding, together with 300 subsidiaries and more than 500 minority holdings (Fernández Rodriguez 1989). It is estimated that between 1980 and 1986 state public enterprises were responsible for 8 to 10 per cent of the total value of production of goods and services (gross value added), and 10 to 16 per cent of the gross capital formation in Spain (Ortiz Junquera and Gómez Rodrigo 1989). In terms of employment they accounted for about 5 per cent of the labour force. In the industrial sector public enterprises represented about 16 per cent of the gross value added and 9 per cent of the industrial labour force (Fariñas et al. 1989). These figures were far smaller than in France, where nationalised industry accounted for about 30 per cent of gross national product in 1989 (Jonquiéres 1990).

Although numerous public enterprises have been shed from the public sector since the mid 1980s, it continues to occupy a significant position in the economy. The public sector embraces some of the largest businesses in Spain, including: Argentaria, Correos, Iberia, Renfe and Telefónica; companies that employed 18,000, 60,000, 24,000, 50,000 and 74,000 respectively in 1993. In 1992 it was estimated that public sector businesses still contributed close to 10 per cent of GDP, much less than in France, Greece, Ireland, Italy and Portugal, and only substantially more than in Britain (Casamayor

1994a). In the same year companies in the Grupo Patrimonio generated value added equivalent to 3 per cent of the total in the Spanish economy and investment represented almost 5 per cent of total national fixed capital formation (Grupo Patrimonio 1993). The companies in the INI group would add some 2 per cent to each of these figures. Employment in the Grupo Patrimonio and INI/Teneo in 1994 amounted to over 2 per cent of the occupied population. The significance of these companies in the economy also varies geographically, for example they are particularly important in Asturias and in parts of Andalucía.

2.4 Major non-financial public enterprise groups

The National Industry Institute (Instituto Nacional de Industria, INI) is the holding company that embraces most of the public sector industrial companies, participating, directly or indirectly, in over 600 companies at the beginning of 1994, employing some 130,000 people. INI operates within the legal framework of a public company (within the Ministry of Industry) subject to private company law (this legal status was adopted in 1989 under the Ley de Presupuestos del Estado, *para* 1989, *artículo* 123, which transformed the company from an autonomous organisation of the state into a state company: 'una entidad de derecho público sometida al ordenamiento privado'). This status allows INI to operate like a private company, simultaneously obliging it to take more account of profit and efficiency in its allocation of resources, thereby placing more emphasis on entrepreneurial activity than in a traditional public enterprise. However, its interventionist role outlined in its 1941 constitution was retained and it remains constrained by political considerations. Along with other public enterprise trading companies, under European Community regulations it should have abandoned its dependence on state funds from 1993.

In 1992 a limited liability company (*sociedad anónima*) was formed within the INI group (Teneo SA) to which direct ownership in 47 INI companies was transferred. These companies were the ones that were considered to be viable businesses and able to operate without public subsidies. Reorganisation allowed INI to go some way towards meeting the business criteria for public companies required by the European Community. Teneo is the largest industrial group in Spain spanning activities ranging across all sectors of the economy from mining to services (Figure 2.2), although the focus of the group is on energy (especially on the electricity utility Endesa) and air transport (primarily Iberia and Aviaco). In 1992 the Teneo group accounted for 35 per cent of all electricity generated in Spain, over 60 per cent of eucalyptus pulp production, almost all potash production, all electrolytic aluminium production and 37 per cent of all passengers passing through Spanish airports. It is also one of the country's leading exporters (exports accounting for over a quarter of group sales in 1992). Despite the

Sector	**Principal companies**
INI group	
Defence	Bazán —— Santa Bárbara
Iron and steel	CSI (Ensidesa, AHV) —— Sidenor —— Productos Tubulares
Minerals	Hunosa —— Figaredo —— Presur
Shipbuilding	Astilleros del Norte (Astilleros de Sestao and Astander) Astilleros del Noroeste (Astano, Barreras, Juliana) Astilleros del Sur (Aesa group)
Other	INI Finance —— Musini
Teneo SA group	
Aerospace, electronics	Casa Indra group (Inisel, Ceselsa, Disel, Enosa, Ensa, Eritel)
Air transport	Iberia (Iberia, Binter, Viva) —— Aviaco
Aluminium, chemicals, minerals	Inespal Group (Aluminio Español, Alúmina Española) Almagrera, Ence, Grupo Potasas (Suria K, Potasas de Llobregat)
Auxiliary industries	Auxini group —— Babcock & Wilcox —— Ensa
Corporate services	Artespaña, Infoleasing, Infoinvest group, Sociedades para el desarrollo industrial
Energy	Endesa group, Carboex, Enusa, Red Eléctrica
Sea transport	Elcano

Teneo SA is 100 per cent owned by INI

Total employment in the INI group at the end of 1994 was approximately 130,000, of whom about 70,000 were in the Teneo group

Figure 2.2 Organisation of INI and the Teneo group, 1994
Source: Adapted from Grupo INI/Teneo *Directorio 1994*

presumed viability of the companies in the Teneo group, in 1993 nearly all the companies lost money (with the notable exception of the electricity utility Endesa).

Having transferred the more viable businesses, INI was left with a rump of companies (about a dozen) for which there was no immediate prospect of survival without public support. These companies are concentrated in the defence sector and in the traditional heavy industries of coal mining, iron and steel, and shipbuilding. In 1994 this rump of unprofitable companies represented about 40 per cent of employment in the INI group but contributed less than one fifth of value added and income. In 1993 the whole INI group lost pta 125 billion (pta 242 billion if the profits of the Endesa group were excluded). All the companies outside the Teneo group suffered substantial losses.

The National Hydrocarbon Institute (Instituto Nacional de Hidrocarburos, INH) is responsible for articulating government policy in the hydrocarbon sector. Its importance has diminished with the partial privatisation of its former oil and gas interests, the oil company Repsol SA and the natural gas company Enagas. INH was formed in 1981 under the Ministry of Industry and Energy to co-ordinate the dispersed interests of the state in the hydrocarbon industry (Chapter 5). Prior to its formation state control was exercised in a variety of companies through both the Ministry of Economy and Finance (especially through Campsa), and the Ministry of Industry and Energy (especially through INI).

The State Assets Office (Dirección General del Patrimonio del Estado,

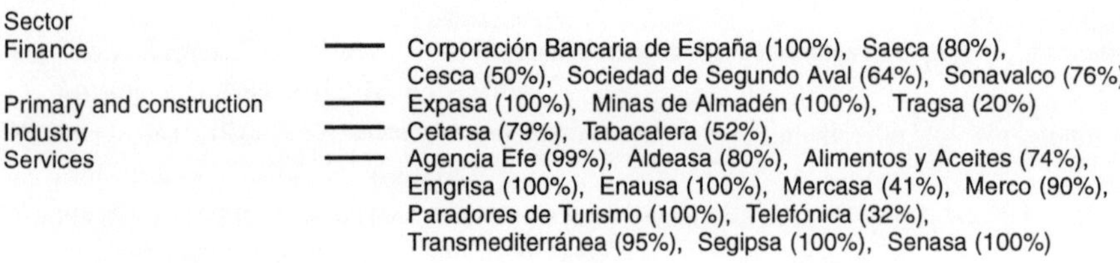

%: Percentage DGPE holding
At the end of 1993 Grupo Patrimonio held 51 per cent of Corporación Bancaria de España

Figure 2.3 Organisation of the Grupo Patrimonio, 1992
Source: Grupo Patrimonio 1993

DGPE; regulated by the Ley de Patrimonio del Estado 1964 and the Texto Refundido de la Ley General Presupuestaria 1988) supervises a loose grouping of companies (financial, industrial, agricultural and commercial) within the Ministry of Economy and Finance (Figure 2.3). Shares in its constituent holding companies are held directly by the state allowing the State Budget Office (Dirección General de Presupuestos) close financial control. Outside of budget control considerable freedom has been granted to management. Traditionally the DGPE has been responsible for those companies yielding important tax revenues (for example the tobacco company Tabacalera) or during the economic recession for those companies that required rapid financial restructuring prior to being reprivatised (for example the Rumasa group). At the end of 1992 the DGPE participated directly in 27 non-financial companies (together with indirect investments in other companies), companies in the group employing some 140,000 people. While the grouping is very diverse, both in activities and in size of companies, it is dominated by holdings in Telefónica and Tabacalera. At the end of 1992 Telefónica (in which the DGPE had a 32 per cent holding) accounted for 60 per cent of employment in the group, three-quarters of fixed capital investment and two-thirds of value added (*El País* 1994). Tabacalera (a tobacco and food group in which the DGPE had a 52 per cent holding) accounted for 8 per cent of employment and 5 per cent of value added (Figure 2.4).

Figure 2.4 Organisation of the Tabacalera group, 1994
Source: Grupo Tabacalera 1994

2.5 Evolution of the public enterprise sector

INI was set up by the government in 1941 as a holding company with 'the objective of strengthening defence industries and promoting self-sufficiency in areas where private resources were insufficient' (Tsoukalis 1981), the only existing state grouping being the DGPE (established in 1874). In the aftermath of the Civil War it was considered essential for the state to provide the substantial investment necessary to underpin private initiative and promote economic take-off. Thus the INI became particularly active in the basic manufacturing area (especially coal, iron and steel, electricity, shipbuilding, vehicles and transport), helping to lay the foundations for Spain's industrialisation (Martín and Comín 1991). By the end of the 1950s public enterprises had become a sizeable element in the economy. In transport, communications and credit there were important nationalisations. In energy, water and manufacturing new companies were created.

Justification for intervention varied between sectors. Air and rail transport were nationalised for strategic reasons, to co-ordinate the different means of transport, to promote development, and to offset decapitalisation. In communications the objective was to reduce the control of foreign capital; while in credit there was a desire to offer privileged facilities to promote development. Intervention in energy was focused on the need to substitute imports of energy and primary products and promote the use of national resources. Similarly, in manufactured goods there was a desire to become more self-sufficient. Thus public enterprises performed a clear, if questionable, role.

The growth of public enterprise in GDP continued during the period 1959-74, along with some diversification both into expanding industries (such as transport materials) and into industries in crisis. Optimism associated with rapid national economic growth led to heavy investment in the early 1970s, consolidating the basic structure of the group but also contributing to the problems of over-capacity in the recession that followed. Public enterprises thereby assumed a more ambiguous role, not only promoting national economic growth but also protecting the industrial and employment base: a role that became much more pronounced in the late 1970s and early 1980s.

Recession between 1974 and 1984 coincided with political transition from dictatorship to democracy, leaving government concerned more with political rather than business strategy. The public sector became a hospital for sick industries (including Astilleros Españoles, Babcock Wilcox, Viajes Marsans and the largest acquisition, Seat, in 1980), developing a deeper involvement in iron and steel, railway materials, shipbuilding and capital goods, while spreading out into a wide range of manufacturing industries, including ceramics, food, shoes and textiles. These acquisitions significantly diversified the portfolio of companies and increased the labour force. From 1976 the financial position of INI and the other state holdings deteriorated. Management problems were increased by the diversity of the group. Excess capacity developed in the heavy industries of steel, shipbuilding and chemicals, and there was generally a low level of productivity. By the early 1980s public enterprises faced mounting debt and it was clearly necessary to clarify their objectives. The most important change in government policy during the latter part of this period was the move away from the nationalisation of companies in crisis at the turn of the decade towards the development of reconversion plans put forward by the private sector and supported by state assistance (García Fernández 1989).

Public sector enterprises evolved in the mid 1980s within the context of a more secure democratic government, an improving international economic climate and the integration of Spain into the European Community. Also, the important political process of devolution continued, resulting in the increased importance of public enterprises operating at the regional and local level. This was reflected in higher levels of assistance from the territorial administrations, which between 1979 and 1986 increased their proportion of total public sector operating assistance from 11 to 26 per cent. In capital transfers their proportion increased from 0.1 to 11 per cent (Ruiz Cañete 1989, p. 86).

The election to government of the PSOE in 1982 heralded a period of greater political stability than before. The government felt able to adopt a more pragmatic approach to industrial policy and attempted to tackle the very serious problems that existed. Set alongside entry into the European Community, the twin policy guidelines became: i) profitability, giving greater emphasis to the balance sheet of public enterprises and reinforcing reconversion programmes (for example in iron and steel, aluminium, fertilizers and railway equipment); and ii) liberalisation, which not only reduced the level of direct government intervention but also overturned the traditional goal of a solid 'national' industrial base to look benignly on multinationalisation.

Reconversion and restructuring were assisted by improvements in the international economic environment (many public enterprises being particularly dependent on international trade and thus influenced by the international market situation; Fariñas et al. 1989). In the energy sector, improvements came as crude oil prices fell, helped by the depreciation of the dollar against the peseta (the cost of obtaining crude oil in Spain fell by 60 per cent between 1985 and 1986), while the government maintained the level of final energy prices. In the manufacturing sector, improvements came with lower financial costs and increasing consumption. Losses became concentrated in specific sectors; notably minerals, shipbuilding and defence (although these sectors embraced a large proportion of the workforce of INI).

Hence, as a result largely of the improved economic environment, public enterprises reduced their losses in the mid 1980s. For example, losses in the INI group fell from a record pta 204 billion in 1982 to pta 42 billion in 1987, the group returning to profit in 1988 for the first time since 1975. As part of this economic regeneration INI tried to move away from its socio-political roles of dustbin for unprofitable industry, adapting sectors in difficulty and cushioning the effects of industrial rationalisation, towards creating a more efficient organisation acting as a catalyst for industrial development. However, losses mounted once again from 1990 through to the end of 1993.

Measures taken by the government during the mid 1980s (particularly after 1984) involved a strategy of financial improvements and rationalisation to increase efficiency. Improvements to the financial position of companies included tighter financial controls and financial restructuring along with measures to reduce costs, for example through energy savings and employment reduction. From 1984 to 1986 the government reduced levels of operating assistance, although capital transfers continued to increase. The main beneficiaries of state assistance were the non-financial public enterprises, with especially large transfers being made to the state railway company Renfe, the coal mining company Hunosa and the agricultural fund Forppa. There were reductions in employment in public enterprises (probably greater than 40,000 between 1984 and 1986, excluding losses through privatisations that would take the total up to about 70,000), reductions that were concentrated in the manufacturing sector (especially in iron, steel and shipbuilding; Fariñas et al. 1989).

Rationalisation embraced: i) disinvestment through a) the liquidation of companies that were not viable (for example Viajes Ita (DGPE), Aplesa (INH), Potases de Navarra (INI)), b) the closure of excess capacity (as with the reduction of 45,000 tonnes of aluminium capacity achieved through the closure of plant at Valladolid and part of the aluminium capacity at Avilés; also the closure of the blast furnace at Sagunto and the Enfersa fertilizer plant at Puentes de García Rodriguez) and c) privatisation; ii) the restructuring of whole industrial sectors (for example in hydrocarbons with the formation of INH in 1981 and Repsol in 1987; iii) the internal restructuring of public enterprises into sub-holdings (in INI for example with Inisel in electronics and defence equipment in the company Santa Bárbara); iv) company mergers (for example in aluminium between Alugasa and Endasa); v) the interchange of holdings between companies in the public sector (for example in the electricity industry and in the sale in 1988 of four food companies of INI to Tabacalera); vi) selective investment (for example the fertilizer company Enfersa converted its ammonia plant in Sagunto to natural gas and added a new nitrates plant); vii) the reorientation of production in some companies; and viii) other measures to increase efficiency including adoption of new technology, improvements in management organisation and better quality of products.

The process effectively brought to an end the policy of incorporating industries in crisis. Although the public sector, including the regional governments, continued to support ailing industries, no new public enterprises were formed (except for Redesa and ERZ, both the result of rationalisation in the electricity sector and the brief nationalisation of the Rumasa companies).

2.6 Privatisation

Privatisation has been defined as 'that wide range of policies designed to reduce the scope, limit the functions and generally weaken the influence of the public sector' (Vickers and Wright 1988). It embraces wider participation by the private sector in areas previously reserved for the public sector, selling land and publicly owned housing stock as well as industrial privatisation. In Spain the policy of industrial disinvestment followed by the state has been attributed more to considerations of industrial rationale or pragmatism than to any political belief in privatisation (Aranzadi 1989). There has been no full privatisation policy underpinned by an explicit market centred ideology as in Britain nor clear privatisation programme as elaborated in France and Italy (Fernández Rodriguez 1989). Indeed, in 1994 there remained significant opposition within the government to an extensive privatisation programme. Nevertheless, privatisation did gain momentum during the 1980s and appears set to continue in the 1990s.

Until 1988 privatisation had not substantially altered the sectoral composition of the public sector, except in transport materials and, apart from the cases of SKF and Seat, had involved the disposal of companies of relatively little significance (in food and textiles) or those in deficit (Table 2.1). Privatisations simplified the portfolio of companies held by the state and improved the efficiency of control. There were also relatively few sales given the number of public enterprises. However, the first round of privatisation of the hydrocarbon group Repsol in 1989, the sale of the fertilizer group Enfersa to the Ercros group and the flotation of almost half the banking group Argentaria in 1993, indicated a shift towards a more market-centred view of the future of public enterprises.

Privatisation has involved the direct sale of companies to the private sector and the flotation of companies on the Stock Exchange. Companies sold wholly or in part directly to private companies have included those sold as part of the process of financial rehabilitation of the banks in crisis and the expropriation of Rumasa, the sale in 1985 of the ball-bearing manufacturer SKF to Asea Brown Boveri and the electronics company Secoinsa to Fujitsu, in 1986 the motor-vehicle manufacturer Seat to Volkswagen, and in 1989 the fertilizer company Enfersa to Ercros, the electrical engineering companies Ateinsa and MTM to GEC-Alsthom and the motor-vehicle manufacturer Enasa to Fiat-Iveco. Overwhelmingly, sales have been to foreign multinational companies.

The other form of privatisation has involved flotation of companies on the Stock Exchange (Table 2.2). In most cases these have been only partial privatisations, broadening the capital base while leaving control in the hands

Table 2.1 Privatisations of public companies, 1984 - 94

Enterprise	Sector	Buyer	Year	% Privatised
Textile Tarazona	Textiles	Cima Eursa (Spain)	1984	70
Secoinsa	Electronics	Fujitsu (Japan)	1985	69
SKF Española	Ball bearings	SKF (Sweden)	1985	99
Viajes Marsans	Travel	Trapsa (Spain)	1985	100
Motores MDB	Veh. engineering	Klockner Humboldt (Germany)	1986	60
Olcesa	Food	Mercosa (Spain)	1986	51
Seat	Motor-vehicles	Volkswagen (Germany)	1986	75
Dessa	Shipbuilding	Forestal del Atlántico (Spain)	1987	80
Purolator	Vehicles	Knecht Filterwerke (Germany)	1987	95
Carcesa	Food	Tabacalera (Spain)	1988	100
Lesa	Food	Tabacalera (Spain)	1988	100
Astican	Shipbuilding	Italmar	1989	91
Ateinsa	Engineering	GEC-Alsthom (France/UK)	1989	85
Enasa	Vehicles	Fiat-Iveco (Italy)	1989	100
Enfersa	Fertilisers	Ercros (Spain/Kuwait)	1989	80
Imepiel	Textiles	Cusi (Spain)	1989	100
Intelhorce	Textiles	Orecifi (Italy)	1989	100
MTM	Engineering	GEC-Alsthom (France/UK)	1989	85
Oesa	Food	Grupo Ferruzzi (Italy)	1989	100
Pesa	Electronics	Amper SA (Spain)	1989	97
Hytasa	Textiles	Integusa (Spain)	1990	100
Seat	Motor-vehicles	Volkswagen (Germany)	1990	100

Source: Adapted from Noceda 1993

of the state; for example a 38 per cent holding in the electricity utility Gesa was sold in 1986, 20 per cent of the electricity utility Endesa in 1988, 30 per cent of Repsol in 1989 and almost 50 per cent of Argentaria in 1993. Further reductions in public sector holdings in what are considered strategically important companies such as Repsol and Endesa raised the question of how the government might retain a veto over key strategic decisions.

Table 2.2 Stock market flotations of public companies

Enterprise	Sector	Year	% Privatised	% State holding
Gesa	Electricity	1986	38.0	62.0
Ence	Paper	1988	39.8	60.2
Endesa	Electricity	1988	25.0	75.0
Repsol	Oil	1989	30.0	54.4
Repsol	Oil	1993	13.3	41.1
Argentaria	Banking	1993 (May)	24.9	75.1
Argentaria	Banking	1993 (November)	24.9	50.1
Repsol	Oil	1994	20.0	21.1
Endesa	Electricity	1994	10.0	65.0

Source: Author compilation

Initially the objectives of privatisation were essentially commercial. Flotations diversified sources of finance, broadened the base of shareholdings and introduced the discipline of the market into management. Sales to other companies (apart from the banks in the early 1980s and the special case of Rumasa) provided the opportunity of gaining access to technological, logistical or commercial expertise and facilities (for example developed networks of international distribution), economies of scale and industrial synergy. These opportunities were considered to offer companies a more secure future, although some of them have been gained simply through co-operation between companies, for example between Enasa and Daf, Casa and Airbus, Iberia and Lufthansa. However, in the early 1990s increasing pressure for the sale of public companies came from the need to control public expenditure and reduce the public sector deficit in an effort to retain international confidence in the economy and meet the convergence criteria set out in the Maastricht Treaty. There certainly remains scope for further privatisation, for example in banking, the postal service, much of the transport system and the water utilities (Table 2.3).

Privatisation, while raising public revenue at the time of sale (for example the sale of shares in Argentaria netted pta 290 billion in 1993), has often only been achieved following considerable public investment in companies to secure their sale (through debt write-offs, cash injections, etc.), although

Table 2.3 Potential privatisations

Enterprise	Sector	Group	% Controlled
Aldeasa	Retail	DGPE	100
Argentaria	Banking	DGPE	50
Tabacalera	Food	DGPE	55
Telefónica	Telecommunications	DGPE	32
Transmediterránea	Shipping	DGPE	100
Repsol	Oil	INH	21
Gas Natural/Enagas	Gas	INH-Repsol	9
Aena	Airport management	MOPTMA	100
Correos	Postal services	MOPTMA	100
Enatcar	Road transport	MOPTMA	100
Feve	Rail services	MOPTMA	100
Renfe	Rail services	MOPTMA	100
Auxini	Construction	Teneo	100
Babcock & Wilcox	Machinery	Teneo	100
Casa	Aerospace	Teneo	99
Elcano	Shipping	Teneo	100
Ence	Paper	Teneo	56
Endesa	Electricity	Teneo	65
Iberia	Air transport	Teneo	100
Indra	Electronics	Teneo	60
Inespal	Aluminium	Teneo	98

The 9 per cent holding in Gas Natural refers to the direct holding of INH
MOPTMA: Ministerio de Obras Públicas, Transportes y Medio Ambiente
Holdings as in mid 1994

Source: Author compilation

the process cuts future government spending on public enterprises. For example, between 1983 and 1988 INI invested pta 1,800 billion in its subsidiaries (of which pta 1,350 billion was provided directly by the state, the rest was raised by INI through sales of companies; Tizón 1989). At the turn of the decade INI was continuing to invest to consolidate the process of reconversion, including the completion of the reconversion programme for shipbuilding. In the case of MTM and Ateinsa, INI invested pta 20 billion (£100 million) to enable it to be sold to the GEC-Alsthom group. The sale of Seat may have cost the exchequer over pta 400 billion (Casamayor 1994b; similar investment in debt write-offs and cash injections have been made by other governments: in 1989 the British government allocated £6 billion to the water authorities prior to their privatisation and the Italian government wrote off most of the £4 billion debt of the public sector steel group Finsider). As in the case of public financial assistance generally to private companies, such injections of public funds may be squandered should the new owners decide at a later date to rationalise the businesses.

2.7 Deregulation

Deregulation and liberalisation have been spreading through the Spanish economy to affect all public enterprises. The process has been hastened by the need to comply with European Union requirements. As a result, national market restrictions are being eliminated, state monopolies broken up, and the whole economy exposed to much more intense competition than before. Trade barriers to imports from the European Union have largely disappeared. In the financial sector, deregulation has created a single capital market, transforming the banking sector, the stock market, insurance and other financial services. Entry to the European Community was directly responsible for the break-up of numerous state monopolies, forcing the public enterprises concerned to adopt new strategies. For example, the long established monopolies of Campsa and Tabacalera were both broken up, land transport began to be reformed by the transport law of 1987 (Ley de Ordenación de los Transportes Terrestres, LOTT) and the law of telecommunications (Ley de Ordenación de las Telecomunicaciones, LOT 1987) began the process of dismantling the monopoly of Telefónica (although voice transmission and the basic telephone network in Spain will not be deregulated at least until 1998). In 1993 the monopoly of Iberia on domestic flights was broken by a new operator on the Madrid–Barcelona route and maritime transport was partly liberalised.

2.8 Restructuring in the public sector

While there has been some slimming down of public enterprises in the economy, it is important not to equate privatisation with any denial of the continued importance of state involvement in the modern Spanish economy. 'The State continues to be a provider, regulator, entrepreneur, purchaser and umpire in industrial affairs' (Vickers and Wright 1988).

The role of public enterprises in Spain remains unclear in the absence of a specific public enterprise policy. The stated position is that privatisations are not founded on any government strategy of denationalisation (Myro 1988), nor on political ideology, but on the industrial logic of securing an efficient public sector ('las decisiones de desinversión del INI no responden a imperativos de carácter político o ideológico, sino a criterios de racionalidad industrial y financiera ligados, en última instancia, al cumplimiento del objectivo prioritario del INI: la maximización del Patrimonio del Grupo.' ; Aranzadi 1989, p. 258) and on meeting the competition requirements of the European Union (Salas 1993). In practice, as companies become profitable they become candidates for privatisation.

Without state subsidies economic efficiency will be essential if public enterprises are to survive. More efficient operation is seen to come at least in part from exposure to market disciplines. Thus both INI and INH shed their previous close ministerial control and now operate under statutes similar to those of private companies, while Teneo, Repsol, Gas Natural and Corporación Bancaria Española are constituted as limited liability companies. However, some public enterprises will continue to find it difficult to achieve profitability. The arguments behind the continued public support of these businesses are largely social (and political), either relating to the maintenance of employment or the provision of public services.

By the beginning of the next century the public sector will contain fewer public enterprises than at present. The case for a smaller public enterprise sector is readily made by reference to its poor record, both operationally and in implementing government policies. Governments have used the INI to implement such policies as guaranteeing the supply of basic products, preventing the formation of private monopolies, contributing to regional development and salvaging loss-making companies. But in terms of the supply of basic products, Spain remains critically dependent on foreign supplies, especially of energy. In preventing monopolies 'the INI never applied any prices lower than those set by private enterprise; in fact it joined forces with private companies in a series of mixed public and private ventures of dubious general interest' (Tamames 1986). In regional policy, public enterprises have played a relatively minor role and the state regional development associations (SODI) have been overshadowed by their regional government counterparts. As for the role of the public sector in salvaging loss-making companies, the policy substantially increased the burden on public finance and may be seen in retrospect to have diverted public funds away from technological development towards redundant technologies and inhibited the growth of more efficient private companies. However, operational inefficiency was at least in part a reflection of the broader inefficiency of government in the past, and in many cases losses were inherited from the private sector.

The rising tide of foreign penetration in the Spanish economy is closely linked to privatisation, as companies have frequently been sold directly to foreign owners or share ownership has passed to foreign owners through flotations. Despite attempts by the government to promote the formation of larger Spanish companies able to compete effectively against foreign multinationals, the prospect of losing national control over large segments of the economy has been viewed as the inevitable price of industrial and economic development, securing employment and reducing the public sector deficit. In fact, the government has actively sought out and encouraged foreign investors.

Thus the government has played an active role in shaping the economy through its industrial policy and the surgery it has applied to public enterprises in an attempt to meet the competitive conditions of an international market-place. This surgery has kept a number of industries alive which would have disappeared if exposed to market forces, although frequently these industries have remained in intensive care at considerable cost to the taxpayer.

The future role of the public sector in Spain, as elsewhere in western Europe, is unclear. It is unlikely to witness the type of job creation that occurred in the 1980s and early 1990s. On the contrary, what is of concern is the scope for staff reductions both in public enterprises and in the public administration, where reforms and efficiency savings are long overdue. The greatest challenge in the public sector will be that associated with defining the welfare state and, indeed, the model of European development in the late 1990s and into the next century. Disillusion with the market mechanism, especially to deliver an acceptable society as opposed to an efficient economy, may bring a return to more of a social market economy: 'At the beginning of the 1990s, attention is switching back to the public sector. This is less a reflection of a desire to expand the sphere of government than a belated recognition that ... the performance of the public sector is a crucial determinant of the quality of our lives' (Prowse 1990). But this will be constrained in an open, integrated, world economy where other regions of the world do not embrace the same welfare state and environmental principles.

References and bibliography

Aranzadi, C. (1989) 'La política de desinversiones en el INI', *Papeles de Economía Española* 38, pp. 258–61

Banco Bilbao Vizcaya, BBV (1994) *Spain's economic overview,* June. Madrid

Casamayor, R. (1994a) 'Todas por la patria', *El País* (sección negocios), 30 January, pp. 8–9

Casamayor, R. (1994b) 'Seat condiciona su futuro a las ayudas oficiales', *El País* (sección negocios), 22 May, p. 10

Comín, F. (1988) 'Las administraciones públicas', in J. García Delgado (ed.), *España: Tomo II, Economía,* pp. 431–69. Madrid: Espasa-Calpe SA

Donaghy, P. and M. Newton (1987) *Spain: a guide to political and economic institutions.* Cambridge: CUP

Edo Hernández, V. (1989) 'Las empresas públicas: concepto, delimitación y clasificación', *Papeles de Economía Española* 38, pp. 68–77

El País (1994) *Anuario El País,* 1994. Madrid.

Fariñas, J., J. Jaumandreu and G. Mato (1989) 'La empresa pública industrial española: 1981–1986', *Papeles de Economía Española* 38, pp. 199–216

Fernández Rodriguez, Z. (1989) 'El alcance del proceso privatizador en España', *Papeles de Economía Española* 38, pp. 243–6

García Fernández, J. (1989) 'La teoría de Stigler sobre la regulación como marco de la política empresarial pública 1973–1988', *Papeles de Economía Española* 38, pp. 224–42

Grupo Patrimonio (1993) *Memoria 1992.* Madrid

Intervención General de la Administración del Estado (1988) *Cuentas de las empresas públicas para 1985.* Madrid: Ministerio de Economía y Hacienda

Jonquiéres, G. de (1990) 'The break with French tradition', *Financial Times,* 17 January, p. 24. London

Martín, P. and Comín, F. (1991) *INI: 50 años de industrialización en España.* Madrid: Espasa–Calpe SA

Ministerio de Economía y Hacienda, MEH (1992) *El sector público estatal.* Madrid

Ministerio de Industria y Energía, MINE (1989) *Informe Anual 1988.* Madrid

Mochón, F., G. Ancochea and A. Avila (1988) *Economía española 1964–1987: introducción al análisis económico.* Madrid: McGraw-Hill

Myro, R. (1988) 'Las empresas públicas', in J. García Delgado (ed.), *España: Tomo II, Economía,* pp. 471–97. Madrid: Espasa-Calpe SA

Noceda, M. (1993) 'A vueltas con la privatización', *El País,* 30 August, p. 34

Novales, A., C. Sebastián, L. Servent and J. Trujillo (1987) *La empresa pública industrial en España.* Madrid: Fundación de Estudios de Economía Aplicada

OECD (1984) *OECD economic surveys: Spain 1983/84.* Paris

OECD (1993) *OECD economic surveys: Spain 1992/93.* Paris

OECD (1994) *OECD economic surveys: Spain 1993/94.* Paris

Ortiz Junquera, P. and A. Gómez Rodrigo (1989) 'La empresa pública en el contexto de la contabilidad económica', *Papeles de Economía Española* 38, pp. 78–84

Papeles de Economía Española 38 (1989) *La empresa pública en España.* Madrid: Confederación Española de Cajas de Ahorros

Prowse, M. (1990) 'Putting a price on the quality of life', *Financial Times,* 11 July, p. 20. London

Ruiz Cañete, O. (1989) 'Empresa pública y transferencias estatales', *Papeles de*

Economía Española 38, pp. 85–100
Salas, J. (1993) 'El futuro de la empresa pública', in *Anuario El País*, 1993, p. 392
Segura, J. (1988) 'Intervención pública y política de bienestar: el papel del Estado', in J. García Delgado (ed.), *España: Tomo II, Economía*, pp. 831–58. Madrid: Espasa-Calpe SA
Tabacalera SA (1994) *Informe anual 1993.* Madrid
Tamames, R. (1986) *The Spanish economy.* London: C. Hurst and Company
Teneo SA (1993) *Annual report 1992.* Madrid
Teneo SA (1994) *Directorio 1994.* Madrid
Teresa López, M. and A. Utrilla (1993) *Introducción al sector público español.* Madrid: Editorial Civitas
Tizón, A. (1989) 'La adaptación a la competencia del INI', *El País* (sección negocios), 20 August, p. 2
Tsoukalis, L. (1981) *The European Community and its Mediterranean enlargement.* London: Croom Helm
Vickers, J. and V. Wright (1988) 'The politics of industrial privatisation in western Europe: an overview', *West European Politics* 11, October, No. 4, pp. 1–30

Chapter 3

Agriculture, forestry and fishing

3.1 Agriculture, forestry and fishing in the economy

For many people employed in agriculture, forestry and fishing the future is bleak, as economic pressures force further contraction in employment placing a question mark over the basis of rural economies. However, the extent of the agricultural area in Spain and the size of the fishing fleet should ensure that these industries continue to represent an important contribution to food supplies in the European Union and to exports from Spain. Further developments in agriculture will occur against the background of reform of the Common Agricultural Policy (CAP), bringing prices more into line with world prices, further technological innovation and increased international competition, prompted in part by agreements reached under the Uruguay Round of GATT, but depending also on the future shape of the European Union.

Agriculture, forestry and fishing remain important elements of the economy, although their relative importance has declined as a result of the more rapid growth of other sectors. Their economic significance can be gauged by their contribution to the gross domestic product, to trade, to employment, to the processing industries that they sustain and to the market that they offer for manufactured products and services. Beyond this these primary activities permeate the life and culture of the country, providing a cushion of resources in times of recession, part-time employment, subsistence income and an invaluable recreation resource intimately connected with the physical environment. Moreover, farming is now recognised to have a crucial role in environmental management and in maintaining rural communities.

The sector contributes a significant part of both national income and employment, dominating the economy of many parts of Spain. Agricultural production represents between 3 and 5 per cent of the gross domestic product, depending upon the climatic conditions experienced during the year. Within the total final value of production of agriculture and forestry (*producción agraria*), agricultural production (*producción agrícola*) contributes between 55 and 60 per cent, livestock production 35 to 40 per cent and forestry 2 to 5 per cent (based on the years 1985 to 1993 inclusive; MAPA 1993a). The Agricultural Census in 1989 recorded 2.2 million farms and farm owners (including 1.4 million farm owners working full-time in farming), 1.4 million members of farm owners families and 155,000 paid farm workers (of whom about half were full-time; ibid.). In addition, fishing provides direct employment for a further 85,000 (occupied population in 1992). Thus, the activities of agriculture, forestry and fishing involve some 3 million people directly, even though the number recorded in the labour force survey as occupied in the sector are much lower. To these statistics it is important to add the direct links that the sector has with the food processing industry, the largest manufacturing sector in Spain.

Agricultural and food products (*productos agroalimentario*) are also important components of trade, where they represent between 12 and 15 per cent of imports and a slightly higher percentage of exports (MAPA 1993a). The trade balance in agricultural and food products is influenced by the size of annual harvests, nevertheless there tends to be a deficit. The source of the deficit is in processed food products. Trade surpluses are normally recorded in fruit, vegetables and drinks. Major exports are fresh fruit and vegetables, cereals, wine, vegetable oils and prepared foods. Spain is a leading world exporter of table olives, olive oil, wine, almonds and cork. Major imports include wood and wood products, feed grains (especially soya beans), fruit, skins, tobacco, meat, dairy produce, fish and prepared foods in general.

An increasing proportion of trade in food and agricultural produce is with the European Union (EU), accounting for 60 per cent of imports (*importaciones agroalimentaria*) in 1992. Until the mid 1980s this trade was roughly in balance. However, food imports from European Community (EC) countries then grew faster than exports (attributable in part to the strength of the peseta and the terms of accession). Between 1985 and 1987 imports from EC countries rose from 22 per cent of total food imports to 42 per cent, while exports to the EC increased over the same period from 65 to 69 per cent (MAPA 1989a).

While the sector remains of considerable importance to the economy, it has none the less experienced a substantial relative, and in some senses absolute, decline. The economically active population in agriculture, forestry and fishing plummeted from 4.9 million in 1960 (40 per cent of the economically active population) to 2.4 million in 1980, then down further to 1.4 million (9.2 per cent) in 1994 (Table 3.1), the occupied population in 1994 being only 1.2 million with less than half a million full-time professional salaried farmers. By the end of the century the proportion of the occupied population in agriculture is likely to have fallen to around 6 per cent. As a proportion of gross domestic product, the sector has fallen by about 10 percentage points since the early 1960s and by a larger amount in trade,

Table 3.1 The decline of employment in agriculture

Year	Economically active	Proportion of labour force
1950	5,271,000	48.8
1960	4,922,700	41.7
1970	3,706,300	29.1
1975	2,852,600	21.5
1980	2,362,700	17.8
1985	2,242,500	16.5
1990	1,766,400	11.8
1994	1,417,900	9.2

Figures refer to the first quarter of each year
Source: INE (*Encuesta de la población activa*, various dates)

reflecting the slower growth of the sector relative to others in the economy.

Employment decline in agriculture has been accompanied by a restructuring process involving a radical transformation away from traditional agricultural practices towards more commercial production. Traditional agriculture was based on farming practices that were closely allied to the physical environment (for example using fallow to maintain fertility – as in the *año y vez* system – and dispersed plots to ensure product variety). Production methods were reliant upon abundant and cheap labour. Marketing was oriented either to local markets or subsistence requirements. This form of agriculture was protected by an extensive web of state intervention and product protection, enabling the survival of small farms while providing an easy income on large farms. Rapid economic growth in the 1960s created a crisis in this system, as the labour force on which it relied melted away to leave behind a decaying rural economy suffering from labour shortages and rising labour costs (García Delgado 1988). The adoption of capital to replace labour and draught animals (Table 3.2) and the

Table 3.2 Methods of production

	1960	1970	1980	1986	1990	1992
Draught animals						
Bulls and oxen	212	67	11	4	—	—
Cattle	1063	1035	306	162	—	—
Horses, mules and asses	1469	914	394	241	—	—
Mechanised equipment						
Tractors	57	260	594	658	741	766
Motorised cultivators	2	72	221	275	280	281
Combine harvesters (for cereals)	2	28	42	47	48	49
Use of nitrate fertilizers	15	36	58	51	64	—

Animals in thousand head; mechanised equipment in thousand units; nitrate fertilizers in kg/ha of cultivated land (excluding fallow) plus natural pasture increased reliance on off-farm inputs (mechanised equipment, new seeds, fuel, feed, fertilizers, pesticides and irrigation) increased other input costs. Simultaneously, farm revenues were squeezed by inflation and weak product prices resulting from increased production, slow growth in demand and poor marketing. Problems were heightened in some sectors by changing patterns of demand. As incomes rose, those products with low or negative income elasticities of demand (such as cereals and field vegetables) faced declining or stagnant markets, while demand grew for those products with high income elasticities of demand (such as horticultural products, dairy products and meat). Agriculture was slow to adjust to these changing patterns of demand, as market controls impeded the translation of changing patterns of demand into appropriate pricing structures. Nevertheless, throughout Spain farms were abandoned, especially in the more remote areas of the interior and in the mountains. Even around the coast agricultural land was lost, the result of land-use competition.

New forms of agriculture are associated with more intensive production, specialisation and the increased reliance on capital and off-farm inputs. Farms are more dependent on markets for both inputs and outputs than they were under traditional farming systems. Production is more scientific and more commercially based, requiring careful cultivation techniques. Marketing has become more sophisticated, depending on specialised marketing channels. These changes in agriculture have been 'triggered by powerful market forces rather than by state policies' (García-Ramon 1985).

The modern face of agriculture is illustrated by commercial citrus fruit production in Valencia, mechanised cereal farms in Seville and horticultural production in southern Spain. Along the coast of Almería, Granada and Málaga, increased horticultural production has been achieved through the use of new techniques, particularly plastic to protect crops, either in the form of greenhouses (*invernaderos*), frequently coupled with sand-bed cultivation *(enarenado)*, or as micro or macro plastic tunnels (*tuneles*), or as black plastic sheeting over the soil *(acolchado)*. Greenhouses conserve moisture, provide proof against frost and ensure higher average temperatures, bringing forward maturity and allowing many 'earlies' (which command higher prices than the main crop) to be produced. Covering the ground with black plastic has a similar effect and also inhibits the development of weeds. The *enarenado* system consists of: i) careful preparation of the ground; ii) application of a thick dressing of organic material; and then iii) covering the peat with beach sand. The latter has two effects: it insulates the soil, thereby advancing the harvest, and it interrupts capillary movement of water through the soil, thereby reducing evaporation loss. The plants develop their roots in the top centimetres of soil below the layer of sand. In this area of soil they find the optimum conditions of aeration, nutrients and humidity for their development. This technique of farming has transformed unproductive land into areas of intensive horticulture and has spread widely around the Mediterranean coast. The Campo de Dalías in Almería is the largest such area in Spain, with over 5,000 hectares under greenhouses. Localities along the coast of Huelva are more recently established, having developed a major export industry in strawberries in the 1980s, while Cádiz has become the base of a significant flower-growing industry.

New agricultural practices along the coast of southern Spain have been accompanied by new economic and ecological problems, threatening continued success. Following a number of years of rapid expansion, markets have been saturated by both the volume of production (including increased competition from countries outside the EU, notably Morocco) and by the concentration of the harvest at certain times during the year. Low profit margins coupled with small farm units have inhibited the introduction of more sophisticated technologies such as hydroponic systems, computer-controlled greenhouse environments and fully automated watering and fertilizer systems. Ecological problems are potentially more serious than economic ones. Rapid expansion of production has dramatically increased water demand, heightening problems of salinity (and possibly lowering the water table in the interior, leading to increased desertification there). As a result, further expansion of the industry has had to be halted in many areas until new supplies of water can be harnessed. Other problems have been associated with the intensive use of agri-chemicals: fertilizers, pesticides and fungicides. Less often mentioned is the staggering visual blight on the landscape resulting from extensive stretches of coastline being enshrouded in plastic, a reflection (along with that of tourist development) of the priority given to economic development and of private initiative uncontrolled by an effective planning system. Finally, there is the problem of plastic waste (the plastic used normally lasts only two seasons), which is being tackled by the construction of plastic recycling plants.

3.2 Changing patterns of agriculture

In market economies, agricultural enterprises expand or contract according to their relative viability. As input and product prices change, so too do agricultural patterns, hence changes in the CAP are of critical importance. In addition, climatic conditions have a major influence on productivity (especially in non-irrigated areas), farmers varying their choice of crop partly according to expectations about climatic conditions. For example, during a prolonged drought in the early 1990s farmers reduced the area sown to barley, maize, cotton and rice and increased that sown to sunflowers. From 1992 to 1993 the area planted to barley fell from 4.1 million hectares to only 3.5 million hectares, that under cotton fell from 75,500 hectares to 32,000 hectares, while that under sunflowers increased from 1.5 million hectares to 2.1 million hectares (MAPA 1994a). Further complications are added by crop rotations, mixed and multiple cropping. As a result, the area under cultivation of different crops fluctuates from year to year, making it difficult to identify long-term trends. Nevertheless, there has been a trend towards the expansion of irrigated areas, horticulture and livestock production, while marginal dry farmed areas and their associated crops have been contracting.

Of the total area of Spain (including the islands, Ceuta and Melilla: 504,750 square kilometres) about 95 per cent is classified as agricultural land, 40 per cent is cultivated (*tierras de cultivo*), 13 per cent is under pasture (*prados y pastizales*) and 32 per cent under some form of woodland (*terreno forestal*; MAPA 1993b). Of the land in cultivation (some 160,000 square kilometres, excluding fallow) about 70 per cent is under herbaceous crops (cereal grains, dried pulses, roots, industrial crops, forage crops, vegetables) and 30 per cent under woody crops (citrus fruits, non-citrus fruits, vines and olives) (Table 3.3).

Physical environmental conditions provide the framework within which different forms of agricultural enterprise are potentially viable. For example, the pasture lands of the north coast of Spain (Asturias, Cantabria,

Table 3.3 Land use in 1991/92

Land use	Dry farmed (000 ha)	Irrigated (000 ha)	Total (000 ha)
Cultivated area	16,738	3,208	19,946
Pasture	6,277	195	6,472
Forest	15,915	0	15,915
Other	8,145	0	8,145
Total	47,076	3,403	50,479
Land in cultivation			
Cereal grains	6,852	961	7,813
Dried pulses	263	37	300
Tubers for human consumption	136	133	269
Industrial crops	972	415	1,387
Forage crops	878	374	1,252
Horticulture	79	403	482
Flowers	0	5	5
Herbaceous crops: sub total	9,180	2,328	11,508
Citrus crops	0	265	265
Non-citrus crops	682	281	963
Vines	1,367	64	1,431
Olives	2,000	127	2,127
Other woody crops	96	4	100
Woody crops: sub total	4,145	741	4,886
Total land in cultivation	13,325	3,069	16,394

Figures for land-use are for 1992 and include fallow

Figures for land in cultivation are for 1991 and exclude fallow

Sources: MAPA 1993b and 1993d

Galicia and País Vasco) contrast with the extensive cereal-growing areas of the interior (Castilla y León, Castilla-La Mancha and Extremadura), which again contrast with the intensive horticulture around the Mediterranean coast. Similarly, across much of the country (excluding the north coast and Galicia) the availability of water supplies determines the intensity of production. Where agriculture relies mainly on intermittent rain-fed water supplies, production tends to be extensive and centred around the traditional Mediterranean triad of cereals, olives and vines. Conversely, where regular water supplies are available, more intensive and diverse agriculture is possible (especially fruit and vegetables).

Herbaceous crops occupy more than 70 per cent of the land in cultivation. About two-thirds of this area under herbaceous crops is sown to cereals (7.8 million hectares in 1991), of which barley covers the largest area (4.4 million hectares in 1991), followed by wheat (2.2 million hectares in 1991). The total area under cereal production has remained relatively stable since 1960, concentrated on the dry farmed lands of central and southern Spain. However, the composition of crops grown has changed, the area sown to wheat (mainly soft wheat) having decreased by about a half and that sown to barley having increased by 300 per cent. Among the other cereals, both oats (0.3 million hectares in 1991) and millet (0.2 million hectares in 1991) have experienced notable reductions in area planted. The area under maize has tended to remain relatively stable (about 0.5 million hectares), while the cultivation of rice has tended to expand (occupying on average 80,000 hectares from 1985 to 1992): production being concentrated in the Guadalquivir delta (Seville), Ebro delta (Tarragona), around Albufera (Valencia) and along the river banks of the Júcar (Valencia) and Guadiana (Badajoz). Dried pulses (legumes, including beans, chick-peas and lentils) have exhibited a long-term tendency to decline (the area under cultivation falling by 70 per cent between 1960 and 1991 to 0.3 million hectares), reflecting changing consumption patterns and the switch from natural means of maintaining fertility through fallow and crop rotations to the addition of artificial fertilizers. The area under rootcrop production has remained stable with about 30 per cent of production arising in Galicia, followed by León. Roots for human consumption are dominated by potatoes, very early varieties being produced in the Canary Islands and along the coast of Andalucía.

Olives and vines are the other crops that dominate the landscape of central and southern Spain. The total area under olives has remained stable since 1935 at around 2 million hectares (of which over 90 per cent is under olives used for producing oil). The olive will grow on steep slopes, its long roots enabling it to survive the summer droughts. Thus even where the trees are old and unproductive they fulfil an important function in stabilising slopes. The plant bears fruit seven years after planting, reaching full production in fifteen years and thenceforth enjoying a long production life in which it requires relatively little attention. The olive formed a vital component of many traditional agricultural systems, providing oil, wood for fuel, a construction material and olive waste for pig food. Modernisation has disrupted this system to leave olive growers more dependent on the olive itself. Olives frequently form a monoculture, covering extensive areas in Andalucía (the region embraces over 50 per cent of the total olive-growing area in Spain; Jaén alone has 20 per cent of the total area in Spain and Córdoba 13 per cent), Extremadura (9 per cent of the total olive-growing area of Spain) and in other parts of central Spain. The major area for table olive production is around the city of Seville (especially the Aljarafe area) and in Badajoz. Extensive areas have been replanted with new olive trees and some areas taken out of production. But many areas remain covered by unproductive trees, especially where there are few alternative crops or where neglecting the land has brought tax advantages.

Vines occupy over 1.4 million hectares, half of which are in Castilla-La Mancha. As with wheat and olives, vines are frequently grown as a monoculture (for example in Valdepeñas and Manzanares in Castilla-La Mancha and Penedés in Cataluña). Poor soils and lack of attention have resulted in low yields. Where more careful cultivation is practised the vines yield table grapes (about 5 per cent of production, concentrated in Badajoz and Valencia) and high-quality wines (many quality wines coming from areas covered by Denomination of Origin Regulation Boards, los Consejos Reguladores de Denominaciones de Origen, CRDO). The trend has been towards a decline in the area under vines (essentially in marginal areas), prompted by government policy. But, as with olives, many of the areas in which vines are grown are unsuitable for other crops.

Production of industrial crops has displayed a strong long-term increase in the area under production (from 461,000 hectares in 1960 to 1,387,000 hectares in 1991). In the early 1990s three-quarters of this area was under sunflowers and 10 per cent under sugar beet. Industrial crop enterprises tend to be more capital intensive than other sectors and more closely tied to industrial production. Production of sunflowers has expanded dramatically since 1970 (from 165,900 hectares in 1970 to 1.2 million hectares in 1990, reaching an estimated 2.1 million hectares in 1993 as farmers adopted strategies to reduce the impact of drought conditions), benefiting first from guaranteed prices and then in the early 1990s from acreage payments made under the CAP to compensate for low market prices (deficiency payments). In 1994 a ceiling on cultivation was introduced of 1.2 million hectares to stabilise production. Sunflowers are grown throughout Spain under a wide range of environmental conditions (although half the area planted is in the provinces of Seville, Cuenca, Badajoz and Córdoba). The plants are able to withstand drought and cost relatively little to grow. In Andalucía sunflowers have frequently replaced olives or are grown in rotation with cereals. The bulk of sugar production is obtained from sugar beet (some 165,000 hectares in 1991), especially in the Ebro Valley (Zaragoza), the Duero Basin (León and Burgos) and Andalucía (Granada, especially the Vega de Genil,

Seville, the Guadalquivir Valley, Málaga, the Antequera Basin and Cádiz). The areas under sugar-cane have declined steadily in the face of more profitable uses of the southern Mediterranean coast where it is grown (the crop occupying some 2,100 hectares in 1990 in Almería, Granada, Málaga and the Canary Islands). Former sugar-cane fields are now more likely to be used for horticulture or covered by urban development.

Other industrial crops include cotton and tobacco; the former being the only textile fibre now of any importance in Spain. Cotton requires a frost-free environment, irrigation, and ample fertilizer and labour (prior to recent mechanisation). The area under production fluctuated in the 1980s around an average of 72,000 hectares. Andalucía is the main region of production, especially Seville, followed by the provinces of Córdoba, Cádiz and Jaén. Tobacco is cultivated in non-irrigated areas of the north of Spain and in the irrigated lowland areas (*vegas*) of the interior in the south. During the 1980s the area under production averaged around 21,000 hectares. About three-quarters of the planted area is in the Jerte and Tietar valleys (Cáceres), followed by the Vega de Genil (Granada).

Horticultural production is one of the most intensive agricultural enterprises. Although it occupies only a small percentage of the cultivated land, it contributes about 30 per cent of the value of crop production *(producción final agrícola)*. Production areas essentially reflect the climatic conditions around the Mediterranean coast and in the Canary Islands. Vegetable production has tended to expand steadily in the 1980s to around half a million hectares. Among the more important crops are artichokes, broad beans, cabbages, cauliflower, cucumbers, asparagus, lettuces (iceberg lettuces having become a particular speciality along the coast of Murcia), melons, onions, peas, peppers, runner beans, tomatoes, water melons, strawberries and flowers. One of the most widely planted crops is the tomato, early varieties being grown in the Canary Islands, Alicante, Almería, Málaga and Valencia. In the interior, horticultural products tend to be grown mostly for the domestic market, with the major exporting area being around the Mediterranean coast and in the Canary Islands.

One element of horticultural production is that of 'forced cultivation' (*cultivos forzados*). In 1990/91 there were 25,786 hectares under greenhouses in Spain (built largely of plastic hung over wooden or steel frames), 10,379 hectares under tunnels (again made of plastic over metal frames), and 62,896 hectares under plastic laid over the ground. Of the total area under greenhouses, 55 per cent were in the province of Almería (especially the Campo de Dalías and Campo de Níjar), 14 per cent in Murcia, 7 per cent in Comunidad Valenciana and 6 per cent in the Canary Islands (mainly Tenerife). As regards tunnels, almost half the area is in Huelva (where they are used predominantly for growing strawberries, particularly around Moguer and Lepe) and almost 40 per cent in Valencia. The use of plastic to cover the ground is mainly a characteristic of Andalucía, especially in Seville and the west of the region.

Citrus and non-citrus fruit contribute around 20 per cent of the value of crop production *(producción final agrícola)*. They are important export crops in addition to supplying the domestic market. Citrus fruits grown on plantations occupy some 265,000 hectares, four-fifths of which are under oranges (including mandarins), with most of the rest under lemons (grapefruit occupying a much smaller area). Production is concentrated around the Mediterranean coast and in the Ebro Valley, the major export region being Valencia. Orange varieties have changed in recent years towards sweeter ones, with more juice and fewer pips (for example the navel orange). In contrast to the limited range and concentrated pattern of citrus fruit production, non-citrus fruits cover a diversity of products and are widely scattered, occupying over 950,000 hectares, over half of which are under extensive almond production. Non-citrus fruits embrace a diversity of products including apples, pears, apricots, cherries, plums and peaches from cooler climatic areas; figs, chirimoyas (custard apples), avocados, bananas and pomegranates from sub-tropical and semi-desert areas; and the dry fruits almonds, walnuts and hazelnuts. The almond-growing areas are distributed widely around the Mediterranean coast (especially in Alicante, the Balearic Islands, Granada and Murcia). In contrast, production of the chirimoya is highly concentrated. Almost all of the 3,500 hectares under production in 1991 being in Granada (especially in the municipality of Almuñécar). Similarly, production of bananas is almost totally confined to the Canary Islands (with limited production from the Costa del Sol). Spain is a net exporter of all the Mediterranean fruits but has net imports of apples, pears and other crops from non-Mediterranean climatic areas.

Livestock production is another sector that has expanded, stimulated by increased consumer demand and access to imported feeds. Climatic conditions have always been a constraint on production, especially on beef and dairy enterprises, but this has been reinforced in the past by the protection afforded to potential animal feeds. The lifting of import restrictions has allowed greater imports of animal feed (imports that explain why there has been little increase in the area under forage crops such as alfalfa, vetch, clover and many cereals despite higher livestock numbers). Cattle production is concentrated along the north coast and in Galicia, where there is adequate rainfall to support pasture, elsewhere production must rely on cattle feed. The most important sub-sector of livestock production is meat, followed by milk then eggs. In 1993 there were about 5 million head of cattle, of which there were about 1.5 million dairy cows (50 per cent Frisians), 24 million head of sheep, 3 million head of goats and 18 million head of pigs (MAPA 1994b). The largest increase since 1960 has been in the size of the pig herd (Table 3.4). Dairy cattle are concentrated in the provinces of Barcelona, Madrid, Oviedo, Santander and Vizcaya (a high proportion of milk produced being processed into butter and cheese). Outside of the north, beef cattle are reared particularly in Andalucía (for example in the Guadalquivir Valley). Sheep are reared widely across Spain with Merino

Table 3.4 Livestock

Year	Cattle	Sheep	Goats	Pigs
1950	3.1	16.3	4.1	2.7
1960	3.6	22.6	3.3	6.0
1970	4.3	17.0	2.6	7.6
1980	4.5	14.2	2.0	11.3
1990	5.1	24.0	3.7	16.0
1993	5.1	24.6	2.8	18.3

Figures in millions of head

The size of the dairy herd in 1991 was 1.5 million head

Sources: MAPA 1993a and 1994c

sheep being bred particularly for their wool in Extremadura. In many areas milk from sheep is used to produce cheese, for example 'Manchego' from La Mancha. Goats are widely kept but are found especially in central and southern Spain where they are a characteristic element of the traditional farming scene, being bred for their skin, milk and meat.

3.3 Problems of agricultural production

The continued drain of people away from agriculture is symptomatic of fundamental problems in the sector. The cause of these problems lies partly in the rapid changes that have occurred in the economic environment of an industry characterised by more deeply embedded traditions and conservatism than most other sectors of the economy. This conservatism was encouraged by the way in which agriculture evolved in a protectionist and interventionist political economy. A difficult physical environment, distorted farm size structure, extensive monocultures, an elderly and low-skilled labour force, under-capitalisation, financial problems, diffuse marketing arrangements and inadequate industrial development of agricultural products have all contributed to the problems of agriculture.

3.3.1 The physical environment

The major long-term threat to agriculture in Spain may not be international competition but long-term climatic change predicted to bring higher average annual temperatures and lower rainfall to Spain in the next century. Low and unreliable precipitation already poses a regular threat to production (roughly 90 per cent of the Spanish peninsular receives on average less than 685 mm of precipitation per year) and is a factor behind soil erosion and desertification. For example, a long period of drought over large areas of Spain in the early 1980s led to a series of poor harvests and consequent agricultural trade deficits, ended in 1984 by heavy spring rains and a record harvest. A further drought in 1992 was estimated by agricultural organisations to have caused losses of pta 300 billion in farm incomes. Those crops that rely on rain-fed water supplies are naturally most affected (especially cereals), but irrigated crops may be affected too as irrigation water is reduced during prolonged periods of drought. Such problems can only be ameliorated either by changing agricultural practices, improved water management or by large-scale investment in schemes to transfer water from the north of Spain to the centre and south as envisaged under the controversial National Water Plan (Plan Hidrológico Nacional under discussion in 1994). Conversely, heavy rain hinders the development of olive flowers and dampness causes disease on olives, especially if it occurs in the autumn just before the harvest.

Apart from rainfall, there are numerous other physical environmental constraints on agriculture, including spatial variations in soil conditions, temperature regimes (especially the occurrence of frosts) and steep slopes. The extent of agricultural activity in adverse environments can be gauged from the proportion of all agricultural land used productively (*superficie agrícola utilizada*, SAU; this includes all the cultivated land, including fallow and pasture during the period of the Census of Agriculture), recorded as being in less-favoured areas *(zonas desfavorecidas:* designated according to physical and economic criteria but notably mountainous and depopulated areas). According to a survey undertaken in 1987 by the Ministry of Agriculture (MAPA 1989b), 46 per cent of the total SAU was in areas classified as unfavourable and 28 per cent in mountainous areas.

3.3.2 *Farm size structure*

One of the most intractable of problems in Spanish agriculture is a farm size structure distorted by a small number of very large farms and a multitude of very small ones. Farm size alone does not necessarily reflect efficiency, which depends on management, product mix, location, physical layout (degree of fragmentation), soil and so forth. Indeed, the dichotomy between small and large farms partly reflects the contrasts between farming potential on irrigated and non-irrigated land. Nevertheless, large estates have frequently been associated with under-utilisation of land and small farms are frequently unable to generate adequate incomes or support capital investment.

Using the standard definition of a farm (*explotación agrícola*) to be a unit of operation and not of ownership, the 1989 Census of Agriculture recorded only 2.7 per cent of all holdings as 100 hectares or more, yet these large farms occupied 62.3 per cent of the total agricultural area. Conversely, 65.3 per cent of all the holdings were recorded as being less than five hectares in size, but they occupied only 5.4 per cent of the agricultural land (Table 3.5). In practice this degree of distortion may be misleading as the total agricultural area includes land not utilised for agriculture (for example woodland,

Table 3.5 Farm size structure

	Percentage of holdings				Percentage of area				Percentage of SAU	
Farm size (ha)	1962	1972	1982	1989	1962	1972	1982	1989	1982	1989
No land or < 0.1	7.4	1.8	1.3	0.9	0.0	0.0	0.0	0.0	0.0	0.0
0.1–0.9	24.4	22.8	25.0	27.8	0.7	0.6	0.6	0.7	0.9	0.9
1.0–4.9	34.3	38.0	37.1	36.7	6.0	5.3	4.8	4.7	7.1	6.1
5.0–9.9	13.9	15.1	14.1	13.2	6.6	5.9	5.2	4.9	7.5	6.5
10.0–19.9	10.0	10.5	10.2	9.5	9.4	8.2	7.5	6.9	10.7	9.3
20.0–49.9	6.5	7.1	7.1	6.8	13.2	12.0	11.6	11.0	17.1	15.5
50.0–99.9	1.7	2.3	2.6	2.5	8.2	8.9	9.6	9.4	13.8	13.2
100.0–499.9	1.4	1.9	2.1	2.1	19.8	21.8	22.9	22.9	24.5	24.9
500 plus	0.4	0.5	0.5	0.5	33.7	37.3	37.8	39.5	18.3	23.6
Total	100.0	100.0	100.0	100.0	100.0	100.0	100.0	100.0	100.0	100.0

Percentages are based on the total area of land included in the census except for the last two columns which are percentages of the utilised agricultural land (SAU)

Source: MAPA (Agricultural censuses)

scrub and mountainous land). If utilised agricultural land only is considered, then according to the 1989 Census holdings of 100 hectares or more occupy only 48.6 per cent of the farmland and holdings of less than five hectares occupy 7 per cent (INE 1991). Comparisons between censuses must be treated with caution but in general the polarisation in size structure appears to have increased.

There are two explanations for the discrepancy between the figures for total agricultural land and utilised agricultural land. The first is that many large estates cover entirely unproductive land (for example in the province of Málaga many large estates are owned by municipalities and occupy high mountainous areas). The other explanation is that large tracts of land in large estates are not used for cultivation or pasture. Medium-sized farms of 20 to 99.9 hectares occupy only 28.6 per cent of the utilised agricultural land. These figures do not of course take into account ownership patterns, which may be more distorted than those of farms with individuals owning more than one holding or the ownership of individual holdings being split between a number of people.

The existence of large estates in the farm size structure has been a crucial factor not just in the development of agriculture but in the evolution of the political economy (Bosque Maurel 1973). Traditionally, large estates *(latifundia)* were associated with extensive agriculture, insufficient capital investment and low levels of productivity, despite occupying some of the best lands (the land reform law of 1932 defined *latifundia* as estates of 200 hectares or more in dry farming or 50 hectares or more in irrigation, *dehesa* being mainly pastoral in the mountains and *cortijo* mainly arable in the lowlands; Martinez-Alier 1971). They are particularly characteristic of La Mancha (notably Ciudad Real), Extremadura (notably Cáceres) and western

Andalucía (notably Cádiz, Córdoba and Seville). In the past, owners had little incentive to improve these lands: the lower the official classification of land the lower the taxes (a situation that may change with the completion of the rural land catastral survey in the early 1990s and the tightening of taxation laws; Bruce 1990). Frequently the land was rented out for grazing and hunting, while absentee landowners lived in the cities. Apart from the economic consequences of *latifundia*, the social consequence was a landless peasantry denied any prospect of improvement (Giner and Sevilla 1977). The *latifundio* was part of a feudal society, which withered only with the death of General Franco.

The presence of *latifundia* was an important political issue in the past, but in contemporary Spain the issue has been defused by the changing production environment: the Common Agricultural Policy, decline of the agricultural population and the modernisation of agriculture. Emigration during the 1950s and 1960s released pressure on the land and diverted attention away from discontent over land ownership. By the time emigration was halted in the mid 1970s and a political regime installed that was more sympathetic with the problem, the problem itself had partly evaporated. Modern large estates are frequently intensively cultivated (especially where they are farmed by personally managing owners; Maas 1983) and in many areas (for example in parts of Seville) they are company farms practising the most modern agro-industrial techniques.

At the other end of the farm size spectrum is the small farm or *minifundio*, occupying only a few hectares (and frequently much less) and/or involving only a few head of livestock. Commonly these small farms are further fragmented into numerous dispersed plots (although fragmentation is also present on large farms), giving a variegated aspect to the landscape. In addition, there may be multi-ownership of single plots and different usufruct rights in the same plot. Efficiency is precluded by limitations on economies of scale: the exclusion of machinery, the loss of land in field boundaries, the restrictions placed on raising loans to finance improvements and the time taken to move from one plot to another. Atomisation of land holdings is common across Spain, being particularly characteristic of the more mountainous areas of Andalucía and Galicia.

Restructuring of agricultural holdings has been substantial, though small farms remain common. According to the Census of Agriculture, there has been a dramatic decline in the number of farm holdings since 1962 (although analysis of trends in farm structure must be treated with caution because of changes in definitions and coverage in the Census). Between 1962 and 1982 the number of farm holdings decreased by a quarter (from 3,007,000 in 1962 to 2,375,000 in 1982) and thence by a further 4 per cent to 1989 (2,284,944 in 1989). Despite this decline, which has been far less than the decline in farm employment, statistics on farm size provide little evidence that the small farm is disappearing from the landscape, although fragmentation does appear to be on the decline (García Delgado 1988). But aggregate statistics mask important structural changes within different sectors of agriculture. Thus in cereal production (where economies of scale are critical) small farms have been declining, while in horticulture the number of small farms has been rising. Overall, the total number of land plots (*parcelas*) decreased by over half between 1962 and 1982 (from 39 million to 18.4 million), resulting in an increase of average plot size from 1.15 hectares to 2.33 hectares. In 1962 the average number of plots per holding was 13.7, while in 1989 it was 8.1 (Census of Agriculture). These average figures conceal enormous spatial variations. Thus the average size of a plot (number of plots to total agricultural land) in 1989 varied from 0.26 hectares in Pontevedra to 17.7 hectares in Cádiz.

3.3.3 *Enterprise combinations*

In many parts of Spain agriculture has been heavily dependent on a single crop, with vast tracts of land given over to the monocultures of cereals, olives or vines, and fallow (fallow and unoccupied lands occupied 21 per cent of the cultivated area in 1990). Irrigation is gradually breaking up this pattern. Monocultures include cereals in the Meseta (for example in the *comarca* - district - of Almazán (Soria) they occupy 87 per cent of the cultivated area), olives in Jaén (for example in the *comarca* of Campiña Sur olives occupy 80 per cent of the land area) and vines in Ciudad Real (for example in Valdepeñas). Strawberry production around Lepe and Moguer (Huelva) provides a more recent example of monoculture. Such cropping patterns expose whole regions to the economic risks of crop-specific diseases or a downturn in the fortunes of the crop produced; a risk that is reduced by enterprise diversification. At the other end of the spectrum many small farms have practised polycultures, providing a subsistence component to household income. Increased commercialisation is forcing greater specialisation.

3.3.4 *The labour force*

One of the most serious problems facing Spanish agriculture relates to the size and quality of the labour force. There are still too many farmers to be supported at an adequate level of income, although the number is falling quickly (an estimated 200,000 left the sector in 1992). In general, it is an elderly labour force, the majority of farm workers are members of families (an estimated 80 per cent of farm labour), many work only part-time in farming, there is a low level of education and a lack of agricultural training. In other traditional industrial sectors reconversion programmes included early-retirement programmes, in agriculture there was no such programme until 1989.

A more youthful labour force is only slowly emerging. Ageing of the agricultural labour force was reversed in the late 1970s as young people found it difficult to find work away from rural areas but the age of those employed on farms continued to fall only slowly despite government incentives for young people in agriculture to start agricultural businesses, modernise farms, acquire land, obtain housing, etc. The average age of the occupied population in agriculture fell from 45.3 in 1982 to only 44.8 in 1991. The proportion aged less than thirty rose from 20 per cent at the beginning of the 1980s to 22 per cent at the end of the decade, while 42 per cent were aged fifty or over in 1991 (Povedano 1993a). Almost 60 per cent of farm owners are aged over fifty-five, only 3 per cent were aged less than thirty in 1989 according to the Agricultural Census. Lowering the age profile has been slowed by the continuing loss of young people from the land and a lack of interest in farming among young people.

A better educated labour force is also only slowly emerging. A high percentage of those working in farming are illiterate and very few have had higher education (*estudios superiores*). Relatively few people working in agriculture have had professional training.

Apart from the quality of the labour force, rising labour costs have been at the heart of the reorganisation of production and a critical factor in the crisis of traditional agriculture. Over the period 1964 to 1984 labour costs rose more rapidly than other farm costs, even during the period of rapidly rising energy prices in the 1970s (García Delgado 1988). Not only has this resulted in the substitution of capital for labour (for example in cotton picking), but also in an increased reliance on temporary labour. Yet despite increased labour costs, negative wage differentials with other sectors still exist. Increased productivity in agriculture has been accompanied by a continued loss of labour and not by equivalent increases in real incomes.

3.3.5 *Productivity*

In relation to other countries in the European Union productivity in agriculture remains low (Povedano 1993a), partly because of the relatively low levels of capital application and the relatively large labour force. Hence the contribution of agriculture to the GDP is far less than the proportion of the labour force employed in agriculture. Low yields are particularly characteristic of cereals but are also typical elsewhere; for example, in milk production yields are only about 60 per cent of the European Union average. There has been a steady increase in mechanisation (associated with a decrease in labour and in the number of draught animals). The mechanisation rate (the horsepower of all motorised equipment per 100 hectares) increased from 23 in 1962, to 76 in 1970, 177 in 1980 and thence to 258 in 1991 (MAPA 1993d). In specific sectors there have been sharp increases in mechanisation. For example, in cotton the number of cotton harvesters increased from 299 in 1985 to 628 in 1986. But in comparison with other European

Union countries mechanisation remains low. Thus in 1986 there were three tractors per 100 hectares of utilised land (SAU) in Spain compared with five in France and twelve in West Germany (MAPA 1989a). A similar picture exists in the application of agri-chemicals. Nitrogenous fertilizer consumption increased by 360 per cent between 1960 and 1989, yet in 1986 Spain used only 43 kilograms per hectare (SAU), higher only than Portugal in the European Community (MAPA 1989a).

3.3.6 *Finance*

Agriculture remains heavily subsidised despite greater competition within the European Union under the CAP. Subsidies from all public sources doubled from 1982 to 1990, absorbing about 11 per cent of the price guarantee section of the European Agricultural Guidance and Guarantee Fund (EAGGF) in 1992 and one-fifth of the guidance section (Povedano 1993a). In 1993 pta 705 billion was paid to Spain under the guarantee section of the EAGGF (almost 50 per cent under the cereal, olive oil and oil-seed regimes). In the same year it was estimated that subsidies represented 25 per cent of farm incomes in Spain (Maté 1994a), while another estimate suggested that 47 per cent of farm incomes in the EC could be attributed to protectionism (OECD estimate quoted in Compés López 1994).

More capitalistic farming methods have meant increased reliance on external finance and an increase in rural indebtedness (Maté 1990a). Credit to agriculture, excluding fishing and food industries, increased by an estimated 100 per cent in real terms between 1984 and 1992 (Povedano 1993b). In 1992 the total debt in the agricultural sector was estimated at pta 1,280 billion (almost two-thirds of the gross value added in the sector; Compés López 1994). The central problem for many enterprises has been that costs have risen faster than revenue, squeezing profit margins and resulting in a deterioration in levels of living. Higher prices for farm products have frequently been associated with rising costs of distribution, leaving farmgate prices low. As a result, average farm incomes remain below those of other sectors in the economy (and only above those in Greece and Portugal in the European Union). Increases in per-capita incomes have come about mainly through a decline in the agricultural work force (although incomes from agriculture are frequently supplemented by income from other activities).

Farming faces a particular financing problem because of the long time interval between investment and returns (and the cash-flow problem of income coming at one time of the year while expenditure is incurred throughout the year) and the indivisibility of many development projects. Simultaneously, the financial returns on many agricultural investments would not normally allow farmers to borrow from the private sector. The Ministry of Agriculture provides grants (for example to subsidise investment in farms) and in the past many farmers relied on government price supports and on the public sector for credit (notably the Agricultural Credit Bank (Banco de Crédito Agrícola), the National Agricultural Produce Service (Servicio Nacional de Productos Agrarios, SENPA) and the National Agricultural Reform and Development Agency (Instituto Nacional de Reforma y Desarrollo Agrario, IRYDA)). Membership of the Common Agricultural Policy has swept away this system replacing it with a new support framework. At the same time the CAP has limited many product prices to control surplus production. The net result has been a more market-oriented form of agriculture, increasingly financed through the private sector (over 40 per cent from the commercial banks, 20 per cent through the rural savings banks and co-operatives, 30 per cent through savings banks and only 5 per cent through official credit; MAPA 1993c).

3.3.7 Marketing

Weak marketing organisation continues to inhibit agricultural development, reducing total income in the sector. Exports are frequently handled by foreign marketing organisations (for example most flowers pass through Dutch auction rooms), often with local agents inspecting the quality of products at their source. Weaknesses in domestic marketing have also contributed to the increased penetration of the domestic market by foreign products as foreign firms and large foreign retailers use more efficient distribution channels (more responsive to demand) and market products with more consistent standards.

In the traditional production system marketing is frequently chaotic with output directed principally at the domestic market. Small family farms (generally with limited management ability and with limited power to negotiate prices) sell their products either directly in local markets or to merchants with small businesses. These merchants transport the products to their stores (which are often small, badly prepared and without refrigeration facilities) and, after some brief selection and packing, they forward them to wholesale markets. Any surpluses are auctioned in small lots without standardisation. The bulk of production tends to arrive in the market at the same time undermining product prices (hence prices tend to be lower in early summer and higher for the majority of products from December to April). In general there is a lack of information (transparency) about all aspects of the market.

The formation of marketing co-operatives has been one means by which farmers have endeavoured to improve their marketing position, but they have frequently been unsuccessful as a result of the inadequate discipline imposed by the co-operative. Producers may continue to decide independently the variety to be produced, the time of sowing, the cultivation methods to be used and the time of harvesting. When prices are high, all or part of the crop may be harvested and auctioned, resulting in market saturation and lower prices. Consequently, it may be impossible for a co-operative to offer consistent quality, quantity and price. For these reasons the big food-processing firms avoid these marketing networks by establishing their own farms or by having direct contracts with farmers.

3.3.8 Technological dependence

Despite the size of the agriculture sector in Spain, it has failed to produce an internationally competitive farm equipment or farm inputs industry. The modernisation of agriculture has been accompanied by increased technological dependence, including increased imports of agricultural equipment, agro-chemicals and plant materials. For example, many of the strawberry plants are imported annually to Huelva from California, Dutch seed suppliers occupy an important position in horticulture and multinationals supply agri-chemicals.

3.4 Government intervention

The dominant theme in agricultural policy from the early 1980s was the adaptation of the Spanish agricultural system to European Community requirements and the concomitant untangling of the extensive web of Spanish intervention measures developed during the Francoist regime (Arévalo Arias 1993). This required the transfer to Brussels of part of the agricultural policy-making process and a rationalisation of assistance provided by the Ministry of Agriculture. Moreover, many of the functions previously carried out by the Ministry of Agriculture were transferred to equivalent organisations in the regional governments leaving the Ministry to formulate central government policy and act as a conduit with Brussels. Reform of the CAP and increased liberalisation of agriculture will require the Ministry to place even more emphasis on promoting efficiency in agriculture, while continuing to lobby in Brussels for policies favourable to Spanish agriculture.

The major concern of national agricultural policy from the early 1980s has been to modernise production structures and increase agricultural efficiency, thereby meeting internal demand for food and supporting an export industry able to meet foreign competition. However, since this has been undertaken within the framework of an interventionist system - the CAP – policy has also been directed towards ensuring interventionist measures beneficial to Spain. The outcome has been that many sectors of agriculture remain uncompetitive in international markets.

Modernisation has included reform of production structures: irrigation, development of underground water supplies, farm modernisation, farm size structure improvements, training, and research and development.

More broadly it has encompassed integrated rural development and the renovation of some sectors of agricultural production (notably vines, olives, milk and cattle). Important programmes have included assistance to establish refrigeration equipment in milk-producing areas, the provision of a modern network of municipal abattoirs (Plan General de Mataderos), the assistance provided in agricultural industrialisation zones (ZPLIA) and assistance to small agricultural enterprises (*Pequeñas y Medianas Empresas agroalimentarias*). Particular emphasis has been placed on promoting the formation of co-operatives for the purchase of inputs, the sharing of equipment and the marketing of produce. Most of these activities are now supervised by the regional governments and supported by the European Union.

3.4.1 Intervention in production and marketing

Prior to entry into the European Community, Spain operated an extensive intervention mechanism covering all stages of agricultural production and marketing. Areas planted were set, input and product prices were fixed and imports were controlled. Agricultural policy emphasised increased output, but this was restricted by the expansion of demand. Intervention inhibited the transmission of market signals to producers, leading to a mismatch between supply and demand.

Examples of intervention can be drawn from across the whole range of agricultural production. Intervention in wheat extends back to the nineteenth century, when production developed in the shelter of the rigidly protectionist laws prevailing between 1820 and 1869. Following strong competition from imports, further tariff protection was applied in 1891 and 1906, then in 1922 an absolute ban was imposed on foreign wheat imports. From 1937 wheat prices were supported by the National Wheat Service (Servicio Nacional del Trigo), which guaranteed to purchase all of the wheat crop at prices that would ensure the survival of small producers and simultaneously prove very rewarding to larger producers (*ad valorem* tariff barriers against wheat imports were also used to support prices). This agency was later broadened to the National Cereals Service (Servicio Nacional de Cereales), which in turn was enlarged in 1971 to the National Agricultural Produce Service (SENPA). SENPA guaranteed the purchase price for a range of crops (including soya seeds, sunflower seeds and rape seeds) and it subsidised seeds and fertilizers.

Agricultural product prices were supported from 1968 through the Fund for the Management of Agricultural Product Prices (Fondo de Ordenación y Regulación de los Precios y Productos Agrarios, FORPPA), an autonomous organisation of the Ministry of Agriculture. In sugar production the Ministry of Agriculture determined the annual area of sugar planting for each region, fixed the price at which the sugar crop would be bought and the price at which sugar was sold to the public and to industry. In tobacco the state intervened in cultivation and preparation through the National Tobacco Service (Servicio Nacional del Cultivo y Fermentación del Tabaco, SNCFT, established in 1944). Manufacturing and distribution were controlled by the Tobacco Monopoly (Monopolio de Tabaco) and through the State Tobacco Company (Compañía Arrendataria de Tabacalera SA). Only the Canary Islands lay outside the control of the tobacco monopoly. In the livestock industry there were guaranteed prices for all meats fixed at the abattoir and the Supply and Transport Board (Comisaria General de Abastecimientos y Transportes) regulated prices in each product distribution channel (skins, frozen meat, etc.).

Other elements of the control system included a network of wholesale markets in agricultural zones owned by the state and the local authorities (Empresa Nacional de Mercados en Origen de Productos Agrarios SA, Mercosa) and a network of wholesale distribution markets (Mercados en Destino, Mercasa; of which there was a network of 22 markets in 1993).

Membership of the European Community required that production and primary processing be liberalised. Frequently, the national regulating organisations took on the responsibility of managing the pricing regime of the CAP. In the case of a wide range of crops this is undertaken by SENPA (with support for the pricing policy being channelled through FORPPA, which also manages intervention stocks) and in the case of tobacco by the SNCFT. In the case of Mercosa, the assets of the company were sold off. Tabacalera attempted to diversify into a broad food manufacturing company then consolidated around its core business of tobacco.

Co-operation between farmers is promoted as a means of overcoming the problems faced by small farms, increasing farm incomes through higher productivity, adoption of new technologies and improved marketing (forms of association include Cooperativas Agrarias, Cooperativas de Explotación Comunitaria de la Tierra, Sociedades Agrarias de Transformación and Cooperativas de Trabajo Asociado). Apart from assistance available from the government, assistance for this type of activity is also available from the European Community through the European Agricultural Guidance and Guarantee Fund (EAGGF, guidance section) and European Social Fund. The phenomenon of association has been growing in recent years (in 1992 there were one and a half million members of Cooperativas Agrarias), but many of the associations that have been formed remain small in size and the extent of development is less than in some other countries of the European Union.

The government also promotes the marketing of produce in a number of ways: for example, through setting up consumer panels to gain a better understanding of demand, through food information campaigns and through the regulation and classification of horticultural and food products (the Fondo Nacional para la Normalización y Tipificación de Productos Hortofruticolas represents one specific action to achieve this end). The government has also attempted to promote quality and differentiate products from Spain through branding products according to their origin (undertaken by the national food classification institute, Instituto Nacional de Denominaciones de Origen). Classifications cover wine, cheese, sausages, asparagus and so forth (for example, Rioja, Queso de Picón, Chorizo de Pamplona and Espárrago de Navarra respectively).

3.4.2 Restructuring and renovation

As part of the process of farm modernisation the government has pursued a number of restructuring and reconversion programmes covering olives, vines, citrus fruit, milk, tobacco and livestock, designed to adjust production to demand (since 1986 undertaken within the framework of the CAP). Producers must apply for assistance, which (in the case of crops) can be used to remove plants from unproductive areas and replant productive areas with improved stock.

In the case of olives at least 25 per cent of the production area has been estimated to be on marginal land, difficult to convert to other uses. On these marginal lands yields are low and mechanisation is difficult. The socio-economic implications of this crop have led government to intervene over a long period of time. Plans for reconversion and restructuring were begun in 1972 and further measures set in motion in 1982 (El Plan de Reestructuración del Olivar Mejorable y Reconversión de Comarcas Olivareras Deprimadas). Under this scheme 250,000 hectares of land then grown to olives were to be put down to other crops. Since 1986 help for improving the structure of the sector has been made through investment projects approved and partly financed by the European Union.

Vines have been another sector that have suffered from over-production and have thus been subject to restructuring and reconversion programmes designed to reduce excess production and improve the quality of wine. However, the CAP regime operating in the early 1990s failed to reduce surpluses. The planting of vines in wine-producing areas was prohibited but was impossible to control. The practise of adding sugar to wine (*chaptalización*, to increase the alcohol content) has contributed to the increase in wine production. Equally, the policy of offering financial assistance towards the removal of vines only reduced acreages in marginal areas (with the exception of Jerez, where the area under vines was reduced from 22,000 hectares in 1980 to 11,600 in 1993), which was more than offset by increases in yields in more productive areas (Yubero 1994). In an attempt to tighten policy in 1994 the EU was seeking further cuts in the output from EU member states, including cuts in Spanish output equivalent to 20 per cent (some 300,000 hectares) of the existing area under vines.

Other restructuring programmes have covered citrus fruit, milk and tobacco. In the case of citrus fruit, reconversion was necessary because of disease. The citrus virus '*tristeza*' caused the death of more than 10 million trees in the early 1980s. To combat the disease problem, and to maintain output in the sector, assistance was provided for the purchase of new disease-resistant stock. Dairy farmers have also been able to apply to restructure production (which has been coupled with a plan to restructure the dairies). Intervention in tobacco cultivation was necessary to shift production to new varieties and to improve the production infrastructure (Plan de Reordinación de la Producción Tabaquera Nacional).

3.4.3 *Agrarian reform*

As mentioned earlier, farm size structure and organisation have been an important constraint on agricultural development. However, successive governments have avoided radical land reform and concentrated instead on irrigation, improving agricultural practices, land consolidation, colonisation and more general improvements in the rural environment. They have made little progress in breaking up large estates (Giner and Sevilla 1977; Naylon 1973).

Following the death of Franco and the implementation of democratic government, renewed attempts were made to effect structural change. A law passed in 1979 permitted the expropriation of large estates where the land was found to be under-utilised, but little progress was made, partly because the ideology of the Francoist regime still survived in the Ministry of Agriculture and partly because of the fear that radical reform might destabilise the emerging democracy. The Law of Agrarian Reform, passed in 1983, provided new measures for the expropriation of land. The regional government of Andalucía was the first to implement the new legislation. In 1984 it designated land for reform in Antequera (province of Málaga). By the beginning of 1990 nine other *comarcas* had been designated for reform, but expropriation made little progress (Maté 1990b) and was quietly dropped. The changing agricultural environment (especially European Union initiatives to take land out of cultivation and further falls in the agricultural labour force) weakened the demand for such reforms (apart from among a declining group of militant agricultural workers). The designation of areas for agricultural reform is now seen more as a means of achieving farming improvements rather than one of achieving land redistribution.

Apart from the problem of *latifundia*, the central government has also attempted to tackle the problem of small and fragmented farms through land consolidation programmes. The first law on land consolidation was passed in 1952 (Guedes 1981) and implemented by the Servicio Nacional de Concentración Parcelaria y Ordenación Rural (SNCPOR). Progress in this complex area of action was inevitably slow, although grants and loans were available at low interest rates for small farms to be increased in size and for all farmers to improve their properties. Vineyards, irrigated land, orchards and woodland are all difficult to consolidate, as are farms in mountainous areas. Heterogeneity of land with different potential and trees of different ages and yields pose particular problems. Hence most headway has been made on uniform lands (for example the grain lands of León and Castilla, where settlement is nucleated). By 1977 4.7 million hectares had been concentrated, affecting 3,375 areas and 937,234 farmers; 13,688,688 plots of average size 0.35 hectares had been reduced to 1,790,971 plots of average size 2.64 hectares (Guedes 1981). By 1982 consolidation had been extended to 5.2 million hectares (Tamames 1983). But, even after reform, farms tended to remain small in size (O'Flanagan 1982). Significant increases in farm size will only occur as the number of farm owners decrease.

Responsibilities for agrarian reform have now been largely transferred from the central government (IRYDA, which was formed in 1971, subsuming the roles of both the colonisation institute, the INC, and the land consolidation organisation SNCPOR) to the regional governments (for example, in Andalucía the Instituto Andaluz de la Reforma Agraria, IARA). These regional agencies continue the work of agrarian reform: crop development, farm modernisation, the introduction of new farm systems, irrigation and settlement. However, in a democratic society (where under the Constitution private property is protected) structural change is inevitably slow, with limited opportunities to break up large estates or consolidate small farms.

Apart from the general programmes of agrarian reform, specific areas now qualify for assistance under both state and European Union schemes. Specific support is available for agriculture in mountainous areas (*indemnizaciones compensatorias de montaña*, ICM) which embrace 3,000 municipalities and an area of 20 million hectares. The scheme complements that for unfavourable farming areas.

3.4.4 Irrigation

In the past, irrigation schemes have been used by the state as the main means of promoting rural development. Irrigation has been installed across the whole of Spain, especially in the main river basins: the Duero, Ebro, Guadalquivir, Guadiana and Tajo. Between 1960 and 1992 the irrigated area (covering both public and private irrigation schemes) increased by 85 per cent from 1.83 million hectares to 3.4 million hectares. Irrigation enables more intensive production (higher crop yields, multiple cropping, year round production), a greater diversity of crops and more consistent output. The principal problems of irrigation are concerned with its cost in relation to the benefits derived from increased agricultural output and employment, the relationship between those who pay for irrigation works and those who benefit from them, the ecological impact of irrigation on surrounding areas (for example the over-use of underground aquifers and other areas of extraction), and the management and technical problems associated with the implementation and running of irrigation schemes. The political dimension of water use was highlighted in mid 1994 when the government of Castilla-La Mancha initially refused to sanction the transfer of water from the Tajo basin to the irrigated areas in the Segura basin of Murcia and Valencia through the 'trasvase' (the 'trasvase' was planned in the 1930s and built in the Franco years, never fulfilling its potential).

Major public works associated with irrigation schemes (dams, reservoirs and irrigation canals) are carried out under the direction of the Ministry of Public Works (Ministerio de Obras Públicas) through the water authorities (*confederaciones hidrográficas*). Schemes are set in motion by the central government in conjunction with the regions (where they are of national concern) and/or by the regions themselves. The regional agencies then implement the irrigation schemes and are responsible for agrarian development (including any colonisation). Assistance from central and regional government agencies is also available for the improvement and development of private irrigation.

3.4.5 *Conservation of nature*

The national rural environmental agency is the Instituto Nacional para la Conservación de la Naturaleza (ICONA), which on its formation in 1971 subsumed the roles of the Patrimonio Forestal del Estado, the Servicio de Pesca Continental, Caza y Parques Nacionales and the Servicio Nacional de Conservación de Suelos. Thus it has broad responsibilities for the environment: for the protection of flora and fauna, the protection of river basins and water, for forestry and the conservation of soils. Like IRYDA it is an autonomous organisation of the Ministry of Agriculture and, as with IRYDA, its role has been reduced by the formation of regional government agencies such as the IARA and the Agencia de Medio Ambiente in Andalucía. Generally, ICONA provides a link between the regional agencies and the central government, channelling national programmes down to the regions. It also represents the central government on supranational environmental bodies. Among the gravest ecological problems are those of desertification, soil erosion and pollution. Thus ICONA continues work on reducing desertification (*lucha contra la desertificación del mediterráneo*), preparing maps of the erosion situation in each of the river basins, monitoring rural resources and on programmes to combat forest fires.

3.5 Application of the Common Agricultural Policy

Following membership of the European Community agriculture was incorporated into the Common Agricultural Policy (CAP), another interventionist system but with free trade within the EC, a different set of regulations, a well-defined policy constructed around the requirements of mainly north-west European countries and policy determined in Brussels. Membership offered greatly increased export opportunities, guaranteed prices (milk and sugar were the only two products with higher prices in Spain than in the EC; Compés López 1994) and assistance under the Agricultural Guidance and Guarantee Fund (EAGGF) for price support and farm modernisation. Unfortunately, the terms of accession were unfavourable to agriculture in Spain and pressures for reform of the CAP were mounting.

Incorporation of Spain into the European Community added about 30 per cent to the cultivated area, to employment in agriculture and to the number of farm holdings in the ten existing member states. Agricultural production in Spain now represents about 12 per cent of that in the European Union. The Canary Islands, Ceuta and Melilla, initially chose to remain outside the customs union of the Community and thus to remain outside the Community agricultural and fisheries policies. From 1991 the Canary Islands adopted a transitional status accompanied by measures to compensate for their insular character and remoteness (the POSEICAN programme). The CAP covers 95 per cent of Spanish agricultural production in its price support section in addition to providing assistance for modernisation under its guidance section and broader rural development under the European Structural Funds. Spanish agriculture, like that in other EU member states, remains protected from competition from outside the Union.

Spanish accession brought conflicts with other Mediterranean producers and added substantially to the problems of agricultural restructuring and maintaining price support within the Community. It also brought problems for third countries trading with Spain, for example the United States feared the loss of a substantial maize market and other third country Mediterranean producers (for example Israel and North African countries) feared greater competition for their products in European Community markets.

The objectives of agricultural policy in the European Union are to: i) increase the productivity of agriculture; ii) seek an equitable standard of living for the agricultural population; iii) achieve stability of markets; iv) guarantee security of food supplies; and v) achieve reasonable prices to consumers (Treaty of Rome, Article 39). This policy has been implemented through the Common Agricultural Policy drawing on the EAGGF. The price support element of the EAGGF (guarantee section) has absorbed the majority of all funding, funds going especially into cereals and milk products. The guidance section has complemented national funding for agricultural improvements including funding for hill farmers, training, modernisation and early retirement.

Pressures for reform of the CAP have come from both inside and outside the European Union. Inside the Union pressures have resulted from the growth of spending under the CAP and its effect of stimulating excess supply (at a time when population growth has been almost static!).

Externally, the pressures have come from GATT and countries seeking the dismantling of the trade barriers and agricultural subsidies. Reforms introduced in 1992 have included more realistic product pricing, quantity restrictions and land set-aside schemes, designed to reduce agricultural surpluses and make agriculture more internationally competitive. They have also introduced the concept of farming as a crucial element of environmental management. Simultaneously, the guidance section of the CAP has been incorporated into the system of Structural Funds, where agricultural improvements are now viewed in the broader context of rural development.

Reform of Spanish agricultural policy necessary to make it compatible with the CAP began before 1986. There were four main differences between the Spanish intervention system and that in the CAP. In Spain there was a more rigid system of intervention. Thus sales of a number of products (wheat, tobacco, sugar beet and hops) had to be directed through a public agency. Secondly, the state controlled trade in cereals, vegetable oils, milk products, cotton, tobacco and meat, which together represented a substantial proportion of total agricultural trade. Thirdly, the breadth of state intervention was less in Spain. Finally, there were a smaller range of structural measures than under the CAP (Reig 1988).

Issues relating to agriculture were critical bottlenecks in negotiations over the terms of Spanish entry into the EC and membership was only gained after the acceptance of some restrictive terms. Thus, while transitional arrangements lessened the immediate impact on Spanish agriculture of increased competition, they also restricted market access for those products where Spain had the greatest competitive advantage, fruit and vegetables. For these products and for vegetable oils, the dismantling of tariffs was slower than for other products. A strict quota was also imposed on milk production, which was far below existing levels of production. The result was that Spain gained less immediate advantage from membership. Spanish exports of fruit and vegetables to the EC were inhibited, and further pressure was exerted on the already struggling dairy industry of northern Spain.

To accommodate Spanish agriculture a two-pronged transitional arrangement was agreed: one extending over seven years and one extending over ten years. The classical model was one of seven years applying to all products, except for fresh fruit and vegetables, and vegetable oils, which allowed only very limited imports during the first four years. In practice, full integration into the CAP was achieved at an earlier date than the 31 December 1992 deadline for many products, including cereals and beef. Institutional price regimes were gradually brought into line (although where the initial difference was less than 3 per cent the price adjustment was instantaneous). Preferential state assistance incompatible with that in the European Community was eliminated and the free circulation of products between Spain and the European Community was established. Tariffs were gradually reduced and other trade restrictions including the state control of agricultural trade were ended. Finally, there was a gradual adjustment to the Common External Tariff, with the exact conditions varying according to products. A special safeguard clause (initially agreed for ten years until 1996) allows for protectionist measures to be taken with the agreement of the European Union to prevent serious market problems. For fresh fruit and vegetables the transition comprised two stages extending over ten years (until the beginning of 1996). In the first four years domestic market protection was maintained while Spain adjusted its internal market mechanisms to those of the European Community. From 1 January 1990 the second stage of six years began during which trade restrictions with the European Community were gradually removed. For vegetable oils there was a special regime also covering ten years based on maintaining the *status quo* for five years (until 1 January 1991), thence following the classical model. In practice, almost complete integration into the CAP was achieved for these products by 1993 (Milan Diez 1993), stimulating the exports of fruit and vegetables to the EU.

Agricultural policy in Spain has sought to address the negative aspects of CAP membership through continued negotiation. Increased funding was secured under the price support section of the EAGGF (from pta 37 billion in 1986 to pta 479 billion in 1992, from 1 to 11 per cent of the total fund, taking Spain from tenth to the fourth largest recipient of funds; MAPA 1993a), together with substantial funding under the guidance section of the EAGGF and from the Structural Funds. Moreover, the transition period for fruit and vegetables was brought forward to January 1993 and the milk quota for supplies to industry was increased in 1992. In general, membership has been beneficial to producers of fruit and vegetables, cotton, rice, sunflowers, olive oil and wine. However, for the latter two products production restrictions have created problems and in the vegetable oil market olive oil will come under increasing pressure from other cheaper oils (notably sunflower and soya oil). Tight regulations on product quality have also had an impact. Thus the export of pork was prohibited up until 1989 because of the disease *porcina africana*. Overall, membership of the European Union has increased competition (including that with countries with which the EU has trade agreements, for example Morocco) and resulted in substantially higher trade with EU countries, especially greater exports of horticultural products and greater imports of dairy products and meat. It has also lead to a gradual specialisation of agriculture around those enterprises in which Spain has the greatest competitive advantage within the existing economic environment.

3.6 Forestry

Changes in the CAP coupled with the land set-aside scheme and subsidies for forestry have combined with replanting for ecological and industrial reasons to renew interest in forestry. For a country the size of Spain the area of productive woodland is relatively small and timber yields are low, reflecting a long history of forest clearance (for example for agriculture and the sheep pastures of the Mesta), timber extraction (for shipbuilding and construction) and inadequate forest management. Of the total area of Spain, 15.9 million hectares are classified as forested land (*terreno forestal*). Within this forested area woodland (*bosque*) occupies 11.2 million hectares, of which only 6.8 million hectares contain useful timber (Fernández Tomás 1985) and 7.2 million are classified as suitable for timber extraction (*monte maderable*). Even these tend to have a low-density tree cover. In fact only 2.5 million hectares of woodland show good or average density stands of timber. Potentially, the most productive areas for forestry are the low lands (below 600 m) in Galicia and Cantabria

Under current agricultural policy in the European Union forestry is being promoted as an alternative to agriculture. Hence in 1994 the EU approved a new five-year forestry plan for Spain involving expenditure of pta 300 billion, of which two-thirds will come from the EU as part of the programme for restructuring agriculture. The plan involves incentives (planting, maintenance and income support) for landowners to turn up to 800,000 hectares (31 per cent of which are in Andalucía) currently under crops (mostly cereals) over to woodland and to replant up to 200,000 hectares of existing woodland.

Increased production of timber and timber products (Table 3.6) has been achieved mainly through the planting of fast-growing tree species, especially eucalyptus. Rapid growing species can produce an average of more than 8 cubic metres of wood per hectare per year. The eucalyptus can produce 10 to 25 cubic metres per hectare per year in a 10 to 20-year growth cycle, compared with pine (*pinus pinaster*, maritime pine) which can only produce 5 to 12 cubic metres per hectare per year after 18 to 24 years to reach maturity. Spain and Portugal are the only two producers of eucalyptus pulp in Europe. Apart from rapid growth, the tree has grown in popularity with paper producers because its fibres are short and easy to dry. By 1985 the public sector had planted 232,691 hectares and private growers 203,082 hectares. Since the early 1980s the planting of eucalyptus by the government has virtually ceased but private growers have continued to plant large areas, some of which has been undertaken without official approval (official planting averaged 3,500 hectares a year 1980 to 1990 inclusive, including 7,250 in 1990; MAPA 1993a). In the late 1980s production was stimulated by economic growth, European Community subsidies and the reduction of tariff barriers. As a result, Spain became a major exporter of eucalyptus fibres. However, recession in the industrialised countries in the early 1990s, increased paper pulp production from countries outside the EU (notably Brazil), competition from North America and tighter environmental regulations have seriously affected the timber industry leading to a restructuring of production capacity.

The forest products industry offers employment in rural areas and a

Table 3.6 Forest products

Year	Wood	Sawnwood	Wood pulp	Paper and board	Cork	Resin
1960	4,513	—	—	—	86.3	47.2
1965	5,705	1,779	301	658	126.2	46.7
1970	8,627	2,098	599	1,280	110.0	43.1
1975	11,340	2,313	919	1,853	82.5	38.2
1980	11,892	2,103	1,258	2,566	107.9	26.4
1985	13,899	2,249	1,394	2,913	73.5	24.0
1990	15,460	3,651	1,489	3,445	73.8	10.6

Wood and sawnwood in thousands of cubic metres, other products in thousand metric tonnes
Sources: MAPA 1977 and 1993a

source of exports in addition to meeting growing domestic demand. Total wood production averaged around 15 million cubic metres in the late 1980s (Table 3.6), output having increased by over a third since the mid 1970s. The greater proportion of output is derived from conifers (particularly *pino pinaster*) and eucalyptus. Despite increased production, consumption during the 1980s tended to exceed production, resulting in a deficit on the balance of trade, with imported products tending to be of a higher value than exports.

Extraction of timber is closely related to the primary timber processing industries of sawmilling and wood pulp. These in turn are linked to the manufacturing of paper and board, and furniture. In 1990 the total value of wood sold (*madera en rollo*) was pta 121 billion. Sawmills are widely distributed across the forested area (in 1991 there were 2,694 sawmills employing 21,000 people compared with 3,149 employing 23,000 in 1983 when sawmilling capacity was 6.73 million cubic metres), with particular concentrations in Galicia (one-third of sawmills), Castilla y León (one-fifth of sawmills) and Valencia (8 per cent of sawmills). Valencia is also the most important region for board, plywood and veneer mills. These industries are characterised by numerous very small plants (for example, in 1990 95 per cent of sawmills employed less than 20 people). Fibre board and particle board mills are larger and more modern, including some of the most modern plant in Europe. Wooden furniture is a major industry in Spain with important exports and an estimated employment of over 70,500 people in more than 11,500 establishments (INE 1993), Cataluña and Valencia being the most important regions.

The paper industry expanded in the 1980s on the basis of growing domestic demand, production increasing from 2.6 million tonnes in 1980 to 3.4 million tonnes in 1990. Part of the increased demand was met by imports, which increased over the decade from 294,000 tonnes to 1,389,000 tonnes, while exports rose from 160,000 tonnes to 511,000 tonnes (MAPA 1993a), leaving a growing trade deficit. Despite the growth of consumption it remains below the average in the European Union. This market situation was a major factor in attracting foreign multinational companies into the Spanish paper industry in the 1980s. Wiggins Teape bought the paper producer Celulosas de Asturias in 1986. Scott Paper of the United States expanded its Spanish operations in 1987 by buying a pulp mill from the state-owned Ence (Empresa Nacional de Celulosas SA), and the Kuwait Investment Office took control of the Catalan paper group Torras Hostench. Jefferson Smurfitt of Ireland and Feldmuehle of Germany were other paper companies that invested in Spain in the late 1980s.

Over-capacity, increased competition and rising costs (occasioned partly by tighter environmental regulations) in the early 1990s led companies to close plants and in some cases withdraw from production altogether in Spain (Jefferson Smurfitt, for example, closed its last plant in Spain at Balaguer, Lérida in 1993). The mixed public/private company Ence also suffered losses in the early 1990s. The company is one of the world's largest producers of eucalyptus pulp, producing 466,872 tonnes of pulp in 1993 from its two factories in San Juan del Puerto (Huelva) and Pontevedra, with a substantial proportion of sales going to exports (about three-quarters by value in 1993). It controls 122,725 hectares of forest (113,000 in Spain and almost 10,000 in Uruguay), of which some 100,000 have been planted with eucalyptus, making it the second largest eucalyptus grower after the government. In 1993, 1.4 million cubic metres of wood were supplied to its factories mostly by its subsidiary companies, 95 per cent of supplies coming from the Iberian peninsular (24 per cent of which was supplied from its own forests; Ence 1994). One of the companies in most serious difficulties has been Sniace (Sociedad Nacional de Industrias Aplicaciones Celulosa Española SA), a cellulose and textile fibre plant in Torrelavega (Cantabria), which after suffering losses throughout the 1980s finally went into receivership in 1992. In 1994 it was operating again with the help of government assistance but continued in a precarious position.

The paper industry has been characterised by small plants and fragmented ownership, but, as in other sectors, increased competition has brought restructuring and the closure of many of the smaller plants. In the early 1980s 44 per cent of plants had production capacities of less than 5,000 tonnes per year and less than 1 per cent had capacities of more than 50,000 tonnes. The industry was not offered a government-sponsored restructuring plan, thus restructuring with the closure of many of the smaller plants was left to market forces. Small size remains a characteristic of firms in the industry, with no Spanish paper company in the world's top 100 in 1994. Cataluña, País Vasco and Valencia are particularly important centres of production.

Other traditional forest products, especially cork and resin, have tended to decline in importance. Cork is obtained from the cork oak (*alcornoque - Quercus suber*), which is estimated to cover 421,000 hectares mainly in western Andalucía (especially Cádiz with 79,750 hectares, Huelva and Seville), Extremadura (Badajoz and Cáceres) and Gerona (Abreu Pidal 1985). The cork oak once formed the core of an agricultural system (Parsons 1962a and 1962b) but its importance has declined (from over 100,000 tonnes in the 1970s to 70,000–80,000 tonnes in the 1980s) as labour costs have increased and cork substitutes (notably plastic) have appeared. Resin is produced from the maritime pine and as a by-product of the cellulose industry. Like the cork industry, the resin industry has also declined, with the number of factories falling from 38 in 1974 to 17 in 1983, while production capacity decreased from 60,000 tonnes to 40,000 tonnes and production from 43,100 tonnes in 1970 to 10,600 tonnes in 1990 (Abreu Pidal 1985).

Apart from their commercial use the forests are an integral part of the natural ecosystem and provide an invaluable leisure facility; as such they require careful management. Exploitation of the forests threatens not only the forests themselves but the whole forest ecosystem. However, while many forested areas are now protected (for example as National or Natural Parks) the pattern of woodland ownership provides only limited opportunities for the state and regional governments to become directly involved in woodland management. Fifty-four per cent of the woodland area (*bosque*) is privately owned, leaving 4.3 million hectares (38 per cent) belonging to local authorities and only 929,000 hectares (8 per cent) belonging to the state and regional governments (much less than in other EU countries). Where the state is involved it operates through ICONA, although woodland management is now essentially the responsibility of the regional governments.

Reforestation and the prevention of forest fires are an important part of forest management. Between 1977 and 1987 an average of 70,660 hectares (0.6 per cent of the woodland area) were replanted each year. Much of this replanting was associated with fast-growing pines and eucalyptus, providing quick economic returns. However, this policy has impoverished the forest and it is claimed that the eucalyptus dries up the soil (increasing the risk of forest fire) and saps the soil of nutrients. Grade I and II forests can no longer be cut down for eucalyptus and regional governments are now supposed to be much stricter about planting applications. But many private landowners continue to plant without permission. By comparison with reforestation, in the years between 1977 and 1987 an annual average of 96,634 hectares of woodland (*superficie arbolada*) were affected by fires (0.9 per cent of the woodland area) and between 1988 and 1992 88,000 hectares. The area affected by fire varies considerably from year to year, thus in 1988 only 36,000 hectares of woodland were affected, while in 1989 the figure was 174,000 (MAPA 1993a). The incidence of drought, accessibility and woodland management are all factors influencing the occurrence and damage caused by fires.

3.7 Fishing

The Spanish fishing industry is the largest in Europe outside of Norway, supporting a large fish processing industry and sustaining part of the shipbuilding industry. Like agriculture it has been experiencing a process of long-term contraction and reorganisation (Laxe 1988). The industry is now regulated by the European Union (through the Common Fishing Policy, CFP) and administered in Spain through the Fund for Regulating the Market in Fish and Marine Products (Fondo de Regulación y Organización del Mercado de Productos de la Pesca y Productos Marítimos, FROM), which operates in a similar way to FORPPA. Under the CFP, fishing within EU waters is tightly controlled to conserve fish stocks through a system comprising the Total Allowable Catch, national quotas and technical standards. Outside of the EU the previous pattern of fishing agreements between Spain and other countries has been replaced by agreements negotiated by the EU. Structural measures are designed to modernise fishing fleets and cushion the impact of decline in the industry.

In 1994 there were some 19,000 registered fishing vessels amounting to over 600,000 gross registered tonnes (GRT), unloading 0.8 million tonnes of fish in Spanish ports (including about 10 per cent from marine fish farms). The industry gave direct employment to 85,000, many others either employed in related activities or supplementing their incomes from fishing (MAPA 1993c; Larrea Ereño 1989). Most of the fleet (16,740 vessels) and the majority of those employed (52,300) operate in Spanish waters, 1,011 vessels operate in Community waters (employing 13,100) and 1,138 in international waters (employing 19,600) (Maté 1994b and 1994c). Although fishing represents a modest part of the total agriculture, forestry and fishing sector, contributing less than 10 per cent of the value of final production and of employment in the sector, it is of critical importance in certain parts of the country.

Growth of the industry was based on the considerable length of Spanish coastline: 5,968 kilometres, of which 3,359 kilometres border the Atlantic and 2,580 kilometres the Mediterranean (3,904 kilometres are around the peninsular and the rest around the islands). The most important waters are those of the Atlantic coastline (Canary Islands and Cantabria), which are much richer than those of the Mediterranean. However, because of the narrow coastal platform around the coast (depths of less than 400 metres extending only 30 to 50 kilometres from the coast, except in the Gulf of Cádiz and Valencia, where the coastal shelf extends 80 to 100 kilometres) and the depletion of fish stocks, the industry is now dependent on fish caught in distant waters (about two-thirds of the fish catch).

The north-west (Galicia) is the leading fishing region accounting for about 50 to 60 per cent of the total fish unloaded in Spanish ports by weight (Table 3.7), about one-third of the fishing vessels (measured by GRT) and one-third of employment. It is also the major centre of shipbuilding for the fishing industry and of the fish processing industry. The fishing industry focuses on Vigo and La Coruña, the two largest fishing ports in Spain. Outside of the north-west, fishing is also important along the rest of the northern Spanish coastline, in Cantabria (for example in Bermeo, Pasajes, San Sebastián and Gijón) and Vizcaya. The port of Santoña (Cantabria) specialises in anchovies. Other Atlantic coastal areas in southern Spain and around the Canary Islands also support an important fishing industry (Las Palmas de Gran Canaria is the third largest fishing port in Spain). The provinces of Cádiz (major ports in Algeciras and Cádiz) and Huelva (major port is Huelva) are the base for the fishing fleet in north African waters, as well as offering local fishing banks. In the Mediterranean, the Tramontana region (Cape Palos to Cape Creus) is the most significant (fishing ports including Castellón de la Plana, Tarragona, Barcelona, Villanueva y Geltria and Valencia). Elsewhere in the Mediterranean fishing is either based on small catches for very localised markets or larger vessels must travel to waters off the coast of Africa or to the Atlantic (fishing ports include Alicante, Cartagena, Málaga and Palma de Mallorca).

Overfishing, the extension of territorial waters (from 12 to 200 miles) and the imposition of fishing quotas and licenses have severely restricted fishing both in waters around Europe and elsewhere (especially around north and west Africa – Morocco, Senegal, Angola, Namibia – the United States and Canada) requiring adjustments throughout the industry and leading to fishing in very deep waters outside of territorial limits (Table 3.8). Two-thirds of the fish catch is now from distant waters. For example, the cod catch dropped from 170,000 tonnes in the 1960s to about 11,000 tonnes in 1983. As a consequence, the industry has been unable to meet the domestic demand for fish and fish products, fish forming a major element in the Spanish diet amounting to 40 kilograms of fish per capita per year or 1.1 million tonnes. This has led to a substantial and growing annual trade deficit in fish, imports rising from pta 64 billion in 1985 to pta 303 billion in 1993. For example, imports of frozen hake *(merluza)* increased from 22,500 tonnes in 1986 to 65,000 tonnes in 1988, and frozen squid from 9,800 tonnes to 44,000 tonnes (Maté 1990c). The trade deficit amounted to pta 222 billion in 1993 compared with pta 50 billion in 1986 (Larrea Ereño 1989 and *El País* 1994), with imports covered only 27 per cent by exports compared with 80 per cent coverage in the mid 1980s.

Because of the size of the Spanish fishing industry and its threat to the markets of other EC member states, Spain had to accept some strict EC entry conditions, which have been the source of continuing friction between Spanish fishermen and their European partners (for example in the conflict over tuna fishing in the summer of 1994). The transition period for the full integration of the Spanish fishing industry into the EC was to stretch into the next century. During the transition period there were additional fishing restrictions and restrictions on market access designed to protect other Community countries. Moreover, the fish canning industry in Spain has

Table 3.7 Regional distribution of fish catch unloaded in 1992

Area	Fresh and salted fish		Frozen fish		Total fish catch	
	Volume (tonnes)	Value (pta bn)	Volume (tonnes)	Value (pta bn)	Volume (tonnes)	Value (pta bn)
Cantábrica	108,166	32.7	—	—	108,166	32.7
North-west	207,737	57.8	216,139	31.1	423,876	88.9
South-Atlantic	61,417	24.1	21,109	22.3	82,526	46.4
South-Mediterranean	28,568	9.2	—	—	28,568	9.2
Levante	34,111	10.6		—	34,111	10.6
Tramontana	75,720	22.7	—	—	75,720	22.7
Balearic Islands	4,967	3.2	—	—	4,967	3.2
Canary Islands	37,149	5.3	46,250	18.7	83,399	24.0
Total	557,835	165.6	283,497	72.1	841,332	237.7

The figures do not include fish trans-shipped on the high seas (*transbordos en alta mar*), those landed in non-Spanish ports, or those unloaded by Spanish vessels flying other flags

Total fish catch includes fresh and frozen fish and those from marine fish farms

Source: MAPA 1993b

suffered from competition from third countries (for example Morocco) where processing costs are lower, being free to buy vegetable oil and cans on the world market (Maté 1990d). In 1984 exports of canned fish were 35,000 tonnes and imports 8,800 tonnes; in 1988 exports were 25,000 tonnes and imports 27,800 tonnes. There is a long tradition of fish canning in Spain (especially in Galicia). In 1980 there were 375 factories with a production capacity of 351,000 tonnes; by 1988 there were only 180 factories with capacity of 360,000 tonnes (although production in 1988 was only about 200,000 tonnes), employing some 40,000 people. Sixty per cent of production in 1988 was of tuna and sardines.

The policy response to the adverse EC entry conditions was to continue to negotiate improvements, seek financial assistance through the CFP Structural Funds and try to ensure that the EC linked access to Community markets with access to fish resources. Between 1986 and 1992 Spain received Ecu 445 million in aid from the EC for the modernisation of its fishing fleet (the largest sum allocated to any EC member state) and it anticipates receiving further large sums to the end of the century. In EC negotiations with the European Free Trade Association (EFTA) countries over reducing trade barriers and then membership of the EU, Spain was particularly concerned to gain access to Nordic waters (especially as Norway had the largest fishing fleet in Europe and therefore posed a considerable threat to Spanish markets). In the event, agreement over the accession of Norway to the EU was bought at the price of bringing forward the transition period for the Spanish fishing industry to 1 January 1996 and allowing Spanish fishing vessels access to the Irish Box. However, the decision by Norway in November 1994 to stay outside the EU complicated the picture. In the Mediterranean the waters around Morocco have been a particular focus of tension, being crucial for both Spain (especially for the fishing fleet of Andalucia) and Morocco (which has sought to protect its fish

Table 3.8 Volume of fish unloaded in Spanish ports, 1961–92

Period	Volume (000 tonnes)
1961–65	786.0*
1966–70	1,171.0*
1971–75	1,273.8*
1976–80	1,218.9*
1981–85	1,167.6*
1986–90	1,020.6*
1987	1,071.2
1988	1,047.6
1989	974.8
1990	953.0
1991	783.9
1992	841.3

* five year annual average

Source: Anuario El País (various dates)

stocks and use access to them as a lever for better access to EU markets. Beyond Europe and the Mediterranean, Spain has pressed the EU to establish new fishing agreements, usually with reciprocal arrangements for access to the EU market (for example the agreement with Argentina).

In mid 1994 the government presented its fishing industry plan to the EU. The plan envisages public expenditure of pta 400 billion over the six years to the end of the century, increasing the efficiency of the industry and improving distribution and marketing. The plan includes the construction of 1,400 vessels, the modernisation of 1,800 vessels, the break-up of 900 vessels and the formation of mixed public/private fishing enterprises in other countries. Overall, the size of the fishing fleet should be reduced by 100,000 GRT. Included in the plan is an allocation of pta 22 billion to fish farming (Maté 1994c).

The response by fishermen to the tighter restrictions was to seek ways of maintaining their livelihood. These included the registration of fishing vessels in other EU countries, the transfer of fish catches at sea and the formation of businesses in third countries (usually in joint ventures with local companies) to gain access to the fish resources of these countries. There were also illegal actions, such as the landing of fish above EU quotas, and evasion of EU regulations.

Despite a process of restructuring, involving the modernisation of the fishing fleet, a shift towards higher value-added fish products, and the promotion of fish farming, the industry continues to suffer from over-capacity, an atomistic ownership structure coupled with the small average size of vessels (especially in Andalucía, where in the early 1980s 61 per cent of boats were less than 20 GRT; Osuna Llaneza 1985) and old ships.

Fish farming (both sea water – especially mussels – and freshwater – dominantly trout) offers one possibility of reducing the substantial fish imports. Recent developments supported by government funding build on a long history of fish farming in many parts of the country, especially in Galicia where production of mussels represents 96 per cent of the Spanish total and half of the world total. About three-quarters of fish farms are in the north of the country (for example along the river Arosa). There also exists considerable potential for development in the Ebro delta and in Huelva. But the growth of the industry has been slow, impeded by technical problems, competing water uses and pollution.

3.8 Restructuring in agriculture, forestry and fishing

Restructuring in agriculture, forestry and fishing has been less publicised than that in other sectors of the economy. Nevertheless it has been substantial in a sector where archaic production structures have persisted for longer than in most other parts of the economy, protected by the state and by the inertia of activities that have been as much a way of life as a means of livelihood. The clearest indication of change has been the continuing decline in employment as labour-intensive production methods have given way to mechanisation. Beyond this, qualitative changes have brought the eclipse of subsistence production, replaced by new production techniques, new products and more efficient marketing methods. Whole landscapes have changed as farmers have responded to movements in crop prices, dry farmed areas have been transformed by irrigation, the land has been buried beneath plastic sheeting, uplands have been replanted with conifers and eucalyptus, and fishing ports have been converted into marinas.

Further restructuring will be driven by the evolving business environment of agriculture, notably the future organisation of the CAP and indeed the future form of the European Union. The degree of international competition will depend on the extent to which current protection is removed in recognition of the agreements reached in the Uruguay Round of trade negotiations.

Given present trends agricultural employment will continue to decline at least until the end of the century. Greater specialisation in agriculture will add to the relative importance of fruit and vegetables in the agricultural production structure. Forestry should also gain in importance. Fishing is likely to become even more dependent on distant waters unless more success is achieved in fish farming. For all these sectors environmental considerations and conservation of natural resources will become more prominent considerations, not least among which will be the management of water resources.

Rural areas will reflect the changes in agriculture and broader patterns of socio-economic development, embracing new agricultural enterprise combinations but also shedding their dependence on the land as the distinction between urban and rural economies becomes more blurred. Improvements in the rural infrastructure, decentralisation of industry, further development of tourism in rural areas and more opportunities for home working through information technology systems are some of the factors that will transform the traditional rural environment.

References and bibliography

Abreu Pidal, J. (1985) 'Resina, corcho y frutos forestales', *El Campo*, No. 98, pp. 66–73. Bilbao: BBV

Arévalo Arias, J. (1993) 'Diez años de política agraria', *El Boletín*, No. 3, May, pp. 48–55. Madrid: MAPA

Bosque Maurel, J. (1973) 'Latifundio y minifundio en Andalucia Oriental', *Estudios Geográficos*, Nos 132–3, pp. 457–500

Bruce, P. (1990) 'The party ends for Spain's rural taxpayers', *Financial Times*, 5 April, p. 3. London

Compés López. R. (1994) 'Política de subvenciones comunitaria y sus resultados en el agro español', *Boletín Económico de ICE*, No. 2404, March, pp. 605–13. Madrid

El País (1994) *Anuario El País*, 1994. Madrid

Ence (1994) *Informe anual 1993*. Madrid: Grupo Teneo

Fernández Tomás, J. (1985) 'Aspectos económicos de nuestros bosques', *El Campo*, No. 98, pp. 21–4. Bilbao: BBV

García Delgado, J. (1988) 'La agricultura: cambios estructurales en los últimos decenios', in J. García Delgado (ed.), *España, Tomo II, Economía*, Chapter 2, pp. 119–52. Madrid: Espasa-Calpe SA

García-Ramon, D. (1985) 'Old and new in Spanish farming', *Geographical Magazine*, March, pp. 128–33

Giner, S. and E. Sevilla (1977) 'The *latifundio* as a local mode of class domination: the Spanish case', *Iberian Studies* V1, No. 2, pp. 47–57

Guedes, M. (1981) 'Recent agricultural land policy in Spain', *Oxford Agrarian Studies*, 10, pp. 26–43

Instituto Nacional de Estadísticas, INE (1989) *Encuesta sobre la estructura de las explotaciones agrícolas, 1987*. Madrid

Instituto Nacional de Estadísticas, INE (1991) *Censo agrario 1989. Tomo 1, resultados nacionales*. Madrid

Instituto Nacional de Estadísticas, INE (1993) *Encuesta industrial 1990*. Madrid

Larrea Ereño, S. (1989) 'La producción pesquera española desde la implantación del limite de las 200 millas nauticas', *Situación*, No. 3, pp. 5–38. Bilbao: BBV

Laxe, F. (1988) *La economía del sector pesquero*. Madrid: Editorial Espasa-Calpe

Maas, J. (1983) 'The behaviour of landowners as an explanation of regional differences in agriculture: latifundists in Seville and Cordoba (Spain)', *Tijdschrift voor Economische e Sociale Geografie*, TESG 74, No. 2, pp. 87–95

Martinez Alier, J. (1971) *Labourers and landowners of southern Spain*. London: George Allen and Unwin

Maté, V. (1990a) 'Las deudas del campo', *El País* (sección negocios), 3 June, p. 34

Maté, V. (1990b) 'Reforma agraria, del rojo al verde', *El País* (sección negocios), 25 March, p. 12

Maté, V. (1990c) 'Volver a casa: la flota congeladora', *El País* (sección negocios), 1 April, p. 22

Maté, V. (1990d) 'El entierro de la sardina', *El País* (sección negocios), 25 March, p. 27

Maté, V. (1994a) 'El campo recibe 700,000 millones en ayudas', *El País* (sección negocios), 15 May, p. 13

Maté, V. (1994b) 'Salir a flote', *El País* (sección negocios), 24 April, pp. 26-7

Maté, V. (1994c) 'El plan sectoral de pesca', *El País* (sección negocios), 10 July, p. 15

Milan Diez, R. (1993) 'La agricultura española y el mercado único: finalización del períodico transitorio', *El Boletín*, No. 1, February, pp. 16–21. Madrid: MAPA

Ministerio de Agricultura, MAPA (1977) *Anuario de estadística agraria, 1975*. Madrid

Ministerio de Agricultura, MAPA (1989a) *Manual de estadística agraria, 1989*. Madrid

Ministerio de Agricultura, MAPA (1989b) *Encuesta sobre la estructura de las explotaciones agrícolas, 1987*. Madrid

Ministerio de Agricultura, MAPA (1993a) *Anuario de estadística agraria, 1990*. Madrid

Ministerio de Agricultura, MAPA (1993b) *Boletín mensual de estadística*, May. Madrid

Ministerio de Agricultura, MAPA (1993c) *La agriculture, la pesca y la alimentación, 1992*. Madrid

Ministerio de Agricultura, MAPA (1993d) *Spanish agricultural statistics, 1992*. Madrid

Ministerio de Agricultura, MAPA (1994a) *Boletín mensual de estadística*, June. Madrid

Ministerio de Agricultura, MAPA (1994b) *Boletín mensual de estadística*, February. Madrid

Naylon, J. (1973) 'An appraisement of Spanish irrigation and land-settlement policy since 1939', *Iberian Studies*, Vol. II, No. 1, pp. 12–18

O'Flanagan, T. (1982) 'Land reform and rural modernization', *Erdkunde*, 36, pp. 48–53

Ortiz-Cañavate, J. (1989) 'Situación actual de la mecanización agraria en España', *El Campo*, No. 111, pp. 3–9. Bilbao: BBV

Osuna Llaneza, J. (1985) 'La pesca Andaluza', *El Campo*, No. 99, pp. 87–95. Bilbao: BBV

Parsons, J. (1962a) 'The cork oak forests and cork industry', *Economic Geography*, Vol. 38, No. 3, pp. 195–214

Parsons, J. (1962b) 'The acorn-hog economy of S.W.Spain', *Geographical Review*, Vol. 52, No. 2, pp. 211–35

Povedano, E. (1993a) 'Evolución de la agricultura española', *El Boletín*, No. 2, March, pp. 6–12 Madrid: MAPA

Povedano, E. (1993b) 'El endeudamiento del sector agrario', *El Boletín*, No. 3, May, pp. 6–13. Madrid: MAPA

Reig, E. (1988) 'La adhesión española al Mercado Común Agrícola', in J. García Delgado (ed.), *España: Tomo II, Economía*, Chapter 3, pp. 153–76. Madrid: Editorial Espasa-Calpe SA

Tamames, R. (1983) *Estructura económica de España*, Vol. 1. Madrid: Alianza Editorial

Yubero, F. (1994) 'La reforma de la Organización común del mercado del sector vitivinícola', *El Campo*, No. 130, pp. 245–57. Madrid: MAPA

Chapter 4
Minerals and mining

4.1 The mining industry

In the early 1990s the mining industry in Spain (with the exception of quarry products) was on the verge of collapse, sustained by government subsidies, direct government involvement and the remnants of protectionism. A long period of weak prices, shifting patterns of demand, liberalisation of markets, rising production costs, exhaustion of deposits and more stringent environmental regulations combined to reduce the industry to a shadow of its former size. In some cases production was only suspended and mines could re-open, but many mine closures will be permanent. In 1994 further contraction in coal mining was certain, metallic mineral mining almost ceased, potash production faced serious economic problems and even the quarry products sector had declined with the cyclical downturn in the construction industry.

Despite a rich variety of resources and important mineral deposits, the mining industry now employs less than 0.5 per cent of the occupied population (less than 50,000 at the end of 1993) and accounts for less than 1 per cent of GDP. Apart from problems endemic to mining itself, domestic markets have shrunk. In some cases raw material processing industries have closed. In other cases markets such as electricity generation, metal manufacturing, heavy chemicals and fertilizers have been liberalised enabling manufacturers to buy raw materials on the open market. The consequent decline of raw material production has left the country dependent on imports, especially of energy and metals. In the early 1990s there was a trade deficit in energy, metallic and non-metallic minerals, with a surplus only on quarry products. Mineral exports tend to be of relatively low-value quarry products.

Energy products represent the largest component of the mining industry by value of output, while quarry products account for 90 per cent of mineral workings. Even with the low energy prices prevailing in the early 1990s energy products contributed over half the value of production and

Table 4.1 Characteristics of the mining industry, 1992

Sector	Mines	Employment	Production (pta billion)
Energy products	160	36,415	251.9
Metallic minerals	14	3,224	30.1
Non-metallic minerals	193	4,968	48.0
Quarry products	3,044	14,900	118.0
Total	3,411	59,507	448.0

Number of mines and value of output for quarry products are for 1991

Sources: MINE 1993a, 1993b and 1994

employment in mining (Table 4.1). Within the energy sector, coal and lignite account for almost 90 per cent of the value of energy mining output and most of the employment. In metallic minerals, zinc and precious metals are the principal products followed by iron and mercury, almost all lead, copper, pyrites and tin production having ceased. Of non-metallic minerals, potash and salt remain important products. Limestone is the most important quarry product, both in terms of value of output and the number of people employed in its extraction, followed by sand and gravel, granite, marble and slate.

Development of the mining industry was restricted by a combination of physical resource limitations (limited or poor quality raw materials), more attractive investment opportunities outside mining in the 1960s and severe economic problems from the mid 1970s. There was always a lack of vertical integration in the industry, with notable weaknesses in backward links to mining equipment manufacturers. During the period of economic growth in the 1960s the mineral sector was neglected because of cheap supplies of minerals on the international market, the higher returns in manufacturing industry, services and property development, and industrial policy measures that were not appropriate to the mining sector. Following the first oil shock, renewed attempts were made to stimulate mining; for example the Law of Mines (Ley de Minas, 1973) made geological reserves public property, exploitable by concessions for thirty years. There followed intensive exploration by Spanish and foreign companies but with little result except in the Iberian pyrites zone, where exploration and development had been underway since the late 1960s. In this zone three new mines were developed after 1970 – Cerro Colorado, Aznalcóllar and Sotiel (Figure 4.1). In each case the discoveries were made in association with existing workings or previous mines (there were also major discoveries across the border in Portugal, for example the polymetallic sulphide deposits at Neves Corvo were discovered in the late 1970s and the mine opened in 1988; Anon 1989). Further attempts to encourage mineral development were made at the end of the 1970s through the introduction of the National Mineral

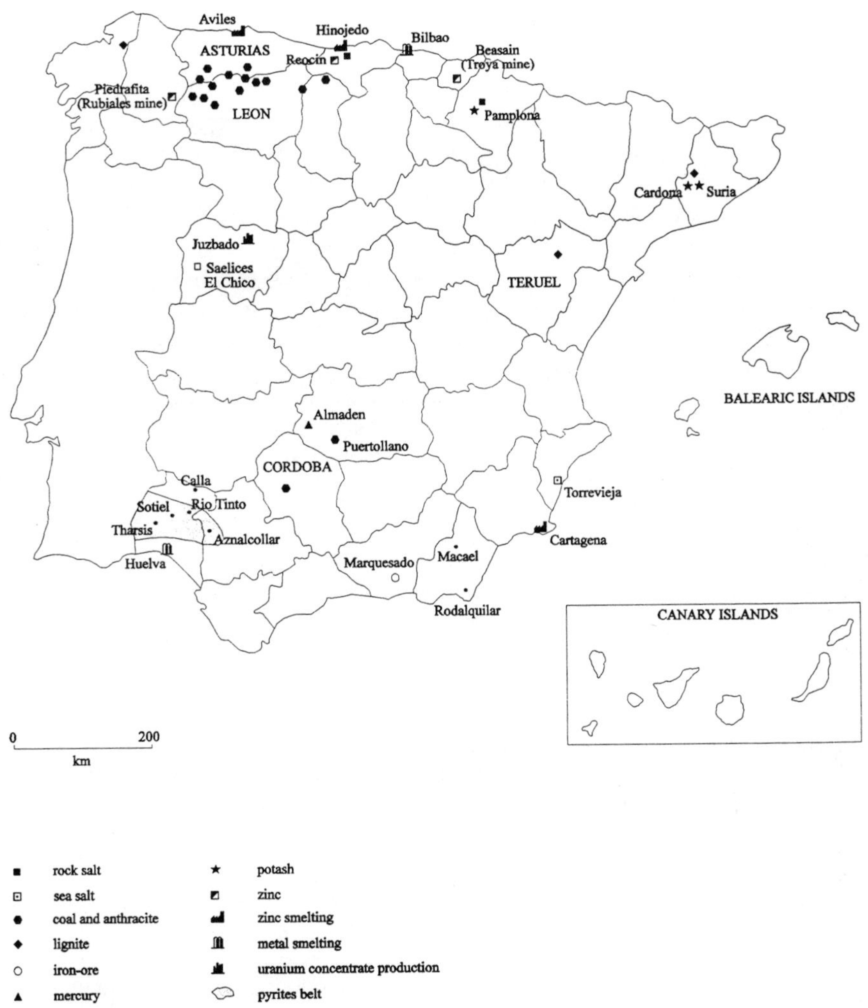

Figure 4.1 Mining activities

Supply Plan (Plan Nacional de Abastecimiento de Materias Primas Minerales, 1979–87) but it was difficult to promote investment in a climate of retrenchment in mineral production. In the late 1980s there was a strong recuperation in non-metallic minerals and quarry products and a brief respite in metallic mineral mining linked to economic growth, but growth ground to a halt or went sharply into reverse with recession in the early 1990s.

Mining activities have frequently spawned settlements, their communities dependent on the mines. Mine closures have threatened these communities, prompting stiff union opposition and government intervention at both state and regional level. Intervention has included production subsidies, subsidies to defray redundancy costs, support for early retirement schemes, nationalisation of companies and measures to diversify the local employment base. The problems have been most serious in the coal mining areas of Asturias and León and in the metal mines of Huelva. In Huelva,

Table 4.2 Large mines in 1994

Mine	Province	Mining method	Size	Product
Cerro Colorado/Alfredo	Huelva	P	1	Copper, silver, gold
Sotiel (closed)	Huelva	U	3	Copper, lead, zinc
Filon Sur (closed)	Huelva	P	5	Gold
Cerro Cinto (suspended)	Almería	P	5	Gold
Agruminsa (closed)	Vizcaya	P	1	Iron
Franco Belga (closed)	Vizcaya	P	3	Iron
Marquesado	Granada	P	1	Iron
Almadén	Ciudad Real	P	3	Mercury
Cardona	Barcelona	U	2	Potash
Llobregat	Barcelona	U	3	Potash
Suria	Barcelona	U	3	Potash
Barruecopardo (suspended)	Salamanca	P	2	Wolfram
Aznalcóllar	Seville	P	1	Zinc, copper, lead
Mantos de Silicatos (closed)	Murcia	P	2	Zinc, lead, silver
Reocin	Cantabria	P	2	Zinc, lead
Rubiales (closed)	Lugo	U	3	Zinc, lead, silver
Troya (suspended)	Guipúzcoa	U	3	Zinc, lead

Mines shown are those producing more than 150,000 tonnes of ore per year in 1990

Size: 1: Over 3 million tonnes; 2: 1 to 3 million tonnes; 3: 0.5 to 1 million tonnes; 4: 0.3 to 0.5 million tonnes; 5: 0.15 to 0.3 million tonnes

Type: U: Underground; P: Open Pit

Source: Adapted from Anon 1992

the company Tharsis closed in the late 1980s, the state company Almagrera closed in 1994 and Rio Tinto Minera (RTM) was saved from complete closure only by government intervention and the sale of the company to an American mining group. Of all the mines in Spain producing more than 150,000 tonnes of ore in 1990 relatively few were operating in 1994 (Table 4.2).

As recently as the early 1970s the characteristics of mining echoed those identified in the nineteenth century: i) a multitude of small-scale workings; ii) lack of profitability and hence a lack of investment; and iii) the presence of foreign ownership (Mallada 1890). An atomistic structure is still apparent in quarrying and in parts of the coal mining industry. But generally the small mines have been closed to leave a dwindling number of large mines operated either by public companies or companies linked to foreign multinationals.

Foreign penetration of the mining industry has ebbed and flowed with the profitability of mining. Foreign involvement has a long ancestry, covering ownership of production resources, supply of mining equipment and control over foreign marketing. For example, the British companies Rio Tinto Zinc and Tharsis played an important role in developing the mining industry in Huelva (Rio Tinto Zinc was formed in 1873 after buying the Rio Tinto mines from the Spanish government), the Belgian company Solvay opened up the salt deposits in Cantabria and the potash deposits in Cataluña, and Rothschild played a key role in marketing mercury. As a result, the potential economic impact of mining in Spain was diluted (Tamames 1983). Foreign ownership of mineral resources is most clearly illustrated in the case of the mining industry of Huelva, dominated first by British capital in the Tharsis and Rio Tinto mines, then by the Ercros group in the late 1980s (the principal shareholder in which was the Kuwait Investment Office) and most recently by the American company Freeport McMoRan, owners of the Rio Tinto mines in 1994. Foreign ownership of production resources also partly explains the foreign domination of the mining equipment industry, restricting the development of competitive domestic manufacturers. The severe crisis that affected the mining industry in the 1970s and early 1980s led to the withdrawal of much foreign investment, leaving the state to absorb failing mining companies. More profitable conditions in the late 1980s attracted some new foreign investment. For example, the Swedish Boliden group took over the company Andaluza de Piritas SA (Apirsa in Seville) in 1988.

The mining industry can be subdivided into energy products (of which only coal is dealt with in this chapter), metallic minerals, non-metallic minerals and quarry products. While this is not a perfect classification, it does have the advantage of grouping most minerals according to the industrial sectors which they supply. Energy minerals supply the energy industry and some manufacturing industries, metallic minerals feed the metals industries, non-metallic minerals the chemical and fertilizer industries, and quarry products the construction industry. The fortunes of each mining sub-sector are closely bound up with these downstream activities.

4.2 Coal mining

In the mid 1990s large parts of the underground coal and anthracite mining industry were threatened with closure, supported only by substantial government assistance and intervention within the framework of the European Coal and Steel Community (ECSC). Despite a series of restructuring plans an internationally competitive industry had not been created nor had the economies of mining areas been significantly diversified to lessen the impact of mine closures.

At the beginning of 1994 the industry employed about 32,000 people (Carbunión 1994). Coal and lignite accounted for about 20 per cent of primary energy requirements and about one-third of domestic primary energy production. After a period of expansion in the late 1970s and early 1980s production stabilised at around 15 million tonnes of hard coal and anthracite and 18 million tonnes of lignite (Table 4.3), the use of coal coming under renewed pressure from other energy sources particularly away from the coalfields. Domestic coal production has suffered from increased import penetration, imports rising from 3 million tonnes in 1975 to over 14 million tonnes in 1992, due largely to increased demand from power stations (especially in 1992 with drought reducing HEP production). Environmental problems have also become a more important issue in the coal industry both in terms of extraction (especially open-caste workings)

Table 4.3 Characteristics of energy extraction, 1992

Energy product	Production (million tonnes)	Value (pta billion)	Mines	Employment
Coal	8.5	93.5	50	22,612
Anthracite	6.2	65.0	79	8,937
Coal and anthracite	14.7	158.5	129	31,549
Sub-bituminous coal and brown lignite	18.7	65.4	26	4,295
Crude oil	1.1	15.1	4	254
Natural gas	1.2	11.4	a	a
Uranium concentrate (tonnes)	219.5	1.3	1	216
Total	—	251.9	160	36,314

a: Figures included in those for crude oil

Natural gas production in millions of tonnes oil equivalent

Sources: MINE 1994; Carbunión 1994

and use (emissions from power stations and cement works leading to air pollution and acid rain).

Spanish coal remains costly to produce as a result of numerous interlocking factors. The coal itself tends to be of low quality, is frequently dirty (containing many impurities, especially a high proportion of sulphur), friable and of low calorific content. Production costs in underground mines are high due to difficult geological conditions involving thin and faulted seams, making the use of modern mechanised equipment difficult. Small-scale production and low productivity continue to characterise the industry, while labour difficulties, often associated with poor working conditions and threats of redundancies, are endemic. Transport too is frequently a problem, adding to the delivered cost of coal.

4.2.1 Coal resources

Given present levels of output and on the assumption of no new deposits being discovered, hard coal and anthracite supplies should be available for forty to fifty years, brown lignite (*lignito pardo*) for thirty years and sub-bituminous coal (black lignite, *lignito negro*) for eighty to ninety years (from 1990). Almost 80 per cent of 'probable' hard coal and anthracite reserves are located in Asturias and León (360 million tonnes and 285 million tonnes respectively of national 'probable' reserves, estimated at around 840 million tonnes; MINE 1993c). The central Asturias Basin alone produces 50 per cent of all Spanish hard coal and contains about one-third of probable national coal and anthracite reserves. Major producing districts are found in the Nalón Valley (districts of Langreo, San Martín del Rey Aurelio and Leviana) and Caudal Valley (Mieres and Figaredo), and in the Camocha depression south of Gijón. In the provinces of León and Palencia mainly anthracite is produced, León producing 60 per cent of the total notably from the north-west in the valleys of the Bierzo district in an arc from Fabero to Bembibre and between Villablino and Caboalles. For other hard coal production Villablino is the major centre, followed by a zone bordering the railway from La Robla (25 km north of León) to Bilbao. Outside this northern area the most important coal and anthracite deposits are at Puertollano in Ciudad Real (proven reserves of 59 million tonnes, all suitable for open-caste working, supplying local power stations and industry as well as providing the nearest supply for Madrid) and in the province of Córdoba in the upper Guadiato valley (at Belmez, Peñarroya and Espiel, proven reserves of 40 million tonnes plus further probable and possible reserves of 40 million tonnes, mostly suitable for open-caste working; Encasur 1994).

The major deposits of brown lignite are located in the province of La Coruña, which contain an estimated three-quarters of all 'probable' reserves (national 'probable' reserves of 385 million tonnes, MINE 1993c). The province is the source of virtually all national brown lignite production (all from two mines at the end of 1992). Large new deposits were found in Orense in 1982. Teruel, with three-quarters of all 'probable' sub-bituminous coal (black lignite) reserves (national 'probable' reserves 353.5 million tonnes), is the source of 90 per cent of all sub-bituminous coal production. There are deposits of sub-bituminous coal at Utrillas, Aliaga and around Ariño-Alloza-Andorra. Many mines in the province were closed in the 1980s and early 1990s, especially those around Utrillas. Other deposits are in the province of Barcelona ('probable' reserves of sub-bituminous coal of 35 million tonnes) and Granada ('probable' reserves of brown lignite of 94 million tonnes but no production; MINE 1993c and García Alonso 1987). In Cataluña the basins of Berga, Figola and Pobla de Lillet in the upper Llobregat Valley produce small quantities of high-calorific lignite.

4.2.2 *Development of the coal industry*

Following the Civil War hard coal and anthracite production expanded from 6.7 million tonnes in 1939 to 11.3 million tonnes in 1960. Apart from hydroelectricity it was virtually the only domestic energy source available to sustain autarchic industrialisation.

The change in economic policy after 1959 opened the way for oil imports and a fundamental restructuring of energy use away from coal. Oil was relatively cheap, more convenient and cleaner to use, and the basis of the new petrochemical industry. Coal was left with only power stations and iron and steelworks as customers. Even in these two industries it faced competition from other sources of energy and imported coal. During this period of crisis in the industry, production was sustained by protection, rapid expansion of electricity generation and iron and steel production. Coal and anthracite output fell from 12.9 million tonnes in 1965 to below 10 million tonnes in 1973 (essentially hard coal production fell while anthracite production remained stable). Employment in coal and lignite mining dropped from over 100,000 people in 1959 to 51,000 in 1973. Atomisation of production impeded planned rationalisation, while government intervention prevented an even more drastic decline that would have resulted from exposure to international market forces. Nevertheless economic circumstances forced closures and amalgamations, reducing the number of coal and anthracite mining companies from 391 in 1959 (84 per cent of which were producing less than 25,000 tonnes per year) to 112 in 1972 (of which 55 per cent were producing less than 25,000 tonnes per year). Similarly, in lignite mining the number of companies fell from 135 in 1959 to 34 in 1972 (Carbunión 1994; García Alonso 1987).

The government took a number of steps to cushion the impact of economic change on the coal industry. One of these steps was to reach an agreement with the industry over production targets in exchange for a package of government assistance including official credit and import tariff protection (this form of joint action – *acción concertada* – was introduced from 1965). This action met with little success. A second step was partially to nationalise the industry by initiating the fusion of 17 loss-making coal mining companies in Asturias into the state-owned company Hunosa (Empresa Nacional Hullera del Norte SA, established in 1967). The process of fusion was difficult and protracted, continuing into the 1970s. In 1970 Hunosa employed 25,000 people at 31 mines, producing 4 million tonnes of mostly coking coal (Terán 1978). During the entire life of this company it has never made a profit!

The sharp increase in oil prices beginning in 1973 and continuing into the early 1980s led to renewed interest in coal by producers (as coal prices rose), by consumers (as coal prices fell below those of oil; coal prices to power stations and coke ovens were fixed by the government but other coal prices were free) and by the government (for both strategic and balance of payments reasons). The government introduced a number of policies to stimulate the use of coal, including the conversion to coal of existing large industrial energy consumers (especially cement works, ceramic factories and power stations). Many power stations were converted to coal (for example Los Barrios, Algeciras) with the help of official credit to cover up to 70 per cent of the investment necessary for conversion. Under the Second National Energy Plan there was an acceleration in the construction of coal-fired power stations, leading for example to the construction of As Pontes de García Rodríguez in the province of La Coruña (1,400 MW) and Andorra (Teruel; 1,050 MW) power stations. As a result, installed capacity in coal-fired power stations increased from 3,060 MW in 1976 to 9,640 MW in 1985 (García Alonso 1987).

These policies resulted in a substantial growth in coal production between 1975 and 1985. Coal and anthracite production rose from 10.7 to 16.4 million tonnes and lignite production from 3.4 to 23.6 million tonnes (Table 4.4). Demand for coal doubled from 14 million tonnes of coal equivalent (mtce) in 1976 to 27.5 mtce in 1985 (García Alonso 1987). This increased demand was accompanied by higher coal imports, which rose from 4 million tonnes in 1975 to 8.4 million tonnes in 1985, coal imports being handled through 3 major ports: Algeciras (Cádiz), Carboneras (Almería), and Gijón (Oviedo). It was also accompanied by a switch in the composition of coal demand, a change in the structure of electricity generation and a reduction in fuel oil consumption. Power stations substantially increased their absolute levels of demand, accounting for over 80 per cent of coal production in 1985 (including virtually all lignite). Industrial demand also increased in absolute terms (notably in the cement industry and in ceramics), although this was tempered by contraction in some traditional heavy industrial markets (notably in the iron and steel industry) associated with industrial contraction and energy conservation. By 1994 virtually all national coal production was consumed by power stations.

Table 4.4 Coal production and imports, 1950-93

Year	Hard Coal	Anthracite	Lignite	Coal imports
1950	9.5	1.5	1.3	–
1960	11.3*	–	1.8	–
1970	7.9	2.8	2.8	3.5
1975	7.5	3.2	3.4	4.0
1980	9.1	4.1	15.4	5.7
1985	10.5	5.9	23.6	8.4
1986	9.5	5.3	22.2	8.7
1987	14.3*	–	20.5	8.9
1988	9.0	5.2	17.6	8.8
1989	9.1	5.3	21.9	10.6
1990	9.1	5.8	21.0	10.5
1991	9.1	5.8	19.6	13.0
1992	9.1	5.8	18.8	14.3
1993	14.1*	–	17.5	12.5

Figures in millions of tonnes coal equivalent

* hard coal and anthracite

Lignite includes sub-bituminous coal (black lignite)

Sources: García Alonso 1986 and 1987; Carbounión 1994

4.2.3 *Coal industry structure and restructuring*

The industrial structure of coal mining remains littered with small firms. During the 1960s there was a significant decline in the number of firms in the industry as primary energy demand switched to oil. But the wave of industrial expansion in the 1970s increased the number of firms by 50 per cent between 1974 and 1982. Small size is most common in hard coal and anthracite mining. In 1992 there were still 123 hard coal and anthracite firms, of which half produced less than 25,000 tonnes per year (Carbunión 1994).

In hard coal production there are a few large firms, mostly public ones, and a multitude of small, mainly family-run, businesses. The public company Hunosa employs about 70 per cent of all employees in this sub-sector (Hunosa employed 12,200 at the beginning of 1994) and produces about half of total output (2.5 million tonnes in 1993). Other public companies include Encasur operating in Peñarroya and Puertollano (the company produced 0.7 million tonnes of hard coal and 0.6 million tonnes of anthracite in 1993 and employed 1,128 people at the end of that year) and Minas de Figaredo in Asturias (the company produced 0.3 million tonnes in 1993 and employed 966 people at the end of that year).

In anthracite production there is less penetration by public companies. Production is concentrated among the companies that exploit the anthracite deposits of Bierzo and its surroundings. In 1994 the largest of these companies was Minero Siderúrgica de Ponferrada (the largest private mining company in Spain employing 2,600 people in 1993 but which was also on the brink of closure). However, the average size of firm in the sector and average output remain small. In 1992 there were an estimated 123 firms in the coal and anthracite industry producing some 12 per cent of European Community (EC) coal output in 1993 but employing around 20 per cent of the EC coal mining labour force.

The lignite sector is dominated by production from the public enterprise Endesa, which accounted for about two-thirds of all production in 1992. There are two contrasting lignite sectors. Brown lignite production is undertaken by only two firms, some 80 per cent coming from Endesa. Sub-bituminous coal production remains fragmented, although the number of firms has declined from the sixteen which existed in 1992 (for example Minas y Ferrocarilles de Utrillas has closed). Endesa produced 10.1 million tonnes of brown lignite from its open-caste mine at As Pontes de García Rodríguez in 1993, supplying its local power station. In Andorra (Teruel) the company produced one million tonnes of sub-bituminous coal from three mines (the underground mines of Innominada and La Oportuna, and the open-caste Corta Barrabasa), supplying its power stations at Andorra (Teruel) and Escatrón (Zaragoza). In 1994 Endesa was developing a new open-caste mine (Gargallo) in Teruel (Endesa 1994).

Rationalisation of the coal industry has been very slow in comparison with other countries in the European Union (EU), especially in relation to the contraction of the labour force in the public sector. Between 1974 and 1988 the labour force remained around 50,000. In the Febero basin in León, where the industry is in private hands, the number of miners declined to a little over 1,000 by early 1993 compared with 5,000 in the 1960s. But the public company Hunosa employed 25,000 in 1970 and still employed 18,000 in 1990. Only after 1988 did numbers in coal mining begin to fall significantly, gathering pace in the 1990s as pressure mounted from market forces and more especially from the European Commission.

Employment in coal mining is set to fall much further in the 1990s. Despite some mechanisation and the opening of new mines, productivity remains below that in other EU countries. In 1993 productivity was estimated to be below 400 kg per man hour in underground hard coal mines in Spain compared with an EC average of 758 (over 1,200 in the UK; Carbunión 1994). The greatest contributions to productivity have come from open-caste developments such as the lignite workings at As Pontes de García Rodríguez, Meirama and Ariño, the hard coal workings at Prado de la Guzpeña, Coto Cortés, Valdesmario and Puertollano, together with smaller, less important ones in anthracite. The slow pace at which rationalisation has proceeded stems essentially from the extent of public sector involvement in the industry, linked to the political problems of pit closures in areas dependent on coal mining.

Further rationalisation will continue through the 1990s within the framework of ECSC rationalisation plans for the European coal mining industry, cuts in capacity and employment being accompanied by financial assistance (Spain was the second largest recipient after Germany of EC financial assistance to the coal industry in the three years 1991 to 1993), access to EU Structural Funds in coal mining areas and approval for the payment of subsidies. Thus a major restructuring plan was requested in 1990 by the EC before further European assistance was granted (a similar condition to that which was applied to the shipbuilding industry, where cuts of up to 30 per cent in the labour force were requested). The Restructuring Plan 1990–93 envisaged cuts of almost 7,000 in employment in the coal industry in exchange for continued financial assistance from the EC. In practice, employment was reduced by over 13,000 and the Plan extended by one year to allow all those companies that wished to participate in the Plan to do so. Restructuring in Hunosa alone cut some 6,000 jobs between 1991 and the beginning of 1994, reducing the company's labour force to 12,000 by that time.

In December 1993 European Commission Decision No. 3632/93 was approved, setting out the framework for assistance to the coal mining industry up to the year 2002 (*OJ* 1993). The Energy Directorate of the EU (which was in broad agreement with the Competition Directorate) believed that state aid in the EU should be allowed to continue to guarantee coal supplies and reduce the socio-economic problems in coal mining areas, but that this assistance should be made transparent and tied to specific restructuring measures. At the same time, prices between coal suppliers and power stations should be freely determined from January 1997 (in 1994 aggregate coal production from mines in Spain was authorised by the New Coal Contracting System Monitoring Committee – Comisión de Seguimiento del Nuevo Sistema de Contratación de Carbón Termoeléctrico, NSCCT).

As a result of the Decision, further cuts beyond those agreed in the initial 1994–97 Rationalisation Plan are likely. For example, in mid 1994 the Ministry of Industry was suggesting that the employment contraction targets should be raised to over 7,000 from 1994 to 1997, cutting the total labour force in coal mining by that date to some 23,000. At Hunosa employment would be cut to around 8,000 (whereas initially the agreement was to cut the labour force by only 2,000 to 10,000 and to close only two of the thirteen mines owned by the company, leaving production roughly the same at around 2.5 million tonnes). The Plan envisaged state assistance of pta 297 billion over the four-year period.

Table 4.5 Characteristics of metallic mineral mining, 1992

Product	Production (000 tonnes)	Metal content (000 tonnes)	Value (pta billion)	Mines	Employment
Iron	2,967	1,334	4.2	3	545
Zinc	423	230	11.9	1	–
Lead	–	–	–	a	–
Copper	32	6	1.1	3	–
Tin (kgs)	11,085	7	–	1	9
Pyrites	264	123	0.4	2	–
Mercury	0	0	0.0	1	0
Precious metals	–	–	9.4	3	–
Silver (kgs bullion content)	–	439,428	–	–	–
Gold (kgs bullion content)	–	7,698	–	–	–
Total	–	–	30.1	14	3224

– refers to no data; a: figures included in those for zinc
Base metal production refers to mineral concentrate

Sources: MINE 1993b and 1994

4.3 Metallic mineral mining

Metallic mineral mining has been very severely affected by contraction, such that in 1993 almost all metallic mineral production in Spain had either ceased or was suspended. Rising costs of production, loss of markets, weak market prices and default on payments have sent many companies into bankruptcy. Zinc and precious metals were the most important metals produced by value of production in the early 1990s (Table 4.5).

4.3.1 Pyrites and sulphur

The Iberian pyrites zone (known reserves of 870 million tonnes of polymetallic sulphides) extends for some 250 km from the Guadalquivir in Spain (province of Seville) through the province of Huelva to the valley of the river Sado and the Atlantic coast of Portugal, constituting the main stock of base metals and sulphur in the European Union (Figure 4.1). All of the pyrites zone is designated as a National Reserve and divided into exploration blocks. Mining production from the zone includes iron, copper, lead, zinc, gold and silver, as well as sulphur. An estimated 60 per cent of pyrites reserves in Huelva were under the control of the British company Tharsis (established in 1866) and 24 per cent under the control of RTM. By the early 1990s both Tharsis and RTM (formally a subsidiary of Explosivos Rio Tinto) had ceased mining pyrites (Tharsis being closed completely). In mid 1994 the state company Almagrera SA, a subsidiary of the state-owned Teneo, closed. The company had operated the Sotiel mine (Huelva), an underground mine that has been developed since 1984 producing copper, lead, zinc and precious metals. This left only two remaining producers of pyrites in the region: the Swedish Boliden group at Aznalcóllar, Seville (an open-caste mine producing copper, lead and zinc as well as pyrites; Fox 1990) and Presur at Cala, Huelva (producing iron and copper). The reserves at Cala were formally owned by Minera de Andivalo but were taken over in 1981 by the newly formed INI subsidiary Prerreducidos Integrados del Suroeste de España (Presur, now part of the Teneo group), another public enterprise which since its inception has lost money.

In 1992 about a quarter of a million tonnes of pyrites were produced (0.1 million tonnes of sulphur content) from iron and copper pyrites (sulphur ore), all from the three mines in the provinces of Huelva and Seville (MINE 1994). In recent years production of sulphur from iron pyrites has declined relative to production from copper pyrites. Sulphur provides the basic material for the production of sulphuric acid and for certain fertilizers.

4.3.2 Copper

The copper mining industry entered a serious crisis in the late 1970s as production costs increased and copper prices fell in response to lower demand, occasioned both by weak demand generally and product substitution (for example the introduction of optical fibre in telecommunications). By 1987 the copper price in dollars had fallen below that in 1950 (low prices continuing into the early 1990s). Companies responded by cutting employment, closing mines, introducing more energy-efficient technology and taking advantage of large-scale production, frequently in less developed countries. For example, copper production at Codelco, Chile's state-owned copper corporation, rose to 572,618 tonnes of copper in the first half of 1992. In Spain the two major copper mining companies, RTM and Tharsis, both ceased production of copper after a long period of serious financial problems, leaving the Aznalcóllar mine as the principal source of production. The industry was only protected from complete collapse in the 1980s by government intervention and investment in new facilities by state-owned mining companies.

The copper industry comprises copper produced from scrap, copper produced from copper ores and copper produced as a by-product from complex metal ores. Smelting or the chemical treatment of ores is the first stage of the production process. For example, Metalquímica del Nervión (in Bilbao) and Presur used a chemical process to treat pyrites residuals to produce copper. Blister copper is produced from copper pyrites that are smelted in a blast furnace with coke to produce black copper, which is then further refined to blister copper (98 per cent copper). In the Huelva industrial complex there is an oxygen furnace (built in 1970) that enables the use of ores with high levels of sulphur impurities. To achieve economies of

Table 4.6 Metal concentrate production from selected mines

Mine/Metal	1990	1991	1992	1993	1994*
Aznalcóllar					
Copper		27,358	35,586	9,728	20,367
Lead		38,201	28,049	15,129	34,852
Zinc		128,760	105,785	44,015	112,390
Pyrites		447,535	355,825	217,700	190,000
Reocín					
Lead	15,004	16,100	16,058	18,535	
Zinc	173,006	189,107	192,108	197,250	
Cala					
Copper	3,620	2,410	2,021	890	
Iron	173,904	138,386	110,921	90,255	

* target figures

Metal content (per cent of concentrate): Aznalcóllar: copper 20.5, lead 49, zinc 47; Reocín: lead 70, zinc 56

Cala: no data for copper, iron is for sinter and pellet feed (iron metal content)

Sources: Personal communications and Asturiana de Zinc 1993 and 1994

scale, the plant has always drawn on imports and now relies on these. Electrolytic refining is the final stage in the production process. Refineries are located in Huelva (RTM: capacity 105,000 tonnes) and in the north of Spain in Bilbao.

More than 90 per cent of the economic reserves of copper in Spain are associated with copper pyrites in the Iberian pyrites zone, from which almost all the blister copper in Spain is produced. In 1992 only 6,000 tonnes of copper metal content mineral were produced in Spain. Three mines were producing copper ore, located in the provinces of Huelva and Seville. The most important copper mine was the open-caste Cerro Colorado, Huelva (opened in 1971 and owned in 1992 by RTM), until it ceased copper production. Production from the mine was about 28,000 tonnes of copper mineral in the mid 1980s with recoverable reserves estimated at 670,000 tonnes. Another three mines in the Iberian pyrites zone are at Aznalcóllar, Sotiel and Cala (production in 1992 of 35,586 tonnes, 7,800 tonnes and 2,021 tonnes of copper concentrate respectively; Table 4.6). Outside of the south-west there were mines owned by RTM in the province of La Coruña (open-caste mines of Arinteiro and Bama at Santiago de Compostela).

4.3.3 *Lead*

The crisis affecting the mining industry in the 1980s resulted in the closure of most of the lead mines in Spain, including all those in the provinces of

Jaén and Murcia, leaving lead production concentrated at the Aznalcóllar mine (production in 1992 of 28,049 tonnes of lead concentrate) and at the Reocín mine in Cantabria (production in 1993 of 18,535 tonnes of 70 per cent lead content concentrate, galena; Asturiana de Zinc 1994). The Aznalcóllar mine ceased production in mid 1993 because of technical difficulties and the Sotiel mine closed in 1994 (it produced 10,500 tonnes of lead concentrate in 1992). In 1991, 44,000 tonnes of lead metal mineral were produced compared with 80,000 tonnes in 1986. Lead is now mainly produced as a by-product of zinc or in association with precious metals.

No lead metal is now produced in Spain following the closure of the country's lead smelters. Lead metal was produced from the smelting of lead ores (essentially galena, lead sulphide). At the end of the 1980s there were two companies involved in smelting: Sociedad Minera y Metalúrgica de Peñarroya-España (owned by French capital), which were the owners of the Santa Lucia smelter in Cartagena, Murcia (closed in 1992), and Compañía La Cruz (Banco Central group), which owned a smelter in Linares, Jaén. Lead metal production in 1985 was 164,000 tonnes (14 per cent of the volume produced in the other EC countries, and about 2 per cent of world production). National production of lead concentrate was insufficient to meet the demands of the lead smelting industry in Spain, hence lead concentrate had to be imported. At the same time consumption of lead in Spain was below the output of the lead smelters, hence part of the lead produced was exported. Lead consumption in Spain (for example in batteries) increased from 77,000 tonnes of refined lead in 1970 to 117,000 tonnes in 1985 and has stabilised at about 100,000 tonnes as substitutes have emerged. Similarly, in the world market consumption has been relatively static since the late 1970s, contributing to weak prices.

4.3.4 Zinc

Zinc mining in the early 1990s was affected by the general malaise in the metal mining industry (production normally being associated with other metals notably lead and pyrites) and in metal manufacturing. Zinc metal production was adversely affected by weak prices arising from over production in Europe, a rise in metal supplies from the former Eastern Bloc countries and recession (thus the average annual price in real terms of zinc in dollars on the London Metal Exchange in 1993 was below the price in the mid 1980s). Zinc production is characterised by high fixed costs, stemming from high capital intensity and the structure of power supply contracts. European zinc producers, who are at a comparative cost disadvantage, have always seen only one way of staying competitive, spreading fixed costs by expanding capacity. Inevitably the result was over-supply in the industry. Attempts to manage the process of contraction in Europe were generally unsuccessful as stronger companies awaited the collapse of weaker ones through market forces. In 1994 the European zinc industry amounted to around 2 million tonnes and world consumption of zinc at about 6 million tonnes.

Zinc concentrate production in Spain increased from 86,100 tonnes (metal content) in 1960 to 98,100 tonnes in 1970, 179,300 tonnes in 1980 and 202,000 tonnes in 1992 (40 per cent of EC production but only a small percentage of world production). As zinc concentrate production fell in the early 1990s (and as part of production is exported) so an increasing volume of zinc concentrate was imported to meet the demands of the zinc producers, zinc imports rising from 80,000 tonnes of metal content in 1990 to over 200,000 tonnes in 1992 (Española del Zinc 1994).

Zinc metal in Spain is obtained mainly from zinc blend (ZnS) in northern Spain and pyrites in southern Spain. In 1994 zinc mineral was mainly being produced at Aznalcóllar (106,000 tonnes in 1992) and at the Reocín mine by Asturiana de Zinc (incorporated in 1957; in 1981 taking over from the Belgian company Real Compañía Asturiana de Minas, which had monopolised the industry up until the 1960s). Reocín is the most important zinc mine in Spain and the second most important in Europe (in 1993 the mine produced 197,250 tonnes of zinc concentrate of 56 per cent zinc content; Asturiana de Zinc 1994). Most other zinc mining has ceased: in Andalucía at the Sotiel mine (the latter produced 51,000 tonnes of zinc concentrate in 1992; Teneo 1993) and in Murcia (notably by Sociedad Minera y Metalúrgica de Peñarroya-España SA at Mina de Silicatos in Cartagena), although deposits at Mazarrón are being studied. Exploración Minera Internacional España SA (Exminesa, founded in 1965 by Asturiana de Zinc with Canadian and South African capital) owned the Rubiales mine in Piedrafita del Cebrero in Lugo (which produced lead and silver as well) and the Troya mine in Beasain (Guipúzcoa), opened in 1986. Both these mines had ceased production in 1994, the former due to exhaustion of deposits and the latter due to operating problems. The company Exminesa was wound up.

Zinc metal production in Spain in 1993 was 326,599 tonnes (about one-fifth of EC production and 6 per cent of world production outside the former Soviet Union and eastern Europe). The principal producers of zinc metal are Asturiana de Zinc (which supplies about three-quarters of the 100,000 tonnes of domestic requirements) and Española del Zinc (constituted in 1956 to treat ores from the Cartagena area). At San Juan de Nieve (Avilés, Asturias) the former operates three roasting plants with a processing capacity of over 500,000 tonnes of zinc concentrate a year, an electrolytic smelter with a capacity of 320,000 tonnes of zinc ingots a year and plant for manufacturing zinc products. There is also a zinc products plant at neighbouring Arnao. The company's smelting plant at Hinojedo (Cantabria) ceased production in 1993 and then closed completely in 1994. About one-third of the zinc concentrate for these plants comes from the Reocín mine, the rest is imported. Española del Zinc operates a plant at Cartagena (Murcia). Zinc smelters also produce heavy metals (cadmium, copper, germanium and mercury) and sulphuric acid. As a result, substantial investment has been required to update them to meet environmental regulations. In 1993 the San Juan plant had a processing capacity of 460,000 tonnes of sulphuric acid a year. Acid from the plant in Cartagena is sold mainly to the adjacent fertilizer plant, Potasas y Derivados.

4.3.5 Mercury

Spain has been one of the world's leading producers and exporters of mercury (and the only producer in the EU), increasing its market share in the early 1980s by maintaining production in the face of falling prices. Production of mercury metal remained static at about 40,000 to 50,000 flasks (one-fifth of world production; one flask is 34.5 kg of mercury), but by 1990 production had fallen to about 26,000 flasks, ceasing altogether between 1991 and 1993 while stocks were reduced. Normally, 90 per cent of mercury production is exported. Reserves would allow production at late 1980s levels at least into the early twenty-first century.

In the 1970s there was widespread publicity concerning the health hazards of mercury, leading to its substitution by other less toxic products. This contributed to falling demand. Three private mercury producers in Asturias/León ceased production (although from 1980 mercury has been produced as a by-product from zinc concentrate by Asturiana de Zinc; for example the company produced 1,054 flasks at its San Juan plant in 1992). Since the mid 1980s prices have remained weak (less than $150 a flask in 1985 falling to less than $100 in March 1994). In the mines the health hazard was recognised by the adoption of special employment conditions. The normal regime was to work six hours per day for only eight days per month. Retirement was at fifty and workers were exempt from taxes and national service. They also received a small plot of land.

The mercury deposits at Almadén (Ciudad Real) are among the largest in the world. They have been known since the fourth century BC and are known to have been in production since 1499. In the early twentieth century marketing was handled by Rothschild, which also controlled mines in Istria (Italy) and California. In 1981 administration of the mines and the marketing of the mercury was placed in the hands of the public enterprise Empresa Nacional de las Minas de Almadén y Arrayanes (under the DGPE, and now constituted as a limited company), which was also given responsibility for other mercury deposits in Spain (in Asturias, Granada, Castellón and Badajoz).

The main deposit that has been worked recently by Minas de Almadén is that of El Entredicho (17 km from Almadén), an open-caste mine with reserves estimated at 500,000 flasks. The mine produced 21,290 tonnes of mineral in 1991 before operations were suspended in 1992 (Grupo Patrimonio 1993). In the late 1980s one other deposit was being worked, that of Almadén (estimated reserves of 65,000 flasks), and a further deposit at Las Cuevas was under development (8 km from Almadén, production from underground deposits with reserves estimated at 200,000 flasks). All the raw material is processed in plants at the mines, which have also processed residual mercury since 1985.

From being an important source of state revenue the mines have become a liability with chronic deficits. Falling demand has been accompanied by cuts in employment, employment in the mining company falling to around 500 at the end of 1992 (a figure that is likely to fall further and only a small proportion of whom are directly employed in the mines; Rivera 1990). Dependence of the local region (covering some 30,000 people) on the activities of the mines has prompted government investment to cushion the impact of industrial decline. Investment has included an exploration programme that led to the discovery of two new mercury deposits and one of lead and zinc at Navalmedio, a mercury-waste treatment plant, and an economic development programme for the region of Almadén involving state investment in new activities and further investment in mercury mining. Further plant for treating and storing toxic industrial waste have been proposed (as one of three sites suggested under the Plan Nacional de Residuos Tóxicos y Peligrosos), met by environmental opposition but matched by support from those who wish to see employment expand. Facilities for recycling mercury residuals were being expanded in 1994.

4.3.6 *Tin and precious metals*

Tin deposits are found mainly along the border with Portugal (in Salamanca), but few mines have been worked since 1959, when tin prices fell following the easing of import restrictions. In 1992 only 7 tonnes of tin metal were produced, all from one mine in Salamanca (MINE 1994). Most tin and cassiterite (tin ore) is imported. At the beginning of the 1990s there were three major companies in tin smelting: Metalúrgica del Estano (with smelters in Villaverde in Madrid and Villagarcía de Arosa in Pontevedra), Ferroaleaciones Españolas (with smelters at Medina del Campo) and Metalúrgica del Agueda (at Villaralbo in Zamora).

Production of precious metals is small, with production normally associated with other minerals. The principal mines which have produced gold and silver in recent years are those in Huelva (Sotiel and Cerro Colorado mines, the latter producing precious metals from Gossan deposits), Seville (Aznalcóllar mine) and Almería (the Rodalquilar mine at Cerro Cinto in the municipality of Nijar).

Table 4.7 Iron-ore production in 1985 and 1992

Province	Number of mines		Employment		Iron-ore output	
	1985	1992	1985	1992	1985	1992
Granada	1	1	409	242	3.7	2.2
Guadalajara	1	0	52	0	0.4	0.0
Huelva	1	1	149	171	0.0	0.1
Murcia	1	0	6	0	0.2	0.0
Cantabria	2	0	118	0	0.2	0.0
Soria	1	0	30	0	0.2	0.0
Teruel	1	0	133	0	0.5	0.0
Vizcaya	3	1	108	132	0.9	0.7
Total	11	3	1,005	545	6.1	3.0

Iron-ore output in millions of tonnes saleable production

Sources: Koerting Wiese 1986; MINE 1994

4.3.7 Iron

Iron mining has been in long-term decline since the 1960s, a decline that accelerated in the early 1980s to leave only one significant mine in 1994, that in Granada. In the 1960s there were about 200 mines employing more than 9,500 people. By 1970 the number of mines had fallen to 72 and by 1976 to 29 with 2,676 people employed (Table 4.7). Contraction in the number of mines and employment was especially severe in the early 1980s as rising production costs (labour, fuel and transport) coincided with weak prices resulting from cut-backs in the iron and steel industry. For example, the Compañía Minera de Sierra Menera SA (CMSM), which mined the deposit of Ojós Negros/Setiles (Teruel/Guadalajara), was closely linked to iron making at Sagunto. At the end of 1992 iron mining employed little over 600 people in three mines, the largest of which was in Granada. Total production had fallen to less than 4 million tonnes of iron-ore, yielding about 1.5 million tonnes of metal (MINE 1994).

Imported ores are generally more competitive than domestic ones, leading to a substantial deficit on the balance of trade in iron-ore. In addition to low export volumes, the value of exported iron-ore has tended to be low (mainly fines), while imports have tended to be of higher value material (mineral and pellets). Successive proposals for pelletisation plants in Spain were rejected, although the state-integrated iron and steel company Ensidesa invested in pelletisation plant abroad (Ensidesa having a holding in the pelletisation plant of Hispanobras, Tubarao in Brazil, which became operational in 1979 with a 3 million tonne capacity; the plant is its main supplier of pellets). Hence Spanish iron mineral output can only be used in iron sintering plants. In 1992 about half of iron-ore production was exported (almost all from the Alquife mine in Granada and mostly to the EC). Imports of iron-ore in 1990 amounted to 4.4 million tonnes (over 50 per cent of national requirements) plus a further 2.3 million tonnes of pellets, sinters and briquettes. Imports were drawn mainly from Brazil (where Ensidesa has mining interests), Venezuela (Ensidesa and Alto Hornos de Vizcaya), Mauritania, Australia (Ensidesa) and Canada.

Iron-ore deposits are generally of relatively low iron content and contain many impurities. Total reserves are estimated at 305 million tonnes. Possible resources may amount to a further 1,700 million tonnes. The largest reserves (82 million tonnes) are found in the south-east, centred on the Alquife and Marquesado haematite deposits in Granada. The deposits, worked by open-caste methods, are situated on the northern slope of the Sierra Nevada on the flood plain of the Marquesado. Ores average 54 per cent iron content with no phosphorous or sulphur impurities. The Alquife mines were opened with British capital but eventually passed to the Compañía Andaluza de Minas SA (CAM). Production increased from 2 million tonnes of iron-ore in 1971 to 3 million tonnes in 1975 and reached 3.7 million tonnes in 1987.

In the north-west there are reserves of 21 million tonnes in Galicia, León and Asturias (Koerting Wiese 1986). These reserves of magnetites and haematites (averaging 48 per cent iron, generally of high phosphoric content and containing silica and alumina) are found in Silurian and Devonian sediments in a series of parallel arcs extending from Astorga (León) to Ribadeo (Lugo). The largest deposits are thought to be near Ponferrada (León) and were worked by Minero Siderúrgico de Ponferrada (part of the Banco Central Hispano group). In the north there are reserves of 60 million tonnes (35 to 40 per cent iron content) in limestones in Vizcaya and Santander. Haematite ores extending from Durango to Santander are now mostly worked out. In the Centro-Levante region there are reserves of 60 million tonnes. The most important deposits (44 per cent iron content with silica and alumina) are found in Silurian limestones in the Sierra Menera (Teruel and Guadalajara). Included in this area were the mines of Albarracín and Moncayo. In the south-west there are reserves of 40 million tonnes (mainly magnetites of iron content 38 to 60 per cent) in Badajoz, Huelva and Seville. Reserves of iron pyrites in this zone are put at 100 million tonnes.

Iron has also been produced from iron pyrites, mainly by plants in Vizcaya and through the state-controlled company Presur in Huelva. Metalquímica del Nervión operated a factory in Axpe-Erandio (Bilbao) that extracted iron and other metals chemically from pyrites brought from Huelva before it went into liquidation in 1991. Production (capacity amounting to almost half a million tonnes annually in the mid 1980s) was sold to Ensidesa and AHV. Presur works the deposit of Cala (also producing copper) and has research and development facilities in Fregenal de la Sierra, Badajoz. In 1993 the company produced 90,255 tonnes of iron (metal content, down from 174,000 tonnes in 1990) supplied mainly to Ensidesa (Presur 1994).

Current problems facing the iron mining industry are the limited domestic demand (constituted by the two state-controlled integrated iron and steelworks), the poor quality of domestic ores (which continues to impede their use despite work by Ensidesa to develop new production technology), high production costs, high transport costs and competition from imports.

4.4 Non-metallic mineral mining

Non-metallic mineral mining provides inputs to the fertilizer and chemical industries. Both these industries have been subject to severe economic pressure and have undergone restructuring. In the late 1980s demand for chemicals and fertilizers recovered only to fall again in the early 1990s. With the liberalisation of markets domestic sources of supply have been undercut by imports. A scarcity of commercial phosphate deposits in Spain already requires fertilizer manufacturers (producing superphosphates) to rely on imports (mostly from Morocco).

4.4.1 Potash

Problems in the potash industry in Spain in the 1980s and early 1990s (associated with high production costs, weak prices arising from a decline in demand for fertilizers and increased competition from imports) forced closures and concentration of production in the hands of the state-owned Teneo group, where companies continued to sustain losses.

Reserves of potash (potassium carbonate) in Spain support an industry that produces between 0.7 and 1.2 million tonnes of potash a year (MINE 1993a; world production 24 million to 30 million tonnes), constituting both an important raw material for the domestic fertilizer industry and an export. Reserves of potash between Barcelona and Navarra are estimated at 107 million tonnes. In Barcelona production is centred around the Cardener and Llobregat valleys (reserves 75 million tonnes), the mineral being exploited by Suria K (Teneo group; production 263,000 tonnes in 1992 and a labour force of 692 in 1991) and Potasas de Llobregat (also part of the Teneo group having been acquired from Ercros in 1991) mining the Sallent and Balsareny deposits (production 165,000 tonnes in 1992 and a labour force of 500 in 1993; Teneo 1993). These deposits are located relatively close to the coast, facilitating exports (mineral lines linking the mines to the port of Barcelona). In Navarra, Potasas de Subiza (jointly owned by the regional government of Navarra and INI) exploited deposits at Cendea de Galar near Pamplona until their closure in 1991.

The Cardona and Suria deposits in Barcelona were the first to be worked in Spain in 1912. The developers of the mine formed the company Minas de Potasas de Suria in 1920 with capital from the Belgian company Solvay, which quickly became the outright owner. In 1929 another company was formed in Cardona, which later became part of Union Española de Explosivos and later part of the Ercros group. Operations in the Llobregat Valley began soon after that, falling under the control of French and German companies. After the Second World War the state holding company INI took control of the German holdings, forming the company Fodina in 1952. Fodina then acquired interests in other potash companies. From 1969 the Llobregat deposits were being worked by Explosivos Riotinto and Fodina. In 1972 Fodina ceded the working of its deposits to Potasas de Suria. Recession forced the integration of the two companies in 1982 (and the withdrawal of Belgian capital), leaving INI as the major partner in Potasas de Suria. With the sale of the interests of Ercros in potash mining all potash production was concentrated in the hands of INI (Teneo group).

In Navarra, Potasas de Navarra was established in 1960 by the state holding company INI to work the potash deposits in the Sierra del Perdón, large-scale production beginning in 1964. High extraction costs, limited reserves, labour disputes and weak market prices brought deteriorating economic circumstances, forcing INI to close the company in 1986. To save the industry, a new company (Potasas de Subiza) was formed by the regional government of Navarra and INI to work the Navarra deposits. This company closed in 1991.

Membership of the European Community forced the break-up of a highly regulated market in fertilizers (which had maintained fertilizer prices generally above world market prices), resulting in economic pressures which prompted mergers in the Spanish fertilizer industry to leave one major company, Ercros. Until 1970 domestic demand was relatively small (reflecting the backwardness of Spanish agriculture), forcing a reliance on exports. The structure of the domestic fertilizer market was oligopolistic, the fertilizer manufacturers ERT and Cros accounting for about three-quarters of demand. As ERT obtained its supplies from within the company, the major consumer was Cros (others included Energía e Industrias Aragonesas, Inabonos, the state company Enfersa, SA Mirat and Induca).

From 1971 marketing of potash was in the hands of the monopoly Coposa (Comercial de Potasas SA), formed by the producing companies. Coposa divided the domestic market between producers and controlled all exports except those to China (which were exported by Marfusa through the port of Tarragona). Coposa gave Spanish producers more power in international bargaining and provided a channel for presenting the producers' case to the government on import protection and domestic prices (which were set by the government and tended to reflect the profitability of INI's potash operations). Coposa is now the marketing arm of the Teneo group's potash operations.

4.4.2 *Common salt*

Production of common salt in 1991 amounted to 3.2 million tonnes (MINE 1993a), the largest proportion coming from rock salt (two-thirds), for which Cantabria is the most important single location (Polanco de la Sal, Cabezón de la Sal and Monte Corona; linked to the Solvay company). The remainder (between half and one million tonnes) comes principally from sea salt produced at various locations around the Mediterranean (especially Torrevieja in Alicante, San Roque and San Fernando in Cádiz and Cabo de Gata in Almería). Production of sea salt is concentrated in the hands of a few companies. Apart from the supply of table salt, the mineral is a basic one in the chemical industry.

4.5 Quarry products

After energy, quarry products constitute the most important sector of mining by both value of sales and employment (Table 4.8). Products include limestone, marble (for example from Macael, Almería), slate, granite (ornamental granite particularly from Pontevedra), clay and aggregates of various types. Quarrying occurs throughout Spain, although high transport costs mean that there is particular pressure to extract materials near to market areas. Activity is bound up with that of the construction industry and thus follows the cyclical fluctuations in the construction industry. It also supports a large ceramics industry. Generally, quarrying has been more buoyant than the other sectors of mining. Many of the materials produced enjoy worldwide recognition both for masonry and decoration. The frantic pace of construction in many areas (especially in the 1960s, early

Table 4.8 Characteristics of non-metallic mineral mining and quarrying, 1991/92

	Production (million tonnes)	Value (pta billion)	Mines	Employment
Non-metallic minerals				
Potash salts	4.8	9.4	3	2,021
Other	–	38.6	207	2,947
Sub total		48.0	210	4,968
Quarry products				
Limestone	126.7	49.7	747	
Sand and gravel	52.0	19.0		
Granite	13.0	10.5		
Other	–	39.4		
Sub total	–	118.6	3044	14,900
Total	–	169.0	3254	19,868

Employment at the end of 1992; production, value and the number of mines in 1991

Production of potash salts refers to potash mineral (683,309 tonnes of potash content produced)

1970s and late 1980s) put particular pressure on sites for mineral extraction, frequently leading to environmental degradation.

4.6 Restructuring of the mining industry

Throughout the mining industry mine closures and industrial restructuring have left a pattern of larger, more highly automated mines, dominated by public enterprises and multinational companies.

The decline of coal mining in Spain was delayed by various forms of protection, including direct financial support and intervention in markets, which began to be removed from the late 1980s. The ECSC have signalled the requirement that European coal producers compete freely with supplies on the world market by the late 1990s. In this environment the closure of coal mines and cuts in employment will continue throughout the decade.

Metallic mineral mining had almost withered away by 1994 in response to greater competition from other sources of metallic minerals and changing patterns of demand. At the international level the business environment is dominated by giant multinational companies, sourcing raw materials from large-scale deposits in countries which frequently have less rigorous environmental regulations and lower-cost labour. Increased demand could reactivate a number of mines but there is probably little scope for increased employment, a conclusion that applies equally to non-metallic minerals.

Employment in quarry products may be sustained, protected by the natural monopoly offered by the cost of transporting low value, bulky materials. Although even here the liberalisation of markets, technological innovation, industrial rationalisation and pressure from imports will cap employment growth as demand recovers.

In former mining areas, centuries of mining have left a legacy of old mine workings, environmental degradation and pollution that will challenge the environmental industry into the next century. One source of alternative employment will be tourism centred on industrial archaeology (as for example around the Rio Tinto mines in Huelva).

References and bibliography

Anon (1989) 'Neves Corvo', *Mining Magazine*, September, p. 184–90
Anon (1992) 'Mines producing more than 150,000 tonnes', *Mining Magazine*, January
Asturiana de Zinc SA (1993) *Annual report 1992*. Madrid
Asturiana de Zinc SA (1994) *Annual report 1993*. Madrid
Carbunión (1994) *Carbunión 1993*. Madrid
Castejon Montijano, R. (1986) 'El síglo crucial de la minería española (1850–1950)', *Papeles de Economía Española* 29, pp. 30–48
Castillo Bonet, M. (1983) 'El carbón en perspectiva', *Papeles de Economía Española* 14, pp. 171–94
Coll Martín, S. and C. Sudriá Triay (1987) *El carbón en España 1770 -1961: Una historia económica*. Madrid: Ediciones Turner SA
Costa Campi, M. (1986) 'Minería potásica', *Papeles de Economía Española* 29, pp. 240–70
Encasur (1994) *Informe anual 1993*. Madrid: Grupo Teneo
Endesa (1994) *Annual report 1993*. Madrid: Grupo Teneo
Española del Zinc SA (1994) *Cuentas anuales, informe de gestión y propuesta de aplicación de resultados 1993*. Madrid
Fox, K. (1990) 'Aznalcollar', *Mining Magazine*, January, pp. 20–5
García Alonso, J. (1986) 'La minería del carbón', *Papeles de Economía Española*, No. 29, pp.110–40
García Alonso, J. (1987) 'El carbón en España', *Situación*, No. 2, pp. 32–53. Bilbao: BBV
García Guinea, J. and J. Martínez Frías (1992) *Recursos minerales de España*. Madrid: Consejo Superior de Investigaciones
Gea Javaloy, R. (1986) 'El sector del plomo en España', *Papeles de Economía Española* 29, pp. 271–81
Gea Javaloy, R. (1986) 'El sector del zinc', *Papeles de Economía Española* 29, pp. 321–31
Grupo Patrimonio (1993) *Memoria 1992*. Madrid
Harvey, C. (1981) *The Rio Tinto Company*. London: Alison Hodge
Koerting Wiese, G. (1986) 'La minería del hierro', *Papeles de Economía Española*, No. 29, pp. 332–47
Mallada, L. (1890) *Los males de la patria y futura revolución española*. Madrid: Manuel Tello
Ministerio de Industria y Energía, MINE (1993a) *Estadística minera de España, 1991*. Madrid
Ministerio de Industria y Energía, MINE (1993b) *Informe anual sobre la industria española, 1992*. Madrid
Ministerio de Industria y Energía, MINE (1993c) *Panorama minero, 1990*. Madrid
Ministerio de Industria y Energía, MINE (1994) *Estadística minera de España, 1992* (Avance). Madrid
Morera Altisent, J. (1986) 'La minería del cobre', *Papeles de Economía Española* 29, pp. 303–20
Muñoz, J., S. Roldán and A. Serrano (1976) 'Minería y capital extranjero', *Información Comercial Española*, No. 514, pp. 59–89
Official Journal of the European Communities (1993) 'Commission decision No. 3632/93/ECSC of 28 December 1993 establishing Community rules for State aid to the coal industry', in L329 Vol. 36, 30 December, pp. 12–18. Brussels
Presur (1994) *Cuentas anuales 1993* (and personal communication). Madrid: Grupo INI
Rivera, A. (1990) 'Almadén se plantea el tratamiento de residuos como medio de subsistencia', *El País*, 8 July, p. 21

Romero Alvarez, J. and J. Oliveros Rives (1986) 'El mercurio', *Papeles de Economía Española* 29, pp. 282–302
Tamames, R. (1983) *Estructura económica de España*, Vol. 1. Madrid: Alianza Editorial
Teneo SA (1993) *Annual report 1992*. Madrid
Terán, M. (1978) 'La minería y las industrias extractivas', in M. Terán and L. Solé Sabaris (eds), *Geografía general de España*, pp. 404–28. Barcelona: Editorial Ariel
Velarde Fuertes, J. (1986) 'Ante la nueva minería española', *Papeles de Economía Española* 29, pp. 2–29

Chapter 5
Energy

5.1 Energy in Spain

A crucial characteristic of the Spanish economy centres on the limited capacity to meet energy requirements from domestic sources and the consequent reliance on imports, especially of oil and increasingly on gas. In 1993 the degree of self-sufficiency in primary energy was only about 36 per cent, 54 per cent of primary energy requirements being derived from oil (Table 5.1). Dependence on imported energy was one of the major causes of the severe economic crisis in the early 1980s and remains a latent threat to the economy, especially as dependence is set to increase over the coming decade.

Primary energy production is shared by coal, nuclear power, hydroelectricity and renewable sources (Table 5.2). Domestic oil supplies are very small (about 2 per cent of requirements), as are those of natural gas. Coal supplies are reasonable but of poor quality. Hydroelectricity continues to grow but its contribution to overall production is erratic, being subject to

Table 5.1 Structure of primary energy consumption, 1950–93

Energy source	1950	1960	1970	1975	1980	1985	1990	1993	
Oil	8.9	27.9	62.2	70.9	68.6	55.8	54.2	54.0	(48.4)
Coal	73.6	47.0	22.3	15.5	18.3	27.0	21.4	20.4	(18.3)
Nuclear	0.0	0.0	0.5	2.5	1.5	10.3	16.0	16.3	(14.6)
HEP	17.5	25.1	14.7	9.7	9.4	3.9	2.5	2.3	(2.1)
Natural gas	0.0	0.0	0.3	1.4	2.2	3.1	5.7	6.6	(5.9)
Other							0.3	0.2	(0.2)
Total	100.0	100.0	100.0	100.0	100.0	100.0	100.0	100.0	(89.6)

Figures in brackets refer to primary energy consumption in millions of tonnes oil equivalent

Other includes wind, urban waste and other residuals consumed in electricity production

Sources: Papeles de Economía 29, 1986; INE 1994

Table 5.2 Structure of primary energy production, 1975–93

Energy source	[1975]		[1980]		1985		1990		1993	
Coal	41.3	–	39.4	–	45.7	(13.6)	39.0	(11.9)	37.1	(10.8)
Nuclear	10.3	–	6.8	–	21.1	(6.3)	46.4	(14.1)	50.0	(14.6)
HEP	36.1	–	48.3	–	24.9	(7.4)	7.2	(2.2)	7.1	(2.1)
Oil	12.4	–	5.3	–	7.4	(2.2)	2.6	(0.8)	3.0	(0.9)
Natural gas	0.0	–	0.2	–	1.0	(0.3)	4.0	(1.2)	2.1	(0.6)
Other							0.8	(0.3)	0.7	(0.2)
Total	100.0	(16.4)	100.0	(22.0)	100.0	(29.7)	100.0	(30.5)	100.0	(29.2)

Figures in brackets refer to production in millions of tonnes oil equivalent

Other includes wind, urban waste and other residuals consumed in electricity production

Sources: *Papeles de Economía* 29, 1986; MINE 1989; INE 1994

Table 5.3 Structure of final energy consumption, 1975–93

Energy source	1975		1980		1985		1990		1993	
Oil	74.8	(31.4)	75.4	(38.1)	68.3	(34.3)	67.4	(40.9)	67.5	(41.6)
Electricity	13.8	(5.8)	15.3	(7.7)	17.8	(8.9)	18.1	(11.0)	18.7	(11.5)
Coal	9.4	(4.0)	7.0	(3.5)	10.4	(5.2)	7.0	(4.3)	5.3	(3.3)
Gas	2.0	(0.8)	2.3	(1.1)	3.5	(1.8)	7.5	(4.5)	8.5	(5.2)
Total	100.0	(42.0)	100.0	(50.5)	100.0	(50.2)	100.0	(60.7)	100.0	(61.6)

Figures in brackets refer to final energy consumption in millions of tonnes oil equivalent

Sources: *Papeles de Economía* 29,1986; MINE 1993; INE 1994

variations in precipitation. Nuclear power expanded rapidly in the late 1970s and early 1980s but further development has been halted by political opposition and shifts in energy production costs. As a reflection of these characteristics energy policy continues to concentrate on the diversification of energy sources, with less attention being given to reducing energy imports and energy conservation. In terms of the organisation of the industry, the liberalisation of the energy market is reducing the extent of state control, gradually opening up the industry to foreign penetration and allowing energy-producing companies to secure raw materials from the lowest cost sources.

The final energy market in Spain is characterised by relatively low levels of consumption per unit of GDP (in relation to other European Union countries), continued dominance by oil (67 per cent of final energy requirements), a high degree of penetration by electricity (Table 5.3) and the dispersal of major markets. Electricity consumption per head in 1993 was 3,901 KWh in Spain, higher only than Greece and Portugal (5,431 KWh per head in the UK; *El País* 1995). The dispersal of major markets is illustrated by the statistic that only 40 per cent of final energy consumption in 1985 was concentrated in the four areas of Barcelona, Madrid, País Vasco and Comunidad Valenciana (Martos Martínez 1987).

5.1.1 National energy plans

The first round of world oil price rises at the end of 1973 highlighted the excessive dependence of Spain on imported oil and the poverty of existing domestic energy resources. The ensuing energy crisis spawned a series of national energy plans (Plan Energético Nacional, PEN), all of which have aimed at energy conservation, reducing dependence on energy imports and expanding the role of domestic resources. However, the strategies adopted have shifted in the light of changing political and economic realities. Thus the First National Energy Plan (approved in January 1975 for the period 1975 to 1985) assumed continued strong growth in energy consumption to be met largely through a massive nuclear energy programme. The Second National Energy Plan (approved in 1979 for the period 1978 to 1987) revised energy demand downwards, attached less urgency to reducing oil consumption and scaled down nuclear energy plans. The switch to increased coal usage in electricity generating stations was to continue and further diversification of the energy base was to be achieved through the increased use of natural gas. The substantial oil price rise in 1979 necessitated an early revision of the Plan, to focus on reducing oil consumption to 45 per cent of primary energy requirements by 1990 (Revision of the Second National Energy Plan, 1981–90).

The Third National Energy Plan (1984–92) provided a thorough review of energy policy following the 1982 general elections. It sought four kinds of medium term action: i) absorption of current surplus capacity by a) scaling down energy investment and b) raising prices to cover costs of production; ii) financial improvement of energy utilities and reform of the institutional mechanisms for transferring earnings among the various utilities; iii) improvement in the efficiency of energy use; and iv) reduction of the vulnerability of Spanish energy supply by increasing the use of coal and hydroelectricity and reducing the import dependency associated with the use of oil. National economic growth and the growth of energy consumption were further revised down from the previous plans to an average of 3.5 per cent per annum (GDP growth) 1986–92, with an elasticity of energy demand of 0.73 x GDP (compared with the actual elasticity of 0.95 in the period 1971–81).

A fourth plan was initially due in 1986 but uncertainty in the energy market on both the supply and demand side (including the Gulf crisis) resulted in delay until mid 1991. The Fourth Plan (PEN 1991–2000; MINE 1991) was drawn up in the context of an expanding economy, continuing weakness in oil prices, problems in the nuclear industry and a growing environmental lobby. Key assumptions in the plan are that GDP will grow at an annual average rate of 3.5 per cent, primary energy demand by 2.4 per cent and that oil and gas prices will remain steady. The principal source of growth in primary energy consumption has been allocated to natural gas, which is projected to increase its share of the national energy market from 6 to 12 per cent by the year 2000. The use of coal will depend on the evolution of its competitive position, while the moratorium on new nuclear generating capacity will continue. Diversification of the structure and geographical origin of energy supplies will continue with the further development of renewable energy and new gas and electricity supply contracts (for example with Norway and France respectively). Dependence on external primary energy supplies will therefore increase.

5.2 Oil

Expansion in oil refining and oil consumption in the 1960s and early 1970s came to a halt during the 1970s as crude oil prices increased and energy consumption switched to non-oil sources. This caused a crisis in the refining sector and a rapid deterioration in the energy trade deficit, while prompting oil exploration and production within Spain. Lower oil prices in the late 1980s and early 1990s (attributable both to low dollar prices and a strong peseta exchange rate) reduced the urgency for domestic exploration, while rekindling demand in refined oil products (although this was offset by oil tax increases). The most significant events in the oil industry were those affecting its organisation as the oil market was progressively liberalised.

5.2.1 Oil industry structure and restructuring

The oil industry is split between the public and private sectors. The public sector is represented by the Repsol group (a mixed public/private company), formed in 1987 from the various public companies owned by INH (Instituto Nacional de Hidrocarburos) involved in the hydrocarbon sector.

On its formation in 1981 INH acquired the state interests and rights in the following: i) the mixed (public/private) refining company Petroliber and the former INI refining and petrochemical company EMP (Empresa Nacional de Petróleo SA); ii) the exploration and extraction companies Eniepsa and Hispanoil; iii) the oil distribution company Campsa (initially INH had a 54 per cent holding, increased to 60.5 per cent by 1985); and iv) the former INI gas distribution companies Butano and Enagas. These companies participated in a further 27 companies. Through Campsa and its affiliate, CEH (Corporación Española de Hidrocarburos), INH had interests

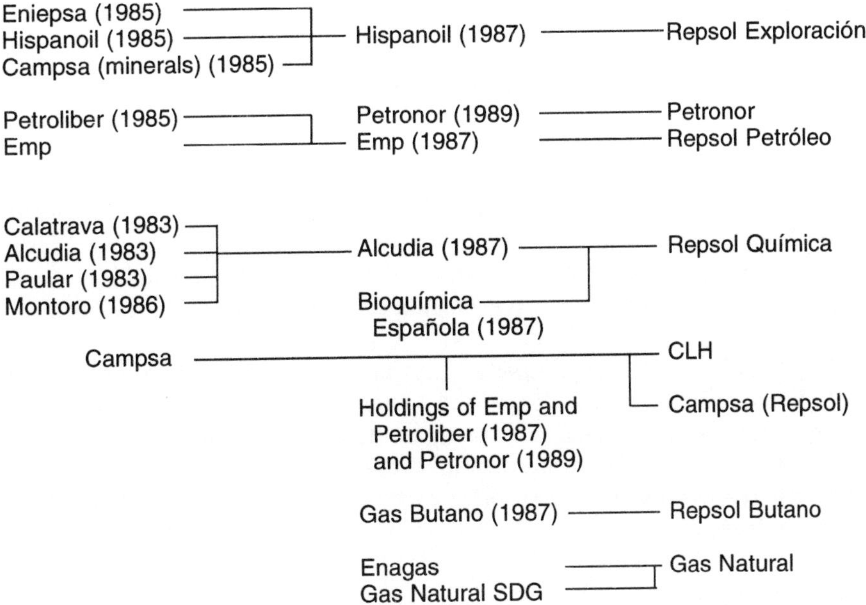

Campsa: Compañía Arrendataria del Monopolio de Petróleos SA
CLH: Compañía Logística de Hydrocarburos SA
Emp: Empresa Nacional de Petróleo SA
INH formed in 1981; Repsol Group formed in 1987
(1985): Date of incorporation into the group

Figure 5.1 Evolution of INH, 1981–94

in the companies Asesa, Proas and Petronor; and through EMP in the petrochemical companies Paular, Alcudia, Calatrava and Montoro.

Co-ordination of public sector interests in hydrocarbons facilitated a policy of restructuring, reducing costs, investing in distribution networks (for example, modernising service stations) and improving the image of public sector companies through advertising campaigns. The process of restructuring began in 1983 and was completed with the formation of Repsol in 1987 (Figure 5.1).

In exploration and crude oil production there were initially two public sector companies: Hispanoil (formed in 1965, initially with 70 per cent INI capital, becoming wholly owned by INI in 1975), concerned with overseas exploration and production, and Eniepsa (owned by INI), concerned with exploration and production within Spain. In 1985 Hispanoil acquired Eniepsa and the mineral exploration rights of Campsa. In 1986 Hispanoil was operating in fifteen countries and producing oil in six (with major deposits in Dubai). The company also produced gas from the Gaviota and Serrablo fields.

In refining INH bought the holding of Phillips in the petrochemical company Calatrava in 1984, thereby increasing its participation in EMP to 99 per cent. EMP was formed in 1973 from the three companies with INI participation: Repesa (Refinería de Petróleos de Escombreras), with a refinery at Escombreras, Cartagena (established in 1949); Empresa Nacional Calvo Sotelo, with a refinery at Puertollano (established in 1965); and Enptasa (Refinería de Tarragona), with a refinery at Tarragona (established in 1974). In 1985 EMP acquired the company Petroliber (Compañía Iberica Refinados de Petróleos, which was owned 54 per cent by INH, 28 per cent by Deutsche Marathon Petroleum and 18 per cent by other private interests). This acquisition brought a fourth refinery located in La Coruña (established in 1966). Together the four refineries have a crude oil refining capacity of 25 million tonnes.

In petrochemicals the company Alcudia absorbed Calatrava and Paular in 1983. In 1986 Alcudia acquired the participation of Arco in Montoro and merged all four petrochemical companies in 1986 under Alcudia, with plants in Santander, Puertollano and Tarragona producing a wide range of products (especially plastics, rubber, carbon black, styrene and butadiene). Alcudia thus became the only subsidiary of EMP and a medium-sized petrochemical company by European standards, exporting a large proportion of its production.

The formation of Repsol in 1987 marked a further stage in the rationalisation of the oil industry. Repsol became the seventh largest oil company in Europe, the largest industrial organisation (by sales) in Spain and one of the country's few multinational companies. The company's main divisions are: Repsol Exploración (formally Hispanoil) with reserves in Colombia, Indonesia, Dubai, Gabon, Angola and Egypt, and stakes in the North Sea (in 1993 Repsol's net hydrocarbon reserves were estimated at 553 million barrels of oil equivalent and it owned about 30 per cent of its crude supply); Repsol Petróleo (formally EMP) concerned with oil refining and distribution and the production of basic chemicals mainly at the refineries of Puertollano and Tarragona; Repsol Química (formally Alcudia) concerned with manufacturing and marketing derivative petrochemicals, the main manufacturing facilities being located at Puertollano, Tarragona and Santander; Repsol Butano (formally Gas Butano); Repsol Naviera Vizcaina (shipping); Campsa (distribution) and Petronor. Petronor (Refinería de Petróleos del Norte) has been controlled by Repsol since 1989. This subsidiary owns the refinery at Somorrostro, 18 kilometres west of Bilbao. Petromex (Petróleos de Mexico) has an equity interest in Petronor (providing a foothold for Mexico in the EU) and a supply agreement with Repsol under which (along with Repsol's own production) more than half of Repsol's supply requirements are met.

In the private sector the largest company is Cepsa (Compañía Española de Petróleos SA; owned mainly by Banco Central Hispano and the French company Elf-Aquitaine). Cepsa is a vertically integrated company involved in production (for example in Venezuela), transportation, refining, petrochemicals and distribution, as well as non-oil-related activities. In refining it has an effective crude oil refining capacity of 18.5 million tonnes split between three refineries, one in Santa Cruz de Tenerife, one in San Roque (Cádiz) and one in Huelva (the result of the acquisition of Ertoil in 1991). The latter two are the centres of Cepsa's petrochemical operations (including asphalt and carbon black production). Faced with the prospect of increased competition, the company first diversified into non-oil-related activities (acquiring the operations of the food and drinks companies Aguas de Lanjarón and Condepols in 1984), and then sought alliances with foreign companies refocusing on its core business of oil refining, lubricants and petrochemicals. In essence, Cepsa is a regional oil company in the European Union with interests in Portugal, France and Spain.

The other private oil refiner is BP Petromed (Petróleos del Mediterráneo SA) acquired from the Banco Banesto Group in 1991. The acquisition not only gave BP a refinery at Castellón but also entitled it to 9 per cent of the assets of Campsa, including use of the oil pipeline system and some 330 service stations.

5.2.2 *Oil production and resources*

Despite substantial exploration, domestic oil production remains minimal (less than 2 per cent of supplies to refineries in 1993), with the bulk of crude oil supplies (52.4 million tonnes in 1992) being met by imports (49 million tonnes in 1993). In 1992 Repsol Exploración (formally Hispanoil) produced 11.2 million tonnes of petroleum equivalent (mtpe) oil and gas (over 90 per cent oil and condensates), less than 10 per cent coming from within Spain in 1993. Exploration first succeeded in oil production in Spain as early as 1900 at Huidobro (Burgos). But large-scale exploration did not really begin until legislation was passed in 1958 (Hydrocarbon Law), which reserved 3.5 million hectares of land for exploration and provided incentives for foreign companies. Even then exploration was not very intensive, resulting in only a small quantity of oil being produced in 1964 from the La Lora region (Burgos), which was used by local industry. The 1958 legislation was fundamentally changed in 1974 and with higher oil prices there was much greater investment in oil exploration, involving both foreign and national oil companies. However, few commercial reserves have been discovered. Oil production rose from 0.2 million tonnes in 1972 to 2 million tonnes in 1974, then peaked at only 2.98 million tonnes in 1983. Since then oil production has fallen back to less than 1 million tonnes (1993). Almost all the oil produced comes from the offshore field on the continental shelf of Tarragona (Casablanca field) and very small quantities from both onshore and offshore in País Vasco (Ayoluengo and Gaviota fields, which are being converted into storage facilities for natural gas). The most promising onshore geological areas are the Guadalquivir Valley and the sub-Pyrenees basins.

5.2.3 *Oil refining*

Oil refining is divided between the mixed public/private sector company Repsol Petróleo (including Petronor), which accounts for about 60 per cent of capacity, and two private companies. There are nine crude oil refineries (excluding a small specialist refinery owned by Asfaltos Españoles, Aesa, owned jointly by Cepsa and the Repsol group) with an effective capacity of 62 million tonnes (Figure 5.2 and Table 5.4). The first oil refinery was installed by Cepsa in 1930 in Tenerife, outside the control of the state oil monopoly Campsa. In 1944 Campsa authorised a refinery at Escombreras (Cartagena) that began operating in 1949. No further refineries were added until the 1960s, when refineries were built at Puertollano, Huelva, La Coruña, Bilbao, Algeciras and Castellón. By 1975 the industry had grown to roughly its present size.

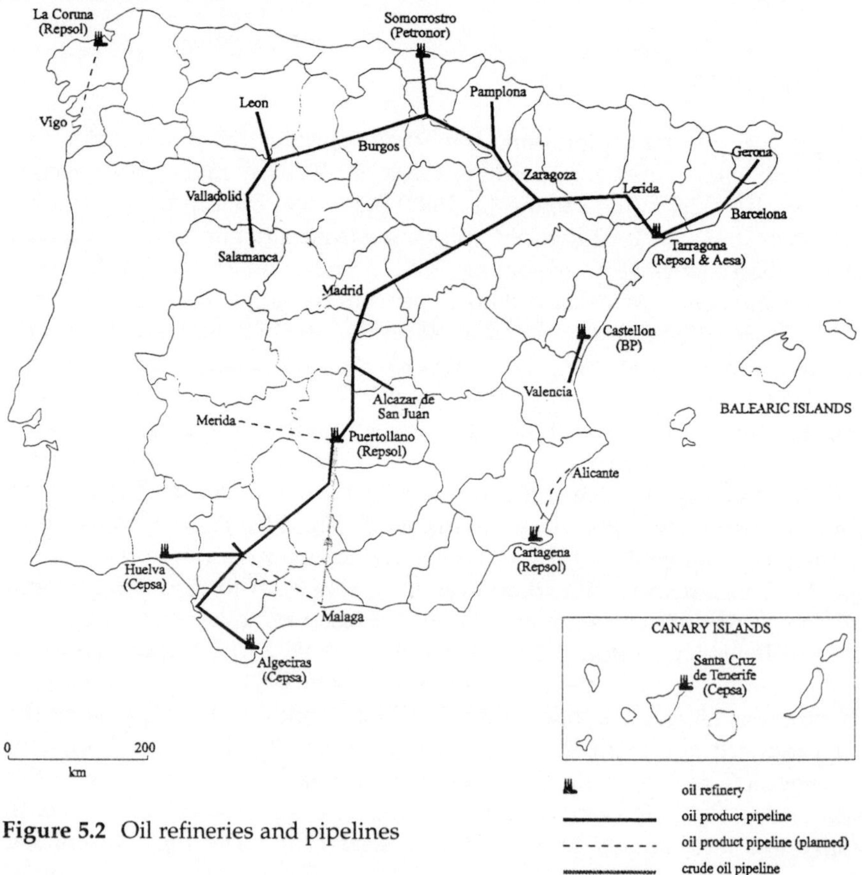

Figure 5.2 Oil refineries and pipelines

Table 5.4 Distribution of oil refining capacity, 1991

Company	Refinery	Authorised capacity	Effective capacity
Repsol Petróleo	Puertollano	7.0	6.0
	Tarragona	11.0	8.0
	Cartagena	10.0	5.0
	La Coruña	7.0	6.0
	Repsol sub total	35.0	25.0
Petronor	Somorrostro, Bilbao	12.0	11.0
Cepsa	San Roque	8.0	8.0
	Tenerife	8.0	6.5
	Huelva	4.0	4.0
	Cepsa sub total	20.0	18.5
Petromed	Castellón	6.0	6.0
Aesa*	Tarragona	1.4	1.5
Total		74.4	62.0

Figures in millions of tonnes; output of all oil products

* Aesa is a subsidiary of Repsol, it processes crude oil for manufacturing asphalt

Source: Aserpetrol 1992

Adjustment to the refining crisis of the early 1980s was slow, although there were organisational changes as multinational companies withdrew. For example, Gulf Oil sold its interest in the Huelva refinery to Unión Explosivos Rio Tinto and Exxon sold its interests in Petromed. Refiners reacted to reduced domestic demand by increasing exports, which rose from 2.4 million tonnes in 1980 to 4.9 million tonnes in 1985. Between 1980 and 1986 refining capacity in Spain was reduced by only 7 per cent (MINE 1989) compared with 31 per cent in the European Community. Moreover, there were no refinery closures, unlike in other parts of western Europe where the industry was controlled by multinationals.

Decline in demand was fundamentally a decline in heavy oil products (fuel oil for power stations, etc.), where substitutes and energy savings were possible. In contrast, there was an expansion in demand at the light end of the market (for aviation and motor fuel). Refiners in other countries switched to lighter products by investing large sums of money in upgrading refineries with catalytic cracking facilities able to take advantage of a greater variety of crude oils (increasing flexibility in supply) and able to produce a greater proportion of light-oil products. In Spain this provision of catalytic cracking facilities was slow, despite government measures introduced in 1980 to encourage the restructuring of output (the Refinery Modernisation Plan; Plan de Conversión Refinería).

5.2.4 Oil distribution

Oil distribution in Spain was a state monopoly from the 1920s. Campsa (Compañía Arrendataria del Monopolio de Petróleos SA) was founded in 1927 by José Calvo Sotelo to administer a monopoly in oil (Monopolio Español de Petróleos), supervised by the Ministry of Economy and Finance. This monopoly covered the whole of Spain except the Canary Islands, Ceuta and Melilla, where multinational companies were able to market oil products. All oil sold in Spain (except in the excluded areas) was thenceforth sold through Campsa. The objective was to increase state tax revenues and to protect the oil industry from foreign domination. Campsa remained primarily concerned with oil refining and distribution, with little interest in downstream integration into petrochemicals.

Campsa was one of Spain's largest companies by value of sales, distributing and marketing oil in Spain (outside the Canary Islands, Ceuta and Melilla). The company owned an extensive supply network, a large transport fleet (including road, rail and sea transport) and all of the country's oil pipelines. A crude oil pipeline supplies the refinery at Puertollano from Málaga and product pipelines link the main industrial areas with refineries, providing a competitive advantage in distribution for those companies with access to this system. Campsa owned about one-third of the service stations in 1989 and branded most of the others, which were run by private concessionaires.

Membership of the European Community required the break-up of the monopoly of Campsa. In 1984 ownership of the monopoly was transferred to Campsa and ownership of Campsa was divided among all the major oil companies in Spain according to their refinery capacity. This left INH with a controlling share. Campsa was eventually broken up in September 1991, Repsol acquired two-thirds of the assets of Campsa (and the trade name of Campsa), Cepsa-Elf a quarter and BP Petromed 9 per cent. The company Campsa was formally wound-up in February 1992 (the Ley de Ordenación del Sector Petróleo 1992 harmonising the law governing the oil industry with that in the EC). From June 1992, Repsol and all the other shareholders in Campsa began selling from their refineries to the service stations linked to them and direct to clients. From January 1993 all aspects of the oil market were liberalised, including imports, distribution and marketing. This ended the distinction between the former Campsa network of service stations (in which there were 3,718 stations) and the so-called 'parallel' network (of 1,712 stations) through which imported oil could be distributed.

In comparison with the size of the market, there were relatively few service stations in Spain (only 2,600 in 1970). The Campsa monopoly had been slow to increase its number, since it had benefited from the very high volume of sales per station. Moreover, foreign multinational companies were inhibited from entering the Spanish market during the run up to liberalisation. During this period Spanish companies were refurbishing and expanding their service station networks, while sites for foreign companies were hard to obtain. Nevertheless, foreign companies managed to buy holdings in Spanish oil companies, thereby gaining access to the pipeline network.

Foreign companies began to establish service stations at the end of the 1980s. Under a new Road Law (Ley de Carreteras) the minimum distance between service stations was reduced (by about a half) and anyone could apply to the Ministry of Industry and Energy to operate one. At the beginning of 1994 there were still relatively few service stations in Spain (5,500 compared with over 25,000 in France and 20,000 in the UK). It is estimated that a further 200 to 250 service stations a year until the end of the century will be opened, taking the number of stations up to between 6,500 and 7,000 by the year 2000. In July 1993 Repsol owned 2,563 service stations (47.9 per cent of the market, selling under the brand names Repsol, Campsa and Petronor), Cepsa-Elf 987 (18.5 per cent of the market) and BP Oil 246 (4.6 per cent of the market) (Casamayor 1993). Total (which was the first to break the monopoly of Campsa) was seeking to have about 200 service stations (5 per cent of the market) by the year 2000. BP opened its first service station in Valencia in November 1989 through the company BPMED; by the end of the century it hoped to have about 400 stations in Spain, controlling 10 per cent of the market. Agip and Texaco opened their first service stations in Madrid in 1990 and Mobil formed a joint company with the drinks firm Larios to establish a network of service stations in Andalucía.

Despite the difficulties of market entry, multinationals operating in Spain that did not have an interest in a Spanish refiner had already gained almost 10 per cent of the petrol and diesel oil retail market by the first quarter of 1993 and competition was growing. Until 1991 it was difficult to find a foreign emblem on a service station in Spain because of the monopoly held by Campsa. With the ending of the monopoly, Agip, BP, Fina, Mobil, Petrogal, Shell, Texaco and Total were all trading in Spain in 1992.

The response by domestic oil companies to the increased competition has been to improve the efficiency and quality of provision in the domestic market (for example, with improvements to service stations), diversification of the range of services and products offered, alliances with foreign multinationals and investment outside Spain. The one strategic alliance that did not materialise was the inclusion of the Petromed group within the ambit of Spanish-owned companies (an initial merger between Cepsa and Petromed was effectively halted at the end of the 1980s by the failure of Banco Central and Banco Banesto to reach an agreement themselves to merge). Instead, Petromed reached an agreement in 1987 with BP to create a mixed distribution and marketing company in Spain (BPMED), giving BP the potential to gain access to the Campsa pipeline and a network of petrol stations. This agreement was criticised as breaking the objective of the new Campsa to retain the dominance of Spanish companies in marketing oil in Spain, once again illustrating the rivalries between Spanish companies. Alliances with foreign multinationals have included the participation of Elf in Cepsa, a joint venture initiated in 1989 by Cepsa with BP to produce and market maleic anhydride (used to produce plastic resins, lubricants and agricultural chemicals) and the merger of Cepsa's business in resins with the European activities of Dai Nippon. In terms of foreign investment, both Repsol and Cepsa have begun to look outside Spain for service stations. Cepsa has owned service stations in Portugal since the 1960s and has expanded into France. Repsol has service stations in Portugal and has bought service stations in Britain (where it operates under the name Anglo Oil) and is seeking to expand into France (Repsol 1993).

To manage the primary oil distribution system for oil products the government created the Compañía Logística de Hidrocarburos (CLH) in 1992, which controls one of the most important oil distribution networks in Europe with over 3,400 km of pipeline and 36 supply depots handling 30 million tonnes of oil products a year (Figure 5.2). Initially, the company was owned along the lines outlined above on the break-up of the former Campsa, but in September 1993 Shell acquired a 5 per cent holding, leaving Repsol with 61.5 per cent, Cepsa-Elf with 25.1 per cent and BP Oil with 7.6 per cent (Casamayor 1993). Other multinationals may try to follow Shell, although Repsol is unlikely to sacrifice its controlling stake. Effectively, CLH is in an oligopoly position with significant supply advantages in the interior of the country, where most operators buy oil from the nearest CLH distribution centre. The company applies distance-linked tariffs for transporting products, varying according to their point of origin and destination.

5.2.5 *State intervention in the oil industry*

The oil industry has been very tightly controlled by a plethora of state intervention, exemplified by the state monopoly over the purchase of most important oil products and the sale of oil products in mainland Spain and the Balearic Islands (through the Monopolio de Petróleo and Campsa respectively). Other forms of intervention have covered: i) ownership and participation in oil companies; ii) determination of oil input prices to refineries; iii) the requirement that all of the oil from Hispanoil was purchased by refineries; iv) sources of supply regulated through a commercial quota system (the percentage of oil products that the refineries were obliged to buy through the state, the 'Cuota de Comercio'); v) the requirement that crude oil was transported in Spanish registered vessels; vi) control over the market price for many oil products (determined in part by the level of taxes applied to the ex-works price, VAT, the special oil tax (Impuesto Especial de Hidrocarburos and Renta de Petróleos); and vii) a broad influence through energy policy.

Thus state intervention moulded the development of the industry. In exploration, companies benefited by having a tied market. Production was a very profitable activity from the early 1970s to the early 1980s. However, the lack of vertical integration in the 1980s meant that profits from refining could not be used to support production. In refining, state intervention prevented vertical and horizontal integration of the industry, as oil companies concerned themselves mainly with refining Vertical integration allowed multinational companies to take advantage of different levels of profitability at different stages of production. Horizontal integration in multinational companies allowed economies of scale and in recession enabled rationalisation to proceed with selective closure and investment programmes. This was not possible in Spain.

State intervention has also been criticised as: i) protecting relatively small companies operating refineries well below an economically competitive size; ii) impeding responsiveness to market conditions (Spanish refineries generally produced heavy oil products that were high in sulphur and generally of relatively low value); iii) protecting inefficiency, especially high-cost structures, as the pricing policy adopted by the administration was based on a formula that covered production costs; and v) leaving experience of distribution and marketing exclusively to Campsa, which itself had little experience of marketing in a competitive environment.

Liberalisation of the oil industry swept most of this regulation away. Oil product prices began to be freed from 1988 with most becoming free by 1990, subject to the administration being able to fix a maximum price. Within this constraint oil companies are free to set their own prices. In practice, official maximum prices for oil products became the market prices in 1993 (perhaps reflecting the oligopolistic market structure). Moreover, the national oil company Repsol has been partially privatised (the state holding being reduced to about 25 per cent in 1994).

5.2.6 *The oil industry and the European Community*

Membership of the European Community required the harmonisation of Spanish energy policy with that of the EC, including the policy to reduce dependence on oil and imported energy, environmental legislation, compliance with EC industrial policy in restructuring oil refining and EC competition policy in reorganising Campsa and breaking-up the oil monopoly. In restructuring oil refining the EC (EC of twelve) cut its refining capacity by 36 per cent (from 934 million tonnes to 598 million tonnes in the mid 1980s) and completely closed 44 refineries between 1977/79 and the beginning of 1987. During the same period in Spain there were no complete refinery closures and capacity was cut by only 14 per cent (Fernández 1987). The Spanish refiners' association, Aserpetrol, argued that the dispersed pattern of refineries in Spain would lead to significant increases in product distribution costs if any one refinery were closed. Capacity reductions were made largely by the public sector, it being difficult for private firms to reduce capacity below a certain level without plant closures and the withdrawal of firms from the sector. More contentious than capacity reductions were the negotiations over the liberalisation of the oil market required by the EC. As outlined above, the prospect of a more liberal market acted as a catalyst for many of the changes that occurred in the industry.

5.3 Gas

The gas market is divided into town gas, liquefied gas (GLP) and natural gas. Further growth in gas supplies will come from natural gas. Natural gas was favoured in the Third and Fourth National Energy Plans as a means of diversifying energy supplies and because there are domestic reserves. A national gas grid was established, gas tariffs set that were competitive with other fuels and the gas sector reorganised to leave one major mixed (public/private) national gas supply company, Gas Natural–Enagas.

5.3.1 *Town gas*

Town (manufactured) gas is on the decline as supplies are replaced by natural gas. Town gas is produced from coal (which was the source of the first town gas produced in Spain, in Barcelona in 1842), oil and natural gas, and distributed over relatively small areas to essentially domestic (three-quarters of consumption in 1992) and small commercial users. In 1955 about 0.4 million tonnes of coal were used to produce town gas but from the mid 1950s many gas manufacturers began to switch to oil. The spread of liquefied gas in the late 1950s limited the further growth of town gas. A number of small companies manufactured gas (some 16 private companies in the mid 1980s), serving most of the large towns in Spain. In the late 1980s there was a process of rationalisation between the town gas suppliers and Enagas (for example, in 1988 Gas Madrid sold its interests around Valladolid to Enagas in return for the gas activities of Enagas in Madrid). Now most town gas companies are subsidiaries of Gas Natural–Enagas. In 1992 2.2 billion therms of town gas were produced, down from 3.95 billion therms in 1980 (Sedigas 1994). Gas Natural SDG (in Madrid), Gas Andalucía (in Málaga) and Gesa (in Palma de Mallorca) were among the largest suppliers. Town gas supplies are generally being converted to natural gas. For example, in 1992 the conversion was completed in Zaragoza and in 1993 in Santander and Valladolid. One new application of gas produced from coal is being developed in Puertollano (Ciudad Real) where coal will be used in a new integrated gasification combined cycle power station (capacity 335 MW). On completion in 1996, the Elcogas facility (being developed jointly by 11 European power and engineering companies, notably Spanish power groups and Electricité de France) will become the largest of its type in the world, part financed by the EU under its Thermie programme (Endesa 1994). Although the technology is currently expensive, it does offer one possible future use for coal, especially when natural gas supplies become short.

5.3.2 *Liquefied gas*

Liquefied gas (Gas Licuados del Petróleo–GLP) is butane/propane gas that liquefies under moderate pressure. Liquefied gas was first imported by Campsa in bottles from France in 1934. In 1953 GLP began to be produced at the Cepsa refinery in Tenerife and in 1955 at the Repesa refinery at Cartagena. Consumption of GLP increased from only 900 tonnes in 1957 to 2.5 million tonnes (34.3 billion therms) in 1992 (of which about three-quarters was produced in Spain), serving almost 15 million consumers (domestic consumers accounting for almost three-quarters of consumption). Although with the spread of natural gas supplies and the increasing penetration of electricity the market for liquefied gas is threatened, the limitations of the natural gas supply network will ensure a continued significant market for liquefied gas.

The market for liquefied gas is dominated by Repsol Butano, the largest liquefied gas distributor in Europe. It had a monopoly over the import, distribution and marketing of liquefied gas in Spain (except in the Canary Islands, Ceuta and Melilla) until the liberalisation of these activities in September 1992. Liberalisation meant that government fixing of buying prices from Spanish refineries was eliminated and the fixed price system governing sales prices to the public was replaced by a maximum price regime. The company was established in 1987 from Gas Butano, which itself had been formed in 1957 (originally with 50 per cent participation from Campsa and the other 50 per cent by INI, Cepsa, Texaco and Standard Oil of California; later it became wholly owned by INH). Under the Gas Protocol (Protocol de Intenciónes para el Desarrollo de Gas en España 1985) and the Gas Plans (Planes de Gasificación), Repsol Butano also participated in the distribution of natural gas (acquiring interests in local distributors such as Gas Madrid SA). In 1991 these interests in natural gas were transferred to the new company, Gas Natural SDG.

5.3.3 *Natural gas*

Natural gas consumption has been expanding rapidly as the gas grid has been extended and energy pricing policy has been set so as to ensure competitiveness (the maximum price of natural gas to consumers is set by the government and there is a uniform system of tariffs across the country). Expansion of natural gas has been viewed as part of the strategy of diversifying energy supplies and reducing reliance on imports. However, in 1993 only 10 per cent of supplies came from domestic resources (Gas Natural

SDG 1994) and unless new supplies of natural gas are discovered and exploited the industry will be wholly dependent on imports by the turn of the century, a significant proportion of which will be drawn from politically unstable areas.

Expansion of the natural gas market has been much more rapid than forecast in the Third National Energy Plan. The Gas Supply Plan (Plan de Gasificación 1986) envisaged the supply of natural gas increasing to 53.8 billion therms in 1992, of which 15.5 billion therms (29 per cent) were to come from domestic supplies. The Gas Plan (Plan del Gas), approved in 1988, predicted growth to 6.3 per cent of energy requirements (56 billion therms by 1992) and 7 per cent by 2000. Under the Fourth PEN, natural gas is envisaged to be supplying 12 per cent of national energy requirements by the year 2000 (151 billion therms, 90 per cent to industrial outlets, especially electricity plants, where it will largely replace fuel oil). In practice, gas consumption reached 55.5 billion therms in 1989 and 69.9 billion therms in 1992, of which only 12.1 billion therms came from domestic sources (Sedigas 1994).

Despite the rapid expansion of natural gas, its share in primary energy consumption remains small in comparison with other EU countries. In 1993 consumption remained at about the same level as in 1992, representing 6.5 per cent of primary energy consumption, compared with an EU average of 19 per cent. The bulk of natural gas (about 80 per cent in 1993) is consumed by industry (especially power stations, integrated steelworks and fertilizer plants) and commercial customers.

The natural gas supply industry is dominated by the mixed (public/private) company Gas Natural–Enagas (headquartered in Barcelona), the result of the takeover by Gas Natural SDG (in which Repsol and La Caixa were the major shareholders) of the state enterprise Enagas in mid 1994. On the formation of the company (in which Repsol held 45 per cent of the capital, La Caixa 25.5 per cent and INH 9 per cent) it became the third largest gas group in Europe (after British Gas and Gaz de France) supplying 90 per cent of the market in Spain. Before the takeover was completed, agreements were reached over gas supplies to the electricity utilities and the Segamo pipeline was transferred from Enagas to a new state company Segane (owned 91 per cent by INH).

Reorganisation of the gas sector was sponsored by the government. It began with the merger of Gas Madrid and Catalana de Gas in 1991 to form Gas Natural SDG and the acquisition by this company of the natural gas distribution interests of Repsol Butano. In 1992 Gas Natural SDG had one-quarter of the natural gas market and a larger domestic customer base, while Enagas had two-thirds of the market, supplying essentially large industrial customers. Most of the rest of the market (essentially in Asturias, Aragón and País Vasco) was in the hands of Gas de Euskadi.

Enagas (Empresa Nacional de Gas) was set up in 1972 as a wholly owned subsidiary of INI (then later transferred to INH). It was formed to acquire and import natural gas, to construct a gas pipeline network and to distribute natural gas in Spain (a monopoly in which there were clearly areas of conflict with the existing monopoly conferred on Gas Butano for GLP supplies). Thus it acquired the installations of a former company named Gas Natural, which had been set up in 1965 by Compañía Catalana de Gas y Electricidad (together with a number of Spanish banks and the multinational Exxon). This former company Gas Natural first imported gas in 1969 from Exxon in Algeria. A regasification plant was built in Barcelona (which began supplying natural gas in 1971 imported from Algeria and Libya) and the Barcelona town gas network was converted to natural gas. Other companies (existing town gas companies, for example Catalana de Gas, Gas de Euskadi and Gas Madrid) were also involved in the distribution of natural gas within particular localities, mainly to domestic and commercial consumers.

The framework for the development of natural gas supplies in Spain was established in 1985 by the Gas Protocol. Under this protocol Enagas assumed responsibility for: i) constructing the trunk gas pipelines; ii) the regasification plants in Huelva, Cartagena and Mallorca; iii) providing the supply of natural gas; and iv) supplying large industrial consumers (those using over 10 million therms per year) directly, except in Cataluña and País Vasco, where Catalana de Gas and Gas de Euskadi assumed this responsibility and that of developing the respective regional gas supply networks. Small industrial users and the domestic market were supplied by the various gas distribution companies. Gas-supply tariffs were unified throughout Spain (the tariff regime is to be revised in 1995). Further rationalisation of the industry was achieved through the transfer of resources between companies. For example, the rights that Enagas had in various gas distributors (for example a 33 per cent stake in Gas Navarra) were transferred to Gas Butano.

5.3.4 *Natural gas resources and supplies*

Domestic gas supplies met only 10 per cent of demand in 1993. Existing supplies continue to fall and are only likely to last until the end of the century. The first natural gas supply in Spain came from the Castillo field in the province of Alava in 1963. Production from the Serrablo field in the Pyrenees (province of Huesca) started in 1982 and supplies were connected to the national gas grid in 1984. In 1992 the field had virtually ceased production. In 1986 the Gaviota field (offshore from Bermeo, Vizcaya; estimated reserves 12 billion cubic metres) was connected to the gas grid and now constitutes the source of almost all domestic natural gas (supplying over 1 mtpe of gas, 87 per cent of domestic production in 1992). In southern Spain, the Guadalquivir field (Ciervo, Palancares and Marisma) has estimated reserves of 0.46 billion cubic metres and was connected to the

Huelva–Seville gas pipeline in 1990. In 1992 the field supplied 0.15 mtpe of gas, 12 per cent of domestic production. In the Gulf of Cádiz there are reserves estimated at 3 billion cubic metres but there are no current plans for the development of this field.

Algeria and Libya have been the source of foreign gas supplies (in 1993 two-thirds of all gas supplies were imported from Algeria and nearly one-quarter from Libya). Supplies from Algeria will be further enhanced by the completion of a gas supply pipeline (the Segamo pipeline) from Algeria (Hassi R'Mel gas fields), through Morocco to Spain in 1995. The first phase of this project is designed to supply 10 billion cubic metres of gas a year (rising to 20 billion in a second phase). In an attempt to diversify supplies, agreements have been made to take supplies from Norway. In 1993 some 3 per cent of gas supplies came from Norway through the Lacq–Calahorra pipeline (the pipeline has a capacity to supply 20 billion therms, equivalent to 13 per cent of total forecast requirements up to the year 2000). A further agreement has been made to take supplies from the Norwegian offshore Troll gas field (which will supply gas via the Zeepipe gas pipeline to Zeebrugge) from the mid 1990s (Enagas had a contract to take 1 billion cubic metres of associated gas from Norwegian oil fields in the two years March 1994 to 1996). Further gas supplies may be drawn from other countries, including the former Soviet Union and Nigeria.

Within Spain natural gas is distributed through the trunk gas grid which, at the end of 1993, was 18,000 km in length, linking all the major industrial areas in Spain (Figure 5.3). In 1994 it was estimated that a further pta 1,000 billion needed to be invested to complete the gas supply programme and extend the gas grid to 27,000 km by the year 2000 (although the pace at which this programme develops will be dependent on the growth of gas demand). The grid was first expanded in the 1970s following the increasing price of oil. Difficulties over supply contracts and institutional factors (relating to established gas producers) slowed growth. The initial network comprised 1,135 km of trunk pipeline (72 kg/cm^2) and 500 km of primary pipeline (16 and 4 kg/cm^2). The network joined: i) Barcelona Ebro–Tivisa–Zaragoza (with a branch to Serrablo) ii) Tudela–Logroño–Haro (with branches to Burgos and Vitoria, and the Gaviota field); and iii) Barcelona–Reus–Tarragona–Tivisa–Castellón–Valencia. A further 118 km were brought into service in 1986 linking Bermeo and Lemona, and Haro to Burgos. In 1987 Madrid was linked to the pipeline from Burgos, and in 1988 Burgos–Santander–Oviedo were linked. In 1991 the link between Seville and Madrid came into service. The network has also been linked to the French one through the Larrau pass to Lacq, thereby tapping the European grid and sources of supply in the former Soviet Union. Further plans include linking Cartagena through Murcia to Valencia, developing the network in Galicia and linking Córdoba through Jaén to Granada. Of most strategic importance is the Segamo pipeline, construction of which began in 1993 and is planned to be completed as far as Córdoba by 1996. Beyond that

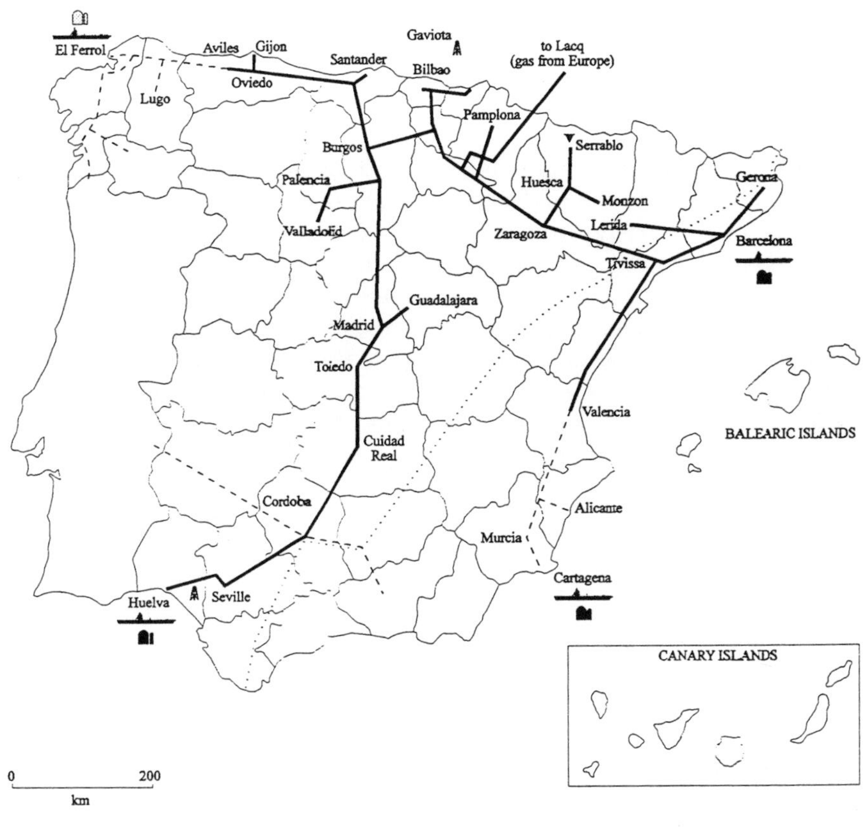

Figure 5.3 Natural Gas

date it is planned to extend the pipeline across Spain with connections into France and Portugal. In addition, underground storage facilities are planned near Puertollano.

The gas network draws on imported liquefied natural gas, which is processed in one of three regasification plants. A plant in Barcelona supplied the whole gas network until the late 1980s, when two further regasification plants were brought on stream; one in Cartagena (completed in 1988) to supply the local market (including a fertilizer plant) and one in Huelva (completed in 1988) to supply the gas link to Seville (and a fertilizer plant in Huelva). In 1994 further plants were under construction in El Ferrol and Setubal (south of Lisbon in Portugal).

5.4 Electricity

Following rapid expansion in the 1960s and 1970s (Table 5.5) the electricity generating industry has undergone a process of restructuring, involving diversification of energy sources (initially to coal and nuclear energy and more recently to gas, with a considerable reduction in the use of fuel oil), measures to increase efficiency and improve financial structures, and major organisational change. The principal challenges in the 1990s will be those arising from the Single European Energy Market, adjustments to complete the restructuring necessary under the new electricity law (Ley de Ordenación del Sector Eléctrico 1994) and financing the new round of investment in electricity generation.

Serious financial problems were encountered in the early 1980s, which had their roots in wildly over-optimistic forecasts of growth in demand made at the beginning of the 1970s. Thus the National Electricity Plan (Plan Eléctrico Nacional 1972–81) sought major new facilities. Demand was forecast to be 117,800 GWh in 1978 (actual net consumption 82,359 GWh), rising

Table 5.5 Electricity consumption and structure of electricity generation, 1950-93

Year	Generation %			Total (GWh)	Net consumption
	Hydro	Thermal	Nuclear		GWh
1950	73	27	0	6,853	—
1960	84	16	0	18,614	14,625
1970	49	49	2	56,490	45,300
1975	32	59	9	82,515	69,271
1980	28	67	5	110,483	92,006
1985	26	52	22	127,363	105,579
1990	17	48	35	153,970	131,416
1991	17	48	35	159,638	135,729
1992	13	53	35	161,105	136,885
1993	16	49	35	159,553	137,131

Renewable energy sources are included in thermal capacity

In 1993 of total electricity generated by members of Unesa, 44 per cent came from domestic coal and anthracite, 18 per cent from domestic brown lignite, 12 per cent from black lignite, 15 per cent from imported coal and lignite, 10 per cent from oil and 0.6 per cent from oil and gas

Source: UNESA 1994

to 154,600 GWh in 1981 (actual net consumption 93,196 GWh). This plan led to major investment (especially in nuclear power), creating over-capacity in the industry in the late 1970s and early 1980s for which the Spanish consumer is still paying. Furthermore, the moratorium on nuclear energy in 1982 left some companies with no return on their investment in the nuclear facilities that had been frozen. Much of the investment by the electricity utilities was financed from outside the industry, increasing exposure to high interest rates and exchange rate fluctuations. Thus increased debt coincided with slower than expected growth in demand.

An important measure to stabilise the finances of the industry was the introduction in 1987 of a set of regulations governing the industry, embodied in the so-called Stable Legal Framework (Marco Legal Estable, Real Decreto 1538), establishing a new electricity tariff-making system which came into effect in 1988 (amended in December 1993).

Completion of the development cycle begun in the early 1970s increased electricity demand and financial restructuring returned most of the industry to an operating profit. However, the industry continued to carry a heavy capital debt that amounted to pta 4,000 million in 1993, a large part of which resulted from the moratorium on nuclear power.

A new cycle of investment to begin in the mid 1990s was implied by increasing electricity demand in the late 1980s (with demand for an additional 3,000 MW by 1995 and between 7,000 and 10,000 MW by the year 2000; Luisa Huidobro 1988; Trinacado 1988; PEN 1991). Plans made in the mid 1980s turned out to be very close in their estimates for the growth in demand over the period to 1992. Thus the Third National Energy Plan envisaged electricity consumption growing at 3.3 per cent annually in the period 1984 to 1992, actual growth turning out at 3.5 per cent. However, growth was higher in the late 1980s, leading to higher forecasts in the Fourth PEN (3.47 per cent annual average growth to the year 2000). As a result of the slowdown in the growth of demand for electricity from 1990 and the economic difficulties faced by the electricity utilities, the new investment cycle will be slowed (net electricity consumption grew by only 0.9 and 0.2 per cent in 1992 and 1993 respectively; UNESA 1994).

In the late 1970s and early 1980s electricity generation and generating capacity were switched to non-oil energy sources. According to Redesa, of 150,886 GWh of electricity produced in 1993, 42 per cent was derived from coal, 37 per cent from nuclear sources, 16 per cent from hydroelectricity and only 3 per cent from oil (oil having provided 21 per cent in 1983). Figures from UNESA for 1993 (UNESA 1994) show that 159,553 GWh of electricity were generated (Table 5.5): 78,389 from coal, oil, gas and renewable energy sources (49 per cent; over 80 per cent of which came from coal with only 10 per cent purely from oil compared with the 37.4 per cent from oil and gas in 1980); 56,060 GWh from nuclear stations (35 per cent compared with 5 per cent in 1980); and 25,104 GWh from hydroelectricity (16 per cent compared with 28 per cent in 1980). Net consumption in 1993 was 137,131 GWh. The use of fuel oil increased in 1991 and 1992, due mainly to the increased demands placed on thermal stations by low hydroelectricity production and the continuing low price of oil. In terms of installed capacity (46,385 MW in 1993), in 1993 47 per cent was in thermal stations (over half of this in coal-fired stations), 37 per cent in hydroelectric stations and 16 per cent in nuclear stations (Table 5.6).

Liberalisation of the energy market is gradually opening the door to increased foreign investment. For example, in 1992 the Belgian company Tractebel had a small holding in Iberduero and the German company Rheinisch-Westfalisches Elektrizitätswerk (RWE) a small holding in Unión Eléctrica-Fenosa. The latter was the first entry of foreign capital into Spain's electricity industry, foreign investment having been cautious of the financial problems in the industry and the uncertainty over its future. Spanish electricity utilities have responded to the more competitive environment by increasing efficiency, diversification (reinforcing core businesses and using existing expertise, for example in telecommunications, environmental and water services), organisational concentration, investment abroad (for example by the Endesa and Iberdrola groups in Portugal and Argentina). International alliances (such as that of Endesa with RWE and La Electricidad de Caracas) allow Spanish companies to join in consortia to bid for projects outside Spain and facilitate future participation in overseas privatisations.

Table 5.6 Structure of electricity generating capacity, 1950–93

Year	Installed capacity %			Installed capacity (MW)
	Hydro	Thermal	Nuclear	Total
1950	75	25	0	2,553
1960	70	30	0	6,567
1970	61	38	1	17,924
1975	47	49	4	25,467
1980	44	52	4	31,144
1985	35	51	14	41,467
1990	37	47	16	45,606
1991	37	47	16	45,794
1992	37	47	16	46,307
1993	37	47	16	46,385

Figures are at 31 December of each year

Renewable energy sources are included in thermal capacity

In 1993 of all thermal capacity belonging to members of Unesa: 53 per cent coal-fired, 37 per cent oil-fired and 10 per cent oil-gas

Source: UNESA 1994

5.4.1 *The structure of electricity supply*

Government policy has sought to create a national electricity industry centred on two large Spanish-owned groups, the mixed public/private group Endesa and Iberdrola. Together these accounted for 80 per cent of the market in 1994, leaving two independent private companies, Hidroeléctrica del Cantábrico and Unión Eléctrica-Fenosa (Table 5.7). A new electricity law passed in 1994 (Ley de Ordenación del Sector Eléctrico, June 1994) will promote the liberalisation of the electricity industry, ensuring that: i) the overall co-ordination of the electricity industry remains in the hands of a single authority; ii) there remains a single national tariff structure (and hence the need to transfer resources from low-cost to high-cost generation areas); iii) the separation of each stage in electricity supply: generation, distribution and sales to final consumers (a move opposed by the private electricity utilities); iv) competitive tendering for new power stations and the opportunity for these to be built and operated by companies outside the electricity sector; and v) financial reforms relating to the bad debt associated with the moratorium on nuclear power stations (Alvarez 1994; Celaya 1994).

The first electricity for public consumption in Spain was produced in Barcelona in 1875. From that time until the end of the century numerous small companies developed, centred on the major towns. During the twentieth century the economics of the industry led to the formation of larger companies. At the beginning of the 1980s the electricity sector was formed principally by ten vertically integrated (generation, distribution and sales), regionally based, companies (involving substantial holdings by the banks) plus the state company Endesa (Empresa Nacional de Electricidad, formed in 1944), which was only involved in generation, and from which the private companies were obliged to buy all of the electricity it generated.

Reorganisation of the electricity industry was necessary as a result of the fragmented pattern of production, arising from the historical evolution of the industry, and as a result of the serious financial problems facing the industry in the early 1980s. In 1985 the state created Redesa (Red Eléctrica de España) to take control over the high-tension electricity grid. There were also mergers and asset swaps (including interests in power stations). For example, in 1984 the three largest companies (Endesa, Hidrola and Iberduero) agreed to take over smaller loss-making companies in exchange for government assistance. In addition, many companies were forced to dispose of assets. For example, Fecsa (Fuerzas Eléctricas de Cataluña), one of the companies in most serious financial difficulties, was forced to sell some of its interests in property and minerals as well as in electricity. The process continued through the 1980s and into the 1990s. For example, in 1992 ERZ acquired the electricity business of Energía e Industrias Aragonesas. A further programme of asset exchanges agreed in December 1993 (including the exchange of installations, markets and shares) should be complete by 1996 (including the sale by Iberdrola to Endesa of all the dis-

Table 5.7 Electricity utilities, 1993

Utilities	Sales (pta billion)	Employment	Capacity (MW)	(%)	Production (GWH)
Empresa Nacional de Electricidad (Endesa)	423	5,629	6,554	(14.1)	40,089
Endesa Group companies					
E.N. Hidroeléctica del Ribagorzana (Enher)	128	1,824	1,730		2,595
Electra de Viesgo	49	1,301	1,080		3,830
Eléctricas Reunidas de Zaragoza (ERZ)	63	1,058	497		1,222
Gas y Electricidad (Gesa)	50	2,091	840		2,916
Unión Eléctrica Canarias (Unelco)	66	2,094	1,179		4,041
Hidroeléctrica de Cataluña (Hidruña)	60	1,032	986	(2.1)	2,050
Endesa group sub total*	779	13,997	11,880	(25.6)	54,693
Endesa associated companies					
Compañía Sevillana de Electricidad	258	6,102	4,457	(9.6)	14,398
Fuerzas Eléctricas de Cataluña (Fecsa)	207	3,321	4,079	(8.8)	11,341
E.N. Eléctrica de Córdoba (Eneco)					
Saltos de Nansa					
Sociedad Eólica de Andalucía					
Iberdrola group	795	14,875	16,714	(36.0)	41,829
Hidroeléctrica del Cantábrico	87	1,034	1,544	(3.3)	7,128
Unión Eléctrica Fenosa	342	5,355	5,406	(11.7)	20,874
Total	2,445	46,759	46,385	(100.0)	156,980

*Endesa group sub total excludes Hidruña, which was acquired from Iberdrola in 1994

Iberdrola group includes figures for Hidruña

Figures for the Endesa group associated companies are for 1992, as are the figures for H. Cantábrico and total sales and employment

The Endesa Group: In 1983 the Endesa group was formed by the acquisition of the electricity utilities owned by INI: Enher, Gesa (which supplies the Ballearic Islands) and Unelco (which supplies the Canary Islands). In 1986 ERZ was acquired. In 1991 the holding in Electra de Viesgo was raised to 87.6 per cent, a 40 per cent holding was acquired in Fecsa, a 33.5 per cent holding in Sevillana, 24.9 per cent in Saltos de Nansa. In 1992 the shareholdings in Fecsa, Sevillana, Fenosa and Saltos de Nansa were raised to 44.9, 33.5, 9.9 and 37.5 per cent respectively. In 1993 the holding in Fecsa was raised to 49 per cent and in 1994 that in Sevillana to 47.5 per cent

Iberdrola: In 1991 Iberduero took over Hidroeléctrica Española (Hidrola) forming one company, Iberdrola SA in 1992. Included in Hidroélectrica Española were Compañía Eléctrica de Langreo, Compañía Eléctrica de Urumea, Electra de Logroño, Fuerzas Eléctricas de Navarra, Vitoriana de Electricidad and Centrales Térmicas del Norte de España

Sources: El País 1994; Endesa 1994; Iberdrola 1994; Celaya 1994

tribution and generation assets of Hidruña, with the exception of the holding in Asco 11 nuclear power station, and the sale to ERZ of the hydroelectricity projects and water rights that Iberdrola owns in the Pyrenees of Aragón, together with all its transmission, production and distribution facilities in Aragón).

Mergers and asset exchanges concentrated the industry around the two companies Endesa and Iberdrola. By the end of 1993 Endesa had embraced many of the larger private companies (Table 5.7). In addition, it had built up major holdings in Fecsa, Sevillana and Saltos de Nansa (described as associate companies). Endesa also owned the coal mining company Encasur and the coal trading company Carboex (in conjunction with Repsol). In 1991 Hidrola (Hidroeléctrica Española) and Iberduero formally agreed to begin to merge, creating the Iberdrola group in 1992 (controlling 50 per cent of national HEP capacity, 36 per cent of total generating capacity, 27 per cent of production and 40 per cent of energy sales in 1993; Iberdrola 1994). By 1994 the only two companies outside these two groups were Hidrocantábrico (5 per cent of the market) and Unión Eléctrica-Fenosa (in which Endesa had a small holding).

Co-ordination of the industry in 1994 was achieved through state control over the high-tension grid, state control over electricity tariffs and a system of compensation for variations in electricity generating costs. Co-ordination of electricity generation and supply in Spain has been the responsibility of Redesa since 1986 (owned jointly by the electricity utilities with majority ownership by the Endesa group). Through Redesa the state controls the high-tension grid and international electricity exchanges. Redesa incorporates electricity into the network according to price, from lowest to highest cost sources (thus optimising supply). Individual utilities can transfer electricity to, or acquire electricity from, the national grid on a swap pool basis, with a flat sale price for the acquiring companies. Nationalisation of the high-tension grid involved compensation to the electricity utilities amounting to pta 61 billion. This represented part of the investment needed to cope with an asset swap programme designed to concentrate electricity production in the hands of companies that had a large market share but insufficient production. For example, Cia Sevillana acquired 33 per cent of the coal-burning Litoral (Almería) plant from Endesa, and 50 MW of the Almaraz nuclear plant from Unión Eléctrica-Fenosa SA (bringing the Sevillana share in this plant up to 670 MW). Secondly, co-ordination is achieved through the private electricity industry utilities association UNESA (Unidad Eléctrica SA). Thirdly, there is a unified system of maximum tariffs fixed by the government (Sistemas de Tarifas Tope Unificadas, established in 1953). Fourthly, the electricity utilities have a contract with Endesa to purchase all of this public company's output. The power purchased is split among the utilities in proportion to their respective share of the end-user market. Finally, co-ordination is achieved through a fund that in view of the uniform pricing structure across the country is used to compensate for the varying costs of electricity generation, distribution and market structures in different parts of the country served by different utilities (administered by the Oficina de Compensaciones de la Energía Eléctrica, Ofico).

5.4.2 Nuclear energy

In 1963 a law on nuclear energy was passed that opened the door to the development of nuclear power in Spain. In the same year authorisation was given for the development of the first nuclear power station (José Cabrera Zorita), which began operating in August 1969. In 1971 Santa María de Geroña and in 1972 Vandellós 1 started operating; these three power stations represented the first generation of nuclear power in Spain (combined generating capacity of 1,200 MW) (Figure 5.4 and Table 5.8).

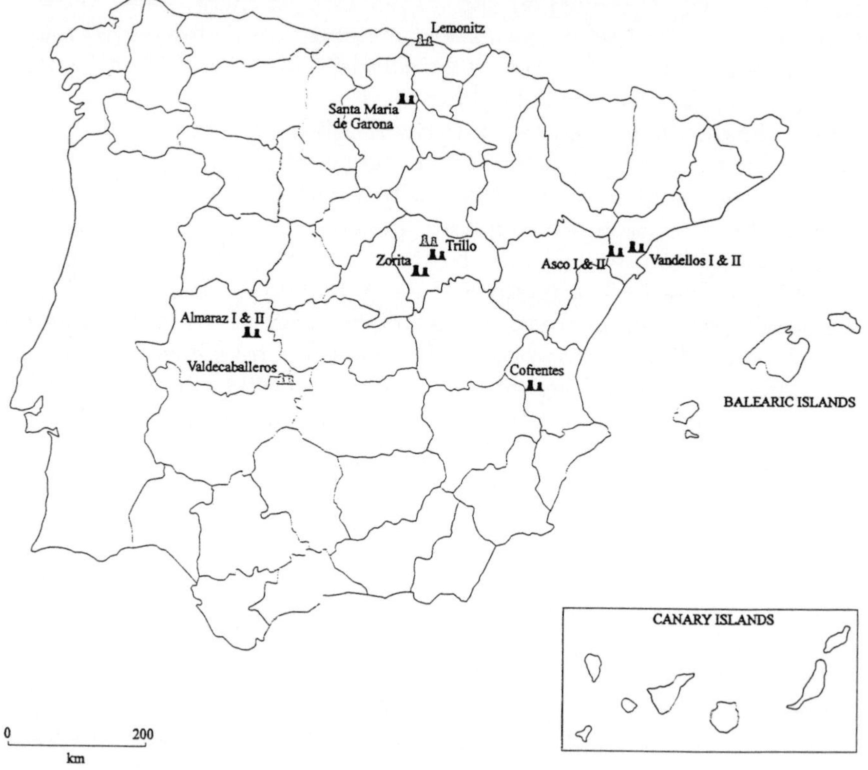

nuclear power station (operational)

nuclear power station (construction frozen)

Figure 5.4 Nuclear power stations

Table 5.8 Nuclear power stations

Power station	Location	Type	Installed capacity (MW)	Authorised	In service	Ownership (1992)
First generation						
José Cabrera	Guadalajara	PWR	160	1963	1969	U.Fenosa
Sta. M. Garoña	Burgos	BWR	460	1963	1971	Iberdrola (50%) E.Viesgo (50%)
Vandellós I	Tarragona	GCR	500	1967	1972*	E.de France (25%) Fecsa (23%) Enher/Endesa (23%) Hidruña (23%) F.E.Segre (6%)
Second generation						
Almaraz I	Cáceres	PWR	930	1971	1981	Iberdrola (53%) C.Sevillana (36%) U.Fenosa (11%)
Almaraz II	Cáceres	PWR	930	1972	1983	As above
Lemóniz I	Vizcaya	PWR	930	1972	Frozen	Iberdrola (100%)
Lemóniz II	Vizcaya	PWR	930	1972	Frozen	Iberdrola (100%)
Ascó I	Tarragona	PWR	930	1972	1983	Fecsa (60%) Endesa (40%)
Ascó II	Tarragona	PWR	930	1972	1985	Fecsa (40%) Endesa (40%) Hidruña (15%) F.E.Segre (5%)
Cofrentes	Valencia	BWR	990	1972	1984	Iberdrola (100%)
Third generation						
Valdecaballeros I	Badajoz	BWR	975	1975	Frozen	Iberdrola (50%) C.Sevillana (50%)
Valdecaballeros II		BWR	975	1975	Frozen	As above
Trillo I	Guadalajara	PWR	1066	1975	1988	U.Fenosa (37%) Iberdrola (49%) H.Cantábrico (8%)
Trillo II		PWR	100	1976	Frozen	Enher/Endesa (60%) U.Fenosa (40%)
Vandellós II	Tarragona	PWR	1004	1976	1987	Endesa (72%) Iberdrola (28%)
Vandellós III		PWR	950	1976	Abandoned	Fecsa (100%)
Sayago	Zamora	PWR	1030	1976	Abandoned	Iberdrola (100%)
Regodola	Jove (Lugo)	LWR	930	1976	Abandoned	U.Fenosa (60%) E.Viesgo (20%) H.Cantábrico (20%)

First generation: Installed capacity in operation 1,120MW
Second generation: Planned installed capacity 6,555 MW; in operation 4,695MW
Third generation: Planned installed capacity 7,914 MW; in operation 2,022MW

Total installed capacity in operation 31 December 1993 7,400 MW

* Vandellos 1 withdrawn from service in 1989 following an accident on 19 October 1989

BWR: Boiling Water Reactor; GCR: Gas-Cooled Reactor; LWR: Light Water Reactor; PWR: Pressurised Water Reactor

Sources: Iranzo, 1987; Nadal and Noceda, 1989; UNESA 1994

The main push towards the development of nuclear energy came at the beginning of the 1970s with the authorisation in 1973 of a further seven nuclear power stations, which on completion would add 6,500 MW. The energy crisis led to increased support for nuclear power in the First National Energy Plan, which envisaged a major expansion of nuclear power to 23 per cent of all primary energy requirements and 56 per cent of electricity generation by 1985. However, in the revised Second National Energy Plan the role of nuclear energy was reduced to supplying 15 per cent of primary energy requirements and 37 per cent of electricity by 1987. Nevertheless, support was given for continuing work on the second generation of reactors and for a third generation of plants.

Enthusiasm for nuclear energy waned in the 1980s, initially in the light of slackening demand and high construction costs, but increasingly amidst worries over safety (inflamed in the mid 1980s by accidents at Three-Mile Island and Chernobyl and then by a fire at Vandellós 1 in 1989), technical problems (such as corrosion in Asco 1 and Almaraz and problems over the disposal of nuclear waste), the problems and costs of decommissioning, and lower conventional energy prices. Thus the Third National Energy Plan envisaged only four more power stations in addition to those operating in 1984 and a number of construction programmes were suspended. Under the Fourth PEN, the moratorium on nuclear energy continued with the contribution of nuclear power anticipated to fall to only 23 per cent of all electricity generation by the year 2000. At the beginning of 1994 there were nine nuclear stations in operation with an installed capacity of 7,400 MW, accounting for 35 per cent of electricity generation.

Nuclear power stimulated development of the uranium industry in Spain. The National Uranium Company, Enusa (Empresa Nacional del Uranio SA), was constituted in 1972 to develop uranium mining, ensure uranium supplies to power stations and provide nuclear technology services. In 1974 the National Plan for the Exploration and Investigation of Uranium (Plan Nacional de Exploración e Investigación de Uranio) was aimed at increasing exploration for uranium in Spain and overseas. Spain participated in overseas exploration, especially in Canada, South Africa, west Africa (notably in Niger where Enusa has a holding in the Akouta mine) and Colombia. In recent years uranium mineral has been extracted in Salamanca (an open-caste mine in the district of Saelices el Chico – Ciudad Rodrigo with estimated reserves of 37,991 tonnes of uranium oxide in 1993 but of low uranium content) and in Badajoz (La Haba, closed in 1989). Further reserves have been located in Badajoz and Guadalajara (amounting to 10,000 tonnes) and exploration has been undertaken in Caceres. Under the Third National Energy Plan production was planned to increase to 1,000 tonnes by 1990, including a project to recover uranium from phosphoric acid in Huelva (project Fuesa, based in the factory of Fosfórico Español SA in the chemical complex of Huelva). In practice, production of uranium oxide peaked in 1988 at 269 tonnes and then fell in each consecutive year to only 216 tonnes in 1993 (Enusa 1994). New uranium concentrate facilities at Saelices (the Quercus plant) have a capacity to produce 950 tonnes a year and to meet over three-quarters of domestic demand (production has been limited to 300 tonnes to conserve domestic resources). Enusa also produces nuclear fuel at its plant in Juzbado (Salamanca), although there are no enrichment facilities in Spain nor plant for treating residuals. Fuel from the plant both supplies the nuclear power stations in Spain and is exported.

As in other countries, there is growing concern over the storage of nuclear waste and the dismantling of nuclear power stations. Currently, nuclear waste is stored at power station sites, although some low-level waste is stored in the El Cabril mine in Córdoba. The task of dismantling power stations will begin with Vandellós 1, work on which was due to start in 1995 (for which mainly foreign technology and expertise will be employed). Control over nuclear waste and responsibility for dismantling nuclear power plants is in the hands of Enresa (Empresa Nacional de Residuos Radiactivos SA). Finally, the state company Equipos Nucleares (part of the Teneo group) produces heavy nuclear plant at its factory in Maliaño (just outside Santander in Cantabria).

5.4.3 *Hydroelectricity*

Hydroelectricity is an important source of electricity production because of its low cost, renewable and indigenous nature. Hence capacity continues to be increased, reaching 16,996 MW at the end of 1993, 37 per cent of all generating capacity (UNESA 1994). However, electricity generation from this source varies considerably from year to year with variations in the pattern of precipitation and river flow regimes. Since 1970 production has fluctuated from 47,473 GWh in 1979 (45 per cent of production) to only 20,570 GWh in 1992 (13 per cent of production and the lowest output since 1965); the ten-year average (1984 to 1993 inclusive) being 33,628 GWh (23 per cent of electricity generation). Lower supplies of hydroelectricity requires utilities to switch to higher-cost sources (coal and oil), reducing profits (and increasing imports).

The rate of development of hydroelectricity has depended on its relative profitability in relation to other sources of electrical energy. Development has been most rapid when assisted by state aid. During the 1970s the utilities tended to invest in nuclear and coal-fired stations. In the early 1980s the strained financial position of many utilities combined with low growth in electricity consumption to restrict investment.

There are both physical and human resource constraints on hydroelectric developments. Relief, precipitation and drainage are obvious physical constraints, leaving the drainage areas of the North, Ebro and Duero with the greatest potential. But restrictions on hydroelectric potential also arise from competing uses of water in river basins, such as domestic and industrial consumption, fishing (and fish farming), irrigation and flood control.

Development of water resources depends on the legal arrangements governing water use. In this respect an important change was made in 1985. The Water Law (Ley de Aguas) was designed to stop the irrational use and contamination of water resources. Under the old Water Law, passed in 1879, subterranean water was regarded as part of land ownership, while surface water belonged to the state. This enabled Spain to produce a national water policy, become a pioneer in the management of its rivers and to develop hydroelectric installations. But soaring demand, new pumping techniques and modern knowledge about the water cycle connecting underground and surface water made the old law obsolete. Thus the new law makes underground water too part of the public domain (although it leaves existing wells in private ownership, protects the rights of well owners and offers them seventy-five-year concessions). The new law should improve the co-ordination of water use within river basins.

5.5 Renewable energy sources and energy conservation

The need to reduce reliance on imported energy has been the principal stimulus for programmes designed to promote renewable energy and energy conservation. However, despite these programmes renewable energy sources (other than HEP) contribute a very small percentage of domestic primary energy production and an even smaller percentage of primary energy consumption. This will remain the position at least until the end of the decade.

Renewable energy sources are derived from biomass, geothermal sources, the tides, rivers, the sun and the wind; of which only river and wind power have been harnessed on any commercial scale. Estimated biomass reserves are in the form of forest and agricultural residuals and urban waste. As yet no geothermal or tidal plants have been built. Possible geothermal sites have been identified in Madrid, Burgos, Barcelona, Orense and Murcia as well as in the Canary Islands (Lanzarote and Tenerife). In relation to harnessing the power of rivers, in 1992 there were 700 mini hydroelectric plants operating. These were concentrated in Cataluña, Huesca and Asturias. Seventy per cent of potential resources lie in northern Spain.

Relatively little energy is expected to be generated from solar power in the near future despite the fact that more than 70 per cent of Spain has over 2,500 hours of sunshine a year. Experimental solar plants have been built in Almería (where there are two 0.5 MW generators, ceded to Ciemat from the International Energy Agency in 1986), Manzanares, Ciudad Real (0.1 MW), Valdepeñas, where the GAST (Generador Solar Torre) wind and solar plant is located (20 MW), in Toledo (1 MW) and at Puebla de Montalbán, Teruel (1 MW). Although generating potential may be small, there are numerous domestic and commercial applications, including solar batteries and solar panels for hot water systems, in addition to the established use in conjunction with plastic and glass shelters in agriculture.

Wind power farms have been installed at a number of sites in Spain. In 1992 the two largest wind-driven electricity generating farms in Europe entered into service in Tarifa (Cádiz): La Planta Eólica del Sur (Pesur) with 184 wind generators (20 MW capacity), and Energía Eólica del Estrecho with 65 generators (10 MW capacity). Operation of these two projects was unified in 1993 with the incorporation of Sociedad Eólica del Estrecho. There are also wind power complexes in the Canary Islands (Los Valles, Lanzarote, 5 MW; Cañada de la Barca, Fuerteventura, 10 MW; Garafía, La Palma, 1.26 MW; Granadilla, Tenerife, 0.4 MW; Barranco de Tirajana, Gran Canaria, 1.26 MW), where a four-year plan produced by Unelco in 1992 envisaged the installation of 60 MW of wind power by 1997, a small centre in Tarragona and one at Camariñas, La Coruña (3MW). The Fourth PEN envisaged 0.2 per cent of electricity production coming from wind power in the year 2000, generating 420 GWh from an installed capacity of 175 MW.

A renewable energy plan emerged in 1986 (Plan de Energías Renovables, PER) from the Third National Energy Plan. The PER envisaged an increase in renewable resources from 0.9 per cent of primary energy supply in 1988 to 2.7 per cent in 1992. A second PER was finalised in 1988 (PER 1989) for the period up to 1995, incorporating the resources available from the European Community for developing renewable energy (particularly under the Valoren programme). This second PER envisages the increase of renewable energy to provide about 4 per cent of primary energy consumption (800,000 tonnes oil equivalent, toe) by 1995. Biomass and urban waste are considered to offer the greatest potential (forecast 190,000 and 330,000 toe respectively by 1995) along with mini-hydroelectric stations.

5.6 Restructuring the energy base

Since the beginning of the 1970s the energy base has been diversified through growth in the use of nuclear power, natural gas and renewable resources. Despite this progress, supply remains heavily dependent on imports and, in the case of natural gas, dependent on a limited number of import sources. Domestic oil and gas supplies are likely to cease by the end of the century and a significant proportion of coal supplies will be met from imports. Without an expansion of the nuclear power programme, and with little prospect of a significant increase in renewable energy, energy dependence will increase. Although growth of energy demand will be slowed by low or negative population growth and a structural shift in the economy towards less energy-intensive activities, the only policy to contain imports would appear to be energy conservation. Yet conservation continues to be given a relatively low priority in energy policy despite the almost inevitable real increase in energy costs in the future.

The energy market will undergo further liberalisation allowing greater penetration by foreign multinational companies. It was with this prospect of a more liberal market in mind that the government successfully sponsored the restructuring of the energy sector, creating a small number of major national energy companies. However, these companies have yet to be fully rationalised and will face increasing foreign competition. In the coal industry further restructuring will be necessary to achieve efficiency and staunch the financial haemorrhage that characterised the industry in the 1980s. The prospects for deep-mined coal are especially bleak. In the oil industry, foreign multinational companies will steadily increase their presence, notably in the number of service stations and their share in the market for oil products. Natural gas will increase its penetration of the market, supplied predominantly through the new Spanish natural gas company. In electricity generation reorganisation will be consolidated around two major companies. The future role of nuclear power remains undecided, with work on a number of stations still shelved and no new stations planned.

References and bibliography

Alvarez, M. (1994) 'El sector eléctrico español hacia el futuro', *Situación,* No. 2, pp. 223–36. Bilbao: BBV

Anon (1988) 'Un Plan del Gas con horizonte en el año 2000', *Economía Industrial,* 259, pp. 7–12. Madrid: MINE

Aranzadi, C. (ed.) (1993) *El sector eléctrico Español en la Europa de 1993.* Madrid: Economistas Libros

Aserpetrol (1992) *Memoria 1991.* Madrid

Badosa Pagés, J. (1986) 'El gas natural en España', *Papeles de Economía Española,* 29, pp. 88–109

Banco de Bilbao (1979) 'Energía', *Situación,* 7, No. 8. Bilbao: BBV

Banco de Bilbao (1984) 'National energy programme', *Situación* July, pp. 28–32. Bilbao: BBV

Casamayor, R. (1993) 'Hasta la bandera', *El País* (sección negocios), 7 November, pp. 3–6

Celaya, C. (1994) 'Corriente alterna', *El País* (seccion negocios), 27 March, pp. 3–5

Díaz-Caneja Burgaleta, F. (1986) 'El potencial hidroeléctrico de España', *Papeles de Economía Española* 29, pp. 163–80

El País (1995) *Anuario 1995* Madrid

Endesa (1994) *Annual report 1993.* Madrid: Grupo Teneo

Enusa (1994) *Informe anual 1993.* Madrid: Grupo Teneo

Fanjul, O. (1986) 'Los problemas de la industría petrolera', *Papeles de Economía Española* 29, pp. 78–87

Fanjul, O. (1986) 'Proceso configurador del INH', *Economía Industrial,* No. 248, pp. 37–40. Madrid: MINE

Fernández, J. (1987) 'El sector petrolero español y la adhesión a la CEE', *Situación,* No. 2, pp. 16–31. Bilbao: BBV

Fernández-Cuesta, N. (1986) 'La liberalización del sector petrolero español', *Economía Industrial* 248, pp. 41–56. Madrid: MINE

Fernández Santamaría, F. and J. Leirado Campo (1987) 'Gas natural', *Situación,* No. 2, pp. 97–104. Bilbao: BBV

García Alonso, J. (1983) 'La energía en la economía española', *Papeles de Economía Española,* No. 14, pp. 2–13

Gas Natural SDG (1994) *Annual report 1993.* Barcelona

Iberdrola (1994) *Annual report and business report 1993.* Bilbao

Instituto Nacional de Estadística, INE (1994) *Boletín mensual de estadística,* May, pp. 234–5

Iranzo Martin, J. (1985) 'El sector energético español: realidades y posibilidades', *Papeles de Economía Española* 21, pp. 271–90

Iranzo Martin, J. (1987) 'La energía nuclear en España' and 'Las energías renovables', *Situación,* No. 2, pp. 75–96 and pp. 105–12. Bilbao: BBV

Lancaster, T. (1989) *Policy stability and democratic change. Energy in Spain's transition.* University Park, Pennsylvania: Pennsylvania State University Press

Luisa Huidobro, M. (1988) 'Sector eléctrico: deuda y financiación', *Economía Industrial* 261, pp. 73–8. Madrid: MINE

Marín Quemada, J. (1986) 'Política de energía', in. Gamir (ed.), *Política económica de España,* pp. 321–48. Madrid: Alianza Editorial

Martos Martínez, R. (1987) 'Consumo final de energía y de electricidad en España',

Situación, No. 2, pp. 54–74. Bilbao: BBV
Ministerio de Industría y Energía, MINE (1989) *Informe anual sobre la industría española, 1988.* Madrid
Ministerio de Industría y Energía, MINE (1991) *National energy plan 1991–2000.* Madrid
Ministerio de Industría y Energía, MINE (1993) *Informe anual sobre la industría española, 1992.* Madrid
Muñoz del Barrio, C. (1983) 'Reconversión de la estructura refino', *Papeles de Economía Española* 14, pp. 293–8
Nadal, F. and M. Noceda (1989) 'Chispas nucleares', *El País* (sección negocios), 3 December, p. 15
Otero Moreno, J. (1983) 'Estructura del consumo energético en España', *Papeles de Economía Española* 14, pp. 52–72
Papeles de Economía Española (1986) *Economía minera en España,* No. 29. Madrid: Fundación CECA
Paya, C. and B. García-Sineriz (1986) 'Hispanoil en la hora actual', *Economía Industrial* 248, pp. 73–9. Madrid: MINE
Perez Cava, F. (1986) 'Estructura del sector de combustibles gaseosos en España', *Economía Industrial* 248, pp. 57–72. Madrid: MINE
Pozo-Portillo, J. (1983) 'La revisión del Plan Energético Nacional', *Papeles de Economía Española* 14, pp. 21–51
Redesa (1993) *Estadísticas de la explotación del sistema eléctrico, 1992.* Madrid
Repsol (1993) *Annual report 1992.* Madrid
Saez García, J. (1986) 'El papel de las compañías distribuidoras en el desarrollo del gas en España', *Economía Industrial* 248, pp. 81–8. Madrid: MINE
Sedigas (1994) *Anuario gas' 94.* Barcelona
Sudria, C. (1987) 'Un factor determinante: la energía', in J. Nadal, A. Carreras and C. Sudria (eds), *La economía española en el siglo XX.* Barcelona: Editorial Ariel
Trincado, J. (1988) 'Algunos temas relevantes para el futuro del sector eléctrico', *Economía Industrial* 261, pp. 33–5. Madrid: MINE
UNESA (1994) *Memoria estadística eléctrica 1993.* Madrid

Chapter 6
Manufacturing industry

6.1 Manufacturing industry

Manufacturing has been shaped by a political economy in which the market mechanism was constrained by a high level of protectionism and state intervention, originating in the nineteenth century, elaborated in the period of autarchy, then modified during the years of the 'economic miracle', the 'economic crisis' and the transition to a single European market. The imprint of this history remains, although fading quickly in the last decade of the twentieth century.

Despite early examples of manufacturing industrial development, industrialisation was late to take off in Spain and never gained the dimensions reached in some more northern European countries (Nadal 1973; Tortella 1994). The peak level of employment in industry (including mining) was reached at the end of the industrialisation decade of the 1960s. In the early 1970s some 3.3 million people were occupied in the sector, 25 per cent of the labour force. Since that time the sector has declined in relative terms and employment has fallen in absolute terms. However, the value of industrial output in real terms continues to display a growth trend and in 1991 was greater than at any time in the past (OECD 1994).

Exposed to the same international market forces, industrial restructuring has followed a similar path to that in other OECD countries, notably a shift away from traditional industries. Substantial employment losses were recorded in these industries in the industrial crises of the 1970s and early 1980s. In the recession of the early 1990s it was not only the traditional industries that suffered but also modern manufacturing industries such as motor-vehicles and electronics. These were more employment adjustments associated with increased productivity rather than trend reductions in the value of industrial output.

Where restructuring has differed from that in some other OECD countries has been in the extent to which the government has attempted to manage the process of restructuring, cushioning employment contraction while attempting to place manufacturing on a more competitive footing. Restructuring has coincided with increased integration into the international economy, especially through the corporate networks of multinational companies, which have themselves been reorganising on a European and often global basis. The result is an increased degree of industrial specialisation largely determined by multinational companies. Six case studies covering iron and steel, fertilizers, textiles and clothing, food, motor-vehicles and electronics exemplify the process of industrial change.

In comparison with Britain, France and Germany, the absolute size of the manufacturing sector is small, though its relative size (as a proportion of the economically active population and GDP) is broadly in line with that in other European Union countries. In 1994 the number of people working in manufacturing industry was 2.3 million, 20 per cent of the total occupied population (INE 1994a).

Spanish industry evolved in a peculiar political economy, which left a distinctive legacy hindering the emergence of full international competitiveness, leaving firms exposed to penetration by foreign capital and Spanish industry open to colonisation by foreign based multinationals. That legacy is characterised by:

i) *The small size of firms and plants*: This characteristic has limited the opportunities for scale economies and made it difficult to raise long-term finance, to participate in research and development and to engage in exports (Segura 1992). Further fragmentation has resulted from many firms being engaged in a diversity of product lines with little specialisation within one segment of the market (García Fernández 1989). Ninety per cent of all the country's industrial companies have fewer than 100 employees, accounting for 50 per cent of industrial employment (Tamames 1986). Only one Spanish group, the mixed public/private company Repsol, was among the one hundred largest manufacturing industrial companies in Europe in 1994 (by value of market capitalisation) (Financial Times 1995).

ii) *An industrial structure weighted towards traditional industry*: In 1991 one-third of all employment and one-quarter of value added in industry arose from the three sectors food, drink and tobacco; textiles and clothing; and wood, cork and furniture (Table 6.1).

iii) *A small defence sector*: Defence spending has tended to represent only a small proportion of the state budget (less than 1.3 per cent of GDP in the early 1990s). Less than 30,000 people were employed directly in the sector in 1986 (Economía Industrial 1987), and less than 20,000 at the end of 1994. Most of these are employed in the public sector (essentially Casa (aircraft), E.N.Bazán (ships), Indra (electronics), Iveco-Pegaso (military vehicles) and E.N. Santa Bárbara (weapons). The latter announced a major rationalisation in early 1994, involving the closure of five of the company's eight factories and contraction of the labour force from 3,128 to only 1,058 (Concha Gil 1994a).

Table 6.1 The structure of industry, 1991

CNAE group	Sector	Employment	(%)	Value added (pta million)	(%)
11–15	Energy	107,986	4.9	2,052,238	17.6
16	Water	33,942	1.5	128,550	1.1
21	Metallic-minerals extraction	3,246	0.1	20,259	0.2
22	Primary processing of metals	60,956	2.8	302,079	2.6
23	Non-metallic minerals extraction	22,828	1.0	120,001	1.0
24	Non-metallic mineral products	138,502	6.3	669,618	5.7
25	Chemical industries	124,261	5.7	965,432	8.3
31	Metal products	239,110	10.9	887,480	7.6
32,33,39	Machinery and mechanical equipment	117,386	5.3	558,983	4.8
34,35	Electrical and electronic goods	114,808	5.2	617,791	5.3
36–8	Transport equipment	204,158	9.3	1,262,894	10.8
41,42	Food, drink and tobacco	362,450	16.5	1,692,273	14.5
43,453–6	Textiles and clothing	205,195	9.3	591,538	5.1
452	Leather and shoes	47,467	2.2	145,374	1.2
46	Wood, cork and furniture	161,597	7.4	400,906	3.4
47	Paper and publishing	129,425	5.9	709,118	6.1
48	Rubber and plastic goods	99,804	4.5	440,505	3.8
49	Other manufacturing	23,934	1.1	87,548	0.8
	Total	2,197,055	100.0	11,652,587	100.0

CNAE: Clasificación Nacional de Actividades Económicas, 1975

Employment figures are for the occupied population

Source: INE 1994b

iv) *Geographical concentration*: The province of Barcelona is the dominant focus of manufacturing in Spain, with one-fifth of all employment. Outside of Barcelona, manufacturing is concentrated in Madrid, País Vasco, Valencia and Alicante (which together with Barcelona account for over 60 per cent of all employment in industry). The Ebro Valley, the Mediterranean coast as far south as Cartagena and a belt north-east from Valladolid through Burgos to Bilbao have become axes of industrial development. The distribution of head offices is still more highly concentrated. Of the 50 largest industrial companies in 1983 (based on sales figures), 45 per cent had their head office in Madrid, 20 per cent in Barcelona and 10 per cent in Bilbao. The provinces most dependent on employment in industry in 1994 were Alava and Guipúzcoa in País Vasco, Barcelona and Navarra, all of which had 32 per cent or more of their economically active population in industry (INE 1994a). This spatial concentration of industry, and especially of those sectors in crisis, continues to have important regional development implications.

v) *Lack of competitiveness*: Low productivity, over-staffing, obsolescent technology and the inefficient use of energy have been common features of Spanish industry. There has been a lower level of technical efficiency in comparison with industry in western Europe (Berges and Simarro 1987). Spanish industry used semi-skilled labour and well-known production techniques (late stage of the production life-cycle) acquired through patents, resembling industry in Greece and Portugal more than that in France.

vi) *State involvement*: The state has exercised a direct involvement across the whole spectrum of manufacturing through the DGPE, INH, INI and through extensive portfolio holdings held by the Bank of Spain in most of the leading companies.

vii) *Involvement of financial groups*: The major financial groups in Spain have had extensive direct involvement in industry. Spanish companies have traditionally relied relatively little on the stock market for raising finance, instead having been heavily dependent on bank finance.

viii) *Family ownership, interlocking directorships and diversification*: Family ownership of companies has been widespread in Spain, as has been the presence of interlocking directorships. Relatively small companies are frequently engaged in a diversity of economic activities.

ix) *Foreign penetration*: Substantial foreign penetration of the economy dates back to the nineteenth century when foreign investment built up in mining, railways, some public services and basic chemicals. Foreign investment was renewed in the 1960s and 1970s, exploding in the 1980s to dominate most profitable industry. More than half the value of manufacturing industrial output now arises within foreign multinational companies (Durán Herrera 1994).

x) *Dependence on foreign technology*: 'Spanish industry is dependent on foreign technology' (Tamames 1986). Many firms in Spain produce goods with foreign patents or under licence. Frequently, these patents allowed production in the domestic market only.

xi) *The widespread existence of monopoly power*: In contrast to the atomistic structure prevalent in many areas of industry (such as clothing and parts of the food industry), there is a very high degree of concentration in sectors such as oil refining, cement, glass and agricultural chemicals.

xii) *Domestic market orientation*: Spanish industry, unlike its foreign counterpart, has been concerned primarily with the domestic market, a reflection both of the protection afforded the domestic market and the lack of international competitiveness. The degree of internationalism can be measured by the percentage of sales and percentage of production in countries outside of that in which the parent company is based. Most of the major Spanish exporting companies are subsidiaries of foreign multinationals (nine of the top ten exporting companies in 1993 being foreign-based multinationals, eight of them in the motor-vehicle industry plus IBM). Overseas production was still very limited in the early 1990s, internationalism being essentially confined to sales and input procurement and focused on the large public or mixed public/private companies. However, increasing competition in the domestic market and the drive to reduce costs are forcing more companies in Spain to develop an international presence.

6.2 Industrial reconversion

From the mid 1970s Spain entered an economic crisis that saw a net loss of 1 million jobs in industry, from 3.6 million in 1975 to 2.6 million in 1985 (a 27 per cent reduction in the occupied population in industry). The economic crisis centred on those industries in which Spain had specialised in the 1960s. For example, domestic steel demand decreased from 11.8 million tonnes in 1974 to 6.9 million tonnes in 1985 and the tonnage ordered in shipbuilding fell to less than one-quarter of a million tonnes in 1986. Changes in the structure of costs and in demand, together with the rise of the Newly Industrialised Countries (NICs), removed the competitive advantage that Spain had enjoyed in these sectors (Nadal et al. 1987).

The response to the recession was slower than in many other countries, a result largely of the combination of a protected economy and the more pressing political problems that dominated Spain in the late 1970s. Industry was partly sheltered from the first oil shock by a cut in taxation on oil products, rapid domestic inflation and the persistence of negative interest rates. Large investment programmes in sectors such as steel and shipbuilding continued to be encouraged until the late 1970s, although demand had fallen substantially worldwide. Moreover, a number of traditional industries, such as textiles, were suffering increasingly from the competition of NICs. The growth of labour costs was proceeding at a pace incompatible with the maintenance of competitiveness, profit margins and employment. The situation came to a head in 1980 when, following the second oil shock, the authorities finally allowed the price of oil to adjust to international conditions while real interest rates turned sharply positive. The crisis found large industrial sectors completely unprepared and burdened with acute problems of over-staffing, excess capacity and indebtedness.

On the industrial front the principal government response to the economic crisis was to promote industrial reconversion (*reconversión industrial*), a term adopted to describe the wide-ranging process of industrial restructuring in Spain in the 1980s. During this period the government introduced a series of measures described as adapting industry to the changing economic environment, with the basic objective of increasing competitiveness (Ortún 1988), thereby aiming to promote a more orderly pattern of industrial restructuring than that which would have resulted from market forces alone. In practice the measures amounted to cushioning traditional industries from the full impact of the industrial crisis.

The first efforts by the government to adjust the economy positively occurred in 1977 with the Moncloa Pacts. But not until 1979 did the government begin negotiations with specific companies over restructuring production. In 1980 'reconversion decrees' were introduced to restructure specific industrial sectors, and measures were introduced to provide encouragement for the merger of firms (Ley 76/1980 provided tax incentives to firms that merged). The process started with kitchen appliances and special steels in 1980 and was extended in 1981 to eleven sectors that were considered to have been especially badly hit by the recession (Real Decreto Ley 9/1981 on Industrial Reconversion). They covered integrated iron and steel, special steels, carbon steels, common steels, semi-manufactured products of copper and its alloys, shipbuilding, textiles, footwear, motor-vehicle parts, electronic components and kitchen appliances. In addition, five companies followed special reconversion programmes: General Electric, Westinghouse, Talbot Automóviles, Asturiana de Zinc and the Standard Group. The programme soon ran into political problems as the negative impact of the restructuring process began to be felt in certain regions. There were also technical problems associated with underestimation of the financial cost involved and problems over monitoring the programme. A large proportion of the state transfers for industrial reconversion between 1979 and 1982 went to absorb losses rather than to tackle the underlying disequilibria.

Reinforcing reconversion began with the introduction of a broad legal framework in 1982 and was completed by a comprehensive White Paper on reindustrialisation published in 1983, followed by a decree in November 1983. This was subsequently converted into a law in July 1984 (Real Decreto Ley 8/1983 and Ley 27/1984, Ley de Reconversión y Reindustrialización) effective as from December 1984. Rapid action was now essential given the imminence of entry into the European Community, which meant both increased competition and adoption of EC regulations limiting further state assistance to industry.

Reconversion strategy was designed to reduce the rate of deindustrialisation and to establish an industrial base capable of meeting international competition. To achieve this it was imperative both: i) to improve productivity and restore company profitability (by cutting excess capacity and over-staffing and by restructuring the financial liabilities of excessively indebted companies; a process described as financial cleansing – *saneamiento financiero*); and ii) to promote investment and technological innovation in those activities with good future profit potential within the sectors affected. Eleven sectors were involved under the 1984 legislation (Table 6.2), essentially the same as the ones identified in 1981. Together they made a significant contribution to employment and exports (they were also mostly covered by EC restructuring policies). In addition to this sectoral programme, specific geographical areas with intense problems of industrial decline were designated as Urgent Reindustrialisation Zones (Zonas de Urgente Reindustrialización, ZUR), within which additional state benefits were available.

Implementation of reconversion policies varied according to the sectors involved. In sectors that were atomistic in structure assistance was generally available to all companies (for example in textiles, where a large proportion of assistance was provided for intangibles such as improving design, image and marketing). In some sectors, notably special steels and kitchen appliances, competition and recession had generated price wars. Co-ordination and rationalisation of these sectors was necessary to take advantage of scale economies and specialisation of production. Thus cartels or industrial groups were formed (*carteles de recesión* and *sociedades de reconversión*; in the period 1980 to 1982 the only *sociedad de reconversión* was in special steels, in which steel companies and central government formed a company to manage the industry). Finally, in sectors where a few produc-

Table 6.2 Reconversion programmes

Sector	Dates	Number of companies	Labour force A	Labour force B	Labour force C
Integrated iron and steel	1980–90	3	42,837	22,761	24,715
Special steels	1980–90	11	13,744	5,016	6,119
Semi–processed copper	1981–84	4	4,503	3,430	3,401
Heavy forgings	1981–84	2	1,277	970	915
Fertilizers*	1984–88	10	8,541	7,232	6,517
Shipbuilding (GA) †	1984–90	2	21,920	9,972	11,249
Shipbuilding (PMA)	1984–90	27	15,427	8,198	9,162
Textiles	1981–86	683	108,844	98,919	98,919
Domestic electrical appliances°	1980–88	18	23,869	11,258	12,272
Vehicle electrical equipment	1981–85	2	6,720	5,378	5,269
Electronic components	1981–85	17	3,744	2,200	2,314
Alcatel Standard Eléctrica	1983–91	1	16,133	7,756	11,459
ERT Group	1983–87	10	10,304	7,811	7,811
Marconi Española	1983–91	1	2,548	450	1,283
Total		791	280,411 (100%)	191,351 (68%)	201,405 (72%)

Labour force: A – Initial, B – Planned, C – At 31 December 1988

† are large shipyards, PM are small shipyards

°Of the 18 firms initially covered in the Domestic Electrical Appliance (White Goods) Sector, six closed and one left the sector.

The labour force refers to the whole sector, including two firms which were not part of the reconversion programme

*The fusion of ERT and Cros has resulted in further reductions in employment

Source: MINE 1989

ers dominated (integrated iron and steel and shipbuilding), they generally became the direct responsibility of the INI. These industries posed the greatest social and political problems as often whole communities were dependent on one firm.

Reconversion programmes required strong measures to achieve rapid results. These measures covered modernisation and rationalisation, financial restructuring (including debt write-offs, rescheduling of debt, new lines of credit, public underwriting of loans, etc.); fiscal measures (tax rebates, extension or fractioning of the payment of tax and social security debts); labour (facilities for the modification, suspension or termination of labour relations and for geographical mobility; aid for early retirement and the possibility of fractioning indemnities for dismissal due to contractual cutbacks stemming from a reduction of employment); and technology (for example the creation of a centre for promoting research and development in companies – the Centro de Desarrollo Technológico e Industrial). Further indirect assistance included protection of the national market (for example controls on steel imports), encouragement of firms to merge and encouragement of unions and employers to work together (the latter especially in the early 1980s).

Substantial public expenditure (in addition to private sector investment) was involved in implementing the measures constituting the reconversion programmes during the 1980s. The cost of the reconversion plan over the three years 1984 to 1986 alone was estimated at pta 1,000 billion (Banco de Bilbao 1984). Investment in modernisation and rationalisation of installations between 1981 and 1989 amounted to more than pta 650 billion, including some pta 50 billion for intangibles such as design (especially in textiles and shoes) and research (especially in information technology) (Ortún 1988). Larger sums went into financial restructuring and labour measures. By sector, probably the largest public investment was in the iron and steel industry.

Labour measures were fundamentally concerned with the treatment of those made redundant and taking early retirement as part of the process of improving productivity and reducing labour costs. The 1984 Plan envisaged a reduction in employment of about 80,000 to 90,000: some one-third of the labour force in the firms affected. About 90 per cent of the reduction was to come from iron and steel, shipbuilding, home appliances and textiles. These planned reductions in the labour force had largely been met by the end of 1988 (Table 6.2). About 25 per cent of the total employment loss was expected to come from early retirements (initially from the age of sixty, then reduced to fifty-five). The rest of the workers involved were given the choice of either a considerable redundancy indemnity and an unemployment allowance, or else surrendering this indemnity to join the Employment Promotion Fund (Fondo de Promoción de Empleo, FPE) for up to three years. In return, the FPE paid them 80 per cent of their last wage, encouraged recruitment by offering a subsidy to would-be employers and provided free retraining.

In retrospect, industrial reconversion was a failure in that it did not create an internationally competitive Spanish-owned industrial base and absorbed resources that could have been directed into promoting new industries and improving infrastructure. Although whole industrial sectors were reorganised, mergers promoted to create larger, more competitive companies, new plant installed and productivity generally increased, it was insufficient to meet the changing international economic environment. In any event, reconversion policy was a major government initiative and one that became unrepeatable under European Community regulations.

6.3 Industrial policy in the late 1980s and early 1990s

While the protectionism and extensive intervention that was characteristic of Spain in the past was being dismantled, an active industrial policy within a market framework (consistent with European Community requirements to increase competition) was still considered necessary in the mid and late 1980s to bring Spain into line with other western industrial nations and to promote the further development of industry. This mixture of market economics and socialist principles reflected the tensions inside the PSOE party. But the emphasis in industrial policy shifted away from support to traditional industries towards producing an economic environment conducive to the emergence of new industry (reflecting the evolution of the political centre of gravity within successive PSOE governments). Until the mid 1980s little public funds had been put into stimulating research and development in Spain, as public spending controls and political considerations ensured that a large proportion of public expenditure went into cushioning the effects of recession and the restructuring programme. To achieve the new emphasis, policies concentrated on increasing the flexibility of factor markets, improving the quality of production factors and infrastructure, reducing the inherent problems of industrial size structure (for example through helping small and medium-sized enterprises and promoting mergers), providing new technologies, improving product design and quality (for example through the state Industrial Design Company which from 1992 managed the Plan for Promoting Industrial Design), promoting the introduction of more environmentally friendly production systems, promoting the internationalisation of Spanish business (especially increasing industrial exports) and privatising public enterprises. However, the fundamental obstacles hindering a real transformation of industry were rooted in cultural factors. For example, despite the declared aim of increasing flexibility in the labour market, it was not until the end of 1993 that the government finally confronted the trade unions on substantive measures to reform labour legislation.

Thus public policy makers sought to establish the coherence of a policy of selective public sector intervention within the framework of increased liberalisation driven largely by external decision makers in the form of greater European integration (evidenced by the introduction of the Single European Market at the beginning of 1993 and the implementation of the Maastricht Treaty in November 1993), increased world trade liberalisation (marked by the completion of the Uruguay Round of trade negotiations in December 1993) and greater international corporate integration. The most important doubt that overhangs this process is whether the state will be able to resist pressures to adopt some form of protectionism (or press for more managed trade) should domestic industry continue to be threatened by increasing import penetration. Any such action would have to be taken within the context of the European Union and World Trade Organisation. The principal strategic risk, is that Spain will be caught between competitiveness based on low-cost production and low technology products, and competitiveness based on new technologies (Maravall 1987).

6.4 Iron and steel

The iron and steel industry illustrates the failure of industrial reconversion policy in Spain to tackle fundamental structural problems. It also illustrates the role of European Union membership in shifting government policy towards more radical restructuring measures, while continuing to provide a cushion of public assistance within the framework of a European Union restructuring strategy that stops short of immediate exposure to market solutions.

As a result of market and political pressures the public company Ensidesa (Empresa Nacional Siderúrgica) and the former private company AHV (Alto Hornos de Vizcaya) were brought together in 1992 under the management of the state-owned group Corporación de la Siderurgia Integral (CSI, part of INI). Nevertheless, in 1994 there remained excess capacity and too many companies in the industry. In the early 1990s (1990 to 1993 inclusive) national steel production ranged between 12 and 13 million tonnes (some 10 per cent of EU production), exports at between 4 and 6 million tonnes and apparent domestic steel consumption at between 9 and 11 million tonnes (Table 6.3).

The iron and steel industry was one of the first targets of government intervention to stem the tide of industrial decline. At the beginning of the 1980s the industry was characterised by over-capacity and obsolescence. Some 80,000 people were employed, of which about half were in the integrated iron and steel sector. Investment programmes implemented in the early 1970s had assumed demand growing to 20 million tonnes by the mid 1980s. This led to the construction of a fourth integrated iron and steel works in Sagunto (Valencia) and production capacity of around 18 million tonnes in 1985. In practice recession cut domestic demand to only about 6

Table 6.3 Steel production and trade

Year	Production	Trade	
		Exports	Imports
1946–50	0.7	–	–
1961–65	2.9	–	> 2.0
1971	5.4	–	> 2.0
1975	11.1	2.1	–
1980	12.7	4.5	1.3
1985	14.2	7.8	1.4
1986	11.9	5.2	2.6
1987	11.8	5.4	2.6
1988	11.9	3.9	2.7
1989	12.8	3.6	3.2
1990	13.1	4.1	3.4
1991	12.9	4.8	3.4
1992	12.3	4.7	3.6
1993	13.0	5.5	2.8

Figures in millions of tonnes

Sources: MINE 1987; Banco de España 1994

million tonnes in 1985, additional production being channelled into exports. Since then exports have remained a significant outlet for production.

The iron and steel industry was slow to adjust to the changing economic environment (to increased world production capacity, especially in the Newly Industrialised Countries, to declining markets, increased imports and over-capacity in the European Community), shielded from market forces by government intervention. Unco-ordinated action to rationalise the sector began in the late 1970s. In 1979 the major shareholders in the Sagunto complex relinquished their holdings to INI and Ensidesa began closing plants in Mieres, La Felguera and later in Avilés. However, in comparison with many other countries, employment contraction was small (only 13 per cent between 1974 and 1982), while steel consumption in Spain fell by one-third to about 200 kg per capita. The first reconversion plan was issued in 1981, although little effective action was taken until new measures were introduced in 1984 that carried the rationalisation process through to the end of the 1980s.

From the mid 1980s one of the most costly reconversion programmes in Spain was initiated with the objectives of reducing capacity (for example with the closure of steel making at Alto Hornos del Mediterráneo (AHM) in Sagunto, owned from 1972 by Ensidesa), improving efficiency through modernisation and rescuing the two integrated iron and steel producers AHV and Ensidesa. The programme cost about pta 1,500 billion from 1984 and involved a planned reduction in jobs of some 25,000 in integrated iron and steel by 1990 (from about 43,000 in the early 1980s; Tizón 1989). About half of the programme cost was associated with refinancing the sector (*saneamiento financiero*) and the social costs of redundancies, involving direct financial compensation to employees coupled with job creation programmes (for example in Sagunto the INI has participated in new firms such as an Italian/Spanish glass venture, a fertilizer factory and the addition of electroplating facilities to the cold rolling mill owned by Sidmed – the public company formed in 1985 from the remains of AHM and partly owned from 1991 by Sollac, a subsidiary of the French company Usinor-Sacilor).

Reconversion in the integrated iron and steel sector came to a close at the end of February 1989 with the inauguration by Ensidesa of a modern LD-oxygen steelworks in Avilés with a capacity of 2.5 million tonnes. Ensidesa was the largest integrated iron and steel group in Spain. The company had a labour force of 10,470 at the end of 1993 (compared with 22,600 in 1982), plants in Avilés (Asturias) and Veriña (3 km from Gijón, Asturias) producing between 3.4 and 3.9 million tonnes of steel in the three years 1991 to 1993 inclusive. The private integrated iron and steel sector was represented by AHV with factories around Bilbao (especially along the river Nervión, for example in Barakaldo, Sestao, Anzio and Basauri) and a labour force of some 6,000 at the beginning of 1994 (compared with 11,400 in 1982). Although the company remained a private one, substantial credit from the state (especially the Banco de Crédito Industrial) left it virtually nationalised.

Despite some respite from continued losses in the late 1980s, the economic downturn in Europe in the early 1990s and over-capacity in the European iron and steel industry demanded further rationalisation measures. In the three years 1991 to 1993 inclusive, Ensidesa shed over 4,000 jobs (Ensidesa 1994). Restructuring plans agreed with the European Commission in 1993 require irreversible cuts in steel-making capacity (total capacity of CSI to be cut from 6.5 million tonnes to 4.5 million tonnes), involving the closure of plant (including the blast furnaces of AHV at Sestao by 1996) and some 15,000 redundancies (over 6,000 from Ensidesa and over 3,000 from AHV). In return, the EU will provide funding for the restructuring process and allow a new mini-mill to be built in Sestao (Bilbao) with a production capacity close to 1 million tonnes (though employing only some 400 people), which must be funded largely from private sources. Such major surgery has repercussions throughout the metal-working complex and indeed throughout the economy of Asturias and País Vasco.

In the special steels sector restructuring had led to the formation of three major groups by 1994, the state group Sidenor (formed in 1992 from the merger of Forjas y Aceros de Reinosa and Aceros del Norte; at that time the group was producing some 1 million tonnes of steel products a year and provided employment for over 3,000 people on three sites: Basauri, Reinosa and Vitoria) and the private groups Acerinox (labour force of 1,800 and production of half a million tonnes of steel in 1993) and Grupo Siderúrgico

Vasco (the result of the merger between two companies in Guipúzcoa: Acerías y Forjas de Azkoitía and the steel-making business of Patricio Echeverría, the new group having a production capacity of some 150,000 tonnes of steel products and a labour force of some 800). Restructuring has been a long process in the sector, involving numerous closures, mergers and reorganisations. Despite this, in 1994 there was still a pressing need for continued rationalisation to further concentrate production both structurally (perhaps to leave one private and one public sector group) and geographically (to reduce the number of plants in each group).

In the more dispersed industry of common steels there has been a similarly long process of concentration, reduction in capacity and strengthening of different industrial groups, resulting in a new map of common steel production in Spain. Aristraín, Celsa (La Compañía Española de Laminación), Marcial Ucín (based in Guipúzcoa), Megasa and Siderúrgica Sevillana (the latter controlled by the Italian group Riva) have emerged as strong groups, along with various independent companies such as Arregui. Once again, however, the process of restructuring still had much further to run in 1994.

Where a sector containing private companies was covered by a reconversion programme, as in the case of common steels, companies could request government assistance in restructuring programmes worked out between them and the government. An illustration of this process was provided by the Celsa group. Following the grouping of companies under the umbrella of Celsa (the companies included the parent company Celsa, Torras Herrería, Nueva Montaña Quijano and Sidegasa), assistance was requested from the Ministry of Industry and Energy to cover the intended closure of Sidegasa (Siderúrgica de Galicia SA), the dismantling of a blast furnace of Celsa and an electric furnace of Torras Herrería, and for retirements (of those aged fifty-five and over) in Nueva Montaña.

From 1986 European Community regulations have covered the iron and steel industry in Spain, although a three-year transition period was allowed, during which the government was able to continue to subsidise steel and to provide substantial aid to the sector. During this time shipments of steel to the EC were limited by quotas. The transition period ran out at the end of 1988, leaving the Spanish integrated iron and steel industry fully covered by the European Coal and Steel Community regime.

Despite the long and costly process of reconversion, further restructuring and investment in new facilities (for example, to produce higher value-added products) will be necessary throughout the steel industry to ensure its long-term survival. The integrated iron and steel sector remains relatively small in scale and split between two producers. The government has been able to foster restructuring from its position as a major shareholder and an institution to whom large debts are owed across much of the industry (indeed, as a consequence of reconversion the steel industry in Spain was virtually mortgaged to the public sector). But the process has been complicated by rivalries within the industry (including significant differences in business culture between companies) and political tensions between central and regional government agencies. Thus, in those companies where there are major public shareholdings (for example in AHV) there has been the difficult problem of who should determine company strategy – the company management, central or regional government.

Further rationalisation and vertical integration will characterise the European steel industry in the 1990s, with steel producers buying control of downstream distributors and processors (in part to secure market share and engage in 'just-in-time' delivery systems). In 1990 British Steel tried to acquire the specialist steel producer Aristraín but had to settle instead for a flat rolled steel business, Laminación y Derivados. Alliances with foreign companies and foreign takeovers in areas of profitable production are as likely as domestic mergers.

Geographical concentration of the iron and steel industry in the Cantabrian Cornise (Asturias, Cantabria, Guipúzcoa and Vizcaya) has contributed to the disintegration of the economic fabric of the region, as traditional primary and manufacturing industries have collapsed. This has left large areas of derelict land and environmental degradation (for example, along the left bank of the river Nervión in, and north of, Bilbao) and some of the most intense problems of economic restructuring in the European Union. These problems have been partly recognised in the designation of the industrial areas as 'zones of industrial decline' (Salmon 1990).

6.5 Fertilizers

Like the iron and steel industry, fertilizer manufacturing is also energy intensive. Thus, following rapid expansion in the 1960s and early 1970s, the industry was severely affected by increasing energy costs which coincided with falling demand. The resulting market pressures brought rationalisation (including the withdrawal of the American multinationals Gulf and Esso, whose interests were acquired by Cros and ERT), hastened in the late 1980s by a reconversion plan. Industrial reorganisation left only one major Spanish fertilizer company, that controlled by the private sector Ercros group, which itself went into liquidation in 1993 following the collapse of the KIO group in Spain. In 1988 the industry produced 5.7 million tonnes but a growing trade gap has appeared, with imports having risen from 200,000 tonnes in 1986 to 1.9 million tonnes in 1993 (*El País* 1994a).

In the early 1980s the fertilizer industry was uncompetitive at the international level, having relied on government subsidies and protection in the domestic market. Production costs were generally higher than those of competitors and prices needed to be reduced to competitive levels (in 1986 urea prices in Spain were pta 40 per kilo compared with pta 30 per kilo for imports). A crucial problem remained that of the spatial distribution of plants, which required reorganisation to achieve a more efficient pattern of supply across the dispersed domestic market. In 1984 there were a dozen companies owning more than 40 plants, many of them obsolete. The greatest problem was in nitrogenous fertilizers: the Spanish industry used naphtha as its main input (subsidised by the government) instead of the natural gas used in competitor countries. To address the problems the government introduced a reconversion plan for the sector in 1985. As this was still incomplete in 1987, the industry was granted two further years of protection from the European Community on imports of urea (covering 1987 and 1988).

The reconversion plan for the fertilizer sector (Plan de Reconversión de Fertilizantes) embraced sweeping changes including: a reorganisation of production through company mergers; financial restructuring; a reduction of the labour force; and rationalisation of the pattern of plants through selective investment, plant closures and a reduction in capacity (about 80 per cent of the Plan was concerned with the nitrogenous division of fertilizer production along with the adjustment of capacity to demand). By March 1989 the number of plants had been reduced to 30, capacity reduced by more than 1 million tonnes and the labour force cut by 1,500. The involvement of the Kuwait Investment Office (KIO) in both of the two major private sector companies, ERT and Cros, paved the way for the merger of these two companies under the name Ercros at the end of 1988, with the formation of Fesa (Fertilizantes Españolas SA) as its fertilizer division. Fesa then controlled about 55 per cent of the fertilizer market, a further 25 to 30 per cent being controlled by Enfersa (Empresa Nacional de Fertilizantes, a subsidiary of INI). As the final act of the Plan the government sold Enfersa to Fesa in 1989, to leave one major private sector fertilizer company. Fesa-Enfersa still contained excess capacity and was carrying substantial debts.

Following its control of Ercros, the KIO speeded-up the restructuring (or asset stripping?) programme. Ercros sold off some of its interests (those in potash to INI, Electro Metalúrgica to Enher and pharmaceuticals to a private company), using the money to reduce the debts of the fertilizer company, cut capacity (closing plants in Castellón, Lérida, Barakaldo, Málaga, Mérida and Santander) and investing in new equipment. In June 1992 Ercros went into receivership (the largest company failure in the history of democratic Spain), taking with it its fertilizer subsidiary. A viability plan for the Ercros group (January 1993) assumed the closure of five plants and the loss of 1,900 jobs (about half the total jobs in the fertilizer group). The plants due for closure were: two plants, Hondón and Escombreras, in Cartagena (leaving one – Asur – open); Seville – San Jerónimo – (and the reduction of the labour force in the four plants in Huelva); Valladolid, Nicas; and Zaragoza, IQZ).

6.6 Textiles and clothing

The textile and clothing sector embraces textiles (cotton, wool, silk, etc.), synthetic fibres, clothing, carpets and shoes (Table 6.4). In 1991 official statistics put the number of people employed in this broadly defined sector at 260,000 people (12 per cent of all industrial employment – including that in energy and mining), contributing about 7 per cent of the industrial product (value added). However, its true sized and importance is understated by official figures (in 1992 even the Ministry of Industry put the employment figure closer to 350,000; MINE 1993), which miss that part of the industry that operates in the submerged economy. In towns and villages across Spain, and especially in Andalucía, Cataluña and Comunidad Valenciana, the textile industry operates partly as a 'cottage industry' invisible to the authorities. The growth of the submerged economy has been one response of textile and clothing producers to the economic pressures besetting the industry, a means of survival in the face of increasing competition. Fragmentation is a problem throughout the industry (except in synthetic fibres), with small and medium-size family firms predominating, especially in clothing and shoes (Table 6.4).

Many problems had their origin in the period of autarchic development, which left an industry with poor management, out-dated plant and low productivity, unable to face growing competition from Newly Industrialised Countries. Expansion in the 1960s was based almost entirely on the small domestic market, resulting in slower growth than elsewhere in north-west Europe, hindering the development of specialisation. There were a series of restructuring plans (for wool in 1962 and particularly for the cotton industry in the 1960s) but they failed to produce a modern, internationally competitive industry, allowing imports to grow in spite of import protection. Falling demand for Spanish textiles in the domestic market during the 1970s forced textile manufacturers to look for export markets and to invest overseas.

Foreign firms remain of relatively little importance in the textile sector (except in synthetic fibres), although their presence grew slightly during the 1980s. For example, the Japanese company Kondobo opened a new factory in 1987 in Gerona to produce cotton thread and textiles mainly for export. Such developments posed a further threat to Spanish producers, who have tended to be insular in outlook, having been protected from the outside world by a high tariff wall (with no more than 5 per cent of textile output exported and imports accounting for about 10 per cent of consumption in the early 1980s).

Since 1986 the textile industry has begun to face direct competition from other producers in the European Community (especially Portugal with its lower labour costs) and from developing countries, which hoped to be able to export larger quantities of goods to western Europe after the Multifibre Arrangement ran out and trade in textiles was subsumed under the new

Table 6.4 The textile sector, 1978 and 1991

Sector (CNAE)	Establishments 1978	Establishments 1991	Employment 1978	Employment 1991	Value added 1978	Value added 1991
Thread and cloth (431 to 434)	2,281	1,182	97,803	39,630	88.1	133.2
Knitted goods (435)	1,717	1,324	37,503	26,198	27.1	69.7
Finished goods (436)	510	421	21,141	12,884	19.2	44.8
Carpets, other textiles (437 to 439)	1,494	888	25,264	15,806	19.3	51.4
Sub total	6,002	3,815	181,711	94,518	153.8	299.1
Tanners (441)	445	297	12,675	9,983	14.6	45.2
Leather goods (442)	1,329	758	14,500	8,394	8.3	20.8
Shoes (451 and 452)	2,893	2,032	65,235	29,090	50.9	79.3
Mass produced clothes (453, 455)	4,510	4,824	118,164	106,661	89.8	283.6
Made to measure clothes (454)	4,495	1,329	9,089	2,405	3.8	3.4
Fur (456)	326	192	3,774	1,611	2.9	5.4
Man-made fibres (2516)	21	19	9,728	7,216	15.1	34.6
Sub total	14,019	9,451	233,165	165,360	185.4	472.3
Total	20,021	13,266	414,876	259,878	339.2	771.4

Value added in pta billion

Sources: INE 1984 and 1994b

GATT agreement. Imports escalated after 1986 as a result of the reduction in import barriers and the appreciation of the peseta. In 1993 imports of textiles and clothing were valued at pta 556 billion and exports at pta 321 billion compared with a small surplus in 1986 (*El País* 1994a).

The textile and clothing industry is concentrated in Cataluña (over 40 per cent of employment) and Comunidad Valenciana (16 per cent of employment) (INE 1994b). Other regions also have significant textile industries, including Andalucía and Galicia (the base of the textile group Inditex with its Zara chain of clothing stores). Specific sub-sectors display greater concentration. In contrast, the finishing industry of clothing is more widespread, Madrid, Barcelona and Valencia being particularly important centres.

Ninety per cent of cotton spinning and 80 per cent of cotton weaving are located in Cataluña (Tamames 1983), predominantly in the province of Barcelona (which alone contains 85 per cent of the industry in the region). Many of the factories are along the Llobregat, Cardona, Besós and Tordera rivers and on the coast. There are also major factories in the urban areas of Barcelona, Manresa and in Gerona. The climate, port facilities, water power and a history of textile manufacturing have all contributed to the present importance of this region. Outside of Cataluña there are isolated cotton textile centres in Andalucía, the Balearic Islands, Extremadura and the Levante.

The wool, silk and leather industries are similarly concentrated in Cataluña, especially in Barcelona. The wool industry flourished in medieval Spain in centres such as Béjar, Medina del Campo, Palencia,

Medina de Rioseco, Segovia, Sabadell and Tarrasa. Now over half the industry is in Cataluña, especially in Barcelona where the main centres are in the city of Barcelona, in Sabadell and Tarrasa. Outside of Cataluña, Alcoy and Crevillente are important centres in Alicante (in Crevillente an estimated 90 per cent of national carpet manufacturing is concentrated) and Béjar in Salamanca (especially rugs). Other woollen centres include: Palencia, Logroño, Zaragoza, Burgos and León. The silk industry too has a long history (especially in Granada) but is now of less importance, pure silk having largely given way to other materials. Raw silk is mainly produced in Alicante and Murcia, while silk production is undertaken in Cataluña, Orihuela (Alicante), Almonacid, Burjasot (Valencia), Valencia, Granada and Palma de Mallorca. The most important centre for the leather industry is in Barcelona, where Igualada is the main centre for the preparation of skins. Outside of Cataluña other important leather centres are in Valencia, Castellón, La Coruña and Ubrique (Cádiz).

The shoe industry in Spain is the second largest in Europe after Italy, producing around 200 million pairs of shoes a year, employing almost 29,000 people in 1993 and with exports (mainly to the EU) running at almost half the value of production (FICE 1994). The industry enjoyed spectacular growth in the 1960s and 1970s (from thirty million pairs at the beginning of the 1960s to 200 million at the end of the 1970s, of which about half were exported). But, as elsewhere in the textile industry, it too now faces problems of growing labour costs, increased competition from Newly Industrialised Countries (imports from all countries grew from 19.5 million pairs in 1987 to 40.9 million pairs in 1991), marketing weaknesses and a fragmented structure. Increasingly the industry has had to adapt to short production runs and rapid response to demand, which displays marked seasonality (demand peaking in summer and winter) as well as longer-term business cycle fluctuations.

The main manufacturing centres are in the province of Alicante (64 per cent of all companies and over half the labour force), the region of Castilla-La Mancha (12 per cent of all companies) and the Balearic Islands (5 per cent of all companies). Within these areas shoe production is highly concentrated. The city of Alicante, Elche, Elda-Petral, Villena and Sax embrace over three-quarters of the shoe companies and employment in the province of Alicante (half of all firms in the industry). In Castilla-La Mancha manufacturing is concentrated in Almansa, Albacete, Fuensalida-Portillo and Toledo. In the Balearic Islands one of the main centres is Inca in Mallorca. In Rioja production is centred around Arnedo. In Zaragoza it is concentrated in the Brea de Aragón and Illueca area, while in Murcia there is local concentration in the cities of Yecla and Alhama. In each of the manufacturing centres a degree of specialisation exists: ladies shoes in Elda and the Balearic Islands, men's shoes in Almansa and children's shoes in Villena, Sax and Fuensalida-Portillo. Elche, Elda and Almansa are oriented especially towards exports. Most companies are very small and there is a high turnover of firms. According to the Spanish Shoe Federation, of the 2,145 firms in 1993 over half employed less than ten workers and over 85 per cent employed less than twenty-five. Moreover, the average size of firm has become smaller (FICE 1994; MINE 1993).

The importance of the textile industry for employment, the extent of the problems that it faced, the prospect of greater competition on membership of the European Community, the assistance being given to the textile sector by other industrial countries and, arguably, the political weight of the main area of textile employment, prompted the early emergence of a textile reconversion plan. The Plan de Reconversión del Sector Textil began to take shape in 1979 and was finally approved in 1981 (Real Decreto 2010/1981). It attempted to foster the adaptation of the industry to meet international competition through measures to promote the renewal of plant and equipment, to improve the financial structure of companies, and to improve 'intangibles' such as marketing, image, quality and design. Twenty-four per cent of investment went into 'intangibles', which were recognised as an important element in competitiveness in the 1984 Reconversion Law.

Under the Reconversion Plan programmes were approved for 691 firms (of which 30 failed to implement their programmes) embracing about 25 per cent of the labour force (including virtually all those in the synthetic fibre sector). Twenty-eight per cent of the reconversion programmes approved contained measures to reduce employment, while 15 per cent contained proposals to expand employment. The net effect was to reduce employment by 9,929 (total losses were 11,156; 28 per cent by early retirements). These relatively small labour force reductions covered by the Plan must be viewed against the very substantial losses that had occurred prior to the Plan, registered employment in the textile sector having fallen from 415,000 in 1978 to only 274,000 in 1986 (Table 6.4). Almost all the large firms in the industry were given financial assistance. Thus of the 661 firms that implemented reconversion plans, 40 had more than 500 workers, 318 had 50–500 workers and 303 had less than 50 workers (MINE 1987). Assistance went especially towards the capital intensive areas of production (for example synthetic fibres), with much of the equipment being imported. Most of the firms assisted (509) were in the textile sector *senso stricto* (for example 131 firms in cotton) and clothing (141 firms). As the textile industry displays a certain degree of spatial concentration, assistance too has been spatially concentrated, with over half of the firms and workers covered by the Plan located in Cataluña and 20 per cent of the firms in Comunidad Valenciana. The total investment realised by the firms in the Plan totalled pta 184 billion, of which pta 111 billion was in textiles (including pta 47 billion in cotton), pta 42 billion in clothing and pta 31 billion in synthetic fibres. Twelve per cent of the total investment came from central government grants above the subsidised loans from the industrial credit bank (Banco de Crédito Industrial) (MINE 1987). The Plan expired at the end of 1986 (although in 1987 the programmes for some firms were still incomplete).

Since the mid 1980s there has been a continued emphasis on investment in research and development, design and improved marketing. For example, in 1992 textile firms received pta 588 million in assistance under national schemes for improving quality, technology and design (MINE 1993). In addition they received pta 520 million under export promotion schemes operated by the National Export Institute (ICEX). Moreover, in 1992 the Textile Competitiveness Plan (Plan de Competitividad Textil) came into force. The Plan envisaged assistance for establishing co-operation between businesses, research and development, financial and management studies, improvements in design, quality and marketing, and in training. The Plan also provides assistance for industrial diversification in textile production areas (within the framework of the European Union restructuring of textile areas scheme, RETEX).

Protection of the industry in the past has left a sector which will need further to rationalise operations and reduce employment during the second half of the 1990s. But it has at least allowed the retention of a large textile sector. The industry will need to continue to promote flexibility, increase research and development, update technology, improve design and marketing, shift production towards higher value-added products and step-up trade promotion. The question is whether this will be enough to retain competitiveness in domestic and international markets and enough to prevent textile manufacturers shifting production facilities out of Spain? Numerous textile companies have opened plants outside of Spain in the early 1990s, mostly in Morocco and Tunisia.

6.7 Food, drink and tobacco

The food, drink and tobacco industry (abbreviated here to the food industry) is the most important manufacturing sector in Spain as measured by employment and value added (in 1993 sales were valued at just below pta 6,000 billion). Approximately 360,000 people are employed in the sector (together with others in the underground economy), representing some 16 per cent of all industrial employment and value added (including that in energy and mining) and close to 20 per cent of all manufacturing industrial employment and value added. The industry also provides a major intermediate market for the agricultural sector. Over 41,000 food companies (60,000 establishments) range in size from the sole trader semi-subsistence business to some of the largest businesses in Spain and multinational companies. The industrial structure is dominated by small firms, although output is more concentrated. In 1992 the 50 largest companies shared one-third of the food market and the 500 largest accounted for 70 per cent. In 1992 about 14 per cent of the 200 largest Spanish non-financial companies (by value of sales) were in the food sector, including foreign multinationals such as Danone (BSN), Nestlé and Unilever, and the nationally based Campofrío,

Ebro Agrícolas, Pescanova and Tabacalera. In terms of employment the largest sub-sector is bread, cakes and biscuits, followed by meat, then conserves, fruit and dairy products (Table 6.5). In brewing Spain is the fourth largest producer in the European Union, with beer production in 1993 of 2.42 billion litres (11 per cent down on 1989; Concha Gil 1994b).

The food industry is dispersed across the country, broadly echoing the distribution of population and reflecting the pattern of agricultural production. Andalucía and Cataluña are the two most important regions. Barcelona and Madrid are the two most important provinces, others being Valencia, Murcia and Seville. Food manufacturing is also particularly important to the regional economy of Murcia and to the local economies of many Andalucian cities such as Málaga, Granada and Seville.

Within this overall pattern of dispersal there are many examples of geographical specialisation in particular sub-sectors related to the distribution of raw materials and the evolution of particular production techniques. Examples include the sherry industry in Jerez de la Frontera, dairy products in Asturias and Cantabria, *turrón* in Valencia and practically 50 per cent of firms registered to the meat sector concentrated in Castilla-León and Cataluña. There are also numerous examples of food industries that dominate local economies such as the biscuit industry of Estepa (Seville), the distilleries of Rute and Montilla (Córdoba), and the mineral-water industry of Lanjarón (Granada).

Table 6.5 Food, drink and tobacco by sector, 1991

Sector		Employment	Establishments	Value added
411/12	Oils and fats	14,457	2,172	76.9
413	Meat products	56,492	4,197	192.2
414	Milk products	24,222	623	155.6
415	Juices and conserves	27,666	692	78.8
416	Fish products	17,253	399	51.1
417	Flour milling	9,387	2,044	30.5
418–23	Diverse food products	23,614	1,330	140.2
419	Bread, cakes and biscuits	99,088	21,646	243.8
420	Sugar	4,639	32	41.3
421	Cocoa, chocolate and sweets	11,836	461	58.5
422	Animal feeds	11,136	1,016	82.0
424	Liquers and alcohol	5,154	271	55.9
425	Wine industry	19,468	4,722	116.7
426	Cider	452	150	2.5
427	Beer	12,257	39	123.6
428	Non-alcoholic drinks	16,804	714	130.2
429	Tobacco	8,525	28	112.5
Total	Food, drink and tobacco	362,450	40,536	1,692.3

Employment refers to occupied population

Source: INE 1994b

As in many other sectors of manufacturing industry the food industry too is characterised by the small size of plants and firms, which remain as limitations to competitiveness despite numerous amalgamations. In 1992 96.5 per cent of all firms employed less than 25 people and only 0.2 per cent more than 250 people (MINE 1993). At the end of 1992 there were only seven food manufacturing companies in the top one hundred non-financial companies in Spain (most of them either subsidiaries of foreign multinationals or with foreign participation) and less than 50 firms employed more than 500 people. Small plants are characteristic of the bread, cakes and biscuits sector, in which there were over 22,000 plants with less than 20 persons and only 10 with over 500 persons in 1991 (INE 1994b). In contrast, brewing and sugar are characterised by large plants, although in sugar the plants are frequently smaller than their counterparts in other EU countries. Thus in 1994 eight of the 21 sugar beet refineries had a capacity of less than 4,000 tonnes of sugar beet a day.

The organisation of the food industry varies between sub-sectors but the most common form of market structure is that of a few large companies (often foreign multinationals) serving national, and sometimes international markets, and a multitude of small ones serving local markets. Direct state involvement in food processing has been small, except in the case of the tobacco industry, which was the monopoly of the state-owned group Tabacalera. In some sub-sectors control of production is confined to a few companies, this being the case in brewing, sugar and tobacco. In other sub-sectors the market is shared by small and medium-sized companies. For example, in the meat industry the four largest firms (Oscar Mayer, Revilla, Campofrío and Estellés) accounted for only 19.4 per cent of the market in 1988 and the eight largest firms for only 28.5 per cent. Outside of these large and medium-sized companies, the multitude of small family firms face increasing competition from national and multinational producers. Many of these small firms will disappear in the wake of increased competition. Equally, there will be further concentration among the larger companies.

Some companies are quoted on the Stock Exchange but many remain in the hands of families. For example, the manufacture of meat products has traditionally been a family business: Campofrío is owned by the Ballvé and Yartú families, Estellés and Fuertes are owned by families of the same names. Other examples of large family-owned companies are Larios (the distillers based in Málaga) and Vall Companys SA (a vertically integrated meat and cereals group) based in Lérida.

Restructuring in the food industry has been market led, there having been no reconversion programme in this sector. This has involved a complex process of spatial, structural and organisational change resulting in a realignment of production, concentration and internationalisation. From 1986 there was a substantial increase in investment in the sector culminating in 1991, after which investment slowed and a wave of rationalisation followed. Added complications in the sector have resulted from exposure to the Common Agricultural Policy (for example, in the dairy products industry) and the food harmonisation measures necessary for the Single European Market. The food industry has also been the recipient of EU funding. For example, in 1994 the Ministry of Agriculture published a Strategic Plan for the Food industry envisaging European and Spanish government funding of pta 220 billion to the end of 1997.

Diversification has been one response to increasing market pressures, although most Spanish companies remain concentrated in one sector (diverse food manufacturing companies being restricted mainly to foreign multinationals such as Nestlé and Danone). In sugar refining the company Ebro Agrícolas has developed backward links to agriculture (with its own farms), horizontal links into other forms of food production and forward links into food distribution. Sociedad General Azucarera markets sugar, alcohol and yeast and has a holding in the meat company Corporación Alimentaria Ibérica (CAI). The big meat companies have also diversified into other food products: Navidul into cheese and Campofrío into fish and dairy products. The increasing importance of distribution has also led to the strengthening of distribution systems and vertical integration.

The most publicised feature of restructuring has involved company mergers and concentration as companies endeavour to rationalise their operations and gain market share. In so doing, many formally local or regionally based companies have become national or even international in outlook. In dairy products the four dairies of Gurelesa, Inlena-Copeleche, Bayena and Urbia, which operate in País Vasco and Navarra, amalgamated to form Iparlat in 1988. The new company was able to take advantage of the economies of scale enjoyed by the major companies in the sector; Lactaria Española (SAM-RAM, owned by Tabacalera), Pascual, Central Lechera Asturiana and Puleva (economies which were insufficient to avoid serious financial problems in the industry in 1994, including Puleva going into receivership). In sugar the three companies, Ebro Compañía de Azúcares y Alimentación, Compañía de Industrias Agrícolas and Sociedad Azucarera Ibérica, merged in 1990 to form Ebro Agrícolas Compañia de Alimentación SA, taking 50 per cent of the market and forming the fifth largest sugar company in the EC in 1992 with a sugar quota of about half a million tonnes (compared with the largest company, British Sugar, with a quota of over 1 million tonnes). This left 22 per cent of the market in the hands of Sociedad General Azucarera and the rest split between Cooperativa Onésimo Redondo (Acor) and Azucarera Reunidas de Jaén. Mergers have led to larger companies but generally these remain relatively small by international standards.

Restructuring in the tobacco industry resulted from the break-up of the tobacco monopoly following membership of the European Community. The state exercised a monopoly (dating back to the seventeenth century) over the production, processing and distribution of tobacco in Spain (except in the Canary Islands where a multinational industry has operated) through the company Tabacalera (Companía Arrendataria Tabacalera SA). The company, which was established in 1945, employs over 8,000 people with factories in Alicante, Cádiz, La Coruña, Gijón, Logroño, Madrid, Málaga, San Sebastián, Santander, Seville, Tarragona and Valencia. In the late 1980s the company diversified into other food industries (including Royal Brands biscuits and the milk products group La Lactaria Española) in addition to developing interests in property and tourism. These ventures were largely unsuccessful and by the early 1990s the company was consolidating around its principal business, tobacco (having sold the food company Royal Brands in 1994).

Greater concentration of production has been accompanied by selective investment and numerous plant closures. For example, in flour milling there were 1,600 mills in Spain in 1978, most of which were small, family-owned concerns. In 1993 there were only about 420 remaining in operation. With milling capacity of 10 million tonnes and demand running at only 3–4 million tonnes further significant contractions will occur accompanied by the introduction of more efficient plant (such as that of Vall Companys in Arévalo (Avila) with a milling capacity of 500 tonnes daily). In sugar refining there has been a reduction in the number of refineries from 32 at the beginning of the 1980s to 21 in 1994, with closures of La Vega, El Carmen and San Isidro in Granada, Antequerana in Málaga, Luceni in Zaragoza, Santa Eulalia in Teruel, Aranjuez in Madrid and Rosales in Seville. Further closures will follow, especially as the sugar regime in the EU is liberalised. Apart from the direct employment effect of the closure of sugar refineries (leading to a reduction of the industry labour force from 9,500 in 1978 to below 6,000 in 1992), the indirect impact has fallen on the farmers engaged in sugar cultivation.

Concentration has been inhibited by strong company loyalties and conflicts of personalities. As a result, precipitous company mergers have sometimes been unsuccessful. An illustration of a failed merger is provided by the history of the two Spanish family-owned olive oil firms, Elosúa (based in Asturias) and Pont (based in Lérida). These two companies joined in 1985 to form the company Aceites Españoles to acquire the second largest olive oil company, Carbonell. It was an action encouraged by the government, which sought to ensure Spanish control over a strategic market segment. Carbonell became part of Elosúa but rivalry between Pont and Elosúa resulted in the failure of their merger and the consequent failure to ensure Spanish control over the sector. The Italian company Ferruzzi gained control of the company Koipe, then Oleaginosas Españolas (Oesa, bought from the government in 1988) and finally formed the Koipe-Elosúa group in 1990 (including Carbonell). In 1994 it was seeking to merge Koipe with Elosúa. A merged company would control over one-third of the vegetable oil market in Spain and be the largest olive oil company in the world. Unilever (operating through the companies Agra and Costa Blanca), the Cargill group and Bunge are other foreign multinationals, which together now dominate the vegetable oil industry.

The other major feature of industrial restructuring has been increased foreign penetration, multinational companies seeking to both gain market share in the domestic market and strategically position themselves for the Single European Market. In so doing foreign capital has grown to dominate the food industry. The antecedents of foreign ownership date back to previous centuries (for example with the development of the sherry industry in Jerez de la Frontera) and some companies established plants in Spain in the 1950s and 1960s (for example Coca Cola established a bottling plant in Barcelona in 1953). However, foreign penetration rose sharply in the 1980s, giving most major food industry multinationals a presence. Of the ten largest food groups operating in Spain in 1993, most were either subsidiaries of foreign multinationals or included significant foreign capital (the main exceptions being Tabacalera, Agropecuaria de Guissona (a co-operative of agricultural producers), Pescanova and Campofrío. The situation may not be untypical of other European countries but it represents a significant change for Spain.

Foreign multinationals are now found throughout the food industry, accounting for close on 40 per cent of the food market in 1993 (refers to companies with a significant foreign holding; MINE 1993). They have control over the two major companies in the mass-produced bread market: Bimbo (owned by the American drinks company Anheuser Busch, which also uses Bimbo to distribute its drinks products in Spain) and Panrico (owned by Allied Lyons of the UK). The meat sector is dominated by three multinationals: Unilever (which in 1986 acquired the meat company Revilla), Nestlé and Oscar Mayer of Germany. The poultry sector is dominated by about four or five multinationals following a wave of acquisitions that have included those by the French firm Doux and the American firm Tyson Foods. In the drinks sector more than half of the Spanish coffee market is divided between the Swiss company Nestlé, the Dutch company Douwe Egberts and General Foods of the United States. In conserves the company Chistu has passed into the hands of Pillsbury (the US food manufacturer, itself now owned by Grand Metropolitan) and Orlando has gone to Heinz. In sugar the company Ebro (with half the Spanish sugar market) fell into the hands of Torras Hostench in the late 1980s (controlled by the Kuwait Investment Office). In the soft drinks market over 60 per cent is taken by the products of the multinational companies Coca Cola, Pepsi-Cola (which acquired Kas from Banco Bilbao Vizcaya in 1992) and Cadbury-Schweppes (although many multinational brands are manufactured or distributed under license by Spanish firms). In brewing five major groups control over 90 per cent of production and all are either foreign-owned or have significant foreign penetration (Table 6.6). Even in the traditional family wine-making and sherry businesses, multinational companies have gradually increased their presence; International Distillers and Vintners have a large holding in González Byass and in 1994 Pedro Domecq was acquired by

Table 6.6 The major brewing groups, 1993

Group	Production in 1993 million litres	(%)	Major foreign shareholder
Grupo Cruzcampo	654	26.9	Guinness (British)
El Aguila SA	420	17.3	Heineken (Dutch)
Mahou SA	420	17.3	Danone/BSN (French)
San Miguel SA	351	14.4	Danone/BSN (French)
Grupo Damm	400	16.5	Oetker (German)
All five major brewers	2,245	92.4	
Others	183	7.6	
Total	2,428	100.0	

Other groups include Grupo Cia Cervecera Canarias with 2.32 per cent of the market, Hijos de Rivera SA with 2.1 per cent, Sical SA with 1.5 per cent, La Zaragozana SA with 1.3 per cent and others with 0.4 per cent

Production in 1993 was 7 per cent less than in 1992

Sources: Concha Gil 1994a and 1994b

Allied Lyons. In 1994 the French company Danone controlled the Spanish dairy products company Danone, the mineral water producers Aguas Lanjarón and Font Vella, the biscuit manufacturer General Biscuits, the cooked food products group Starlux and the brewing company Mahou. It was also building a controlling stake in the brewing group San Miguel.

While the dominant flow of foreign investment has been inward, some Spanish companies have been expanding abroad; predominantly through increasing exports and seeking contracts with foreign distributors rather than through direct investment, although a few have become true multinationals (for example Campofrío and Pescanova). Numerous companies have built up important export markets, including the drinks company Freixnet (the manufacturer of Cava champagne; the company has significant markets in the United States and Japan), Campofrío, Nutrexpa (the manufacturer of the chocolate drink Cola Cao) and Hernández Pérez Hermanos. Generally, Spanish food companies have not been oriented towards exports, being more concerned in the late 1980s with defending their domestic markets. But in the 1990s there has been growing interest in exports. Where Spanish direct foreign investment has occurred it has frequently been concentrated in southern Europe (especially Portugal). The sugar refiner Ebro Agrícolas has a significant holding in the Portuguese company Vasco de Gama (which produces fish and oil), Sociedad General Azucarera, a holding in Unión Sacárica Emiliana de Italia and in the Turkish yeast company Ozmayyas.

Growth in demand (by value) and changes in consumer tastes have characterised the food market. Demand expanded on the back of rising disposable incomes and increasing consumer spending. The industry grew by about 8 per cent per annum in the three years 1987 to 1989 (compared with 5 per cent growth in GDP) after which growth slowed with the downturn in the business cycle. Alongside this growth has been a shift in consumer tastes away from traditional products towards higher value-added processed foods and higher quality products, and those products considered to be more healthy and environmentally friendly. Meat and meat products accounted for over one-quarter of household food expenditure in 1992, followed by fish and fish products (12 per cent). These trends also demonstrate an element of consumer convergence, changes in demand that are gradually aligning consumer behaviour in different European countries. Hence beer consumption in Spain rose from 30.3 litres a person in 1970 to 70.5 litres in 1992, while wine consumption fell.

On the supply side there have been fundamental and far-reaching shifts in the pattern of distribution, with the rapid growth since the 1970s of supermarkets and hypermarkets and the decline of the traditional small store. As distribution has become more concentrated, so power to determine the evolution of the food industry has passed from manufacturers to the distributors, of which many of the largest are foreign companies. Distributors, selling an increasing range of their own brand products, are able to promote imported products. They also provide a much closer interface with the consumer and can quickly respond to (and shape) shifts in consumer tastes.

Traditionally, Spain had a net surplus on trade in agricultural and food products (*balanza agroalimentaria*) but that surplus has disappeared as the domestic market has been opened up to competition, especially from other countries in the European Union. In 1993 exports of agriculture and food products rose to pta 1,319 billion (of which food, drink and tobacco represented pta 368 billion) and imports to pta 1,473 (food, drink and tobacco pta 482 billion), leaving a deficit of pta 154 billion (90 per cent import coverage) (*El País* 1994a). Exports of agricultural and food products are concentrated on relatively unprocessed products (for example horticultural produce and vegetable oils) and alcoholic drinks, while imports tend to have a higher value-added content.

Other EU countries have pursued a strategy of entering the Spanish market, with good results. For example, in 1988 food products exported from France to Spain increased by 22.4 per cent (on 1987) to reach pta 114 billion. Such success may be partly attributed to the aggressive action of the private sector in other countries and better foreign government promotion of products. Spain has been less successful with exports. The private sector has been less active and government agencies (such as the Trade Agency, Instituto de Comercio Exterior) may have been less efficient. Part of the problem is image, Spanish products often being shipped to France or Italy for packaging before sale to final consumers.

On the import side, changing tastes have fuelled imports. For example, imports of fruit from the southern hemisphere have increased spectacularly.

Import quotas on these products disappeared in 1990. In 1983 almost all the fruit and vegetables passing through the Mercabarna (wholesale market for Barcelona) were Spanish; in 1988 12 per cent of the vegetables and 3 per cent of the fruit was imported. Fresh fruit imports especially are on the increase, although the major import items are fish, crustaceans and molluscs (which rose from pta 64 billion in 1985 to pta 303 billion in 1993), drinks (from pta 15 to pta 104 billion), meat and fish products (from pta 8 to pta 35 billion) and sugar and sweets (from pta 3 to pta 43 billion) (*El País* 1994a).

The major weaknesses of the Spanish food industry are the small size of many of the companies and limited product research. It also lacks experience of international markets, suffers from a low quality product image and generally displays insufficient management and work force training. Competitiveness in the 1990s will depend on improving distribution networks, professional training and, perhaps most importantly, improving the image of products. Much of this is likely to be achieved by the incorporation of Spanish businesses into foreign multinational companies.

6.8 Motor-vehicles

The motor-vehicle industry has been a leading sector in Spanish modern industrial development. It demonstrates how foreign investment transformed a backward industry oriented to the domestic market into a modern internationally integrated industry incorporating the latest automated and robotised production techniques in factories linked to multinational production systems, presaging change elsewhere in the economy. Equally, it demonstrates how major investment decisions affecting the Spanish economy are now made according to the corporate goals of multinational companies headquartered outside Spain: foreign companies controlling all car assembly (following the sale of Seat and Enasa in 1989) and 70 per cent of motor-vehicle components manufacturers.

Motor-vehicle manufacturing is one of the major industries in Spain and, with a car-manufacturing capacity approaching two million units per year, it is one of the leading car producers in the world. The motor-vehicle industry also makes a significant contribution towards exports. Exports of vehicles represented over one-fifth of the value of all merchandise exports in 1993 and eight of the leading ten Spanish export companies were motor-vehicle manufacturers (*El País* 1994a). Some 72,000 people were employed in car assembly in 1992 with a further 19,000 employed in assembling other motor-vehicles. Substantial cuts in employment in 1993 and 1994 may take these numbers down closer to 56,000 and 16,000 at the end of 1994 (Table 6.7). If the numbers employed in components (some 172,000 in 1994) and all other motor-vehicle production are added, the figure at the end of 1994 was closer to 300,000.

Cars were being produced in Barcelona at the end of the nineteenth century. In the first quarter of the twentieth century production spread to other centres in Spain but remained small in scale. In Barcelona the companies of Hispano-Suiza and Elizalde were particularly important. The Civil War diverted production to military equipment. Following the war the policy of import substitution and autarchic development isolated the industry, directing output to the domestic market. Enasa (Empresa Nacional de Autocamiónes) was established by INI in 1946 and Seat (Sociedad Española de Automóviles de Turismo) in 1949, both initially in Barcelona. Components factories grew around an existing engineering base.

During the 1950s the domestic industry expanded and some French manufacturers managed to secure production facilities. The industry was opened up to a larger number of mainly European motor-vehicle manufacturers in the 1960s, attracted by the low labour costs and protected domestic market. The industry was still largely nationalised, displayed a high degree of technological dependence on foreign companies and was oriented to supplying the domestic market. A policy of import substitution was supported by a local content requirement of 90 per cent and an almost complete prohibition on car imports (Lagendijk and Knaap 1993).

The giant American and Japanese manufacturers Ford, General Motors

Table 6.7 Motor-vehicle companies in Spain

Company	Employment	Production	Sales
Seat Volkswagen	14,500	578,047	741
(Seat)	10,000		
Fasa-Renault	12,800	364,282	483
General Motors	9,000	378,428	466
Ford España	8,200	310,753	354
Citroen Hispañia	6,700	314,300	305
Peugeot Talbot	5,000	120,300	185
Nissan Motor Ibérica	6,000	300,000	190
Santana Motor	1,700	36,412	49
Iveco-Pegaso	4,300	7,254	70
Mercedes-Benz	2,800	26,461	103
Renault V. Industriales	1,000	2,649	28
Component Suppliers			
Michelin	10,500	–	153
Firestone Hispania	4,000	–	58
Pirelli	1,460		24
Bosch	4,500		85
Bendix	1,100		19
Tudor	1,400		20

Employment figures are author estimates for the end of 1994; sales figures in pta billion for 1993; production figures are for all motor-vehicle units in 1992.

Sources: El País 1994a and 1994b

and Nissan arrived in the 1970s and early 1980s and the emphasis in production switched to exports. The agreement reached with Ford marked a change in policy towards the motor-vehicle industry as it involved important concessions in terms of state involvement and the national content of cars produced. Through the 1970s and early 1980s there was a gradual reduction of duties on imported components, especially after 1979.

Major losses in motor-vehicle manufacturing world-wide from the mid 1970s to the mid 1980s were associated with increasing production costs and over-capacity. A round of global restructuring followed, involving substantial investment in new plant and equipment as well as structural, technological and spatial reorganisation of the industry. Vehicles became lighter in weight (involving a switch in materials) and began to be marketed world-wide. Manufacturers merged or sought strategic alliances. Input sourcing was reviewed to minimise production costs.

Membership of the European Community opened the way for greater integration into the European motor-vehicle industry, enabling further spatial specialisation of production and intra-industry trade. Production in Spain also offered a degree of continuing protectionism until the early 1990s. Access to the European Community market, coupled with expanding demand in the late 1980s, attracted further American, Japanese and other non-Community investment. Scale economies were possible as a result of the large, established motor-vehicle industry in Spain, including a substantial components industry. Finally, various forms of assistance were available from the government for motor-vehicle manufacturers and foreign investment. Hence, during the 1980s Spain continued to attract investment for reasons of relatively low labour costs, a protected and expanding domestic market, access to the European Community, economies of scale and government assistance.

The boom in the late 1980s was followed by a severe contraction in demand in Spain and across Europe at the beginning of the 1990s. Higher labour costs in Spain and the changing world pattern of competitive advantage reduced the attraction of Spain for new investment. All manufacturers sought ways of further reducing production costs and all began reducing their labour forces (a phenomenon which swept through plants across Europe). Rationalisation of production around more integrated European-wide or global operations was intensified. The sense of crisis in Spain was heightened in 1993 by the planned closure of the symbol of national car production, the Seat car-assembly plant in the Zona Franca of Barcelona, with the loss of 12,000 jobs directly (prompted by enormous losses suffered by Seat in 1992 and 1993) and many more indirectly. Simultaneously, Volkswagen (the owner of Seat) was increasing its investment in former eastern Germany and eastern Europe. The crisis in Barcelona (compounded by redundancies at Nissan) was mirrored in early 1994 in Linares (Jaén), where production at the Japanese-owned Suzuki Motor Company ceased and the company threatened to close unless the work force could be trimmed by 60 per cent, productivity improved and financial assistance provided. In Madrid another Japanese company, the agricultural tractor manufacturer Ebro-Kubota, also closed its plant.

The motor-vehicle market reflects the fluctuations in the business cycle. Motor-vehicles are supplied to the market through production in Spain, imports and the sale of second-hand vehicles. The car market absorbed 638,000 units in 1977, then fell to around 500,000 in the early 1980s. The slump also affected the second-hand market, in which the number of car transfers remained static at around 650,000 to 700,000 per year. As the purchase of new vehicles fell, so the average age of vehicles increased (postponement of new purchases). In 1985 more than 35 per cent of cars in Spain were over ten years old (*Economía y Finanzas* 1987). Demand recovered to 689,000 registrations in 1986 before escalating to over a million between 1988 and 1990 inclusive (Table 6.8). After 1990 the market stabilised before collapsing in 1993 (car sales falling by 25 per cent). A similar pattern was followed by motorcycles and mopeds. Record sales were reached in the early 1990s (311,000 mopeds sold in 1990 and 118,000 motorbike registrations compared with 33,000 in 1983; *El País* 1992) before they too collapsed in 1993. In 1994 car sales recovered as replacement occurred (over one-third of the estimated 13 million cars in Spain were estimated to be more than ten years old), in response to lower interest rates, a government sponsored car exchange scheme (Plan Renove; applied initially for six months to cars and seventeen months to commercial vehicles) similar to that first introduced in France, and as car rental companies increased their purchases in the light of buoyant tourism demand.

Although Spain is an important vehicle exporter, its position within the spatial division of labour of multinational companies has become one in which it specialises in the assembly of small cars and vans (lower value-added products) and generally in relatively less sophisticated components. Hence many types of vehicle and many components (generally higher value-added ones) are imported. Furthermore, imports have become increasingly -competitive as the tariff protection around the Spanish market has been reduced (import duties on EC and EFTA vehicles falling from 33 per cent in 1986 to zero in 1993 and for third country imports from 45 per cent in 1986 to 10 per cent in 1993; although voluntary export restraints remain on Japanese cars with a limit of about 30,000 being agreed in 1992 and 1993). From being a negligible part of the market in 1975 and only 11 per cent of the market in 1980, imports represented 56 per cent of the new car market in 1993 with only a relatively small trade surplus being recorded in the category 'vehicles and tractors' in the early 1990s. The picture is worse in motorcycles where imports now represent some 60 per cent of new registrations (from less than a quarter in 1984; *El País* 1994a). Higher imports reflect a greater integration in the motor-vehicle industry; increased imports being offset by a larger volume of exports (the latter helped by devaluation of the peseta in 1993).

Table 6.8 The car market in Spain

Year	Number of cars in Spain	Production	Domestic sales	Registrations	Imports	IP	Exports
1960	290,500	39,732	–	–	–	–	–
1970	2,377,726	450,426	414,702	399,171	12,103	3.0	40,882
1975	4,806,833	696,128	534,067	572,188	9,126	1.6	156,354
1980	7,556,511	1,028,813	504,051	538,989	60,545	11.2	525,845
1985	9,225,111	1,130,071	480,081	575,051	75,508	13.1	865,304
1990	11,996,000	1,679,301	1,178,487	1,007,014	398,429	39.6	1,066,007
1991	12,537,000	1,773,752	1,060,168	914,061	382,290	41.8	1,284,447
1992	13,102,000	1,790,615	979,895	1,008,454	482,492	47.8	1,274,468
1993	13,457,000	1,505,949	743,927	775,439	435,375	56.1	1,182,218

Imports refer to registrations of imported cars

Figures refer to saloon cars and derivatives in units

IP: Import penetration calculated from imports/all registrations

Sources: Farré Terre 1986; *El País* 1994a; Banco de España 1994

Substantial government assistance has been provided towards investment by motor-vehicle companies under a variety of schemes including trade measures, tax incentives, incentives for job creation and training, research and development loans and subsidies, support to enable privatisations and support under the heading of regional development. In the 1970s and early 1980s re-equipment was fostered by reduced duties on imported plant and equipment. In the mid 1980s financial assistance towards modernisation and training was made available under the Plan General de Promoción Industrial y Technológica del Sector Fabricante de Automóviles, set up in 1985 (under the Ley de Reconversión y Reindustrialización 1984). This recognised the importance of the motor-vehicle industry in Spain and sought to consolidate its position. More recently, assistance towards modernisation and the introduction of new technology has been provided under the Industrial Technology Action Plan (Plan de Actuación Tecnológico Industrial, PATI). For example, in 1994 General Motors received a substantial grant under this scheme towards technology associated with the production of a new model at the Zaragoza plant. The sale of the two public motor-vehicle companies, Enasa and Seat, were also accompanied by the injection of public funds.

Regional governments (and municipalities) have competed to attract investment in motor-vehicles and provided assistance to keep plants open. Frequently, this assistance has been made available under regional development programmes. For example, Citroen benefited from being in the former Large Area of Industrial Expansion of Galicia (now an Objective 1 region of the European Union) and General Motors in the Industrial Zone (Poligono Industrial) of Figueruelas, Zaragoza. In 1988 Ford was given substantial government assistance to build a new auto-electronics plant in Cádiz. In the 1990s component suppliers in Zaragoza have received assistance towards modernisation from the regional government of Aragón and Suzuki Santana only remained open in Linares with assistance from the regional government of Andalucía. The largest tranche of government funding, however, was agreed with Seat in July 1994 ostensibly to support technological development (the PSOE government depending on support from the Catalans for their continued stay in office). The decision was greeted with protests from other vehicle manufacturers in Spain who were also claiming more assistance for investment and to cushion the costs of redundancies.

Five foreign multinational companies were involved in saloon-car manufacture in Spain in 1994, the largest volume of cars being produced by the Seat company. Seat was set up in 1949 by INI with the participation of Fiat (which provided the patents) and other private capital. In 1967 Fiat took a 36 per cent holding in the company but after sustaining substantial losses pulled out in 1981, leaving the state (INI) to find a new partner. An agreement was reached with Volkswagen (VW) in 1983, which finally led to a majority shareholding in 1986. Initially, production of Seat cars was centred in Barcelona on the Zona Franca site, then in 1974 Seat took over the former British Leyland plant in Landaben (Pamplona), which became its second major production centre. Following the takeover by VW a major investment programme was begun, aimed at raising capacity and incorporating the Spanish plants into the VW organisation (including sourcing many components in Germany). A completely new car assembly plant was built for Seat in Martorell, Barcelona (inaugurated in 1993 to be fully operational by 1995), with an eventual capacity to produce 1,500 units a day (some 500,000 cars a year) in three shifts (planned employment some 6,500). Closure of the assembly facilities at the Zona Franca plant will leave production of all Seat cars at Martorell. As part of the negotiations over the future of VW in Barcelona, the company planned to promote the Zona Franca site as a components supply complex and began the development of a European vehicle design centre in Sitges (south of Barcelona) in 1994. The Landaben plant was also substantially modernised in the early 1990s to produce the small VW Polo (capacity about 1,200 units a day, employing 4,500). In 1993 VW transferred this plant from Seat to VW (the subsidiary named Industrias Automovilísticas de Navarra).

The French companies Renault and Peugeot Citroen were established in Spain in the 1950s. The Fasa-Renault company (Fabricación de Automóviles SA) was established in 1955 with factories in Valladolid (producing engines in 1994) and technical collaboration and patents from Renault. A factory producing transmission systems in Seville was acquired in 1966 (expanded to 3,100 gearboxes a day in 1994) and in 1977 a further vehicle assembly plant began production in Palencia (expanded to 900 cars a day in 1994 and where Renault were producing the mid-range Laguna model). Until the 1980s production was directed at the domestic market but the plants have been increasingly integrated in the company's international operations with a large percentage of the transmission systems built in Seville being exported. Peugeot Citroen was established in 1957 as Citroen Hispañia based in the duty-free zone at Vigo. This site enabled it to import fully assembled cars, as well as kits from France for final assembly, and to export cars. In 1994 the plant was producing the small AX and ZX vehicles and a light van. The other part of the company's activities in Spain grew out of the takeover of Chrysler's operations in 1978. In 1963 Chrysler had developed an association with the then independent truck producer Barrieros Diesel, producing vehicles under the Simca and Dodge marks at the company's plant in Villaverde, Madrid. Following the takeover by Citroen, vehicles were sold under the Talbot name (the Talbot truck factory was later sold to Renault Industrial Vehicles). In 1994 the Villaverde plant was producing the 205 and 306 car models and commercial vehicles.

The arrival of Ford in the early 1970s marked the beginning of a new wave of motor-vehicle investment in Spain, directed towards developing an export base within an integrated multinational organisation. Authorisation for a factory at Almusafes (Valencia) was given in 1973 on the basis of the level of investment involved and the guarantee of exporting a specified quantity. The factory began producing engines in 1975 and cars in 1976. In 1994 the Ford plant was producing 1,540 car units a day and had a capacity to produce about 1,950 engine units per day. Production is concentrated on small cars (Fiestas, Escorts and Orions) and engines (below 1300cc). The company opened a motor-vehicle electronics factory near Cádiz (Cádiz Electrónica) in 1988, which was being extended in 1993, and extended its plant in Valencia in the mid 1990s to build a new range of engines (the Sigma range).

General Motors followed Ford into Spain at the end of the 1970s. Agreement was reached in 1979 for a car assembly plant on the industrial estate at Figueruelas (24 km from Zaragoza), plus component factories at Logroño (bodywork) and Puerto Real, Cádiz (suspensions); the latter provided valuable employment in an area suffering from serious unemployment problems resulting from the decline of the shipbuilding industry. The project represented the largest-ever foreign investment in Spain and involved a package of development incentives. From the outset, the plant was built as an export platform for small car production in Europe (initially the Corsa model), producing on average 365,000 cars a year.

Japanese manufacturers have concentrated on the production of light vans and all-terrain vehicles. Nissan entered Spain in 1977 through participation in Motor Ibérica. Motor Ibérica had emerged in 1954 with a factory in the Zona Franca (Barcelona) producing trucks (Ebro) and tractors under licence from Ford. Massey Ferguson took a 36 per cent holding in 1965, which was sold to Nissan in 1980. Nissan has since increased its holding in Nissan Motor Ibérica to 67 per cent (1991). The company is centred in Barcelona, where it has produced the Nissan Patrol since 1983 and in the mid 1990s began producing an all-terrain vehicle in conjunction with Ford: the Nissan Terrano 11/Ford Maverick. In addition, it produces heavy trucks and an increasing number of light vans. Light vans are also built at a plant in Avila. Suzuki Motor (formally Suzuki-Santana) was formed from Metalúrgica de Santa Ana in Linares (Jaén), which began life producing agricultural machinery in the 1950s, then from 1959 built vehicles under licence from British Leyland and Willys Overland of the United States. In 1980 the company formed an agreement with Suzuki to build a light all-terrain vehicle, the Suzuki Santana. Suzuki acquired a small equity stake in 1984, increasing it to 17 per cent in 1986 (while the Land Rover holding fell to 33 per cent), and was finally left with an 82 per cent holding in 1993. Apart from the plant in Linares, the company also have a plant in Manzanares (Ciudad Real). As the only motor-vehicle assembly plant in Andalucía, and the mainstay of the economy of Linares, any closure of the plant would have severe regional development repercussions. Consequently, in 1994 the regional government was seeking a new multinational investor to replace Suzuki, who had announced their intention to abandon the company.

Apart from the companies mentioned above, industrial vehicles are produced by the Iveco-Pegaso group, the enterprise created from the sale of the former public enterprise Enasa to Fiat in 1990 (60 per cent of the capital sold, leaving INI with a 40 per cent holding), Mercedes Benz de España and Renault Vehículos Industriales. Enasa was fully owned by INI, having been established in 1946 with factories in Barajas (Madrid), where it now assembles heavy trucks, and Barcelona, where it used to produce components but now produces doors and transmission systems for heavy trucks on the site of the old factory of Hispano-Suiza. In 1966 it took over the Sava truck plant in Valladolid (established in 1957), where it now assembles vans and produces components. Enasa also has a plant in Mataró (Barcelona), where it assembles buses. Initially, Enasa received technical assistance from Leyland but then built original vehicles, buses and trucks under the trade name Pegaso. In the 1980s the company developed collaborative links with other European manufacturers, notably MAN (now part of VW) and DAF. Sales were concentrated in the domestic market, where it has a significant proportion of the heavy vehicle market (sixteen tonnes and more), including buses. Exports have since increased, partly in relation to intra-industry trade within the Fiat group. Mercedes Benz began making light industrial vehicles with Enmasa (an INI company) in 1960. From 1969 this operation became Mercedes Benz de España with plants in Barcelona (constructed in the 1950s) and Vitoria. Then in 1981 Daimler Benz took a majority holding in Mevosa (a company established in 1950 with German capital) in Vitoria, where it builds vans and a 'people carrier'. In 1986 the bulk of production was still oriented to the domestic market but by the early 1990s an increasing proportion of vehicles were being exported. Restructuring of the company's operation in the mid 1990s will concentrate production in Vitoria (where production will increase to 40,000 units by 1996) with major components being imported and the Barcelona plant supplying small parts only. Renault Vehículos Industriales has a plant at Villaverde, Madrid (formally belonging to Talbot), producing trucks, coaches, buses and vans mostly for the domestic market.

The two-wheeled motor-vehicle market is divided into mopeds/scooters (*ciclomotores* from 50cc to 150cc) and motorbikes (*motocicletas*). Like the other parts of the motor-vehicle industry, it too has been engulfed by foreign multinational companies, especially the Italian and Japanese, and reoriented towards exports. Vespa (about one-third of the market), Nacional Motor Derbi (located at Martorelles, Barcelona, with one-quarter), Yamaha, Puch (now controlled by Suzuki) and GAC (Mobilettes) are the main companies producing mopeds and scooters. The Japanese have taken complete control of the motorbike market, absorbing the relatively small Spanish manufacturers such as Sanglas, Butaco, Ossa and Montesa (the latter acquired by Honda). Honda has the largest market share followed by Yamaha. Yamaha began commercial collaboration with Sanglas in 1977 and later became the major shareholder. Production of motorbikes is concentrated in Barcelona (a new site having been acquired for Yamaha on an industrial estate in the Urgent Reindustrialisation Zone of Cataluña).

Spain has a well-established motor-vehicle components industry, embracing over 1,000 manufacturers, estimated to employ some 172,000 people at the beginning of 1994, concentrated in the north of Spain and with over 80 per cent of turnover being accounted for by a handful of foreign multinational companies.

The industry experienced a wave of restructuring in the 1990s in response to a renewed drive by vehicle assemblers to reduce costs (bought-in components accounting for well over 50 per cent of the cost of a car) and reorganisation of vehicle assembly production systems. Many activities formally undertaken within the assembly companies have been shed to outside suppliers (vertical disintegration of vehicle assembly and the externalisation of production processes). Restructuring has included new alliances, consolidation to achieve economies of scale (particularly to meet demands for enhanced research and development) and new opportunities arising from the externalisation of production processes in vehicle assembly.

As the components industry undergoes transformation, the front-rank component suppliers are having to establish a global presence to meet the demands of vehicle makers for global sourcing. Components producers are also having to develop into suppliers of systems rather than simply of components. A pyramid organisation comprising tiers of producers is emerging throughout the industry. Companies in the top tier are growing in size and technological capability but are becoming fewer in number as assemblers radically reduce their number of suppliers. Lower down the supply chain, the companies with whom the system suppliers deal are also being cut in number. The consequences of this restructuring in Europe could be a decline of at least 40 per cent in employment from 1992 (Done 1994). As a reflection of this trend, 12,000 jobs were lost from the vehicle components industry in Spain in 1993 (Prada 1994).

Component supply complexes have developed around the major vehicle assembly factories partly in response to 'just-in-time' or 'immediate' delivery systems and closer co-operation between assemblers and suppliers in design and quality assurance. These complexes include many suppliers from the assembler's home country (Costa Campi et al. 1991). For example, the US company Johnsons have set up a car seat factory in the Almusafes industrial park. Spanish suppliers 'already disadvantaged in aspects of technology and foreign marketing, now face the problem of "closed doors" at home' (Lagendijk and Knaap 1993, p. 1674) leading the larger component companies to seek new markets and production facilities overseas. In 1986 the bulk of components for vehicles manufactured in Spain were sourced in Spain, by 1992 the proportion had been reduced to less than half (by value). As in the motor-vehicle assembly industry increased trade reflects greater integration in the industry and a higher level of intra-industry trade.

Component supply is dominated in Spain by European and American multinational companies. Valeo España SA is the Spanish subsidiary of the French group Valeo. It includes the companies Faespa, Ferodo España (which acquired Fraymon tyres in the 1970s) and Valeo Distribución. Femsa, a major electrical equipment manufacturer, was acquired by the German company Bosch in the 1970s. Fiat has extensive parts manufacturing facilities in Spain including Weber España (with headquarters in Guadalajara) and Magneti Marelli. Among the US groups are subsidiaries of General Motors (including a number of plants in Cádiz) and the US group Allied Signal which own Bendix España, a leading supplier of brakes and hydraulic equipment to the Spanish car market. The company has its headquarters and three factories in Barcelona, two factories in Santander, one in Pamplona and one in Bilbao. Among the tyre manufacturers, Michelin is the largest tyre company in Spain in terms of sales as well as being a major exporter. In 1993 it had plants in Arranda del Duero (established in 1970), Lasarte (Guipúzcoa), Vitoria and Valladolid (employing a total of 10,000 people). The Japanese company Bridgestone (Firestone Hispania) has production facilities in Basauri (Vizcaya), Burgos and Torrelavega (Cantabria), while Pirelli has one plant in Manresa (Barcelona). Among the few remaining Spanish-owned large companies in early 1994 were Grupo Tudor (one of Europe's leading battery manufacturers, since acquired by the American company Exide), Grupo Antolín, Ficosa and Mondragón. No Spanish company is large enough to enter the top tier of component manufacturers. Furthermore, despite the size of the components industry there was a trade deficit in components and vehicle equipment in 1993.

6.9 Electronics

The electronics industry forms part of the high-technology base of contemporary economic development. It can be divided into telecommunications, informatics (software and computer hardware), professional electronics (for example defence electronics), microelectronics and domestic electronics (industries estimated to employ some 60,000 people in Spain in 1992). Spanish involvement in these sectors has always been closely linked with foreign multinational companies (notably Telefónica with ATT, and IBM), there being relatively little indigenous development. With the one exception of Telefónica, foreign multinational companies dominate production in Spain, while consumption of personal computers and software is largely met through imports. Manufacturing is concentrated on those products for which production technologies are well established. Linked to this, there is only a modest volume of research and development.

Industrial policy has sought to expand the high-technology base in Spain through specific sectoral policies and through increased international collaboration, especially within Europe (for example through programmes under Brite, Esprit, Eureka, Race and the European Space Agency). Government assistance has also been widely used. For example, government assistance involving $60 million in grants out of a total investment of $200 million was provided for the ATT-Microelectrónica plant at Tres Cantos north of Madrid, opened in 1987 and designed to produce 1.75 micras custom integrated circuits (semi-conductors) especially for export. Similar substantial assistance was offered to a GEC silicon and plastics plant in Cartagena. The Technological Infrastructure Plan (Plan de Infraestructura Technológica, PIT), provided a framework in the 1990s for technology policies such as the Industrial Technology Action Plan (PATI) and the third National Electronics and Information Technology Plan (Plan Electrónico y Informático Nacional, PEIN 111, in operation in 1994) providing assistance covering microelectronics, telecommunications and advanced automation. Industrial promotion schemes are illustrated by the development of science parks, representing part of the drive by regional governments to attract high-technology industry. Despite these initiatives, investment in research and development facilities still lags behind that in production plant, reflecting a skills shortage that the government is attempting to overcome through promoting technological education and training and closer scientific collaboration with European research institutes.

The electronics sector provides a further example of the reorganisation policy pursued by the government in an endeavour to establish more competitive Spanish companies, safeguard employment and reduce government support to industry, although in practice, rationalisation and employment cuts have generally followed mergers. The state holding company INI grouped its electronics companies into the sub-holding company Inisel. Other companies were exchanged between public enterprises. For example, the INI holding in Fujitsu was transferred to Telefónica, Inisel shed its military telecommunications interests (the company Pesa) to Amper (a subsidiary of Telefónica) and the INI software subsidiary Eria was merged with Entel (a subsidiary of Telefónica) to form Eritel. Other public companies were sold to the private sector, many of them having been acquired in the late 1970s and early 1980s. For example, Intelsa was sold by Telefónica to Ericsson.

Reorganisation of the defence electronics sector was also prompted by the state. In 1992 the public company Inisel was merged with the private company Ceselsa to form the major Spanish defence electronics group, Indra (including Eritel, Disel and Ceselsa). The aircraft group Casa also has defence electronics interests.

Many major foreign multinational electronics companies, including Fujitsu, IBM, Olivetti, Rank Xerox and Siemens, have production plants in Spain. IBM has factories at Fuente del Jarro and Puebla de Vallbona (both in Valencia) and a research facility in Madrid. During the 1980s it was the only significant export company in this sector (computer equipment), being one of the top ten exporting companies in Spain. In the supply of telecommunications equipment Alcatel-Standard Eléctrica (a subsidiary of Compagnie Generale d'Electricite of France) was joined in 1990 by ATT-Network Systems and LM Ericsson-Intelsa.

Multinational companies have mostly chosen Madrid or Barcelona for the centre of their operations, especially marketing (coinciding with an estimated two-thirds of the market for information technology equipment and being the centres of decision making for company development strategies involving electronics provision, especially the banks) but also for research and development. Examples include the ATT-Microelectrónica plant, Siemens, Marconi and IBM research in Madrid. In Barcelona there are numerous high-technology and domestic electronics firms located on the new industrial estates outside the city, including the Korean company Samsung and the Japanese companies Pioneer, Matsushita, Sony and Sharp. Sharp opened a factory in 1987 in San Cugat del Valles, designed to produce televisions and hi-fi equipment, moving to a new factory in the same area in 1992. Over half the value of production in 1993 was exported. Outside of these two cities, IBM have a manufacturing plant in Valencia; Alcatel, Siemens and Fujitsu have plants in Málaga. Fujitsu entered Spain in 1975 through a joint venture with Telefónica and INI in the company Secoinsa. In 1985 Fujitsu became the major shareholder, forming Fujitsu España in 1986. The company also has research, development and production facilities in Madrid and Barcelona. General Electric is building a silicon and plastics production complex at Cartagena (Murcia) oriented towards exports.

6.10 Industrial restructuring

Four key trends have characterised the industrial restructuring process in the last quarter of the twentieth century: a decline in the volume of employment in the sector; a shift in the employment structure away from heavy manufacturing industry and textiles towards lighter manufacturing industry (with its consequent implications for old industrial areas, notably País Vasco); concentration of production (especially where entry is difficult for small firms and where the state or foreign capital have had significant interests); a slimming down of the public sector; and a growing penetration of foreign investment linked to an increased integration into multinational production systems headquartered outside of Spain. These trends are set to continue.

Spatial adjustments in the distribution of industry are proceeding at a number of different geographical scales. Locally, manufacturing industry has decamped from the centre of urban areas to re-establish itself on the urban periphery in industrial estates and along major arterial roads (leaving a number of fine examples of urban industrial heritage). Regionally and nationally, improvements in communications and the consequent reduction in transport costs are allowing the spatial concentration of production in large-scale facilities and the reorganisation of distribution to cover wider areas. Internationally, production and distribution is being rationalised to serve the European and, in some cases, the global market.

Following the flood of industrial investment in the late 1980s, the key questions for the 1990s are: i) how large a manufacturing industrial base will Spain be able to retain?; ii) what will be the precise composition of that base?; iii) will Spain be able to grow and attract new technology industries?; and iv) will Spanish capital retain control over significant businesses?

A more open economy entails a number of strategic risks. The principal risk is that shorn of market protection and exposed to a tighter regulatory environment, large segments of Spanish industry will be insufficiently competitive to survive, caught between competitiveness based on traditional technologies and competitiveness based on new technologies. A second risk is that foreign multinationals will dominate industrial production, leaving the country exposed to remote decision-making centres, peripheral to multinational empires and peripheral to the European market. Balanced against these risks is the possibility that manufacturing industry in Spain will grow more vigorously within a competitive environment open to international investment than it did within the framework of extensive intervention.

References and bibliography

Banco de Bilbao (1984) 'Industrial reconversion', *Situacion,* January, pp. 15–16. Bilbao: BBV

Banco de España (1993) *Cuentas financieras de la economía española, 1983–1992* Madrid

Banco de España (1994) *Boletín estadístico,* May. Madrid

Berges, A. and R. Simarro (1987) 'Eficiencia tecnica en las grandes empresas industriales de España', in F. Maravall (ed.), *Economía y política industrial en España,* pp. 40–58. Madrid: Ediciones Pirámide

Carlos Fariñas, J. (1993) *La pyme industrial en España.* Madrid: Editorial Civitas

Concha Gil (1994a) 'Como un rayo', *El País* (sección negocios), 27 March, p. 7

Concha Gil (1994b) 'Cambio de pluma', *El País* (sección negocios), 6 March, p. 12

Costa Campi, M., M. Callejón and E. Giráldez Pidal (1991) *Estudio de impacto general por la ubicación de la empresa Seat en Martorell.* Barcelona: Centro de Estudios y Planificación

Done, K. (1994) 'A pyramid of many parts', *Financial Times,* 3 August, p. 15. London

Donges, J. (1976) *La industrialización en España.* Barcelona: Oikos-Tau

Durán Herrera, J. (1994) 'Las empresas multinacionales en España', *Anuario El País 1994,* p. 392. Madrid

Economía Industrial (1987) *La industria de defensa en España,* No. 253, pp. 31–124

Economía y Finanzas (1987) *Numero extraordinario dedicado al Salon Internacional del Automovile,* No. 91, March

El País (1992) *Anuario 1992.* Madrid

El País (1994a) *Anuario 1994.* Madrid

El País (1994b) *'Ranking de las principales compañías españolas no financieras',* special supplement, 27 November. Madrid

Ensidesa (1994) *Informe anual 1993.* Madrid: Grupo INI

Escudero Bernabéu, A. (1991) 'El sector de piezas y componentes de automóviles', *Información Comercial Española,* Nos 2305–6, pp. 4094–103

Espina, A. (1992) *Recursos humanos y política industrial.* Madrid: Fundación Fundesco

Farré Terre, A. (1986) 'La regulación de la industría de automoción en España y sus relaciones con el desarrollo del sector', *Economía Industrial* 252, pp. 27–43

Federación de Industrias del Calzado Español, FICE (1994) *Anuario del calzado de España 1993.* Madrid

Financial Times (1995) *FT 500,* special supplement, 20 January. London

García Fernández, J. (1989) 'La teoría de Stigler sobre la regulación como marco de la política empresarial pública 1973–1988', *Papeles de Economía Española* 38, pp. 224–42

Hawkesworth, R. (1981) 'The rise of Spain's automobile industry', *National Westminster Bank Review,* February, pp. 37–48

Instituto Nacional de Estadística, INE (1984) *Encuesta industrial 1978 a 1981.* Madrid

Instituto Nacional de Estadística, INE (1994a) *Encuesta de la población activa, primero trimestre* 1994. Madrid

Instituto Nacional de Estadística, INE (1994b) *Encuesta industrial 1988 a 1991.* Madrid

Lagendijk, A. and G. van der Knaap (1993) 'Foreign involvement in the Spanish automobile industry: internalising versus networking, '*Environment and Planning A,* Vol. 25, No. 11, pp. 1663–76

Maravall, F. (ed.) (1987) *Economía y política industrial en España.* Madrid: Ediciones

Pirámide
Ministerio de Industria y Energía, MINE (1987) *Informe anual sobre la industria española, 1986.* Madrid
Ministerio de Industria y Energía, MINE (1989) *Informe anual sobre la industria española, 1988.* Madrid
Ministerio de Industria y Energía, MINE (1993) *Informe anual sobre la industria española, 1992.* Madrid
Nadal, J. (1973) 'The failure of the industrial revolution in Spain, 1830–1914', in C. Cipolla (ed.), *The Fontana economic history of Europe* Vol. 4, Pt. ii, pp. 532–626. London: Collins
Nadal, J., A. Carreras and C. Sudria (1987) *La economía española en el siglo XX: una perspectiva histórica.* Barcelona: Editorial Ariel SA
OECD (1994) *OECD economic surveys: Spain 1993-94.* Paris
Ortún, P. (1988) 'Las ayudas e intervenciones públicas en los procesos de reconversión industrial', *Economía Industrial* 259, pp. 103–12
Prada de, C. (1994) 'El sector de componentes pierde 12,000 empleos', *El País* (sección negocios), 22 May, p. 11
Quinto, J. de (ed.) (1994) *Política industrial de España.* Madrid: Ediciones Pirámide
Robles Teigeiro, L. (1988) 'La concentración en la industría española de fertilizantes en España', *Boletín de Estudios Económicos,* Vol. XLIII, August, No. 134, pp. 307–29
Salmon, K. (1990) 'Regional policy and incentives', in *Spain: Trade and investment opportunities,* pp. 59–68. London: Caversham Press
Seers, D. (ed.) (1979) 'Spanish Industrialization', in D. Seers (ed.), *Underdeveloped Europe,* Chapter 9. Hassocks, Sussex: The Harvester Press
Segura, J. (ed.) (1989) *La industría española en la crisis 19–1984.* Madrid: Alianza Editorial.
Segura, J. (ed.) (1992) *Un panorama de la industria Española.* Madrid: Ministerio de Industria
Tamames, R. (1983) *Estructura económica de España,* Vol. 1. Madrid: Alianza Editorial
Tamames, R. (1986) *The Spanish Economy.* London: C. Hurst and Company
Tizón, A. (1989) 'La salida del túnel', *El País* (sección negocios), 19 March, p. 7
Tortella, G. (1994) *El desarrollo de la España contemporánea. Historía económica de los siglos XIX and XX.* Madrid: Alianza Editorial
Velarde, J. (ed.) (1990) *La industria española.* Madrid: Economístas Libros

Chapter 7
Services

7.1 The service sector

The service sector is the largest, most diverse and least well-documented sector in the Spanish economy, encompassing such activities as commercial services, communications, distribution (wholesaling and retailing), education, health, public administration, transport and tourism. These activities have provided the main source of employment growth in the second half of the twentieth century. Moreover, services lend themselves most readily to employment in the black economy. As a consequence, the proportion of the labour force in work attributed to the service sector is almost certainly higher than that recorded in the official statistics.

The accumulation of employment in the service sector marks the most general characteristic of restructuring in the Spanish economy. Some 60 per cent of the occupied population are employed in the sector and a further 8–10 per cent in construction. Services offered from within the public sector have been associated with particularly strong employment growth, public sector employment growing by 25 per cent between 1988 and 1993 inclusive (sectors: public administration, education and health), representing over half of all employment growth in services over that period (Table 7.1). However, a decline in employment in services from 1992 to 1993 raises a question over future employment growth. Increased competition in services and economies in the public sector will be two significant factors limiting that growth in the second half of the 1990s.

Each of the sub-sectors mentioned above deserves its own chapter, but space alone must limit examples of structure and restructuring to financial services, retailing and telecommunications. Construction, with its close links to property development, is included briefly to emphasise its significance in the economy. Tourism, as the most important industry in Spain, is dealt with in the final chapter.

Table 7.1 Structure of employment in the service sector, 1993

Sector	Employment	(%)	(%) Change 1988-93
Commerce; repair of motor vehicles and domestic appliances	2,054.7	29.3	5.0
Hotel and catering industry	657.4	9.4	*
Transport, distribution and communications	672.7	9.6	7.2
Financial services and insurance	334.3	4.8	12.7
Estate agency and business services	599.1	8.5	48.8
Public administration, defence and social security	754.3	10.8	25.3
Education	635.4	9.1	*
Health, veterinary and social services	577.8	8.2	*
Other community and personal services	385.4	5.5	-6.1
Households that employ domestic help	343.5	4.9	*
Organisations operating outside Spain	1.8	–	*
Total in services	7,016.4	100.0	12.0
Construction	1,040.5		2.0
Total services and construction	8,056.9		11.3

Occupied population, figures in thousands

* rate of change included in the above figure

Sources: INE 1994; rates of change from Banco de España 1994

7.2 The changing environment of financial services

The liberalisation of capital movements, the globalisation of financial markets, the adoption of a new regulatory environment, the privatisation of public sector financial businesses, financial innovations, new ways of providing financial services, new financial products and the development of enabling information technologies have all contributed to a more competitive environment. This has induced a radical transformation of the system of financial services.

As in other sectors financial services evolved in an isolated environment, focused on the domestic market, protected from foreign competition and regulated by government controls. This environment spawned a unique financial system in which inefficient practices were protected and a multitude of small companies were allowed to survive. A more open and liberal regime has spurred competition, leading to a wave of restructuring covering the merger of domestic institutions, alliances with foreign companies, expansion abroad and the increased penetration of domestic markets by foreign firms. In the public sector financial services have been completely reorganised and partially privatised.

7.3 Banking

The banking system comprises the central bank (Banco de España), the government's financial agency (Instituto de Crédito Oficial, ICO), the mixed public/private sector banking group Corporación Bancaria de España (CBE, trading under the name Argentaria), the commercial banks, savings banks, rural savings banks and credit co-operatives, and foreign banks. One result of liberalisation in the banking sector has been to blur the distinction between these institutions.

Liberalisation has increased competition in the banking sector: among domestic banks, between commercial banks and savings banks, between domestic banks and other financial services, and between domestic and foreign companies. Increased competition has led to a search for greater efficiency and greater market share. This has brought mergers and alliances, which in turn have revealed opportunities for rationalisation including the elimination of functional duplication and duplication in the geographical pattern of branches. Rationalisation will include the sale of some branch networks (possibly to foreign banks), as has already occurred in the commercial bank sector. For example, following the merger of Banco Central and Banco Hispano Americano, Banco Central Hispano sold two of its second tier banks in 1993 (Banco Gallego and Banco de Granada) and in 1994 sold many of the branches of Banco de Fomento to Caja España. Greater efficiency has also been sought through automation, opening the door to staff reductions in many traditional areas of retail banking. If staff reductions in the British banking system are any guide, then staff reductions in existing banking institutions in Spain have much further to run. Rationalisation poses a major challenge to the banking sector in the second half of the 1990s.

7.3.1 Government intervention

Government policy has been directed at unifying the treatment of all banking institutions, liberalising the financial markets and reinforcing the system of regulation. Overseeing this process is the Bank of Spain (Ontiveros and Valero 1988).

The Bank of Spain was established in 1856 and nationalised in 1962 as an autonomous organisation within the Ministry of Economy and Finance. The Bank has played an extremely influential role in shaping economic policy as well as in regulating the banking system and channelling funds to government agencies. It also embraces the most prestigious economics research department in Spain. In May 1994 its autonomy statute was approved by parliament in line with the provisions for such central bank status in the Maastricht Treaty. The Bank now has responsibility for setting monetary policy and controlling inflation. In line with the Maastricht

Treaty's provisions on central bank independence, the new law prohibits the institution from financing the Treasury or any other public agency. However, as elsewhere in the EU, the Spanish government has reserved for itself the responsibility for exchange rate policy. In terms of the Bank's organisation, if regional representation on the board of the Bank is achieved, then narrowing the gap between the rich and poor regions could also become a significant theme in Bank decision making.

7.3.2 The state sector

The state sector of banking was completely reorganised in the early 1990s into the government financial agency (Instituto de Crédito Oficial, ICO) and the banking group Argentaria. During 1991 the former state banks were transferred from ICO to Argentaria and the lines of official credit, which were handled by the state banks, were transferred back into ICO. Hence ICO was redefined from a holding company to the government's financial agency and development bank (as established under Royal Decree 3 May 1991). As the government's financial agency, the main aim of the ICO is to support certain economic policy programmes. This includes attending to the financial requirements of specific sectors of the economy (such as iron and steel, fertilizers, etc.), contributing to the implementation of the Social Housing Policy, managing the aid scheme for small and medium-size dbusinesses, and providing support for the export sector (although official loans for export and their financing are now handled by Banco Exterior). As a development bank, ICO provides finance for those sectors of the economy regarded as strategic, including the promotion of regional development to mitigate regional economic imbalances. In addition, the ICO acts as an agent of the Spanish government in transactions involving the overseas development aid fund (Fondo de Ayuda al Desarrollo, FAD) (ICO 1994).

At the beginning of the 1990s there were six state banking institutions, of which five were constituted as Official Credit Entities (Entidades de Crédito Oficial, ECO) and were dependencies of ICO. The six banks were:

i) Banco de Crédito Agrícola (BCA) was founded in 1925 as the Servicio Nacional de Crédito Agrícola, providing agricultural credit and dependent on the Ministry of Agriculture. It was transferred to the Ministry of Economy and Finance in 1962.

ii) Banco de Crédito Industrial (BCI) was established in 1920 to provide finance to the industrial sector. In 1982 it absorbed the failed Banco de Crédito para la Construcción (established in 1939 to finance reconstruction after the Civil War), which had the largest volume of lending among the ECOs and had a major involvement in shipbuilding. The BCI was one of the main recipients of loans from the European Investment Bank. In November 1991 the absorption of BCI by BEX was approved (with the nonperforming loans of BCI being transferred to the ICO).

iii) Banco de Crédito Local (BCL) was established in 1925 to provide loans (mostly long-term ones) to town councils, provincial councils and small firms. In 1994 it was Argentaria's leading agency for financing the territorial administrations.

iv) Banco Exterior de España (BEX) was established in 1923, operating as a private bank until it was nationalised in 1971 (in 1994 69 per cent of the bank was owned directly by Argentaria). The bank became the agency for channelling export credits from official funds (Crédito Oficial a la Exportación). Its virtual monopoly of export finance came to an end when the market was liberalised in 1985. Reorganisation of the bank in the late 1980s and early 1990s transformed it into a modern international bank with 87 branches in 27 countries at the end of 1993 (although assets on its international network amounted to only 15 per cent of the total assets of BEX at the end of 1993, and almost two-thirds of international assets were in Europe; Argentaria 1994).

v) Banco Hipotecario de España (BHE) was established in 1872. The bank specialises in housing and construction finance, the majority of BHE's lending consisting of long-term loans secured on residential property. Traditionally, it provided finance for the purchase of 'protected' dwellings (Viviendas de Protección Oficial, VPO), but it has extended its lending to finance the construction, purchase and improvement of all housing.

vi) Caja Postal (Post-Office Savings Bank) was established in 1909 as a public enterprise. Before it became part of the Argentaria group it was controlled by the Ministry of Transport, Tourism and Communications and was thus the only bank outside the ICO. Within the Argentaria group it now specialises in retail commercial banking.

Table 7.2 Argentaria group

Bank	Assets	Employment	Branches in Spain	Branches abroad
BEX (Banco Exterior)		10,044	483	
Banco de Alicante			110	
Banco Simeón			59	
BGF			18	
BEX group	5,401	10,687	674	87
Caja Postal	2,459	4,899	664	
BHE	2,098	1,270	53	
BCL	1,502	276	14	
BCA	478	495	21	
Argentaria Group	11,193	17,682	1,426	87

All figures at 31 December 1993; assets in pta billion

BGF: Banco de Gestión e Inversión Financiera

Source: Argentaria 1994

In May 1991 these institutions (by then all transformed into limited liability companies, *sociedades anónimas*) were grouped into the Corporación Bancaria de España, representing about 13 per cent of the banking system in Spain (Table 7.2). The group adopted a federated model of organisation in which the group was structured into business units specialising in different areas of banking and financial activities (including a merchant banking division - Banco de Negocios Argentaria and Argentaria Bolsa – and insurance, where it has a majority holding in Hércules Hispano), co-ordinated by a corporate centre responsible for overall planning and strategic management. In May 1993 24.9 per cent of Banco Argentaria's capital was floated on the international stock market, followed by a second tranche in November 1993, reducing the state holding in Argentaria to just over 50 per cent. The new group joined Banco Santander, Banco Bilbao Vizcaya (BBV) and Banco Central Hispano as one of the leading four banks in Spain and one of the top ten largest banking groups in Europe. The group became the only one in Spain to embrace both commercial and savings bank subsidiaries. Its specific potential lay in the cross-selling opportunities in the group, for example blending BHE's home-buying client base with the Caja Postal nationwide branch network (offering savings accounts to home buyers) and opening up the services of the other specialist banks. Until the formation of the group, most of BHE's mortgage holders held their accounts through other banks (BHE having only 50 branches in 1991). The new group also offers domestic customers an international banking network through BEX and has sought to increase its presence abroad, especially in Europe and Latin America.

Shifting the state banking sector into the private banking environment presented numerous challenges, including increasing efficiency, broadening the capital base of constituent banks and integrating the disparate activities. Increasing efficiency required changing management mentality from a public sector to a commercial one (partly achieved through bringing in managers from the private sector, including the chairman), rationalising banking activities, co-ordinating the different banking entities and introducing new information technologies. The principal challenge for the group is to integrate fully and rationalise its business, while the question remains as to whether or not the state should proceed further with the privatisation process.

7.3.3 Commercial banks

Most of the commercial banks were established in the middle and late nineteenth century. In 1857 the Banco de Bilbao was established by the Chamber of Commerce in Bilbao. In 1901 the Banco de Vizcaya and Banco Hispano Americano were established. In 1902 Banco Español de Crédito (Banesto) was established in Madrid, followed by Banco Central in 1919.

Restructuring was forced on the sector following the collapse of 50 banking institutions (including 20 in the Rumasa group) during the banking crisis in the late 1970s and early 1980s. In response to the crisis, the Deposit Guarantee Fund (Fondo de Garantía de Depósitos, FGD) was set up in 1977 to ensure the security of deposits and the major banks were obliged to assist in rescue operations. For example, the industrial banks Banca Unión and Banca Urquijo merged to become Banco Urquijo Unión and were taken over by Banco Hispano Americano, then sold in 1988 to Banco March. Banca Catalana, which collapsed in 1982, is now a subsidiary of Banco Bilbao Vizcaya. The period was also marked by an expansion in bank branches. Between 1974 and 1985 the number of bank branches increased by 10,957.

Liberalisation and modernisation (especially the adoption of new technology) gradually penetrated the sector during the early 1980s, bringing the system into line with the norms and practices of the banking nations of Europe. The time frame for adaptation was set by the seven-year transition period (from January 1986) granted to Spain under its European Community accession agreement.

An example of the process of liberalisation was provided by the package of measures for deregulating the banking industry that were introduced in March 1987. This scrapped ceilings on interest rates on sight and short-term deposits (previously set by the Ministry of Economy and Finance), which had provided a source of cheap funds. Commissions for banking services were also freed. These measures followed a sharp reduction in the share of deposits (*coeficientes*) that banks were obliged to channel into government directed investments. The system of *coeficientes* (virtually eliminated by the early 1990s) involved a complex system of ratios whereby the government directed a large part (up to 50 per cent) of bank deposits into privileged sources of finance for the Treasury and other sectors. This privileged finance was available at below market rates of interest, providing both a source of budget finance and a means of monetary control. Although the Bank of Spain can still require compulsory deposits to be retained with it (allowing control over monetary growth), the measures signified the virtual disappearance of privileged credit channels in Spain and gradually liberated bank funds as existing bonds reached maturity.

The largest Spanish commercial banks are of only small to medium-size by world banking standards. None are in the top 50 by value of assets. In Europe BBV was only half the size of Barclays by market capitalisation in 1993 (*Financial Times* 1994a). There remain numerous small and medium-size regional and local banks (although many are subsidiaries of the majors; Tables 7.3 and 7.4). In 1994 the Spanish-owned private commercial bank sector comprised 4 majors and over 60 small and medium-sized banks (Portela 1994a). From the mid 1980s the government encouraged consolidation, but the process was slowed by inter-bank rivalries. For example, Banco Bilbao failed to takeover Banesto in 1987 and in 1989 the merger between Banco Central and Banesto failed. Nevertheless, in 1989

Table 7.3 Spanish commercial banks

Commercial bank	Assets	Customer funds	Branches	Employment
Banco Central Hispano	11,209	5,175	2,780	26,231
Banco Bilbao Vizcaya	8,919	4,825	1,934	19,938
Banco de Santander	7,350	3,098	1,334	11,827
Banco Español de Crédito (Banesto)*	5,497	3,097	2,249	15,271
Banco Exterior de España (a)	4,719	1,719	502	7,502
Caja Postal (a)	2,342	1,532	664	4,357
Banco Hipotecario de España (a)	2,038	950	54	1,270
Banco Popular Español	1,742	1,258	984	7,515
Bankinter	1,618	673	253	2,019
Crédito Local de España (a)	1,502	435	14	276
Banco Pastor	1,388	764	418	3,521
Banco de Sabadell	1,281	906	359	4,611
Banco Santander de Negocios (b)	1,190	138	30	320
Banco Atlántico	937	670	246	3,083
Banca Catalana (c)	880	553	396	3,144
Comercio (c)	821	643	220	1,809
Bancotrans (e)	758	277	107	1,624
Banco Urquijo (d)	740	465	169	2,173
Barclays Bank, SAE	640	484	235	1,852
Morgan Guaranty	631	51	1	146
Zaragozano	626	413	352	2,352
America	466	43	3	179
Banco de Crédito Agrícola (a)	462	90	21	494
Sub total	57,756	28,259	13,325	121,514
Other	10,402	5,347	4,130	31,316
All banks (including public sector)	68,158	33,606	17,455	152,830

All figures are for 31 December 1993

Assets and customer funds (*recursos de clientes*) in pta billion

* Banesto acquired by Santander in April 1994
a: Argentaria group; b: Santander Banesto group, c: Banco Bilbao Vizcaya group; d: Banca March group; e: Deutsche Bank group

Source: Portela 1994a

Table 7.4 Spanish banking groups

Bank group	Assets	Customer funds A	Customer funds B	Employees	Branches
Santander (Banesto)	15,386	5,822	7,429	45,500	4,000
Central Hispano	12,950	5,264	6,504	34,400	3,450
Bilbao Vizcaya	11,635	6,214	6,879	28,700	2,902
Argentaria	11,193	4,617	5,054	17,682	1,513
Popular Español	2,865	2,112	2,173	12,000	1,800

All figures except 'A' are at 31 December 1993 and include international operations

'A' refers to customer funds at 28 February 1994, excluding international operations

Assets and customer funds in pta billion

Sources: *Financial Times* 1994b; Noceda 1994

Banco Bilbao and Banco Vizcaya merged to form the Banco Bilbao Vizcaya group and in 1991 Banco Central merged with Hispano Americano to form Banco Central Hispano (BCH). A third major banking group emerged with the formation of the Argentaria group. Further consolidation occurred in 1994 following the near collapse of Banesto in December 1993 (prevented only by the injection of funds from the FGD), its reorganisation under the guidance of the Bank of Spain, and the sale of a controlling block of shares in the bank to Banco Santander in April 1994. The sale left Spain with four major banking groups of roughly equal size, controlling almost three-quarters of bank deposits (though much less of all bank and savings banks deposits). Further mergers in the late 1990s are certain, including those between banks and savings banks.

The banking system is characterised by a dense network of commercial bank branches numbering 17,455 on the 31 December 1993 (including state bank branches), one office to every 2,239 inhabitants (more than in any other EU country except Luxembourg). The average of credits per bank worker in 1992 was barely half the level of the European Community average, and there were few employees per branch (less than 10 employees per branch in 1993 compared with about 18 in France; Lerena 1989). These characteristics contribute towards high costs (although the large number of branches also provides an excellent distribution system for selling financial products), which in the past were offset by the higher price of services. Profitability was ensured by the dense branch network tapping relatively cheap savings (in an unsophisticated market) and then lending at relatively high rates. Competition has squeezed these margins and necessitated cost reductions; reductions that are being found in increased automation, in staff reductions (although staff are also being redeployed to market a broad range of financial services) and through branch rationalisation (particularly where bank mergers occur and exemplified by the sale of the chain of bank branches in the Banco de Madrid by Banesto). Across the banking sector, staff reductions in individual banks were offset in the late 1980s and early 1990s by the increased number of foreign banks, leaving total employment in the sector at 153,000 in 1993 (Portela 1994a). This number is likely to fall during the 1990s as rationalisation gathers pace.

In many cases Spanish commercial banks control substantial commercial and industrial interests, giving them a significant role in restructuring outside the banking sector. In 1994 BCH and Banco Santander (Banesto) controlled the largest industrial empires (in 1990 Banesto separated its industrial holdings in a new holding company – La Corporación Banesto – which it claimed accounted for 1 per cent of Spain's economy). The industrial portfolio of Banco Santander (Banesto) included shareholdings in the construction company Agromán, the mining and metals company Asturiana de Zinc, the agricultural group Quash, the battery manufacturer Tudor, as well as financial and property companies such as Inmobiliaria Urbis. That of BCH included shareholdings in the industrial companies

Campofrío, Cepsa, Dragados y Construcciones, Española del Zinc and General Azucarera. Banco Bilbao Vizcaya (BBV) had important shareholdings in food (for example the wine producer Bodegas AGE) and food distribution (for example, in BBV Continente). All the banking groups embraced other financial subsidiaries and property companies.

Difficult trading conditions, new capital adequacy ratios and more transparent accountancy practices introduced as part of Single Market legislation led the banks to review their industrial portfolios in the mid 1990s. In some cases this appeared to equate with a withdrawal from direct control of manufacturing companies: for example, the declared intention of Banco Santander in 1994 to dispose of most of Banesto's industrial holdings. But this was a special case, more often the banks appeared simply to be reorganising their industrial holdings. Thus Banco Bilbao Vizcaya sold its holding in the drinks company KAS and in the food companies Miko, Avidesa and Castillo de Marcilla to Nestlé, but immediately acquired a large holding in Bodegas Age.

Traditionally, Spanish banks have not been internationally oriented. However, internationalisation became a strategy favoured in the late 1980s and early 1990s as a means of expansion and to offset increasing competition in the domestic market. Spanish banks are not large enough to become global or even pan-European banks, hence securing an international presence has been achieved mainly through forming alliances with foreign banks (for example BCH with the German bank, Commerzbank). The European Union (notably Portugal) has been the principal focus of investment, followed by Latin America (Morocco has also attracted attention). At the end of 1993 73.4 per cent of the total assets of the BBV group were in Spain (69 per cent of which were in the European Union; BBV 1994). Banesto led the way into Portugal acquiring a stake in the Portuguese Banco Totta e Acores (BTA) during the latter's privatisation. For the BBV group the Portuguese operation (with 50 branches in 1993) was the main investment outside Spain (in 1991 it had acquired Lloyds Bank Portugal). BCH has a holding in Banco Comercial Portugués and Banco Santander has acquired Banco de Comercio e Industria. Overall, it was estimated that in 1993 Spanish banks controlled 15 per cent of the Portuguese market. Outside of Portugal, examples of overseas expansion and foreign alliances include the holding of Banco Santander in the Royal Bank of Scotland (RBS), acquired in 1989 (RBS has a reciprocal holding in Banco Santander). Banco Santander also acquired a German subsidiary (CC Bank) and a Belgium subsidiary (Credit du Norge Belge). Outside of Europe, Banco Santander has agreements with Japanese and United States companies (for example its holding in the First Fidelity Bank Corporation of New Jersey). In 1992 Banco Santander earned one-third of its income from abroad and was seeking to raise this to half. Investment in Mexico was stimulated in the early 1990s by the prospects of the formation of the North American Free Trade Association (NAFTA), for example BCH acquired a holding in Banco Internacional de México and BBV has a holding in the finance group Probursa.

More intense competition in the domestic market has prompted structural, organisational and geographical changes in the Spanish banking system, which are set to continue. In addition, banks have been diversifying into a broader range of financial services and have set up investment banking divisions as part of the world-wide move towards securitisation (for example Banco Santander de Negocios). Banks have evolved to become the financial intermediary between investors and borrowers, as well as being responsible for the payment systems and for liquidity in the economy.

7.3.4 Savings banks (cajas de ahorros)

The savings banks expanded rapidly in the 1980s and early 1990s, following a series of liberalisation measures beginning in 1977 that allowed them to operate on a similar footing to commercial banks. However, they have a different legal constitution and are oriented more to families and small business customers. The number of savings bank branches increased by 4,000 between 1975 and 1985 and thence by almost 2,000 more to the end of 1992. Their share of total residents deposits increased from 33 per cent to 47 per cent in the period 1979 to 1993 (Table 7.5), making big inroads into mortgages, leasing, life insurance and a number of traditional banking services. While the banks have been withdrawing from some of their industrial holdings in the mid 1990s, the savings banks have been increasing their participation in non-banking businesses, notably in expanding sectors such as environmental services, leisure and

Table 7.5 Distribution of deposits within the private banking system

Sector	Deposits	%
Spanish commercial banks	24,238	47
Foreign banks	628	1
Sub total	24,866	48
Savings banks	24,533	47
Credit co-operatives	2,354	5
Sub total	26,887	52
Total	51,753	100

Figures for deposits are *recursos ajenos* at 31 December 1993 in pta billion

Savings banks includes all the Cajas de Ahorro Confederades

Source: *El País* 1994b

Table 7.6 Savings banks

Savings bank	Assets	Customer funds	Branches	Employ-ment
La Caíxa	7,134	5,640	2,362	12,079
Caja Madrid	4,324	3,394	1,199	8,875
Caixa de Catalunya	1,423	1,184	668	3,359
Bilbao Bizcaia Kutxa	1,268	1,126	266	2,132
Bancaja	1,191	1,065	655	4,207
Galicia CA	1,183	916	484	2,835
Mediterráneo	1,180	961	615	4,484
Ibercaja (Zaragoza, Aragón y Rioja	1,091	903	721	3,754
Unicaja	995	853	710	4,366
Guipúzcoa y San Sebastián	931	703	186	1,669
Caja España	785	654	346	1,837
Castilla-La Mancha CA	657	539	418	2,185
Salamanca y Soria CA	590	435	402	1,531
Sub total	22,752	18,373	9,032	53,313
Other	9,132	7,779	5,232	30,036
Total all savings banks	31,884	26,152	14,264	83,349

All figures are for 31 December 1993

Assets and customer funds (*recursos de clientes*) in pta billion

Source: Portela 1994b

telecommunications. They also often have key holdings in the regions within which they are based, for example Caja Bilbao Bizcaia Kutxa based in País Vasco had major holdings in Construcciones Auxiliar de Ferrocarriles and in Petronor in 1994.

At the beginning of 1994 there were 51 savings banks grouped into the Confederación Española de Cajas de Ahorros (CECA, which excludes the rural savings banks), with 14,264 branches open to the public at the end of 1993 (Portela 1994b). In addition to these, there are the branches of the Caja Postal. The two largest savings banks, La Caixa (the Caja de Ahorros y Pensiones de Barcelona) and the Caja de Madrid account for about one-third of the deposits in the private savings bank system (Table 7.6). The third largest savings bank is the publicly owned Caja Postal, with access to over 1,000 post offices across the country.

There are two types of savings bank – general savings banks and rural savings banks. They can be privately or publicly owned (state, provincial or municipal ownership). Many general savings banks were initially founded by the Church in the eighteenth century as non-profit-making institutions, and a small number are still owned by the Church. Roughly one-third were founded by local governments (especially provincial governments, *diputaciones provinciales*).

Savings banks are run as foundations through councils consisting of a prescribed mix of savers, employees and representatives of local authorities (there are no shareholders). Government legislation has required these councils to become more democratic and 'visible' (the majority of management boards in ordinary savings banks were renewed in elections in 1977). The governing councils then elect a president. The composition of these governing councils, on which political parties have seats, has meant that local political considerations have influenced management policy, including policy on expansion and mergers. Profits must be ploughed back into operations (thus ensuring that conditions of employment in savings banks are very favourable) or else put into public works benefiting the community (in 1992 Unicaja spent pta 1.5 billion on socio-cultural projects and in 1993 La Caixa spent pta 8.4 billion).

Savings banks have been tightly controlled by the state, predominantly concerned with private savings, and sometimes seen in the past as channels through which capital has been transferred from the less-developed to the more-developed regions. All savings banks have been required to invest a substantial proportion of their deposits in fixed interest securities (targeted by compulsory investment coefficients) and a slightly smaller proportion of their deposits in credits at privileged rates for specialised companies and projects (for example, INI or subsidised housing schemes). Until 1951 they had to invest at least 60 per cent of their money in public funds. Since then the level of investment in official funds has been steadily reduced, declining to 41 per cent of deposits in 1977 and then 35 per cent in early 1984. These investments were never evenly distributed. The principal recipients were the more advanced and industrialised regions in the north. In Andalucía in 1982 it was estimated that roughly 55 per cent of the savings banks' obligatory deposits were invested in the north. There were also imbalances in those investments that were free, even though 75 per cent of them were meant to be distributed in the regions in which the banks operated. The formation of regions has directed attention towards this territorial dimension of savings banks' investments, prompting pressure for a greater level of investment in the home region and close relationships between the regional governments and the savings banks based in their regions.

Restrictions limiting the savings banks to their home regions were lifted in 1989 in return for restrictions on insurance activities (the decree concerning the expansion of savings banks was announced in June 1988 – Real Decreto 29.12.88). Savings banks can now open offices outside of their region of origin (they were previously limited mainly to taking over rural savings banks in crisis outside of their home region), although La Caixa and Caja Postal had already developed a nation-wide branch network. Lifting of geographical restrictions followed a lengthy debate dating back to the late 1970s. Until 1977 all savings banks were restricted to the region in which they originated. Then in 1977 the largest were allowed to open branches in the five largest cities in Spain. The large savings banks (notably

La Caixa and Caja de Madrid) favoured liberalisation to allow branch networks throughout Spain, with at least 50 per cent of their offices outside of their region of origin by the end of 1992. They argued that this would allow them to compete on equal terms with the commercial banks and with any foreign savings banks that became established in Spain. They were supported in their proposals by the government and the Bank of Spain (which also wanted the large savings banks to absorb some of the ailing rural savings banks). In contrast, the smaller and medium-sized savings banks sought strict limits on territorial expansion, with no more than twelve branches of a savings bank outside its region of origin by the end of 1992. They argued that nation-wide expansion would result in a drain of savings away from poor regions to be invested in more prosperous ones, that foreign savings banks had not been inclined to expand outside their country of origin, and that there was the implicit threat of greater competition and a reduction in the number of savings banks. They were supported by the regional and local governments and by the commercial banks.

The prospect of a single European market left little alternative to liberalisation. As a result, the two leading savings banks rapidly expanded their branch networks outside their home areas, La Caixa and Caja de Madrid increasing their number of branches outside their region of origin by 1,071 by the end of 1992 (concentrating on Madrid and Cataluña). Expansion included the acquisition of existing banks, for example La Caixa bought Banco de las Canarias and Caja de Madrid bought Banco de Crédito y Ahorro. However, apart from these two, the other savings banks have tended to consolidate their regional or local position, relying on strong local loyalties and extensive branch networks to maintain their competitive position.

Liberalisation has paved the way for sweeping mergers among the savings banks (Table 7.7) and for acquisitions of commercial banks, actions which have often been achieved against a background of intense personality conflicts and local rivalries. Before the end of the century there will be a significant further decline in the number of Spanish-owned savings banks and other banking institutions.

Regional governments have promoted mergers within their territory to ensure banks large enough to remain based there. For example, in País Vasco the merger of local savings banks created the fourth largest private savings bank group in Spain, Bilbao Bizcaia Kutxa; in Andalucía Unicaja and in Castilla y León Caja España. However, by far the most important merger was that between La Caixa (Caja de Pensiones para la Vejez y de Ahorros de Cataluña y Baleares) and Caja de Ahorros y Monte de Piedad de Barcelona (implemented in July 1990), creating in the new La Caixa one of the largest financial entities in Spain and one of the largest savings banks in Europe (by deposits). At the end of 1993 La Caixa had 5.4 million customers, 2,362 branches (two-thirds in Cataluña) and 11,580 employees, owning a broad portfolio of commercial and industrial interests including

Table 7.7 Mergers among the savings banks

New group	Former savings banks
Bancaja	Cajas de Alicante, Castellón, Sagunto and Valencia
Bilbao Bizcaia Kutxa	Merger of savings banks in País Vasco
La Caixa	La Caixa and CA de Barcelona
Caja España	Cajas de Palencia, León, Zamora, Popular and Provincial de Valladolid
Caja Mediterráneo	CA de Murcia, CA Provincial de Alicante y Valencia
Cajasur	MP y CA de Córdoba
Castilla-La Mancha CA	Cajas de Albacete, Cuenca-Ciudad Real, Toledo
La General	Caja General de Granada, Caja Provincial de Granada
El Monte	Caja MP de Sevilla and Caja de Huelva
Extremadura CA y MP	Caja de Cáceres, Caja de Plasencia
Ibercaja	Cajas de Aragón, Rioja and Zaragoza, Caja Rural de Cataluña
Salamanca and Soria CA	CA y MP de Salamanca, CA de la Provincia de Soria
San Fernando and Jerez	Caja de San Fernando de Sevilla and Caja de Jerez
Unicaja	MP y CA de Almería, CA de Antequera, CA y MP de Cádiz, CA Provincial de Málaga, MP y CA de Ronda

MP Monte de Piedad; CA Caja de Ahorros
Source: Author compilation

important stakes in Aguas de Barcelona, Autopístas Concesionaria Española, Gas Natural, Fecsa, Tabacalera and Telefónica (La Caixa 1994).

Domestic rivalries have tended to divert attention away from policies designed to internationalise the savings banks. Until the mid 1990s there had been little attempt to establish branches abroad. At the end of 1992 there were only six savings bank branches abroad, five of them belonging to La Caixa (all in Andorra) and one to La Caixa de Catalunya. Instead, savings banks have sought international alliances such as the agreement in 1989 between La Caixa de Catalunya and the Italian savings bank la Cassa di Risparmio di Genova y Imperia (Carige) to share services.

The rural savings banks (*cajas rurales*) were co-operative ventures set up at the beginning of the twentieth century (numbering 501 in 1926). In 1941 they were integrated into the Organización Sindical, with the provincial rural savings banks forming the Caja Rural Nacional (CRUNA) in 1957. Smaller, local rural savings banks (*cajas rurales locales*) were grouped into the Central de Cajas Rurales (CECAR, which had balances equal to about 10 per cent of CRUNA). In 1971 the CECAR group became the direct responsibility of the Bank of Spain. Rural savings banks only provided official credit and became characterised by poor loan management. CRUNA did not operate effectively as a supervisory body, becoming directly involved with the banks it was supervising (through, for example, common directorships). By the early 1980s the CRUNA group was in serious financial difficulties, threatening the stability of the financial system.

Severe economic problems among the rural savings banks led the government to seek reforms (including greater transparency in operation and tighter financial controls), rescue operations from other banks (many rural savings banks being absorbed by other savings banks), and mergers. Among the mergers proposed was that between the rural savings banks and the state agricultural bank (BCA). In 1983 all the rural savings banks made a global agreement with the BCA, followed in 1984 by individual agreements (between 50 rural savings banks and the BCA) made for three years. Thus in 1984 the Grupo Asociado Banco de Crédito Agrícola-Cajas Rurales (BCA-CR) was formed. If this grouping had solidified it would have become a major banking force in Spain. The group specialised in finance for agriculture, fishing and related industries (including lines of official credit and short-term loans) and technical assistance to agriculture. The bank also channelled funds into agricultural projects from the Agricultural Fund of the European Community and from the BCI.

In the late 1980s many rural savings banks rejected the arrangements with the BCA and began to look for a foreign partner when ICO insisted that its subsidiary should have a controlling interest in any merged group. Twenty-four rural savings banks (representing about 70 per cent of the deposits held by the 90-odd rural savings banks) joined with Deutsche Genossenschaftsbank (DG Bank, the umbrella organisation for West Germany's co-operative banks) to apply to open a new bank called Banco Cooperativo Español (BCE). The new bank centralised information and established overall policy for its members, who retained their existing branch networks. At the end of 1992 there were some 100 rural savings banks and credit co-operatives, with Laboral Mondragón and Almería accounting for about one-quarter of deposits.

7.3.5 Foreign banks

Adoption of EU banking directives allowed banks from other EU countries to open branches and supply services in Spain. In addition, there are significant foreign shareholdings in Spanish banks (for example, Banco Popular was about 50 per cent foreign-owned in 1992 and BBV 18 per cent). Nevertheless, it is a difficult and slow process for foreign banks to gain acceptance in retail banking, hence the strategy has generally been to innovate new products and provide specialist business services. At the beginning of 1994 there were over 30 banks based in other countries of the European Union operating in Spain (20 in 1987) and over 20 from outside the EU.

Foreign banks have gradually built up their presence after they were allowed to open full branches in 1978, although some foreign banks had established a much earlier presence (for example Credit Lyonnais, Société Générale, Banco Nazionale del Lavoro, Bank of London and South America – the latter opened in Spain in 1916). Bank of America went to Spain in 1965 to form a joint venture with Banco Santander, subsequently buying out its Spanish partner. During the 1980s foreign banks were limited to three branches (which required official authorisation) and there were limits on access to peseta savings. This meant that the only way to gain access to the full retail banking system was through the acquisition of 'lame' Spanish banks. Following the 1978 banking crisis and the first liberalisation, Banque Nationale de Paris, Barclays Bank, Arab Banking Corporation, Citibank and Bank of Credit and Commerce International bought networks from the Deposit Guarantee Fund. For example, Barclays acquired 38 branches from its acquisition of Banco Valladolid and Citibank acquired Banco de Levante. In 1985 Chase Manhattan took over a small industrial bank (Banco Finanzas) and National Westminster Bank formed a joint venture (Nat West March) with the Mallorca based Banca March (which had 81 Spanish mainland branches). In 1988 Nat West March acquired a Basque-based banking group and took a holding in Banco Hispano Americano and Banco Popular Español. In 1989 National Westminster Bank raised its participation in the joint venture to 83 per cent.

Foreign interest in the Spanish banking system grew in the 1990s, the problems of market access being overcome by buying-up existing bank networks. In 1993 Deutsche Bank became the largest foreign bank operating in the retail banking market through its acquisition of Banco de Madrid (concentrated in the Madrid region), adding to its existing ownership of Banco Comercial Transatlántico (Bancotrans) based in Cataluña (acquired in 1989). Crédit Lyonnais and National Westminster Bank followed a similar pattern of acquisition, the former buying two bank networks, Banco Jover in Barcelona (in 1990) and Banco Comercial Español in Madrid (in 1991), both bought from Banco Santander; the latter added Banco de Asturias to its existing holdings. In 1992 it was estimated that foreign banks controlled about 6 per cent of current and deposit accounts in Spain and 11 per cent of bank loans. Further acquisitions of Spanish banks are likely, increasing the market penetration of foreign banks. Moreover, in the early 1990s foreign savings banks began to establish themselves in Spain, including the two largest ones in Britain – the Halifax and Abbey National.

7.4 Insurance

Within Europe a widespread restructuring of the insurance market has been taking place, prompted in part by the prospect of a single European insurance market. Commitments relating to the insurance industry under the Uruguay Round GATT agreement will also increase competition (and open up new markets) in the late 1990s. The process of achieving a single market culminated in July 1994 after which insurance companies could sell their products throughout the EU on the strength of a single license granted in the country of their head office (EU Third Insurance Directive). The impact of this measure will significantly increase competition and lead to the disappearance of numerous insurance companies across Europe. It is probable that a number of insurance companies currently headquartered in Spain will be taken over and thus control over yet another industry in Spain will pass beyond its frontiers. Fragmentation in the European industry has already brought alliances in domestic markets and a search for foreign outlets (for example the acquisition of the German insurance company Colonia by the French company Union des Assurances de Paris, UAP). Banking and insurance interests have converged, the growth of life-insurance business has attracted banks, while the distribution networks of banks have attracted insurance companies. As with banks, deregulation, competition and technology are converting insurance companies into international all-purpose financial institutions. One-stop financial shopping has become an increasingly attractive proposition. Moreover, the trend towards direct telephone sales of insurance and other financial products is likely to increase.

Many European companies have been increasing their capital base to expand. For example, the French insurer UAP (privatised in 1994), Europe's second-largest insurance group, announced plans in 1990 to raise £1 billion in preparation for expansion and the Single European Market. The deal also sealed the alliance with Banque Nationale de Paris (BNP). The other two French state insurers, Assurances Générales de France (AGF) and Groupement des Assurances Nationales (GAN), were allowed to sell stakes to banks and foreign investors after February 1990.

The insurance industry in Spain is relatively small in size and oriented to the domestic market (the only multinational insurance group based in Spain in 1994 being Mapfre). Small size is reflected in the number of people employed in the sector (46,800 at the end of 1992). A degree of under-insurance is indicated by the relatively low level of premiums in relation to GDP (4.4 per cent at 31 December 1993 compared with 12.1 in the UK and 6.6 in France) and low expenditure on premiums per capita (only 40 per cent that in the UK and France; DGS 1994). Under-insurance was especially true in the mid 1980s when in 1986 total premiums written were only 2.2 per cent of GDP, compared to over 8 per cent in the United States and the United Kingdom. However, both employment and premiums have been growing and premiums gradually converging with north-west European levels.

As in other sectors of economic activity in Spain, the insurance industry comprises a few relatively large companies dominating market share together with numerous small companies (Tables 7.8 and 7.9). In 1994 only Mapfre was among the top 50 insurance companies in Europe (and its gross premium income in 1989 was less than 10 per cent of the largest European group, Allianz). At the end of 1993 there were 564 registered insurance companies, of which 101 were in receivership, leaving 463 in operation (many of them operating only in health and death benefits) (DGS 1994). Market fragmentation has been highest in the non-life sector, especially in personal accident, fire and motor insurance (although there was a substantial increase in concentration in the motor sector in the early 1990s in response to severe financial problems). In 1993 the top fifteen companies in the Life sector accounted for roughly two-thirds of all premium business in the sector, while in non-life the same percentage was shared between 39 companies (*El País* 1994a).

By far the largest volume of business in 1993 was non-life (two-thirds of all premiums written), within which motor insurance was the biggest element (almost half of all non-life business), just exceeding the total of all life business (Table 7.10). As a consequence of the initially small market and the high growth of the economy in the late 1980s, most forms of life and non-life income grew rapidly in the late 1980s and early 1990s, making it attractive to foreign investment. Net income from life premiums experienced exceptional growth as a result of the introduction in 1986 of 'single premium life policies' (*seguros de prima única*). Over 40 per cent of all life premiums written in 1992 were for single premium policies.

Since the mid 1980s a process of consolidation has been working through the industry, encouraged by the government, by new solvency regulations and competition, and given a time frame by the seven-year transition period for financial services and the Single European Market in 1993. Nevertheless, concentration had failed to produce a major international

Table 7.8 Size structure of the insurance industry

Volume of premiums written	(%) of companies		(%) of premiums written	
	1991	1993	1991	1993
<50	18.6	11.4	0.1	–
50–125	11.2	7.0	0.2	0.1
125–250	8.4	8.4	0.3	0.2
250–750	15.2	14.5	1.7	1.1
750–1,250	8.0	9.6	1.8	1.5
1,250–2,500	11.8	13.5	4.7	3.9
2,500–5,000	9.8	9.8	8.1	5.3
5,000–10,000	6.4	10.5	10.4	12.2
>10,000	10.4	15.4	72.6	75.6
Total	100.0	100.0	100.0	100.0
Number of companies	641	564	Vol.of premiums	2,659.2

Volume of premiums written in pta billion

Source: DGS 1994

Table 7.9 Major insurance groups in Spain, 1993

Company	Premiums	Market share	Main shareholder
1 Mapfre	236.1	9.0	Independent
Mapfre Mutualidad			
Mapfre Vida	55.8		
2 Grupo Central-Hispano/Generali	194.2	7.4	Generali, BCH
Grupo Vitalicio	108.0		
La Estrella	50.1		
3 Grupo Banco Bilbao Vizcaya	106.8	4.1	Banco Bilbao Vizcaya
Euroseguros	106.8		
4 Holding Caifor	99.0	3.8	La Caixa and foreign investment
Vidacaixa	66.0		
5 Holding Banesto AGF	85.9	3.3	Assurances Générales de France
La Unión y el Fénix			
6 Zurich	73.3	2.8	Foreign-owned
7 Winterthur	66.6	2.5	Foreign-owned
8 Mutua Madrileña Automovilista	65.5	2.5	Foreign-owned
9 Axa-Aurora	65.4	2.5	Foreign-owned
10 Suiza-Re	62.4	2.4	Foreign-owned
Sub total	1,055.2	40.3	
Total (premiums and charges)	2,613.6	100.0	

Figures for premiums written in Spain, in pta billion

Source: Mapfre 1994

Table 7.10 Structure of insurance premiums

	1991		1993	
	Volume	%	Volume	%
Life	546.9	30.9	882.2	33.2
Non-life	1,225.1	69.1	1,777.0	66.8
Vehicles				30.3
Health				9.2
Multi-risk				8.2
Personal accident				4.1
Other				15.0
Total	1,772.0	100.0	2,659.2	100.0

Figures in pta billion

Figures cover the volume of premiums written and charges

Source: DGS 1994

Spanish-owned insurance company by 1993 and the industry remains too fragmented. The insurance law of 1984 (Ley de Ordenación del Seguro Privado) was very important in providing the basis for the adaptation of the insurance industry to an open market in insurance. Tighter capital regulations have forced many companies to close (the official regulatory body is the Comisión Liquidadora de Entidades Aseguradoras, CLEA). Regulation was further increased in 1994 by a new law governing supervision in the industry (Ley sobre Supervisión de Seguros Privados, 1994). The new law raised minimum capital requirements, tightened government regulations and enabled Spanish companies to operate anywhere in the European Union.

Many of the insurance companies in Spain are controlled by the banks, providing an extensive distribution network for selling insurance. For example, La Estrella and Vitalicio are part of the BCH group, Hercules Español part of Argentaria, Cénit part of Banco Santander, Euroseguros and Axa Aurora part of Banco Bilbao Vizcaya, Rentcaixa and Vidacaixa part of La Caixa. Such holdings or alliances between banks and insurance companies are reflected at the wider European level in, for example, the alliance between Dresdner Bank and Allianz in Germany.

Apart from consolidation, Spanish insurance companies have been looking for foreign outlets. Many have opened offices in Portugal, while Mapfre bought the Belgian reinsurance company Compagnie Internationale d'Assurances et Reassurances (CIAR) and has pursued a policy of expansion into Latin America, for example taking control of the South American reinsurance company Caja Reaseguradora de Chile.

Foreign penetration of the insurance industry has existed for some time (examples including the Swiss companies Winterthur and Zurich), but increased notably in the late 1980s. At the end of 1993 foreign capital (in the form of foreign subsidiaries and foreign participation in Spanish companies) represented 43 per cent of all the capital in the insurance industry (two-thirds being capital from the EU and one-quarter from Switzerland; DGS 1994). Companies with majority foreign ownership (over 50 per cent) were responsible for about one-third of all premium business (ibid.). Allianz owns the company Cresa, BUPA owns Sanitas, in 1990 Norwich Union acquired Plus Ultra from Banco Bilbao Vizcaya, in 1992 the Italian company Assicurazioni Generali formed the holding company Central Hispano Generali embracing La Estrella and Vitalicio, in 1993 BBV and the French insurance group Axa set up the holding Axa-Aurora, and in 1994 the ailing insurer La Unión y el Fénix was acquired by the French insurance group AGF.

7.5 Other financial services

The Spanish stock market is the smallest in Europe (after London, Frankfurt, Paris, Milan and Amsterdam) and has played only a very limited role in providing funds to the private sector. There are four markets: in Madrid (established in 1831), Bilbao (established in 1890), Barcelona (established in 1915) and Valencia (established in 1981). Madrid accounts for over 90 per cent of all business. Overall, the stock market has been characterised by a narrow range of companies traded (mainly Telefónica, banks, utilities and construction companies), lacking a broad representation of the corporate sector, limited trading times and excessively restrictive practices. Trading in shares, bonds and debentures was exclusively controlled by 87 *agentes* and insider dealing was rife.

A new law governing the Stock Exchange in Spain was introduced in 1989. This set up a national stock exchange commission (Comision Nacional del Mercado de Valores, CNMV) made up of five members appointed by the government plus the deputy governor of the Bank of Spain and the director general of the Treasury. Continuous trading was introduced and greater transparency in the market was sought. From 1989 any European Community company has been able to buy up to 30 per cent of a stock market firm; this rose to 50 per cent in 1991, and by 1992 any non-Community company was entitled to do the same.

Accountancy was another area dominated by practices uncommon elsewhere in Europe. As companies have sought stock market quotations and a more public profile, so more transparent and internationally acceptable company accounts have had to be produced. Reform of accountancy practices (prompted by European Community accountancy regulations) and the need for companies to present a reliable image (especially on the international scene) have allowed the major multinational accountancy firms to corner the Spanish market.

7.6 Retailing

Distribution in Spain (retailing and wholesaling) represents about 12 per cent of the GDP and employs 1.7 million people directly (15 per cent of the labour force, larger than in many other European Union countries). Following a long period of inertia, distribution has been undergoing rapid change, involving increased concentration (overseen by the banks, public sector companies such as Mercasa and Tabacalera, and foreign investment), greater foreign penetration, new forms of retailing and the wider application of new technologies.

Retailing has a dual structure. The traditional sector is made up of a dense pattern of small, family-owned businesses. The modern sector embraces large stores, supermarkets, hypermarkets, shopping centres and small specialist shops. This dual distribution system is reflected in the density of distribution outlets, lack of concentration in the business structure, and a highly skewed pattern of sales. In the late 1980s there were three points of sale for every 1,000 inhabitants; 95 per cent of the points of sale represented only 54 per cent of sales, while 5 per cent of points of sale (the modern sector) accounted for 46 per cent of sales (Barrio et al. 1990).

Changes in retailing have been associated with changes in consumer behaviour and work patterns, growing consumer demand and more efficient distribution systems. As elsewhere in Europe, traditional shops and street markets are yielding to supermarkets and hypermarkets, and routine shopping is shifting to edge-of-town and out-of-town shopping centres. Given the number of small stores in Spain, this trend presages a significant change in both the pattern of employment and, more broadly, in the pattern of life. In addition, the traditional mixture of land-use across urban areas is changing (and will change further with the new urban property rental law in 1994, Ley de Arrendamientos Urbanos) to a pattern of greater spatial specialisation.

The traditional shop has been an integral part of Spanish society, frequently part of the family home and providing little more than a small supplement to household income. These small shops were often supplied through a lengthy chain of agents (adding significantly to prices). Such shops are still important but are on the decline (especially in the food sector) in the face of increased competition from modern shopping facilities. For example, one survey estimated that traditional shops declined from 71 per cent of food sales in 1975 to only 30 per cent in 1987 (Barrio et al. 1990), with a forecast further decline to only 16 per cent in 1995. Another survey put the share of food sales from traditional shops in 1990 at about 25 per cent (Nielson Company 1990). The Ministry of Agriculture estimate that the share of traditional shops in all food sales to households fell from 53.3 per cent in 1987 to 46.1 per cent in 1992, while food sales to households from supermarkets increased from 30 to 35 per cent and from hypermarkets from 3.5 to 8.9 per cent (*El País* 1994b). Strategies for the survival of small shops have been specialisation and niche marketing (boutiques and delicatessens), the provision of value-added services, or the formation of associations for bulk purchasing.

The modern sector arrived very late in Spain (the first large department store opened in 1956, the first supermarket in 1960 and the first hypermarket in 1973). Its development was further retarded by the economic crisis of the late 1970s and early 1980s. However, from the mid 1980s there has been rapid growth, driven by rising consumer expenditure and fuelled in part by foreign investment, adding the names of an increasing number of multinational stores (including C&A, Marks and Spencer and Sears Retail) to well-established ones such as El Corte Inglés, Galerías Preciados and Cortefiel.

Table 7.11 Leading hypermarkets, 1993

Hypermarkets	Sales	Employment	Stores	Major shareholders
Pryca	491	13,600	42	Carrefour, Grupo March
Continente	353	10,900	32	Promodés, BBV
Alcampo	233	8,076	19	Auchamps
Hipercor	181	6,500	10	El Corte Inglés

Sales in pta billion
Source: *El País* 1994c

Since the mid 1980s there has been an explosion of supermarkets, hypermarkets and shopping centres. The first hypermarket was opened in Barcelona in 1973. Development was slow during the 1970s, making them a phenomenon of the 1980s, with more than 80 being built during the decade. At the beginning of 1994 there were about 180 such establishments, with further stores under construction and one estimate suggesting a capacity in Spain for 500. The majority of the stores belong to one of four companies (accounting for about 75 per cent of hypermarket sales), three of which – Pryca, Continente and Alcampo – are owned by French groups, only Hipercor (a subsidiary of El Corte Inglés) being Spanish (Table 7.11). Continente opened its first store in Valencia in 1976. By the beginning of 1994 it had 32 stores and planned to open a further ten by 1996 (five of which were already under construction). Eighty per cent of Continente stores were located around the Mediterranean coast.

Shopping centres too mushroomed in the late 1980s. For example, between the summer of 1988 and November 1989 a dozen new shopping centres were opened, including Colombia, Galéria del Prado and Arturo Soría Plaza in Madrid, Boulevard Rosa Diagonal in Barcelona, Las Huertas in Palencia and the Kuo Centre in Santander. Parquesur opened at the end of 1989 to become the largest shopping centre in Madrid, embracing 140,000 square metres, overtaking in size the 125,000 square metres of La Vanguada (opened in 1985). Parquesur contains 320 shops (and 6,000 parking spaces) including the hypermarket Alcampo, the department store Galerías Preciados and C&A.

Foreign penetration of retailing is gradually building, although hypermarkets have from the outset been dominated by foreign businesses. Galerías Preciados was bought from the government by a South American group after the collapse of the Rumasa empire, then sold on to the British Mountleigh group in 1988 before returning to Spanish hands in the early 1990s. C&A have developed a significant number of outlets in the 1980s and in early 1990 the first branch of Marks and Spencer opened in Madrid as a joint venture with Cortefiel. The company envisaged opening a further ten stores throughout Spain by 1995.

A number of strategies for expansion in Europe are evolving among retailers. These include the construction of new stores, acquisitions of store chains, cross-ownership of shares and alliances. In the supermarket sector, the Dutch group Unigro has expanded into Spain through the acquisition of existing store chains (supermarkets) and through franchising agreements. Alliances are especially suited to more competitive and saturated retail markets. Alliances can take the form of buying groups, retail development based groups, skills-based groups and multifunctional groups (the latter including elements of the other three, an example being the European Retail Alliance).

Although not strictly part of retailing, the restaurant sector deserves a brief comment. Part of the expanding hospitality industry, there were over 50,000 registered restaurants in 1993 (establishments classified in the one to five star categories, hence excluding the multitude of other catering establishments such as cafeterias and the country inns, *ventas*) offering approaching three million places (SGT 1994). Despite what might appear to be a saturated market, foreign penetration of this sector too grew more visible in the 1990s as foreign restaurant chains exploited niche positions in the market. For example, Burger King (owned by the British group Grand Metropolitan) opened 21 restaurants in 1993, taking its total to 80 (of which 40 were in Madrid and most were franchises) and planned to open a further 20 by the end of 1994. Similarly, Pizza Hut had only 20 establishments in 1992 but had close to 100 by the end of 1994. McDonald's followed a similar pattern of rapid growth, growth that was occurring during a period of economic recession! A similar picture was developing elsewhere in the leisure and hospitality industry as market opportunities arose for modern cosmopolitan facilities.

7.7 Telecommunication services

One of the sectors which appears to offer both prospects for employment growth and the underpinning of business competitiveness in the late 1990s and twenty-first century is that associated with the convergent technologies of electronics, telecommunications and audio-visual systems. Much of this complex is already dominated by multinational companies operating in a global market, the only significant Spanish-owned company being Telefónica. Nevertheless, there will be opportunities for employment creation in activities related to this sector and it will be important for overall business efficiency to establish a full telecommunications infrastructure.

At the beginning of the twentieth century the telephone network was operated by a multitude of concessionaires (the service itself having been designated a monopoly of the state in 1884). In 1924 the state granted the running of the service to a single company Compañía Telefónica Nacional de España (CTNE), the main shareholder in which was the American company ITT (International Telephone and Telegraph Company). CTNE was nationalised in 1946. Since that time the company (now renamed Telefónica) has grown into the largest company in Spain in terms of turnover, shareholder funds, total assets and number of employees (over 74,000 in 1994). Gross value-added in 1993 represented 1.79 per cent of GDP in Spain (Telefónica 1994).

Telecommunication services are developing in a rapidly changing business environment. Liberalisation of the market in Spain was introduced through the Telecommunications Law in 1987 (Ley de Ordenación de las Telecomunicaciones), which began the process of breaking up the monopoly of Telefónica (for example in the sale of telecommunication accessories and value-added services). At the end of 1994 a licence was granted to a business consortium (including foreign capital) to develop a second pan-European global system of mobile communications to compete with the one to be installed by Telefónica. Voice transmission and the basic telephone network was not due to be deregulated until the year 2003, but the date will probably be brought forward to 1998 to coincide with that in most other EU countries. As a result of liberalisation foreign investment in the sector has been growing, gradually increasing the competition for Telefónica.

In response to this changing business environment Telefónica has been reducing its holdings in supply companies, concentrating on its core business of providing telecommunication services and rapidly expanding abroad through acquisitions and alliances. For example, Telettra was sold to Alcatel Standard and Telefónica's holding in Alcatel Standard (one of Telefónica main suppliers of telephone transmission and switching systems) reduced to 13 per cent in mid 1994. Similarly, Telefónica sold its holding in ATT-Microelectrónica de España, taking in exchange a small holding in ATT-Network Systems International BV. In terms of overseas expansion, Telefónica has invested heavily in Latin America – in Argentina, Chile, Peru, Puerto Rico, Uruguay and Venezuela. Globalisation of multimedia services has required companies to form international alliances, thus in 1993 Telefónica joined Unisource (a consortium of Dutch, Swedish and Swiss operators).

7.8 Construction

The construction industry is one of the largest sectors of the Spanish economy, accounting for between 7 and 10 per cent of both GDP and employment (some one million people), depending on cyclical and seasonal factors. In addition, spiralling property prices in the late 1980s and property tax loopholes (currently being closed through a detailed national catastral survey and changes in tax and property laws) attracted a large property services industry, drawing finance from across the whole spectrum of the

Table 7.12 Major Spanish construction companies, 1993

Company	Assets	Income	Employment
FCC	307	302	22,352
Dragados y Construcciones	261	260	11,406
Cubiertas y MZOV	182	180	6,783
Ferrovial group	169	123	3,790
Entrecanales y Tavora	137	65	2,874
Hasa-Huarte	121	90	2,505
Agromán	99	103	4,117
OCP Construcciones	85	77	2,452
Tragsa	59	49	1,213

FCC: Fomento de Construcciones, the company formed from Focsa and Construcciones y Contratas

Assets and sales in pta billion

Source: *El País* 1994c

Spanish economy. The sector is generally recognised to carry with it important economic multiplier effects, especially within the local economy, and represents a larger proportion of the economies of the less developed regions.

A complex ownership structure in the industry embraces interlocking links with other construction companies, construction materials, financial institutions and property-development companies. For example, Banco Central Hispano has an important holding in Dragados y Construcciones; Banco Santander (Banesto) has holdings in the construction companies Agromán and FCC (the latter owns the cement company Portland Valderrivas, which in turn has the majority holding in the Torre Picasso in Madrid); and the family-run Entrecanales y Tavora has moved into the finance business with a merchant bank (Baninvest).

Even the largest companies are only of medium size by world standards (Table 7.12). Ease of entry into the less sophisticated areas of construction has enabled a multitude of small businesses to develop (many operating in the submerged economy), although the majority of public sector works and a large part of all construction activity is undertaken by members of SEOPAN (Empresas de Obras Públicas de Ambito Nacional), comprising about 100 medium-sized companies. Recession in the industry in 1992 and an even worse year in 1993 prompted some mergers, including that between the companies Construcciones y Contratas and Focsa, which merged in 1992 to form Fomento de Construcciones y Contratas (FCC). The larger construction companies have tended to diversify forwards into property, water, cleansing, power and urban environmental services and backwards into cement.

The 'economic miracle' in the 1960s brought an enormous volume of work for the construction industry, as urbanisation spread around the coastline, cities expanded and some of the infrastructure necessary for a modern industrial nation was established. Economic problems brought contraction in the late 1970s and early 1980s, followed by a renewed construction boom in the second half of the 1980s, with growth averaging over 9 per cent a year from 1986 to 1990 inclusive (reaching 13 per cent in 1989 on the back of the property boom and public sector projects oriented especially to the 1992 Olympic Games in Barcelona and Expo '92 in Seville). Deceleration of growth in the economy began to effect the sector in 1991, plunging it into recession in 1992 and 1993 as both public and private sector projects contracted. By the end of 1993 some renewed optimism in the sector was returning with lower interest rates, higher rental incomes from urban property forecast as a result of the new urban property rental law (Ley de Arrendamientos Urbanos), pledges by the government to maintain infrastructure spending (for example as outlined in the Plan Director de Infraestructuras) and the subsidised housing programme (Plan de Viviendas 1992–95, under which the state planned to subsidise 460,000 dwellings between 1992 and 1995: demographic trends indicate that the housing deficit will be a problem until the end of the century in a country where only 15 per cent of families live in rented accommodation).

The complexity of company ownership structures, coupled with the uniquely Spanish environment within which Spanish construction firms have operated, have made it difficult for foreign firms to gain access to the Spanish market and to gain control of Spanish construction companies. Nevertheless, foreign firms began to penetrate the market in the late 1980s, many redirecting their efforts from the Third World to establish cross-border acquisitions and joint ventures in Europe. For example, in 1989 the German company Philipp Holzmann (one of the largest construction firms in Europe) acquired a 50 per cent holding in Jotsa, having previously signed an agreement with Agromán; the French company Bouygues has several Spanish holdings and Hasa Huarte was taken over in 1987 by a group headed by the Fiat civil-engineering subsidiary, Impresit. In the related industry of cement (national production capacity of 36 million tonnes and consumption in 1993 of 26 million tonnes), an estimated 65 per cent of national production in 1993 was in the hands of companies with foreign holdings (including Asland, part of the French Lafarge Copée group and Valencia de Cementos y Sanson part of the Mexican Cemex group). Moreover, imports of cement increased in the early 1990s from 2 to 11 per cent of the domestic market.

Largely in response to the decline in the domestic market in 1992/93, the larger construction companies have once more been looking abroad (for example, both Huarte and Dragados have acquired companies in Portugal and Ferrovial has acquired an Italian construction company) after virtually abandoning overseas work in the late 1980s. Particular opportunities are considered to exist in Latin America.

Further penetration of the domestic market by foreign multinational construction and property companies will lead to mergers among Spanish companies. Greater competition in the domestic market (in part the result of liberalisation of major public construction projects) will also force Spanish companies to seek more work outside Spain.

7.9 Restructuring of the service sector

The service sector has emerged as the main source of employment and income in Spain in the late twentieth century, in this it is similar to other western industrialised countries. What distinguishes the service sector in Spain is the importance of tourism, the scale of employment in distribution and construction, and the low level of exports outside of tourism.

Various factors have combined to protect services from international competition for longer than most sectors of the economy. These factors have included legal restrictions, which in large measure have now been removed, the natural market protection offered by the 'good-will' of consumers and their familiarity with particular institutions and practices, and the requirements of professional organisations. For example, in the insurance market liberalisation in 1994 left such factors as national variations in taxes, legal conditions (for example the settlements awarded by courts for accident victims), frequency of claims and consumer buying patterns as barriers to a single European market. Such protection partly accounts for higher inflation rates in services than in industrial goods (OECD 1992): 'inflation stickiness in the service sectors and the associated wide inflation gap between goods and services had been particular characteristics of the strong inflation pressures and expectations in Spain since the mid-1980s.' (OECD 1994, p. 19).

The results of protection have been a high degree of atomisation throughout the service sector and almost certainly a significant level of over-staffing. The lifting of protection from services is resulting in a wave of restructuring including the slow disappearance of semi-subsistence businesses, the emergence of larger firms, greater concentration, a more international orientation and the increasing presence of foreign capital. The process is also being accompanied by a shake-out in employment, which will retard further employment expansion in the sector.

In the late 1990s, restructuring in the service sector will be the most visible feature of economic change in Spain; new names will appear on the 'High Street', many traditional small businesses will disappear and more European-wide business practices will be adopted. Such changes represent a further dimension of a process which is transforming the Spanish economy into a modern European one.

References and bibliography

Argentaria (1994) *Annual report 1993.* Madrid

Banco Bilbao Vizcaya (1994) *Annual report. 1993.* Bilbao

Banco de España (1994) *Boletín estadístico,* June. Madrid

Barrio, J., A. González and M. López (1990) 'La distribución comercial en España', *El País* (sección negocios), 22 April, pp. 12–13

Berges, A., E. Ontiveros and F. Valero (1990) *Internacionalización de la banca: el caso español.* Madrid: Espasa-Calpe SA

Casares, J. (ed.) (1987) *La economía de la distribución comercial.* Barcelona: Editorial Ariel SA

Casilda Béjar, R. (1993) *Sistema financiero español.* Madrid: Alianza Editorial

Castells, M. and P. Hall (eds.) (1992) *Andalucía: innovación tecnológica y desarrollo económico.* Madrid: Editorial Espasa-Calpe SA

Chislett, W. (1992) *Spain business and finance.* London: Euromoney publications

Cuadrado Roura, J. (1988) 'El sector servicios: evolución, características y perspectivas de futuro', in J. García Delgado (ed.), *España: Tomo II, Economía,* pp. 231–70. Madrid: Espasa-Calpe

Cuadrado Roura, J. (1990) 'La expansión de los servicios en el contexto del cambio estructural de la economía española', *Papeles de Economía Española* 42, pp. 98–120

Cuadrado Roura, J. and M. González Moreno (1988) *El sector servicios en España.* Barcelona: Ediciones Orbis

Cuervo, A. (1988) *La crisis bancaria en España 1977–1985.* Barcelona: Editorial Ariel SA

Diaz de Castro, E. and C. Carlos Fernández (1993) *Distribución comercial.* Madrid: McGraw-Hill

Dirección General de Seguros, DGS (1994) *Informe sector seguros.* Madrid: Ministerio de Economía y Hacienda

El País (1994a) *Anuario de economía y finanzas 1994.* Madrid

El País (1994b) *Anuario El País 1994.* Madrid

El País (1994c) 'Ranking de las principales compañías españolas no financieras', special supplement, 27 November. Madrid

Financial Times (1994a) *FT 500,* special supplement, 20 January. London

Financial Times (1994b) 'Spain: banking, finance and investment', survey, 20 June. London

Fundación Mapfre Estudios (1993) *The Spanish insurance market in 1992.* Madrid

Hernández, S. (1990) 'La resaca de las fusiones', *El País* (sección negocios), 23 April, p. 18

Instituto de Crédito Oficial, ICO (1994) *Annual report 1993.* Madrid

Instituto Nacional de Estadística, INE (1994) *Encuesta de la población activa,* fourth quarter 1993; resultados detallados. Madrid

La Caixa (1994) *Informe anual 1993.* Barcelona

Lerena, L. (1989) 'La estrategía de la banca española ante el reto del mercado unico', *Situación,* No. 1, pp. 5–17. Bilbao: BBV

Mapfre (1994) *El mercado español de seguros en 1993.* Madrid: Fundación Mapfre Estudios

Nielsen Company (1990) *Anuario/evolución Nielsen 1990.* Madrid

Noceda, M. (1994) 'El revulso de Banesto', *El País,* 19 June, p. 48

Ontiveros, E. and F. Valero (1988) 'El sistema financiero. Instituciones y funcionamiento', in J. García Delgado (ed.), *España: Tomo II, Economía*, pp. 367–430. Madrid: Espasa-Calpe SA

OECD (1992) *Economic surveys: Spain 1991–1992.* Paris

OECD (1994) *Economic surveys: Spain 1993–1994.* Paris

Pelegri y Giron, J. (1985) 'El sector de seguros', *Papeles de Economía Española* 25, pp. 173–88

Portela, M. (1994a) 'Ranking de la banca de 1993', *El País* (sección negocios), 30 October, pp. 3–28

Portela, M. (1994b) 'Ranking de las cajas 1993', *El País* (sección negocios), 13 November, pp. 3–21

Secretaria General de Turismo, SGT (1994) *Movimiento turístico 1993.* Madrid: Ministerio de Comercio y Turismo

Telefónica (1994) *Annual report 1993.* Madrid

Torrero, A. (1989) *Estudios sobre el sistema financiero.* Madrid: Espasa-Calpe SA

Unespa (1994) *Informe económico 1993.* Madrid

White, D. (1985) 'Spanish banks gear up for EEC entry', *The Banker*, October, pp. 25–9

Chapter 8
Tourism

8.1 The tourist industry

The popular image of Spain is the one struck by tourism. While this may be a distorted image, it nevertheless focuses on what is Spain's most important industry, which unlike most other sectors of the economy has always been closely linked to international business. With 60 million foreign visitors in 1994 bringing in pta 3,000 billion in foreign exchange, the industry is a key propulsive force in the economy. Apart from generating growth, tourism has been at the centre of both structural and spatial change; attracting investment in services, providing many of the new jobs in the service sector and stimulating development around the coast.

Activities related to tourism permeate the economy, so increasing the difficulties of defining the sector. In major tourist areas almost all activities are either directly or indirectly linked to tourism and yet few activities provide goods or services exclusively for tourists. The leisure and hospitality industries (focused on the hotel and catering industry) are interwoven with tourism, but an important component of their demand arises from changing lifestyles and patterns of domestic consumption not strictly related to tourism. In the early 1990s these activities were among those where employment continued to rise, as illustrated by the rapid expansion of a number of foreign restaurant chains. Beyond these activities, transport, the food and drink industry and construction are among the many closely allied sectors.

8.2 Growth of tourism

Tourism began to grow steadily during the 1950s, annual growth rates in the number of foreign visitors averaging about 15 per cent and the number of hotel beds increasing from 78,771 in 1951 to 150,821 in 1960 (Table 8.1). The momentum for growth was reinforced in 1959 by devaluation of the

Table 8.1 Growth of tourism in Spain

Year	Visitors (million)	Hotel accommodation (Number of beds)	Income (current)	Index	Income (constant)	Index
1951	0.7	78,771	–	–	–	–
1960	6.1	150,821	–	–	–	–
1970	24.1	545,798	130,328	100	130,328	100
1975	30.1	785,339	230,682	177	130,476	100
1976	30.0	798,985	207,073	159	99,602	76
1977	34.3	803,747	313,163	240	121,006	93
1978	40.0	808,015	416,497	320	134,354	103
1979	38.9	806,552	435,300	334	121,449	93
1980	38.0	814,394	500,649	384	120,813	93
1981	40.1	811,700	628,400	482	131,964	101
1982	42.0	825,959	787,650	604	144,975	111
1983	41.3	834,536	990,000	760	162,562	125
1984	42.9	835,200	1,247,798	957	184,095	141
1985	43.2	843,337	1,374,700	1055	186,425	143
1986	47.4	864,834	1,671,900	1283	208,388	160
1987	50.5	886,699	1,826,400	1401	216,193	166
1988	54.2	907,921	1,961,200	1505	221,529	170
1989	54.1	918,649	1,924,000	1476	203,490	156
1990	52.0	929,533	1,820,400	1397	180,220	138
1991	53.5	972,808	1,991,100	1528	185,172	142
1992	55.3	1,003,199	2,123,200	1629	184,718	142
1993	57.3	1,009,041	2,540,000	1949	210,820	162
1994*	60.0		2,900,000	2225	229,100	176

Hotel accommodation embraces that in *hoteles* and *hostales*

* 1994 figures are estimates

Tourism income in pta million

Constant values based on the 1970 value of the peseta given in *Anuario El País* 1995

Sources: SGT 1993 and 1994a

peseta and the opening of the economy to foreign investment occasioned by the Stabilisation Act. The following year growth in the number of visitors increased by 46 per cent over 1959 and thereafter continued to grow strongly throughout the 1960s and into the early 1970s. Growth was fed by an increasingly affluent population in north-west Europe, who were offered guaranteed sun in a country with a low cost of living, stable society and government controlled prices. The number of foreign visitors escalated from 4.2 million in 1959 to 34.6 million in 1973 and the number of beds in hotels from 142,000 to almost 700,000. Simultaneously, the Spanish economic miracle of the 1960s increased disposable incomes within Spain, stimulating domestic tourism.

The burgeoning tourist industry transformed fishing villages like Torremolinos into international tourist playgrounds. It engulfed regional economies, fuelled land speculation, spawned a multitude of service sector activities, stimulated demand for agricultural and manufactured products, contributed to the high level of activity in the construction industry and was a significant force behind cultural change. These developments, together with industrialisation in País Vasco, Cataluña and Madrid, were accompanied by a redistribution of the population away from the agricultural regions of the interior towards the expanding industrial areas and the emerging urban tourist complexes around the coast. By 1981 75 per cent of the population of Spain lived either in Madrid or in one of the provinces with a coastline. In the province of Málaga the population living in coastal municipalities increased from 50 per cent in 1950 to 73 per cent in 1986, swelling the resident population of Marbella, for example, from 9,629 to 74,807.

Faced with escalating demand, the private sector saw highly profitable opportunities in land speculation and development. The Spanish planning system was both unequipped and unwilling to control this sudden tide of development, offering as it did the opportunity for not only local and national economic growth but also personal gain. For the Franco regime it provided an invaluable economic support (especially as a source of foreign exchange) as well as tacit approval of the government (Valenzuela Rubio 1985). During this period tourist facilities grew like Topsy, leaving it for another generation to count the cost of disorderly urbanisation, much of which lacked an adequate infrastructure.

The boom in tourism faltered in 1974 with the onset of recession in the world economy. The number of visitors fell sharply and then stagnated for three years until 1977 (Table 8.1). Provision of new hotel accommodation was drastically cut back and many developments were left unfinished; thus the 798,985 beds in hotels in 1976 increased to only 806,552 in 1979. Similarly, income from tourism fell in the mid 1970s from its peak in 1973, real income not fully recovering until the 1980s. This period of crisis initiated a round of restructuring in the tourist industry, including the formation of larger hotel groups, a reduction in labour intensity (for example through the more widespread use of self-service facilities in hotels) and a switch towards the provision of apartment rather than hotel accommodation.

The late 1970s saw a recovery in the number of visitors but growth was once more interrupted by economic problems at the turn of the decade. Spectacular rates of growth resumed in the mid 1980s, reflecting the consumer boom in north-west Europe (especially in Britain, which accounted for over 30 per cent of the growth in foreign visitors between 1982 and 1987). Domestic tourism also grew rapidly within the buoyant Spanish economy. Optimism based on another pulse of tourism growth in the mid 1980s prompted significant further expansion of tourist accommodation taking the number of hotel beds up to 907,921 in 1988. This upsurge in growth faltered again in 1989, catching many unprepared. Thus tourism in the Canary Islands was forecast to grow by 30 per cent in 1989; in fact it was negative. In 1990 a further fall in the number of foreign visitors sent shivers through the whole tourism industry, casting doubt over its future.

Just as over-optimism characterises periods of buoyant demand, so more pessimistic scenarios dominate troughs. A number of short-term factors could easily explain the interruption of growth in 1989: high interest rates and recession reducing disposable incomes in north-west Europe (especially in Britain), a strong peseta coupled with domestic inflation, exceptionally good weather in north-west Europe and air transport difficulties. Of more serious long-term concern were changing patterns of consumer demand (influenced in part by the public image of Spanish tourism), new forms of tourism, long-haul holidays and more competitive alternative destinations (for example Morocco, Tunisia, Turkey and eastern Europe).

What is probable, is that the sun-and-sand tourism market in Spain has reached a stage of maturity, in which the underlying trend in this market segment will be one of slower growth around which there will be annual variations dependent on the competitive position of Spain in the international market. However, other market segments have yet to be fully developed. The staging of the Olympic Games and Expo '92 helped lift hotel accommodation to over one million beds in 1992, while civil war in the former Yugoslavia, instability in Turkey and north Africa, and devaluation of the peseta in 1992/93, contributed to a record year for foreign visitors in 1993, followed by further growth in foreign visitors in 1994.

Ensuring future growth will require strategic shifts in tourism development, especially the promotion of new tourism areas, new forms of tourism and improvements and remodelling of existing major tourist areas. The crucial problem is that an enormous supply of accommodation now exists that can only be filled through retaining a mass tourism market in which price competition is acute (the package holiday market is estimated to represent about half the total foreign tourism market). The size of this mass market will inhibit moving the industry away from mass tourism and the mass tourism image towards a higher value-added product.

8.3 Distribution of tourist accommodation

Tourist accommodation is provided in a variety of guises, from hotels to campsites and private accommodation (the term hotel is used here to refer to both *hoteles* and *hostales*). The total number of beds available for the use of tourists runs into many millions. Of this total over one million are in hotels (the third largest provision of hotel beds in the world after the United States and Italy) and a further million in other forms of registered tourist accommodation, the remainder are unregistered and escape the official statistics. In 1993 46 per cent of registered accommodation was in hotels, 18 per cent in apartments, 8 per cent in guest houses and 28 per cent on campsites. As a proportion of all tourist accommodation, that in hotels may represent between 5 and 20 per cent (Anon 1987a). Hotels are graded into five gold star (*hoteles*), and three silver star categories (*hostales*). Over 80 per cent of hotel accommodation is provided in gold star hotels (the largest proportion of this in the three star category; Table 8.2). In 1993 there were 633 five and four gold star hotels, 1,625 three gold star hotels, 2,774 two and one gold star hotels, and 4,702 silver star hotels (SGT 1994a). In the late 1980s and early 1990s growth in hotel accommodation was concentrated in the three and four gold star categories, while there was a substantial decline in one silver star hotels. A number of five star hotels downgraded their rating in search of more profitable markets. Outside the hotel sector there are tourist apartments (118,300 in 1993), guest houses (*casas de huéspedes*), inns (*fondas;* 12,679 guest houses and inns in 1993), farm houses (*casas de labranza*) and tourist campsites (1,039 in 1993). Between 1988 and 1993, the only sector of accommodation that did not show significant growth was that of guest houses.

Unregistered accommodation is estimated to offer a potential supply of tourist accommodation amounting to 16.2 million beds, of which 6.7 million beds are exclusively for use by tourists (FEH 1994). The figures for potential tourist accommodation include second homes (which have increased in number from 800,000 in 1970 to over 2.6 million in 1991, concentrated around the coast; Serrano Martínez 1993), apartments, rooms let in family houses and unofficial campsites. Such facilities provide a flexible reservoir of accommodation against which registered accommodation must compete.

Registered accommodation is concentrated around the Mediterranean coast and in the major cities (Table 8.3). Over one-quarter of all hotel accommodation is located in the Balearic Islands and about three-quarters of all accommodation is provided around the Mediterranean coast (including the Atlantic coast in the south). Urbanisation sprawls out around this coast, coalescing in high-density, high-rise agglomerations such as Torremolinos, Benidorm and Arenal; monuments to the tourist boom of the 1960s. Away from the Mediterranean coast, a further 8 per cent of accommodation is provided in Santander and in Galicia and 4 per cent in Madrid. Outside of these areas pockets of accommodation are provided in the winter sports

Table 8.2 Number of beds and bednights in hotels by type of accommodation, 1993

Accommodation	Number of beds	%	Number of bednights	%
Hotel 5 Star	22,616	2.2	3,448,784	2.3
Hotel 4 Star	182,380	18.1	29,758,012	20.0
Hotel 3 Star	387,080	38.4	63,774,648	42.8
Hotel 2 Star	157,768	15.6	23,039,273	15.5
Hotel 1 Star	87,797	8.7	9,712,045	6.5
Hostal 3 Star	9,385	0.9	8,370,637	5.6
Hostal 2 Star	92,040	9.1	a	a
Hostal 1 Star	70,175	7.0	10,763,531*	7.2
Total	1,009,041	100.0	148,866,930	100.0

a: figures for 2 star *hostales* are included in those for three star ones

* figure for 1 star *hostales* is for 1992

Sources: SGT 1994a and 1994b

resorts of the Pyrenees and across Spain in line with the distribution of population. In the early 1990s there was a tendency towards a slowdown in the growth of coastal hotel accommodation, growth being more noticeable inland and in the cities.

The spatial concentration of tourism has brought a form of saturated development to some areas (Torremolinos for example) together with substantial capacity, forcing fiercely competitive pricing and frequently allowing profitable operation only during the summer months. Some of this accommodation could be converted to residential use should tourism demand evaporate (such a measure was proposed by the regional government of the Canary Islands in 1990). By contrast, the majority of the interior has been developed more slowly. Many sites of notable scenic and cultural interest, including the many national parks and nature reserves (such as Cazorla in the province of Jaén and Covadonga in Oviedo) have only recently been provided with modern tourism facilities.

Although the promotion of tourism away from the Mediterranean coast will help raise regional incomes, the lessons of earlier development must be learnt and tighter planning control enforced. Throughout the length of the coastline lack of effective planning control has allowed many attractive landscapes to be blighted (Morris and Dickenson 1987). In major resorts visual pollution has been compounded by noise and water pollution. Additional public service provision can go some way towards reducing these environmental problems but they can only be installed at substantial public costs. Yet without such investment tourists may begin to look elsewhere. Parts of many major tourist resorts are now over thirty years old, further investment in infrastructure and maintenance will be necessary if they are not to deteriorate rapidly into slums.

Table 8.3 Distribution of registered tourist accommodation (beds), 1993

Province	Hotel	%	Guest house	Apartment	Campsite	Total	%
Baleares	258,357	25.6	3,934	118,362	3,683	384,336	17.7
Gerona	75,494	7.5	14,692	20,781	112,634	223,601	10.3
Barcelona	75,923	7.5	15,155	4,147	65,029	160,254	7.4
Tarragona	37,641	3.7	3,656	36,098	62,288	139,683	6.4
Las Palmas	36,826	3.6	2,534	94,638	800	134,798	6.2
Málaga	52,994	5.3	7,673	30,351	14,257	105,275	4.8
Tenerife	47,900	5.4	2,295	40,078	700	90,973	4.5
Madrid	51,335	5.1	16,742	3,823	15,083	86,983	4.0
Alicante	49,843	4.7	2,990	7,870	23,346	84,049	3.9
Cantabria	14,599	1.4	2,540	1,338	27,529	46,006	2.1
Castellón	14,548	1.4	1,817	6,185	21,297	43,847	2.0
Valencia	14,982	1.5	3,678	2,538	17,019	38,217	1.8
Other	278,799	27.6	99,246	20,987	238,705	637,737	29.3
Total	1,009,241	100.0	176,952	387,196	602,370	2,175,759	100.0

Hotels include *hoteles* and *hostales*, guest houses include *fondas* and *casas de huéspedes*

Figures for guest house and apartment accommodation are for 1992

Sources: SGT 1993 and 1994a

8.4 Inbound tourism

Foreign tourists account for more than half the demand for hotel accommodation (SGT 1994b). In 1993 they accounted for 60 per cent of 137.8 million bed nights (excluding those in one star hostales; ibid.). The magnitude of the foreign tourist market can be gauged in terms of the number of foreign visitors. In 1994 there were 60 million such visitors to Spain (including almost 3 million Spanish people resident abroad), 43 million of whom stayed for longer than twenty-four hours (and were thus strictly tourists). Over 90 per cent of all foreign visitors are Europeans (Table 8.4), over half of the Europeans coming from the neighbouring countries of France and Portugal (a large proportion of these are excursionists). The most important groups in terms of consumption are the Germans, the British and the French (about 50 per cent of all visitors). The former two nationalities dominate the hotel bednight statistics. In 1993 for example, visitors from Germany and Britain represented only 15 and 13 per cent respectively of all foreign visitors, yet they accounted for 20 and 16 per cent respectively of all bednights recorded in hotels (excluding one star *hostales*; SGT 1994a and 1994b). The dominance of these two nationalities in terms of hotel bookings is especially marked in the Balearic and Canary Islands. The British have also been particularly important for hotel bookings along the Costa del Sol. Such a con-

Table 8.4 Nationality of foreign visitors to Spain

Nationality	1976	%	1980	1986	1990	1993	%
French	9.5	31.7	10.1	11.3	11.6	12.1	21.1
Portuguese	4.9	16.3	9.1	9.5	10.1	11.4	19.9
British	3.0	10.0	3.6	6.4	6.1	7.5	13.1
German	3.9	13.0	4.7	5.9	6.9	8.7	15.2
Scandinavian	1.2	4.0	1.1	1.8	1.6	1.2	2.1
Dutch	1.0	3.3	1.4	1.6	2.0	2.1	3.7
Belgian	0.9	3.0	1.0	1.1	1.3	1.5	2.6
Italian	0.4	1.3	0.5	1.1	1.7	2.1	3.7
Other	1.1	3.7	1.7	2.1	3.0	2.8	4.9
European	25.9	86.3	33.2	40.8	44.3	49.4	86.2
American	1.3	4.3	1.5	1.5	1.5	1.5	2.6
African	0.9	3.0	1.5	2.7	2.4	2.4	4.2
Asian	0.2	0.7	0.2	0.3	0.5	0.5	0.9
Oceanian	0.1	0.3	0.1	0.1	0.1	0.1	0.2
Total Foreign	28.4	94.7	36.5	45.4	48.7	53.9	94.1
Spanish (A)	1.6	5.3	1.5	2.0	3.3	3.4	5.9
Total	30.0	100.0	38.0	47.4	52.0	57.3	100.0

Number of visitors in millions

Spanish (A): Spanish residents abroad

About half the Americans are from the United States and half of those from Asia are from Japan; almost 90 per cent of Africans are from Morocco.

Sources: SGT 1993 and 1994a

centration of demand indicates the sensitivity of Spanish inbound foreign tourism to variations in market conditions in European countries, especially Britain and Germany. They emphasise both the need to diversify the geographical pattern of demand and the need to extend the appeal of Spain to new market segments within established national markets.

Since 1978 growth in the number of foreign visitors has come primarily from France, Portugal, Britain and Germany in Europe, and from Morocco in Africa. Many factors affect the foreign demand for tourism, including the growth of disposable incomes in tourism source regions, holiday costs (affected by exchange rate variations), exchange-control regulations, consumer tastes (influenced by publicity) and the organisation of marketing. Thus the miners strike in Britain was a factor contributing to lower bookings from Britain in 1985, as was the bad publicity relating to bombing campaigns, crime and pollution in Spain. Conversely, devaluation of the peseta against the pound sterling helped boost the number of British visitors in 1993. Mass tourism to Spain is recognised as being very price sensitive and thus vulnerable to price increases (arising either from appreciation of the peseta or domestic inflation) as was reflected by the fall in tourism numbers at the end of the 1980s. However, given the volume of accommodation offered in Spain compared with that elsewhere in the Mediterranean, it is unlikely that a significant proportion of demand can be switched in the short term to other Mediterranean regions.

8.5 Domestic and outbound tourism

The domestic market for tourism is drawn from a population of 39 million (1994), relatively more youthful and with a lower disposable income than in north-west European countries. These characteristics are reflected in the extent to which Spanish people use unregistered tourist accommodation and the small size of the outbound foreign tourism market.

Spanish domestic tourism has been increasing, but remains distinctive in character to that of foreign tourism. The majority of Spanish people organise their holiday independently, with less than 20 per cent using the services of a travel agent. Less than 10 per cent of all bednights spent by Spanish tourists are in hotels (Anon 1987a), most people preferring to use their own second home, an increasingly common characteristic (Salvá Tomas and Socias Fuster 1985; Barke and France 1988) or the house of a friend, which results in relatively stable tourism patterns. Most of the others prefer alternative self-catering accommodation. As a result, less than half of all bednights spent in hotels were attributable to Spanish residents in 1993 (many of these were in fact in association with business). Their average length of stay in hotels is also less than for foreigners (2.9 nights compared with 7.2 for tourists from the EC in 1993 – a figure almost identical to that in 1984; SGT 1994b). In contrast, over half of all bednights in campsites are taken by Spanish people.

Outbound foreign tourism has expanded rapidly from a very low level in the mid 1980s. In 1975 only 5.7 million visits by people resident in Spain were made abroad (0.5 million by air), by 1990 the figure was around 20 million (1.6 million by air). Recession and devaluation of the peseta in 1993 halted the growth of outbound visits, the number falling to 17.7 million (SGT 1994a). The most popular destinations are in Europe, especially France, Portugal, Italy and the UK. Excursions are frequent to the neighbouring countries of Andorra, France and Portugal.

8.6 Provision of hotel accommodation

Hotel accommodation is provided essentially through the private sector. This sector has been characterised by a few large hotel chains and a multitude of small ones and independent establishments with a high proportion of family ownership. Increased competition has stimulated a process of concentration in the industry as hotels seek economies of scale through hotel chains (integrated through management, leasing or franchising arrangements) or associations. In 1993 there were 106 hotel chains embracing over 1,000 establishments (compared with 76 chains and 592 hotels in 1981), mainly in the three gold star category and above (categories which accounted for over 80 per cent of all hotels in hotel chains; ACHE 1993). Although only 10 per cent of all hotel establishments were part of hotel chains in 1993, these hotels embraced 33 per cent of all hotel beds. Other hotels have been joining associations using central reservation systems and shared marketing. In 1993 the Hotusa group was the largest with 285 hotels, followed by Best Western España with 59.

Despite the process of concentration, only five companies offered more than 10,000 beds in Spain in 1992 (ACHE 1993). Grupo Sol-Meliá was the dominant hotel group. In 1993 this Mallorca based chain (specialising in beach hotels in the Balearic and Canary Islands) owned 120 hotels offering 61,550 beds in Spain. The group was the sixteenth largest in the world and the fourth largest in Europe after Accor, Forte and Club Med. By the end of 1994 it envisaged operating close to 200 hotels. Other major hotel groups include the Barcelona based Hoteles Unidos SA (Husa) with 77 hotels offering 18,663 beds in Spain (the group is the largest catering company in Spain, owning Entursa), Riu Hoteles (based in Mallorca) with 50 hotels and over 22,000 beds, Med-Playa Hoteles with 30 hotels and 11,750 beds, and Fiesta Hoteles with 24 hotels and 11,296 beds in Spain (all figures except those for Riu Hoteles are for 1993). Hoteles Barceló and NH Hoteles are other leading groups. Over half the hotel chains are headquartered in the Balearic Islands and Cataluña.

Increasing competition has tended to hold prices down in the hotel sector, while operating costs have risen. Moreover, increased investment has often not been matched by increased profits. This has resulted in rationalisation and more concerted action by hotel owners over purchasing and over the pricing of accommodation. Even in marketing, which has been left largely to the tour operators in the past, there has been an attempt to market particular hotel groups directly in foreign countries.

Competition has brought the same trends as elsewhere in the economy; the formation of larger companies, foreign alliances and diversification. In 1984 Cadena Sol, in conjunction with the Kuwait Investment Office, bought the 32 hotels of the Hotesa group (Hoteles Agrupados SA, part of Rumasa which had been appropriated by the government in 1983) and in 1986 acquired the Meliá chain. In 1990 the Husa group (a family-owned firm) sold a 27 per cent holding to the Arab investment group Agico (Arabian General Investment Corporation) and planned to float the whole group on the stock market, both measures designed to expand the capital base to support further growth. In 1993 the group took over the Lihsa hotel chain and in the same year the Riu group acquired the Iberotel chain.

Part of the increased competition has come from the growing interest of large multinational hotel groups in the country, including Accor, Club Med, Forte, Holiday Inn and Marriot. In 1994 Forte controlled, directly or indirectly through the Italian Ciga group, the five star Palace de Madrid, the Ritz and Villamagna in Madrid, Alfonso XIII in Seville and the María Cristina in San Sebastián, among others. Holiday Inn opened its first hotel in Spain (Madrid) in 1985. It has also invested in the construction of hotels in Seville, Barcelona and the Costa Blanca (three star hotels aimed at the business traveller), and in another ten establishments called Holiday Inn Garden Court. The latter offer low priced functional accommodation in towns of over 100,000, competing directly with more traditional Spanish accommodation. The pace of inward investment has continued to expand. In 1990 Forte concluded a joint-venture agreement with the oil company Repsol to develop roadside restaurants and hotels (Little Chef and Travelodges) in Spain and the French hotel groups Accor and Air France were looking to create hotel chains in Spain (especially through franchising arrangements under which hotels will operate mainly under the Ibis and Meridien names respectively; three star hotels located on the edge of cities and aimed at the business traveller market). In 1993 the Accor group was already operating a small number of hotels under the names Novotel (business hotels) and Sofitel (Forte acquiring the Air France holding in the Meridien hotel group in 1994).

Partly in response to increasing competition in the national market, Spanish hotel companies have been investing abroad, including the development of franchising and management operations. Overseas ownership of hotels was concentrated in ten companies in 1993, the largest numbers being owned by Grupo Sol-Meliá (35), Occidental Hoteles (25) Hoteles Barceló (14) and Iberotel (11). The most important locations were in the Caribbean (Dominica, Mexico, Cuba, Costa Rica and Venezuela) and in Turkey.

In the public sector the state owns a chain of hotels (*paradores and albergues*) through the company 'Paradores de Turismo SA' constituted in 1991 (in mid 1994 partial privatisation, of this group was being considered, involving the sale of 25 of the coastal and city hotels). The first parador was inaugurated by King Alfonso XIII in 1928 in the Sierra de Gredos to provide a comfortable base for hunting. This one was followed in 1929 by the Hotel Atlantic in Cádiz. Between 1928 and 1960 35 buildings were opened. During the 1960s the chain was expanded with the addition of 50 new establishments. In 1993 the chain provided over 9,655 beds in 86 establishments dispersed throughout Spain, offering a high standard of accommodation in traditional surroundings (frequently old castles and palaces). Following a period of reorganisation in the early 1980s, during which five *paradores* were closed (Villacastín in Segovia, Pajares in Asturias, Marín in Pontevedra, Ojén in Málaga and Santa María de Huerta in Soria), the investment budget in 1989 provided for renewed expansion, including the opening of the parador of Cáceres (opened in 1993). In the mid 1990s it is anticipated that new *paradores* will open in Cuenca, Ronda (Málaga) and Santiponce (Seville). These new locations owe much more to careful consideration of viability criteria than previous sites.

8.7 Travel agency and charter airlines

Travel agency and tour operators in Spain have increased with the growth of domestic tourism. Overall, the travel agency sector remained atomistic in structure at the beginning of the 1990s, with only a few major groups, frequently owned by hotel companies or other tourism businesses (for example, Viajes Barceló). In 1993 there were 2,466 travel agency companies (SGT 1994a), each one having an average of only two offices and between five and ten employees. In total they employed some 30,000 people. Large companies include Viajes Barceló, Ecuador, Halcón, Iberia, Marsans and Pullmantur. Tour operators include Club de Vacaciones, Iberojet, Juliá Tours, Mundicolor, Travelplan and Turavia.

The air-charter market is dominated by foreign companies, although in the late 1980s Spanish companies began to increase their participation. It is a high-risk business in which there is strong competition (especially from the major charter companies such as Britannia, Monarch and Airtours) and a downturn in the market can quickly result in casualties. Spantax ceased operations in 1987 and was transferred to the Dirección General del Patrimonio del Estado (DGPE). Another charter company, Hispania, also ceased operations in 1989 (in Britain, British Island Airways ceased operation in early 1990, Danair in 1992 and Air Europe in 1993). Aviaco (the domestic routes subsidiary of Iberia) transferred its charter operations to Vuelos Internacionales de Vacaciones (VIVA), owned jointly by Iberia and Lufthansa. Iberia also created the regional companies Binter Canarias and

Binter Mediterráneo. Spanish charter airline companies include Air Europa and Spanair. In granting licenses to companies the Civil Aviation Authority (Dirección General de Aviación Civil; part of the Ministry of Transport) seeks assurance in respect of experience in the business and some security that the companies will be able to find customers. Thus many of the Spanish air-charter companies have been formed with the participation of foreign capital. With the gradual liberalisation of air transport the charter companies are beginning to establish more scheduled services such as Air Europa between Madrid and Barcelona.

8.8 Foreign tour operators

In contrast to the atomistic supply of accommodation, a substantial proportion of foreign demand for tourism is channelled through a few large foreign tour operators (estimated at 50 per cent of inbound tourists; Ruiz 1994), such as Tourlatik Union International in Germany, Spies in Scandinavia, Airtours and Thomson in Britain. These groups have gained their strength through control over the marketing of Spanish tourism in Europe. But they have also increased their proportion of tourist revenues through internalising a large part of the holiday package (for example using affiliated charter flight companies). The oligopolistic power of the foreign tour operators has allowed them not only to dictate the prices and conditions under which accommodation is offered, but also to exercise a strong influence over the pattern of tourism development. Their influence has been especially strong in the Balearic and Canary Islands, and in the 'Costas'. Of particular concern has been the tight grip they have exercised on hotel prices, hotel owners arguing that low prices have left them with little margin to invest in modernisation.

8.9 Foreign investment

Since the 1970s foreign companies have been investing in tourism development. There is now significant foreign penetration in the hotel sector, including that in Spanish hotel chains (for example the German company TUI has holdings in the Mallorca based hotel groups Riu Hoteles and Iberotel, and a majority holding in Ultramar Express; there is French capital in the hotel group Med-Playa; the NH Hoteles group is majority owned by Italian capital), and most of the air-charter companies have foreign participation (for example the Swedish company Vingresor has a holding in Spanair and the German company TUI a majority holding in Iberojet).

Investment in property development has been a major component of overall foreign investment. In many cases tourism facilities are provided in conjunction with broader property development schemes. An early example of a combined property and tourism development was Sotogrande (Cádiz). In the 1980s the leisure company Brent Walker developed the marina complex of Puerto Santa María (Puerto Sherry). Finally, after many years during which potential theme parks were mooted (including the siting of the European Disneyland) Port Aventura opened in Spring 1995 (40 per cent owned by Tussauds–itself part of the British Pearson Group – 30 per cent by La Caixa, 20 per cent by Anheuser Busch and 10 per cent by Fecsa) on a 115 hectare site in Salou (Tarragona) the second largest theme park in Europe.

8.10 Economic and social dimensions of tourism

The relative merits of tourism as an agent of socio-economic development have been widely discussed (Pearce 1981; Kadt 1979; Torres Bernier 1979), revealing significant costs alongside demonstrable economic benefits. Nationally, the growth of tourism provided an underlying dynamic to the economic miracle of the 1960s, while drawing the Spanish economy into a closer relationship with external centres of decision making and demand especially in Europe.

In tourist areas the benefits of increased incomes, tax revenues, consumption and employment must be weighed against the additional costs of infrastructure investment, pollution, congestion (costs which show up as growth in regional incomes; Friedmann 1983), loss of land to non-tourist uses, land and house price inflation, the distortion of the labour market and investment patterns, and the alienation of the local population. During the major phase of tourism expansion local regional development was subordinated to national economic growth requirements, including generating income which was then reinvested in the industrial areas of northern Spain and Madrid (Torres Bernier 1979).

The importance of tourism within the national economy is borne out by the value of tourist consumption. Direct and indirect consumption has averaged between 8 and 10 per cent of GDP since 1970 (in some regions its contribution is much higher, for example both the Balearic and Canary Islands are heavily dependent on tourism and even in Cataluña tourism is estimated to contribute some 15 per cent of GDP).

The foreign exchange element of this consumption is also of fundamental importance in the balance of payments. The net balance on the travel and tourism account has always been positive and has enabled the financing of deficits elsewhere, notably on the balance of merchandise trade. The trend has been for the balance on the travel and tourism account to grow consistently in nominal terms. In the late 1980s income from foreign tourism represented between 37 and 43 per cent of the income from merchandise exports and between 20 and 24 per cent of the total income on the balance of payments current account. Although, in the three years 1991 to

1993 inclusive, travel and tourism income as a proportion of income from merchandise exports fell to about one-third and as a proportion of all income on the current account fell to between 17 and 18 per cent (Banco de España 1993 and 1994).

Although Spain has received substantial income from tourism, there has been concern over the level of this income in relation to the volume of tourists. Income has been reduced as a result of the structure and organisation of the tourism industry, especially the extent of mass tourism through package holidays. In the 1980s it was estimated that less than half the cost of a package holiday finds its way into the Spanish economy (Anon 1987b; SGT 1989). Research by the Tourism Institute in Spain (Instituto de Estudios Turísticos) has consistently shown that average earnings per tourist are low in comparison with the world average. Thus, although Spain occupied second place in the world in terms of the number of foreign tourists and foreign tourism earnings in 1987, it was only seventeenth in terms of foreign tourist expenditure per head (Trigo Portela 1988). Expenditure per head appears lower still when calculated on a tourist/day basis. As a result, while Spain received over 117 per cent more foreign tourists than Britain in 1986, foreign receipts were only some 52 per cent higher (Trigo Portela 1988). The multiplier effect in Spain of total holiday expenditure by foreign tourists is reduced through tour operators commissions, through money paid to the foreign charter-flight companies (often owned by the tour operators) and through money repatriated from Spain by foreign-owned activities. Even in 1993 the hotel industry was still facing serious financial problems due to very low prices negotiated by tour operators and recession in the domestic travel market.

An estimated 10 to 12 per cent of the labour force are employed in the tourism industry. The diffuse nature of the tourism sector together with seasonality and the volume of informal employment mean that only rough estimates are possible (Anon 1987c). In 1993 the total number employed in tourism was estimated at 1.4 million; 820,000 directly employed (mostly in the hotel and restaurant sector) and 580,000 indirectly employed (Alcaide Inchausti 1984; Ruiz 1994). Of the total directly employed, it was estimated that 147,000 people worked in the hotel sector, 137,000 of whom were salaried employees. The seasonality of employment is illustrated by the fact that only 41 per cent of the salaried employees in the hotel sector were on year-round permanent contracts and only some 88,000 were employed in the low season (FEH 1994). In spite of measures to cut labour costs, the tourist industry remains labour-intensive, drawing on casual labour as one means of holding down labour costs to retain competitiveness in the international market. While there are social pressures to increase wages and minimum wage legislation, average wages in the sector are unlikely to rise much in the face of very high levels of unemployment and with substantial numbers of people still in the agricultural sector.

Seasonality is an endemic problem in tourist areas, especially those that rely on climatic attractions. Over 40 per cent of all foreign visits to Spain and over 40 per cent of demand for hotel accommodation is recorded during the three months from July to the end of September. In contrast, only 15 per cent of all foreign visits and demand for hotel accommodation occurs in the three months from December to the end of February. The problem of seasonality varies both geographically and with the type of tourism product offered. The north of Spain tends to have a much shorter season than the south and hotels exhibit less seasonality than campsites. Some inland spas have a season as short as two months and ski-resorts tend only to have a four-month season. But even the Canary Islands and the southern Mediterranean coast, which offer warmth and sunshine for most of the year, cannot avoid the mould that traditional holiday periods impose on the length of the season.

This seasonal pattern of demand creates financial problems in the tourist industry, distorts the labour market, necessitates the provision of expensive additional capacity in public services and infrastructure and creates an annual cycle of apoplexy in season and anaemia out of season. Many hotels and other tourist businesses find it uneconomic to remain open out of season and those that do remain open tend to reduce their staffing levels. As a result, substantial seasonal unemployment is a common characteristic of tourist resorts. Public transport, roads, water supply and sewerage facilities must all be able to deal with peak levels of demand but seasonal congestion is still inevitable. Out of season, services and facilities are underused. Diversification and discriminatory pricing policies are used to ameliorate these problems. Lower prices are charged out of season and there has been a particular attempt to attract the retired, who are not tied to fixed holiday periods. Attempts have also been made to break away from the narrow appeal of the climate, diversifying the tourism product for example by encouraging business conventions, activity and special-interest holidays.

The spatial pattern of tourism development has resulted in shifts in the pattern of regional incomes. In 1991 the province of Gerona was estimated to have the second highest regional income per capita of the fifty provinces in Spain, compared with its position in twelfth place in 1960. Over the same period the Balearic Islands had moved up from fifteenth to fifth place, Las Palmas from twenty-seventh to twenty-fourth place and Málaga from forty-third to thirty-third place (Banco de Bilbao 1987; El País 1993). These changes in regional income reflect the stimulus provided by tourism to local economic activities and the resulting increased levels of income, consumption and employment. However, as mentioned above, significant costs accompany these benefits. Furthermore, a tourism monoculture leaves regions vulnerable to fluctuations in the fortunes of this industry.

The social dimension of tourism is less easy to measure than the economic one. Many factors, as well as tourism, have affected the evolution of Spanish culture. Undoubtedly the increased mobility associated with domestic tourism and cultural contact with foreign tourists have served to reduce isolationism and contribute to a process of cultural convergence with north-west Europe. On the positive side this may be viewed as a process of enrichment and liberalisation. Conversely, the weakening of traditional social bonds, coupled with the conspicuous consumption of tourists in areas frequently characterised by high levels of unemployment, have contributed towards rising crime rates in major tourist areas. Similarly, there is a danger that traditional culture will be overwhelmed and reduced to another form of tourist entertainment.

Tourism has also had a dramatic impact on the physical environment; a combination of natural amenities which have been fundamental to the growth of the industry. Rapid growth in the past has overwhelmed the planning system, leading to the despoilation of large expanses of coastline and creating intense local pressure on natural resources and public infrastructure in the vicinity of tourism complexes. This may have been forgivable in the past as the price of economic development, but a more prosperous economy can no longer afford to destroy the very basis of its most important industry. In this, support has been provided by stronger planning controls, a more adequate planning system, new environmental legislation and a growing awareness of environmental issues (Salmon 1989).

8.11 Government intervention

Articulation of government policy has been complicated by the devolution of most tourism development responsibilities to the regions and local authorities. Regional governments have assumed responsibilities for regional economic and structure planning, and for regional tourism development, while municipal governments are responsible for their own detailed planning, development control and promotion. This has left central government with an essentially co-ordinating role, devising framework strategic plans and promotion.

Tourism policy has been further complicated by the fact that tourism has been shunted around between ministries (Transport, Tourism and Communications, Industry, Trade and Tourism, then Trade and Tourism) and that actions influencing tourism, and services provided to the tourism industry, are shared across many government ministries and departments. For example, the infrastructure progammes (roads, railways, ports, coastal development, water supply, etc.) undertaken by the Ministry of Public Works have a direct impact on tourism development. Along with other sectors of the economy, tourism is also influenced by general policies shaping the economic environment, including policy on foreign investment, regional policy, exchange rate, monetary and fiscal policy, policy on official credit provision and labour market measures. In an attempt to improve the co-ordination of government agencies, a new plan published in mid 1994 (Plan Estratégico del Turísmo) proposed strengthening the role of the main central government tourism agency, including strengthening the co-ordinating committee for developing tourism strategy, which involves the central administration and representatives from the regions.

Within the central government, the Tourism Secretariat (Secretaría General de Turismo, SGT) of the Ministry of Trade and Tourism retains responsibility for national tourism policy and the co-ordination of tourism developments. The main agencies under the authority of the SGT in mid 1994 were the Tourism Policy Office (Dirección General de Política Turística), responsible for the formulation of national tourism policy and research, and the promotion agency Turespaña (which also manages the two conference centres and exhibition halls in Madrid and Torremolinos). However, under the Plan Estratégico 1994 it was proposed to widen the role of Turespaña to include all the tourism agencies of the central administration. The Tourism Planning Office would disappear and two new departments (*Direcciones Generales*) created: 'Tourism Strategy' and 'Marketing'.

Regional, provincial and municipal administrations also sponsor tourism organisations and are increasingly promoting themselves, although outside of Spain this promotion is normally channelled through the national tourism offices. In most regions, grants have been available to municipalities to establish tourism offices and there is regional public investment in tourism promotion. In the province of Málaga, the Patronato de Turismo de la Costa del Sol markets the Costa del Sol both nationally and internationally. At the municipality level Almuñécar (Granada) has promoted itself at international exhibitions outside of Spain as 'a tropical valley on the Mediterranean shore'.

A chain of hotels (*paradores* and *albergues*) are owned by the central government together with a number of official tourism and hotel schools. A large proportion of the transport system falls within the public sector – the national airline Iberia, its subsidiary Aviaco and the charter airline Viva (in conjunction with Lufthansa), the railway system RENFE and FEVE, the coach operator Enatcar and the shipping company Transmediterránea. In addition, municipalities own and operate their own urban transport.

State credit, involving lower rates of interest and longer repayment periods than generally available through commercial channels, has been used extensively to stimulate private initiative; although the majority of funding for tourism development has come from the private sector, either internally financed or from private sector finance houses (Anon 1987d). Grants have been available from the early 1970s under a series of hotel modernisation plans, with the main emphasis being on re-equipment, repair and refurbishment of existing hotels. Funds from the public sector have been available through the official credit agencies since 1942: from 1965 until the early 1990s specifically through the Banco Hipotecario de España and now through the Official Credit Institute (ICO) working in conjunction with the regional governments. However, to put the scale of public sector finance in perspective, in the 3 years 1985 to 1987 tourist credit (*crédito turístico*) represented less than 3 per cent of all annual credit provided under the policy of preferential credit (the majority being allocated to subsidised housing, VPO); a small amount of other credit was also offered to the tourist sector under market conditions. In 1987 the tourist sector accounted for only 0.5 per cent of all official credit (Banco Hipotecario 1988). Since 1986 an increasing number of tourism projects have been co-financed by the European Community.

Central government policy in the 1980s and early 1990s has been directed at encouraging the continued growth of tourism (consolidating Spain's market leadership in the Mediterranean), while attempting to correct distortions and constraints on further development. The most serious problems have been perceived as over-reliance on a narrow market segment, the spatial and temporal concentration of tourism and lack of sufficient product differentiation and quality.

In confronting these problems the government has relied on measures to stimulate investment by the private sector (especially on hotel modernisation), on infrastructure provision, on measures to stimulate training and on promotional campaigns. The latter directed at more 'up-market' tourism, promoting the interior (unknown Spain), diversifying the appeal of Spain ('diversity under the sun' and 'passion for life') and on emphasising the security of the tourist in Spain. For example, the strategic planning document providing the framework for increasing the competitiveness of the tourism industry in Spain, 'Futures 1992–1995', earmarked only a quarter of its budget to financial assistance towards the modernisation of facilities, other monies going towards national tourism promotion (60 per cent of the budget), training and research (SGT 1994c). However, national advertising campaigns continue to be overshadowed by the literature supplied by tour operators and the established image of tourism in Spain.

Diversification has been sought both in tourism products and in the client base. Numerous segments of the tourism market have been developed, including conference tourism (promoting conference centres), activity tourism (especially golf), health (with the promotion of spas), tourism focused on the natural environment and cultural tourism (promoting the cultural heritage). Diversification in the age structure of tourists has been sought, especially through promoting holidays for the elderly (Bardón Fernández 1986). Campaigns have also been waged to increase market penetration in North America and Japan, although these markets have remained very small alongside those in Europe. Product diversification not only reinforces demand but also helps reduce seasonality.

8.12 Improving the coastal environment and promoting inland tourism

The pattern of tourism development has left coastal areas in need of renovation and protection while neglecting inland areas. The Law of the Coasts (Ley de Costas: Teixidor Roca 1988; Osorio Páramo and López Peláez 1988) was an important piece of legislation affecting coastal tourism development. Under this law the coast has been placed under state authority (Zona de Dominio Público Estatal) in an attempt to improve current tourism provision, ensure public access to the coast (avoiding the privatisation of the coast) and prevent further deterioration of the coastal environment.

The new regulations confer much wider powers on the state in respect of the coast than existed before (Salmon 1989). They also raise constitutional questions in relation to the treatment of private property and create potential conflict with the authority of the regional governments in relation to matters effecting the coast, ports, waste disposal and urban development. As a result the implementation of the law has been slow.

Numerous initiatives have been taken to improve the coastal environment. In the mid 1990s they included continuing improvements in waste disposal, beach and promenade facilities, a coastal infrastructure investment plan (Plan de Costas), a plan for the reform of tourism areas (Plan de Reformes de Zonas Turísticas) and the '*planes de excelencia turística*' incorporated in the plan 'Futures 1992– 1995'. The latter includes government funding for environmental improvements, modernisation of hotels and improvements in tourist information. By 1994 plans had been approved for Benalmádena (Málaga), Calviá (Mallorca), Gandia (Valencia), Peñiscola (Castellón), Torremolinos (Málaga), Valle de la Orotava (Tenerife) and the south of Gran Canaria. Plans to renovate tourist areas include supporting action to reduce accommodation capacity by demolishing some of the older and least attractive developments, as has already occurred in Calvía, and converting buildings to other uses.

The promotion of rural tourism is seen as one of the means of revitalising rural areas and conserving the rural heritage, while diverting growth away from the congested coast and diversifying the tourism product (Bardón Fernández 1987; Bote Gómez 1987). Most regional governments have adopted appropriate policy measures. A variety of locations (historic towns, places of landscape quality, spas) and activities (climbing, fishing, horse riding, hunting, winter sports) lend themselves to potential development, especially those areas in the vicinity of large towns and cities which can cater for the growing demand for excursions and weekend breaks. All these open up new sources of local employment and income.

A number of rural tourism initiatives have emerged, including the development of family farms for tourism use and the improvement of information. Farm houses (*casas de labranza*) were introduced by the Ministry of Agriculture and the Ministry of Transport, Tourism and Communications in 1967. In 1983 the government of Cataluña began providing incentives to promote the establishment of similar rural tourist accommodation (*casa pagés*) to complement the income of farm families; by 1987 the first guide to these had been produced listing 48 establishments. Better information has included improved signposting and the establishment of tourist routes such as the Route of the White Villages in Andalucía. In 1983 the CSIC (Consejo Superior de Investigaciones Científicas) began to look for measures to manage and promote the rural areas. It undertook pilot studies in Vera (Cáceres) and Taramundi (Asturias) – both with natural tourism attractions – designed to identify and implement a series of tourism projects compatible with conservation and integrated with local life. The projects involved improved information and promotion, refurbishment of old buildings for accommodation, the improvement of recreational facilities (sports facilities, museums), commercialisation of local crafts and improved signposting. By 1984 a rural tourism policy had emerged (*Boletín Oficial del Estado* 1984), involving small-scale, non-standardised, dispersed facilities, adapted to the natural and human environment (for example restoration of local architecture) within small units of space with their own mini infrastructure (an example of such a programme being PRODINTUR, Programas de Desarrollo Integrado de Turismo Rural en Andalucía). Developments should involve the local community, with the public sector providing funds for stimulating further private investment. A special programme exists providing assistance to spas anywhere in the country.

Rural development projects now tend to incorporate a strong sustainable development emphasis, fostering economic activity while conserving natural resources; a necessary prerequisite for securing funding from the European Union. For example, in 1994 work began on implementing the sustainable development plan for the area surrounding the Doñana National Park in south-west Andalucía. Of the pta 60 billion budgeted in the plan up to the year 2000, 75 per cent is to come from the European Union (Ambiente 1994).

These initiatives provide the opportunity for diversifying economic activity, improving the provision of services and infrastructure, raising rural incomes and helping rural areas retain their populations. However, in many rural areas, although tourism may help complement income from other sources, it is unlikely to form a commercially viable activity in itself. For this reason it may be difficult to attract private finance. Even where potentially viable projects exist it may be difficult to find local entrepreneurs. Where larger-scale projects are identified, the challenge will be in enabling a form of sustainable development which does not destroy the rural environment, which ensures environmental conservation and the maintenance of the cultural heritage.

8.13 The European Union and tourism development

European Union policies provide the context within which Spanish tourism policy is now framed: legislation, criteria for assessing the eligibility of tourism projects for EU funding and policy initiatives are echoed in Spain.

This European context extends from general EU policies to specific tourism policy, rural development policy and financial assistance for regional development. In terms of general policy for example, the Single European Market has important implications for tourism, with the consequent freedom to establish tourism services anywhere within the EU and greater freedom of movement for people and capital.

Tourism policy in the European Union is designed to: i) foster the development of tourism within the EU; ii) spread tourism more evenly through time and space; iii) provide a better integration of financial assistance through the various Structural Funds and other financial instruments; iv) provide better information and protection for the tourist; v) improve the working environment in the tourist industry; vi) improve understanding of the sector through research; and vii) integrate conservation of the natural environment into development (Molina del Pozo and Pedernal Peces 1987; *OJ* 1986).

European Structural Policies have provided assistance for many tourism and tourism-related projects (including infrastructure projects such as the high speed railway link between Madrid and Seville); a large proportion of Spain being classified as relatively less prosperous (Objective 1 areas under the Structural Funds) and therefore eligible for financial assistance in the form of both grants from the Structural Funds and loans from the European Investment Bank. Old industrial areas facing decline (especially steel, shipbuilding and mining areas) are specifically eligible for assistance, including that for tourism projects. In rural areas assistance for tourism projects is also available under the programme for rural development (LEADER) and from the guidance section of the European Agricultural Fund (EAGGF), designed to diversify economic activity and to promote environmental conservation.

8.14 Restructuring tourism

Unquestionably, tourism is a vital ingredient of the Spanish economy and will remain so into the next century. Together with the related leisure and hospitality industries, it forms a mutually supportive dynamic complex of economic activities on which a significant segment of the economy hangs. This complex is intensely competitive and dominated by a multitude of small firms from which are emerging a number of larger firms able to operate not only on a national but also an international stage.

Diversification of tourism products and tourism markets, raising the value-added content of products together with the renovation of existing tourism facilities, are the keys to the continued growth of tourism into the next century. If this growth is to be sustainable, then the role of the public sector must be not only to provide the necessary infrastructure and encourage private investment, but also to ensure that future development is environmentally sensitive, avoiding the destruction of the cultural and physical heritage on which much of the development will hinge. Implementation of tighter planning controls should be possible given the adoption of sustainable development practices throughout the economy, underpinned by European Union initiatives and supported by a growing environmental awareness among the population.

In contrast to most other sectors of the Spanish economy, tourism has developed within the context of an international industry, in which Spain has found itself in a peripheral relationship to the core centres of demand and decision making in north-west Europe, supplying an essentially low value-added product. Foreign companies have controlled international marketing and many components of the tourism package, leading to a 'leakage' of income from inbound tourism. Nevertheless, the rewards have been large enough to attract an enormous volume of investment into the tourism industry, an industry which has proved more resilient and long lasting than those heavy manufacturing industrial sectors into which the government channelled investment in the 1960s.

Despite changes in the business environment (larger hotel groups to negotiate with the tour operators, increased marketing from Spain, the changing character of inbound tourism, changing patterns of tourism demand, the growth of outbound tourism), the grasp of foreign capital over the tourism industry is likely to strengthen rather than weaken. This has been a theme repeated in each of the sectors discussed in this book, apart from agriculture and energy, reflecting a transformation in the ownership of business in Spain in the final two decades of the twentieth century. Naturally this is a cause of concern, especially in a country used to domestically owned business. However, a higher level of international integration is more likely to generate employment and income than to undermine them. Hence, while disputing the magnitude of the economic benefits derived from tourism, few would argue with the conclusion that the benefits have been significant and that tourism has been a crucial formative influence in the emergence of the modern Spanish economy.

References and bibliography

Alcaide Inchausti, A. (1984) 'La importancia de nuestra economía turística', *Situación*, No.1, pp. 26–49. Bilbao: BBV

Ambiente (1994) 'Plan de desarrollo sostenible de Doñana', *Ambiente*, No. 21, May. Seville: Junta de Andalucía

Anon (1987a) 'Estudio de la demanda extrahotelera en España (informe resumen)', *Estudios Turísticos* 96, pp. 19–53.

Anon (1987b) 'El gasto turístico', *Estudios Turísticos* 93, pp. 3–26

Anon (1987c) 'El empleo en el sector hotelero', *Estudios Turísticos* 94, pp. 3–37

Anon (1987d) 'La financiación interior del turismo en España', *Estudios Turísticos* 95, pp. 49–72

Asociación de Cadenas Hoteleras Españolas, ACHE (1993) *Las cadenas hoteleras en España 1993*. Madrid

Banco de Bilbao (1987) *Renta Nacional de España 1985*. Bilbao

Banco de España (1993) *La balanza de pagos de España en 1991 y 1992*. Madrid

Banco de España (1994) *Boletín estadístico*, May. Madrid

Banco Hipotecario (1988) *Memoria 1987*. Madrid

Bardón Fernández, E. (1986) 'Viajes de vacaciones de la tercera edad en Europa', *Estudios Turísticos* pp. 77–94

Bardón Fernández, E. (1987) 'El turismo rural en España', *Estudios Turísticos* 94, pp. 63–76

Barke, M. and L. France (1988) 'Second homes in the Balearic Islands', *Geography*, Vol. 73, pp. 143–5

Boletín Oficial del Estado (1984) *Tourism policy*. 2 August. Madrid

Bote Gómez, V. (1987) 'Importancia de la demanda turística en espacio rural en España', *Estudios Turísticos* 93, pp. 79–91

Clark, J. (1988) 'Spain and the Balearic Islands: National Report No. 146', *International Tourism Reports*, No. 1 (Economist Intelligence Unit), pp. 5–28

Díaz Alvarez, J. (1988) *Geografía del Turismo*. Madrid: Editorial Síntesis

El País (1993) *Anuario El País 1993*. Madrid

Federación Española de Hoteles, FEH (1994) *El sector hotelero en España 1993*. Madrid

Friedmann, J. (1983) 'Life space and economic space: contradictions in regional development', in D. Seers (ed.), *The crises of the European regions*, Chapter 8. London: Macmillan

Kadt, E. (1979) *Tourism: passport to development?* Oxford: OUP

Molina del Pozo, C. and J. Pedernal Peces (1987) 'Una contribución al desarrollo de las regiones europeas: iniciativas de la Comunidad Europea en materia de turismo', *Situación*, No. 3, pp. 78–88. Bilbao: BBV

Morris, A. and G. Dickinson (1987) 'Tourist development in Spain: growth versus conservation on the Costa Brava', *Geography*, Vol. 72, No. 1, pp. 16–25

Naylon, J. (1967) 'Tourism, Spain's most important industry', *Geography*, Vol. 52, No. 1, pp. 23–40

Official Journal of the European Communities, OJ (1986) *Tourism policy*. Brussels

Osorio Páramo, F. and L. López Peláez (1988) 'Proyecto de Ley de Costas', *Urbanismo*, No. 4, pp. 16–19

Pearce, D. (1981) *Tourist development*. London: Longman

Ruiz, J. (1994) 'España obtiene con el turismo el 10% de su riqueza', *El País* (sección negocios), 31 July, pp. 3–5

Salmon, K. (1985) 'Spain: National Report No. 103', *International Tourism Quarterly* (Economist Intelligence Unit), pp. 20–41

Salmon, K. (1989) 'Tourism, the public sector and regional development in Spain', *Journal of the Association for Contemporary Iberian Studies*, Vol. 2, No. 1, pp. 32–43

Salvá Tomas, P. and M. Socias Fuster (1985) 'Las residencias secundarias y la agricultura a tiempo parcial', *El Campo*, No. 100, pp. 59–62. Bilbao: BBV

Secretaria General de Turismo, SGT (1989) *Concentración y asociacionismo empresarial en el sector turístico*. Madrid

Secretaria General de Turismo, SGT (1993) *Anuario de estadísticas de turismo, 1992*. Madrid

Secretaria General de Turismo, SGT (1994a) *Movimiento turístico: año 1993*. Madrid

Secretaria General de Turismo, SGT (1994b) *Movimiento de viajeros en establecimientos hoteleros: año 1993 datos definitivos*. Madrid

Secretaria General de Turismo, SGT (1994c) *Futures: Plan marco de competitividad del turismo español*. Madrid

Serrano Martínez, J. (1993) 'Dinámica de crecimiento y difusión espacial de las viviendas secundarias en España en los inicios de los años noventa', *Situación*, No. 2, pp. 45–64. Bilbao: BBV

Teixidor Roca, J. (1988) 'Proyecto Ley de Costas', *Horizonte Empresarial*, No. 1981, pp. 30–4

Torres Bernier, E. (1979) 'El sector turístico en Andalucía: instrumentalización y efectos impulsores', *Estudios Regionales* 1, pp. 377–442

Trigo Portela, J. (1988) 'El Turismo: variable fundamental de la economía Española', *Horizonte Empresarial*, No. 1981, pp. 6–9

Valenzuela Rubio, M. (1985) 'Everything under the sun', *Geographical Magazine*, Vol. LVII, May, pp. 274–8

Williams, A. and G. Shaw (eds.) (2nd edn, 1991) *Tourism and economic development: Western European experiences*. London: Belhaven Press

Appendix 1
Glossary of Spanish terms

Government and business organisations

Acuerdo General sobre Aranceles y Comercio, AGAC: General Agreement on Tariffs and Trade, GATT
ayuntamientos: municipal councils
Boletín Oficial del Estado, BOE: Official State Bulletin
Comisiones Obreras, CCOO: Workers Council, a trade union
Comunidades Autonomas, CCAA: administrative regions
Confederación Española de Organizaciones Empresariales, CEOE: Spanish Employers' Federation
Delegación Provincial: provincial office of a central government ministry
Diputación Provincial: a local authority operating at the provincial level
Dirección General del Patrimonio del Estado, DGPE: Directorate General of State Assets
Instituto de Crédito Oficial, ICO: Official Credit Institute
Instituto Nacional de Empleo, INEM: National Institute of Employment
Instituto Nacional de Hidrocarburos, INH: National Hydrocarbons Institute
Instituto Nacional de Industria, INI: National Institute of Industry
Instituto Nacional de la Pequeña y Mediana Empresa Industrial, IMPI: National Institute for Small and Medium-Sized Industrial Companies
Instituto Nacional de la Seguridad Social, INSS: National Social Security Agency
Instituto Nacional de Reforma y Desarrollo Agrario, IRYDA: National Institute of Agrarian Reform and Development
Instituto Nacional para la Conservación de la Naturaleza, ICONA: National Nature Conservation Institute
Ministerio de Agricultura, Pesca y Alimentación: Ministry of Agriculture, Fisheries and Food
Ministerio de Comercio y Turismo: Ministry of Trade and Tourism
Ministerio de Economía y Hacienda: Ministry of Economy and Finance

Ministerio de Industria y Energía: Ministry of Industry and Energy
Ministerio de Obras Públicas, Transportes y Medio Ambiente: Ministry of Public Works, Transport and the Environment
Ministerio de Trabajo y Seguridad Social: Ministry of Labour and Social Security
Organización Mundial de Comercio: World Trade Organisation
Partido Popular, PP: Spanish political party of the right
Partido Socialista Obrero Español, PSOE: Spanish Socialist Party
Red Nacional de los Ferrocarriles Españoles, RENFE: Spanish National Railways
Teneo SA: state enterprise holding company
Unión General de Trabajadores, UGT: General Workers' Trade Union

European terms

Banco Europeo de Inversiones, BEI: European Investment Bank, EIB
Comunidad Económica del Carbón y del Acero, CECA: European Coal and Steel Community, ECSC
Comunidad Económica Europea, CEE: European Economic Community, EEC
FEOGA, Sección de Orientación: EAGGF Guidance Section
Fondo Europeo de Desarrollo Regional, FEDER: European Regional Development Fund, ERDF
Fondo Europeo de Orientación y de Garantía Agraria, FEOGA: European Agricultural Guidance and Guarantee Fund, EAGGF
Fondo Social Europeo, FSE: European Social Fund, ESF
Fondos Estructurales, FE: Structural Funds
Montantes Compensatorios Monetarios, MCM: Monetary Compensation Amounts, MCA
Operaciones Integrades de Desarrollo, OID: Integrated Development Programmes, IDP
Pólitica Agraria Común, PAC: Common Agricultural Policy, CAP
Programa Integrado del Mediterráneo, PIM: Integrated Mediterranean Programme, IMP
Programas Nacionales de Interés Comunitario, PNIC: National Programmes of Community Interest, NPCI
Sistema monetario europeo, SME: European monetary system, EMS
tipo de cambio verde: green exchange rate of the Common Agricultural Policy
Tratado de Maastricht: Maastricht Treaty
Tratado de Roma: Treaty of Rome
Unión Europea, UE: European Union, EU
Unión Monetaria Europea, UME: European monetary union, EMU

Agriculture

agraria: refers to agriculture, livestock, hunting and forestry
agrícola: refers to non-livestock farming only
cajas rurales: rural savings banks
Cámara Oficial Sindical Agraria, COSA: Agricultural Chamber of Commerce, operating at both the provincial and municipal level
Catastro de la Riqueza Rústica: Rural land catastral record office (est. 1906) maintaining records of land ownership and land-use for taxation purposes
Confederación Nacional de Agricultores y Ganadores, CNAG: National Farmers Organisation
huerta: irrigated upland area
regadio: irrigated land
secano: land farmed without irrigation
superficie agrícola utilizada, SAU: utilised agricultural land including cultivated land and pasture
tierras labradas: cultivated land including land in fallow
tierras no labradas: uncultivated land including pasture, scrub and woodland
Unión de Federaciones Agrarias de España, UFADE: Farmers employers organisation
vega: irrigated lowland area

Economy and business

activos: assets
balanza de pagos: balance of payments
banco de negocios: merchant bank
bienes de equipo: capital goods
caja de ahorros: savings bank
compañía del holding: holding company
cotizaciones: contributions
debe: debit (as in financial accounts)
empresa: company
filial: subsidiary
formación bruta de capital fijo: gross fixed capital formation
franco a bordo, fab: free on board, fob
fusión: merger
haber: credit (as in financial accounts)
Impuesto sobre el Valor Añadido, IVA: value added tax, VAT
Impuesto sobre la Persona Física, IRPF: Personal income tax
impuestos: taxes
Indice de Paridades de Poder de Comprar, IPPC: Index of purchasing

power parities
Indice de Precios al Consumo, IPC: Retail Price Index, RPI
mercado de valores: stock market
pagarés de tesoro: treasury bills
pasivos: liabilities
patrimonio del estado: state assets
Pequeñas y Medianas Empresas, PYMES: Small and Medium-sized Businesses
Presupuestos Generales del Estado: State Budget
Producto Interior Bruto, PIB: Gross Domestic Product, GDP
Producto Nacional Bruto, PNB: Gross National Product, GNP
recargos: surcharges
reconversión: rationalisation and renovation
rentabilidad: profitability
saneamiento financiero: placing business on a sound financial footing
sede: headquarters
sociedad anónima: limited liability company
sociedad colectiva: partnerships
sociedad conjunta: joint company
sucursales: branches
tasas: charges
tipos de cambio: exchange rates
tributos: taxes

Legislative terminology

anteproyecto de ley: preliminary draft law
legislación básica: basic legislation; comparable to framework laws
leyes de base: basic laws; these have the same rank as ordinary laws
leyes marco: framework laws; these have the same rank as ordinary laws
leyes ordinarias: ordinary laws; these constitute the bulk of laws passed
leyes orgánicas: organic laws; these are the highest ranking laws below the Constitution they can only be approved by the Cortes
ordenes: orders; the next highest ranking laws to royal decrees
proyectos de leyes: draft laws
reales decretos: royal decrees; the highest ranking laws emanating from national or regional government departments
reales decreto leyes: royal decree laws; temporary legislative provision which must be debated by the Congress within 30 days, if approved becomes an ordinary law
reglamentos: standing orders
titulos: sections of a legal document

Regional development

comarca: a group of municipalities
incentivos regionales: regional incentives
Sociedad para el Desarrollo Industrial, SODI: State-owned regional industrial development agency
Sociedad para la Promoción y Reconversión Económica de Andalucía, SOPREA: Andalucian Economic Development Agency
Zonas Industrializadas en Declive, ZID: Industrial Zones in Decline
Zonas de Promoción Económica, ZOPRE: Industrial Promotion Zones
Zonas Promocionables: Assisted Areas

Appendix 2
Research sources

General economy

Aduanas, revista de comercio internacional y estudios fiscales: Esic Editorial, Madrid; monthly, academic/factual

Anuario del mercado español: Banco Santander (Banesto), Madrid; annually, detailed statistical and geographical analysis

Anuario El País: El País, Madrid; annually, journalistic/statistics

Boletín económico de ICE: Ministerio de Comercio y Turismo, Madrid; weekly

Boletín de estudios económicos: Universidad Comercial de Duestro, Bilbao; monthly, academic

Boletín Oficial del Estado: Madrid; daily record of the state

Cuadernos de economía: Centro de Estudios Económicos y Sociales, Barcelona; tri-annually

Cuadernos económicos de ICE: Ministerio de Comercio y Turismo, Madrid; quarterly

Estudios de historia económica: Banco de España, Madrid; normally about three editions a year

Estudios económicos, revista del Instituto del Estudios Económicos: Instituto de Estudios Económicos, Madrid; quarterly, academic

Guía fiscal: Albiñana, C., Dunbar Vida y Pensiones; annually, tax guide

Información comercial española, revista de economía: Ministerio de Comercio y Turismo, Madrid; monthly, analysis of the contemporary economy

Investigaciones económicas: Fundación del Instituto Nacional de Industria, Madrid; tri-annually

Moneda y crédito: Editorial Moneda y Crédito, Madrid; monthly, academic analysis

OECD economic surveys (Spain): Organisation for Economic Co-operation and Development, Paris; annually

Papeles de economía española: Fundación Fondo para la Investigación Económica y Social, Confederación Española de Cajas de Ahorros,

Madrid; quarterly, analysis of contemporary topics

Pensamiento iberoamericano: Instituto de Cooperación Iberoamericana, Madrid; bi-annually

Presupuestos Generales del Estado: Ministerio de Economía y Hacienda, Madrid; annually

Revista de economía: Madrid; quarterly, academic

Revista de economía aplicada: edited by J. García Delgado, Facultad de Ciencias Económicas, Universidad de Zaragoza; quarterly

Revista de historia económica: Centro de Estudios Constitucionales, Madrid; tri-annually

Situación: Banco Bilbao Vizcaya, Madrid; quarterly

Statistical series, censuses and surveys

Banco de España:

a *Balanza de pagos de España*: annually
b *Boletín económico*: monthly
c *Boletín estadístico*: monthly
d *Cuentas financieras de la economía española*: annually
e *Informe anual*: annually

Instituto Nacional de Estadística:

a *Anuario estadístico de España*: annually
b *Boletín mensual de estadística*: monthly
c *Censo agrario de España*: decennial census, most recent 1989
d *Censo de población*: decennial census, most recent 1991
e *Censo de viviendas*: decennial census, most recent 1991
f *Encuesta de la población activa*: monthly labour force survey
g *Encuesta industrial*: annual industrial survey
h *Movimiento migratorios*: annually
i *Movimiento natural de la población*: annually

Ministerio de Economía y Hacienda:

a *Estadística del comercio exterior de españa*: annually

Ministerio de Trabajo y Seguridad Social:

a *Anual de estadísticas laborales*: annually
b *Boletín de estadísticas laborales*: monthly

Agriculture

Ministerio de Agricultura, Pesca y Alimentacion:

a *Agricultura y sociedad*: quarterly, academic
b *Anuario de estadística agraria*: annually, statistics
c *Boletín mensual de estadística*: monthly, statistics
d *El Boletín*: monthly, academic
e *La agricultura, la pesca y la alimentación española*: annual survey of MAPA activities
f *Manual de estadística agraria*: annually, statistics
g *Revista de estudios agro-sociales*: quarterly, academic

Agricultura, revista agropecuaria: Editorial Agrícola Española SA, Madrid; monthly trade journal
Alimarket: Alimarket SA, Madrid; weekly
Aral, semanario de artículos alimenticios y bebidas: Tecnipublicaciones SA, Madrid; weekly trade journal
El Campo: Banco Bilbao Vizcaya, Madrid; quarterly, factual/analytical/academic
Encuesta sobre la estructura de las explotaciones agrícolas, 1987: Instituto Nacional de Estadística, 1989, Madrid
Encuesta sobre la estructura de las explotaciones agrícolas, 1993: Instituto Nacional de Estadística, 1995, Madrid

Industry, minerals, mining and energy

Ministerio de Industria y Energía:

a *Economía industrial*: bi-monthly, detailed factual
b *Estadística minera de España*: annually
c *Informe anual sobre la industria española*: annually

Instituto Geológico y Minero de España:

a *Boletín del IGM*: bi-monthly
b *Revista minera*: tri-annually

Annuals

Agenda financiera: Banco Bilbao Vizcaya, Madrid; basic data on companies quoted on the Stock Exchange
Anuario financiero y de empresas de España: Grafinter; information on selected companies
Censo oficial de exportadores: Instituto Nacional de Comercio Exterior,

Madrid; information on the main exporting companies

Dicodi, Directorio de sociedades, consejos y directivos: Grupo INCRESA, Madrid; basic information on more than 20,000 companies

Duns 40000: Principales empresas españolas: Dun and Bradstreet International, Madrid; basic company information

Empresas extranjeras en las ciudades españolas: EDINSA, Madrid; basic company information

Kompass España: Ibericom SA, Madrid; basic company information

Services

Ministerio de Economía y Hacienda:

a *Hacienda pública española*: Instituto de Estudios Fiscales, Madrid; bimonthly
b *Informe sector seguros*: Dirección General de Seguros, Madrid; annual report and statistics on the insurance industry
c *Memoría del crédito oficial*: annually

Ahorro: Confederación de Cajas de Ahorros, Madrid; monthly

Banca española, revista del sistema financiero y mundo empresarial: Bank Marketing Association, Madrid; monthly, trade journal

Informe anual sobre la construcción: Associación de Empresas Constructoras de ámbito nacional (SEOPAN), Madrid; annual review of the construction industry

Tourism

Ministerio de Comercio y Turismo:

a *Anuario de estadísticas de turismo*: annually
b *Estudios turísticos*: quarterly
c *Movimiento turístico*: monthly

Instituto Nacional de Estadística, Madrid:

a *Movimiento de viajeros en establecimientos hoteleros*: monthly and annually

Editur: Semanario profesional del turismo: Barcelona; weekly

Transport, regional development and environment

Ministerio de Obras Públicas y Transportes:

a *Revista ciudad y territorio*: quarterly
b *Revista estudios territoriales*: quarterly
c *Revista estudios de transportes y comunicaciones*: quarterly
d *Revista MOPT*: monthly

Business magazines

Actualidad económica: S.A.R.P.E., Madrid; weekly, includes an annual special edition listing the 100 largest companies in the world and the 1,500 largest Spanish companies (by sales)
Dinero: Servicio de Publicaciones Económicas SA, Madrid; weekly, includes an annual special edition listing the 500 largest private companies in Spain (by sales)
Economía y finanzas españolas: Revista de Economía, Industria, Bolsa y Finanzas: Ediciones Periódicas Especializadas SL, Madrid; weekly, includes an annual special edition listing the 200 largest companies in Spain divided into 20 sectors
El economista: Editorial Defide SA, Madrid; weekly news sheet
Fomento de la producción: Ramón Baratech Sales, Barcelona; bi-monthly, includes an annual special edition listing the 2,000 largest Spanish companies (including their distribution)
Mercado: Semanario de Economía y Negocios: Estructura Grupo de Estudios Económicos SA, Barcelona; weekly, includes a special edition listing basic information on the 500 largest Spanish companies
Spanish trends: Madrid; monthly, English language journal reporting on current business trends in Spain

Business newspapers

Cinco Dias: Estructura Grupo de Estudios Económicos SA, Madrid; daily
El País: El País, Madrid; daily (especially the Sunday edition)
Expansión: Madrid; daily

Appendix 3
Select bibliography

Almarcha Barbado, A. (ed.) (1993) *Spain and EC membership evaluated.* London: Pinter Publishers

Aranzadi, C. (ed.) (1993) *El sector eléctrico Español en la Europa de 1993.* Madrid: Economístas Libros

Carlos Fariñas, J. (1993) *La pyme industrial en España.* Madrid: Editorial Civitas

Casilda Béjar, R. (1993) *Sistema financiero español.* Madrid: Alianza Editorial

Chislett, W. (1992) *The internationalisation of the economy.* London: Euromoney publications

Chislett, W. (1992) *Spain business and finance.* London: Euromoney publications

Cremades, B. (ed.) (2nd edn, 1993) *Business law in Spain.* London: Butterworth

Díaz Alvarez, J. (1988) *Geografía del turismo.* Madrid: Editorial Síntesis

Diaz de Castro, E. and C. Carlos Fernández (1993) *Distribución comercial.* Madrid: McGraw-Hill

Donaghy, P. and M. Newton (1987) *Spain: a guide to political and economic institutions.* Cambridge: CUP

Espina, A. (1992) *Recursos humanos y política industrial.* Madrid: Fundación Fundesco

Gámir, L. (ed.) (2nd edn, 1993) *Política económica de España.* Madrid: Alianza Editorial

García Delgado, J. (ed.) (6th edn, aumentada y actualizada 1993) *España: economía.* Madrid: Editorial Espasa-Calpe

García Delgado, J. (ed.) (1993) *Lecciones de economía española.* Madrid: Editorial Civitas

García Guinea, J. and J. Martínez Frías (1992) *Recursos minerales de España.* Madrid: Consejo Superior de Investigaciones

González Laxe, F. (ed.) (1992) *Estructura económica de Galicia.* Madrid: Editorial Espasa-Calpe

Harrison, J. (1985) *The Spanish economy in the twentieth century.* London: Croom Helm

Harrison, J. (1993) *The Spanish economy: from the Civil War to the European Community.* London: Macmillan

Hooper, J. (1987) *The Spaniards: a portrait of the new Spain.* Harmondsworth: Penguin

Laxe, F. (1988) *La economía del sector pesquero.* Madrid: Editorial Espasa-Calpe

Lieberman, S. (1982) *The contemporary Spanish economy.* London: George Allen and Unwin

Martín Rodriguez, M. (ed.) (1993) *Estructura económica de Andalucía.* Madrid: Editorial Espasa-Calpe

Mochón, F., G. Ancochea and A. Avila (2nd edn, 1991) *Economía española 1964–1990.* Madrid: McGraw-Hill

Nadal, J., A. Carreras, and C. Sudria (eds) (1987) *La economía española en el siglo XX: una perspectiva histórica.* Barcelona: Editorial Ariel SA

Nadal, J. and A. Carreras (eds) (1990) *Pautas regionales de la industrialización española (siglos XIX y XX).* Barcelona: Editorial Ariel SA

Paloma Sánchez, M. (ed.) (1993) *Los grandes retos de la economía española en los noventa.* Madrid: Ediciones Pirámide

Parellada, M. (ed.) (1991) *Estructura económica de Cataluña.* Madrid: Editorial Espasa-Calpe

Pedreño, A., J. Martínez Serrano and E. Reig (eds) (1992) *Estructura económica de la Comunidad Valenciana.* Madrid: Editorial Espasa-Calpe

Quinto, J. de (ed.) (1994) *Política industrial de España.* Madrid: Ediciones Pirámide

Segura, J. (ed.) (1989) *La industría española en la crisis 1978–1984.* Madrid: Alianza Editorial.

Serrano Sanz, J. (1992) *Estructura económica del valle del Ebro.* Madrid: Editorial Espasa-Calpe

Tamames, R. (1986) *The Spanish economy.* London: C. Hurst and Company

Tamames, R. (22nd edn, 1993) *Estructura económica de España.* Madrid: Alianza Editorial

Teresa López, M. and A. Utrilla (1993) *Introducción al sector público español.* Madrid: Editorial Civitas

Tortella, G. (1994) *El desarrollo de la España contemporánea.* Historia económica de los siglos XIX and XX. Madrid: Alianza Editorial

Velarde, J. (ed.) (1990) *La industria española.* Madrid: Economístas Libros

Velarde, J., J. García Delgado and A. Pedreño (eds) (1991) *Apertura e internacionalización de la economía española.* Madrid: Economístas Libros

Index